Bernard Denvir
is the author of a four-volume documentary history
of taste in art, architecture and design in Britain, as well as of
books on Chardin, Impressionism, Post-Impressionism and
Fauvism. A contributor to many journals and magazines, he
was head of the Department of Art History at Ravensbourne
College of Art and Design, a member of the Council for
National Academic Awards, and for several years President
of the British section of the International Association of
Art Critics. A complementary volume in the World of Art
series is the author's *The Impressionists at
First Hand* (1987).

WORLD OF ART

This famous series
provides the widest available
range of illustrated books on art in all its aspects.
If you would like to receive a complete list
of titles in print please write to:

THAMES AND HUDSON
30 Bloomsbury Street, London WC1B 3QP
In the United States please write to:
THAMES AND HUDSON INC.
500 Fifth Avenue, New York, New York, 10110

The Thames and Hudson Encyclopaedia of

IMPRESSIONISM

Bernard Denvir

245 illustrations, 15 in colour

THAMES AND HUDSON

For all my family

©1990 Thames and Hudson Ltd, London

Printed and bound in Singapore

Contents

A reader's guide to the use of this book

Few periods in the history of art have received such intense examination over the past half-century as the comparatively short one which saw the flowering of Impressionism. During the past decade a great deal of revisionism has been taking place in our perception of the movement and the artists who participated in it. Much of this is to be found in recently published books such as T.J. Clark's *The Painting of Modern Life* (1985), John House's *Monet; Nature into Art* (1986), and Robert L. Herbert's *Impressionism; Art, Leisure, and Parisian Society* (1988); but much is also enshrined in specialist periodicals and in the catalogues of the many important exhibitions relating to the Impressionists which have recently been mounted. An inevitable consequence of this great wealth of material is that it is not always easy for the general reader to obtain convenient access to information about specific individuals, themes or related matters, without having recourse to a variety of books and periodicals, some of which are contained only in specialized libraries. An additional complication is the fact that even the most exhaustive works, such as John Rewald's *History of Impressionism*, do not list in their indices thematic subjects, such as patronage, politics, social background or techniques.

The aim of the *Encyclopaedia of Impressionism* is to present a concise compendium of information, based for the most part on recently published work, relating to Impressionism, its practitioners, ancillary figures such as patrons, models, dealers and critics, as well as to relevant general themes which concern the movement as a whole, covering its social, political, economic and general historical context. Inevitably, such a work is bound to be selective, but it aims to provide an accessible introduction to Impressionism in all its aspects, as well as a permanent source of reference.

To enable the reader to investigate further the necessarily concise information contained within the text, virtually every individual entry is provided with a selected bibliography. Works which recur frequently are indicated by the author's name followed by the date of publication, e.g. Rewald (1973); a key to these abbreviated references will be found in the **general bibliography** on pp. 232–33, which also lists works dealing with the movement and its practitioners as a whole.

The **subject index** opposite is intended to indicate the range of entries contained in the encyclopaedia and in particular to draw attention to thematic entries which might not suggest themselves alphabetically. Within each entry, subjects dealt with elsewhere are given in SMALL CAPITALS.

Black and white **illustrations** have been specially selected to expand on information in the text, with a particular emphasis on documentary material. Where relevant illustrations appear under separate headings, rather than in the immediate vicinity of a particular entry, a page reference is given in square brackets at the end of the entry. The **colour plates** on pp. 49–56 and 217–224 have been chosen to illuminate aspects of Impressionist painting which would not have been revealed in black and white. **Maps** of contemporary Paris and of sites connected with Impressionism will be found on pp. 10–12.

A comparative **chronology** on pp. 233–37 sets the movement within its general historical context, and a world **gazetteer** of public galleries which contain important holdings of Impressionist works can be found on pp. 238–40; this is necessarily selective, and is to be complemented by reference to the subject entries. Acknowledgments for the illustrations appear on p. 240.

Subject index

THE SOCIAL AND POLITICAL CONTEXT

cafés
cafés-concert
Clemenceau, Georges
dancing
France
Franco-Prussian War

literature
music
Napoleon III
Nieuwerkerke, Comte
Emilien de
Paris

politics
prices
railways
social background

THE ARTISTIC CONTEXT AND IMPRESSIONIST TECHNIQUE

Académie Julian
Académie Suisse
atelier system
colour
critics and criticism
drawing
Ecole des Beaux-Arts
flochetage
illustration
Impressionism
Impressionist exhibitions
Indépendants
Institut de France
literature
Luxembourg, Musée du
music
pastels
patrons and collectors
peinture claire
plein-airisme
Pointillism
portraiture
Post-Impressionism
prints

Realism
Salon
Salon des Refusés
sculpture
Société Anonyme des
Artistes
Society of French Artists
technique
L'Union

Influences
antecedents
Barbizon
Bonvin, François
Boudin, Eugène
Chevreul, Eugène
Chintreuil, Antoine
Corot, Camille
Courbet, Gustave
Daubigny, François
Delacroix, Eugène
Diaz de la Peña, Narcisse
Virgile
Guys, Constantin

Japanese art
Jongkind, Jean-Baptiste
Lecoq de Boisbaudran,
Horace
Millet, Jean-François
photography
Rousseau, Théodore

Academic painters
Besnard, Albert
Carolus-Duran, Emile-
Auguste
Cormon, Fernand
Couture, Thomas
Gérôme, Jean-Léon
Gervex, Henri
Gleyre, Charles
Guichard, Joseph
Puvis de Chavannes, Pierre

THE ART MARKET

Patrons and collectors
Arosa, Gustave
Barnes, Alfred
Bellio, Georges de
Bérard, Paul
Bruyas, Alfred
Charpentier, Georges
Chocquet, Victor
Davies Collection
Dépeaux, Félix-François
Deudon, Charles
Doria, Count Armand
Ephrussi, Charles
Faure, Jean-Baptiste
Flornoy, Louis
Gachet, Dr Paul
Gangnat, Maurice

Gaudibert, Louis-Joachim
Gaugain, Paul-Octave, Abbé
Havemeyer, Henry Osborne
Hecht, Albert
Hoschedé, Ernest and Alice
Khalil Bey
Lane, Sir Hugh Percy
May, Ernest
Mellon, Paul
Morozov, Mikhail and Ivan
Murer, Eugène
Pellerin, Auguste
Phillips Collection
Proust, Antonin
Rouart, Henri
Shchukin, Sergei
Wagram, Louis-Marie

Dealers
Boussod and Valadon
Durand-Ruel, Paul
Gogh, Théo van
Goupil, Adolphe
Hôtel Drouot
Joyant, Maurice
Latouche, Louis
Manzi, Michel
Martin, Père
Martinet, Louis
Petit, Georges
prices
Tanguy, Julien, Père
Vollard, Ambroise

WRITERS, CRITICS AND PERIODICALS

L' Artiste
Astruc, Zacharie
Baudelaire, Charles Pierre
Blanc, Charles
Bürger, Wilhelm
Burty, Philippe
Castagnary, Jules
Champfleury, Jules Husson
Charivari
Chesneau, Ernest
Claretie, Jules
Daudet, Alphonse
Delvau, Alfred
Dewhurst, Wynford
Duranty, Louis Edmond
Fénéon, Félix
Fourcaud, Louis de

Gasquet, Joachim
Gautier, Théophile
Geffroy, Gustave
Gill, Louis-Alexandre
Goncourt, Edmond and
    Jules de
Halévy, Ludovic
Hamerton, Philip Gilbert
Houssaye, Arsène
Huysmans, Joris-Karl
L' Impressionniste
James, Henry
Lafenestre, Georges
Laforgue, Jules
Leroy, Louis
Maccoll, D.S.
Mallarmé, Stéphane

Mantz, Paul
Martelli, Diego
Mauclair, Camille
Maus, Octave
Mirbeau, Octave
Moore, George
Rashdall, Edward
Rivière, Georges
Rutter, Frank
Silvestre, Armand
Silvestre, Théophile
Stevenson, R.A.M.
Venturi, Lionello
La Vie moderne
Wedmore, Sir Frederick
Wolff, Albert
Zola, Emile

THE IMPRESSIONISTS AND THEIR CIRCLE

The major painters
Bazille, Frédéric
Caillebotte, Gustave
Cassatt, Mary
Cézanne, Paul
Degas, Edgar
Fantin-Latour, Henri
Gonzalès, Eva
Guillaumin, Armand
Manet, Edouard
Monet, Claude
Morisot, Berthe
Pissarro, Camille
Renoir, Pierre-Auguste
Sargent, John Singer
Sickert, Walter Richard
Sisley, Alfred
Tissot, James
Whistler, James Abbott
  McNeill

**Their families and
  confidants**
André, Albert
Baudot, Jeanne
Bellelli family
Closier, Zoé
Emperaire, Achille
Fiquet, Hortense
Gasquet, Joachim
Leenhoff, Léon
Marion, Antoine Fortuné

Oller y Cestero, Francisco
Pissarro, Félix
Pissarro, Julie
Pissarro, Lucien
Renoir, Edmond
Renoir family
Valabrègue, Antonin
Valernes, Evariste de

Their models and sitters
Ambre, Emilie
Andrée, Ellen
Angèle
Callias, Nina de
Dobigny, Emma
Laurent, Méry
Meurent, Victorine
Perrot, Jules
Rouvière, Philibert
Stora, Clémentine
Tréhot, Lise
Valadon, Suzanne

Their close associates
Balleroy, Comte Albert de
Bartholomé, Paul Albert
Béliard, Edouard
Blanche, Jacques-Emile
Braquemond, Félix and
  Marie
Cabaner (Jean de Cabannes)
Cals, Adolphe Félix

Cordey, Frédéric
Desboutin, Marcellin
Duret, Théodore
Forain, Jean-Louis
Guigou, Paul
Guillemet, Antoine
Lamy, Pierre
Lebourg, Albert-Charles
Le Coeur, Jacques
Legros, Alphonse
Lepic, Vicomte
Lerolle, Henry
Maître, Edmond
Nittis, Guiseppe de
Piette, Ludovic
Raffaëlli, Jean-François
Schuffenecker, Emile
Sommier, François-Clément
Stevens, Alfred
Tillot, Charles
Vignon, Victor

Their followers
Bernard, Emile
Denis, Maurice
Gauguin, Paul
Van Gogh, Vincent
Seurat, Georges
Signac, Paul

PLACES ASSOCIATED WITH THE IMPRESSIONISTS

England
France
Germany
Holland
Italy
Scandinavia
Spain
USA

Aix-en-Provence
Algiers
Argenteuil

Auvers-sur-Oise
Barbizon
Batignolles
Belgium
Bougival
Boulogne
Brasserie des Martyrs
Cabaret de la mère Anthony
Chatou
Eragny
L' Estaque
Etretat

La Grenouillère
Honfleur
Louveciennes
Médan
Montmartre
Paris
Pontoise
Sainte-Adresse
Trouville
Vétheuil
Ville d'Avray

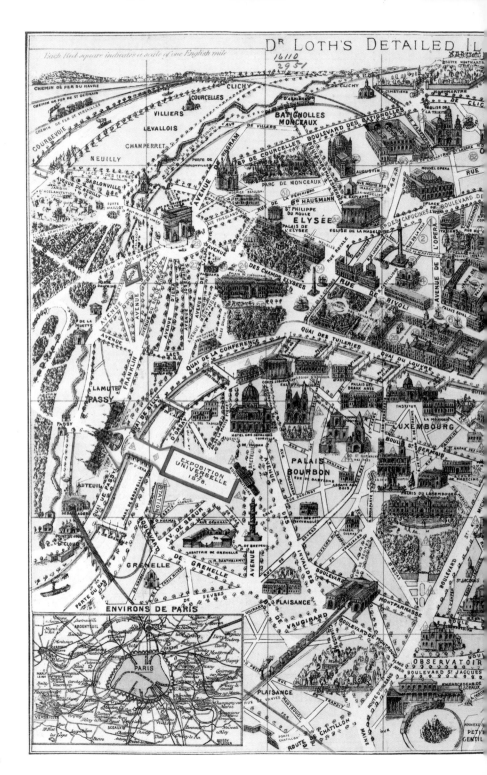

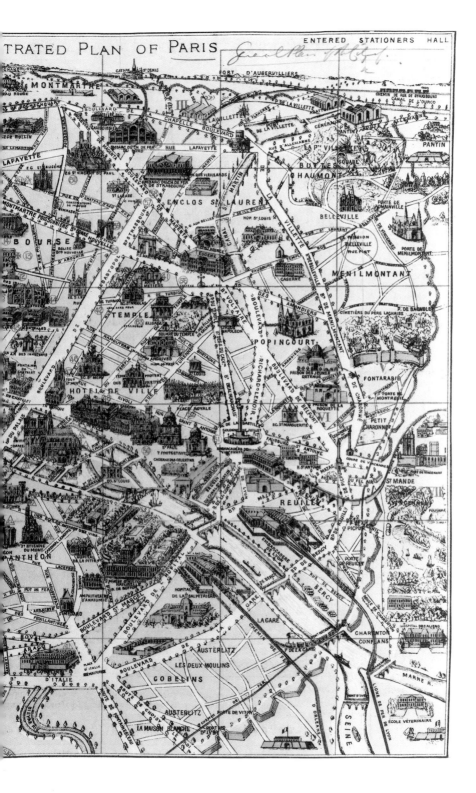

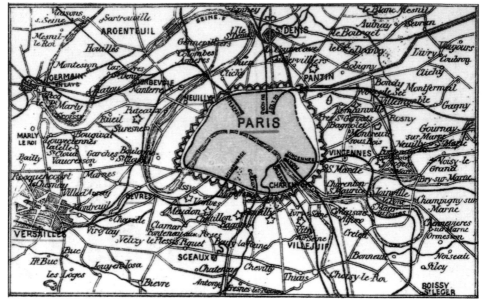

Overleaf: Dr Loth's illustrated plan of Paris, published by Scott and Ferguson of Edinburgh for British visitors to the Exposition Universelle of 1878. *Above:* The environs of Paris, showing the villages along the Seine which attracted the Impressionists, from Dr Loth's map of Paris, 1878.

The Channel coast around the mouth of the Seine with the many resorts visited by the Impressionists, from Baedecker's guide to Northern France, published in 1884.

A

Academic art Forced by the necessary over-simplifications of cultural journalism and the stylistic antitheses evolved by crusading critics, academic art and its traditions have been forced into the role of villain in a melodrama in which 'modern' or avant-garde art is invariably the hero. Nowhere is this more clearly evident than in the history of 19th-c. French painting, partly because of the accidents of history, and partly because of the national character, with its passion for rationalizing even the most intractable areas of human activity. Basically initiated by Colbert in the reign of Louis XIV, the Académie Royale des Beaux-Arts was officially constituted in 1664 and represented an attempt – a successful one at that – to harness art into the service of the state, to which it would be bound not only by systems of control, but by patronage too. It was indeed this identification with the state that, in an age of unrest and revolution such as the 19th c., exacerbated the division between academic art – seen as the art of the establishment – and 'revolutionary art', which at various times could mean the realism of COURBET, the technical innovations of Impressionism, or even the bucolic nostalgia of MILLET.

In essence, the structure of the academic system was based on the guild system that had survived from the Middle Ages. For instance, it retained the principle of apprenticeship, though this level of training was not carried out within the Academy but in the ATELIER of a master, with whom the *élève* worked and, indeed, until the end of the 18th c., lived. The creation of the ECOLE DES BEAUX-ARTS in 1795 more or less coincided with the dissolution of the Academy as such (1793), though the change was one of nomenclature rather than of intention, its place being taken by the INSTITUT. This had a fine arts division – eventually renamed the Academy in 1816 – which recruited teachers for the Ecole des Beaux-Arts; it supervised those competitions that allowed artists to make their way up the scale of promotion, including especially the all-important Prix de Rome; requested help and patronage from the government; and gave expert advice or assistance on those matters of national interest that touched on the fine or applied arts. There were constant administra-

A.W. Bouguereau's *Nymphs and a Satyr* (1873) typifies the classical connotations of **academic art**.

tive and pedagogic changes. The Ecole des Beaux-Arts established a closer relationship with the ateliers of individual artists and, in the shake-up of the French educational system which took place in 1863, the Ecole des Beaux-Arts was taken away from the Academy and transferred directly to the state. However, the effects were so catastrophic that the move was rescinded ten years later.

The authoritarianism of the academic system – with its emphasis on tradition rather than on the new Romantic conception of originality, its belief that by controlling art education you could control style, and its virtual stranglehold on most forms of official patronage – was clearly defined in the early part of the century by Quatremère de Quincy (1755–1849), who became the *secrétaire perpétuel* of the Academy. He emphasized both the importance of tradition and the relative values of certain genres of painting, the most important being history painting (which also included religious and biblical subjects). But it would be a gross exaggeration to think of this as being in any way a consistent element. Changes were constantly taking place within the overall concept of 'official' art. DELACROIX had been patronized on an official level, and by the 1870s there was a considerable overlap between pure academic, official art, and other, newer forms. The success which the Impressionists were achieving by this time meant in fact that they could not be disregarded. In 1881 there was a project for getting MANET and his 'pupils' together which CAROLUS-DURAN, Jean-Charles Cazin and BESNARD, who were more or less accepted academic painters, to decorate the newly built Trocadéro, and in 1879 Manet himself had made an official request to the Prefect of the Seine to paint one of the ceilings in the rebuilt Hôtel de Ville. It must be noted, too, that many of the Impressionists confessed their debt to the academic painters who had been their teachers. Of GLEYRE, who in the generally accepted art histories of the first half of this century was usually dismissed as a bumbling traditionalist, RENOIR said to VOLLARD 'It was from Gleyre that I learnt my trade as a painter'; and BAZILLE said that Gleyre had taught him all he knew as a painter. Artists as disparate as WHISTLER, Georges du Maurier and Edward Poynter were his pupils, and all paid tribute to his fostering of originality.

Albert Boime has pointed out that the 19th c. saw the evolution of a painting as consisting of two phases, the generative and the productive, and that, in the course of the century, the emphasis was shifted from the second to the first – a process mainly represented by Impressionism. The shift occurred within the framework of academic teaching, which by emphasizing the difference between the preliminary sketch and the 'smooth', finished work confirmed the independence of the former, thus allowing the INDÉPENDANTS to systematize it and create an aesthetic climate in which spontaneity, individual vision and immediacy of sensation came to be seen as criteria of excellence. The period, he concludes, should be seen not as a heroic struggle of progressives against reactionaries, but as one in which the Academy made a contribution, albeit often unintentional, to the evolution of 'progressive' tendencies. *See also* CORMON, COUTURE, GÉRÔME, GUICHARD, TECHNIQUE *[64, 100, 150, 151, 192]*

□ N. Pevsner, *Academies of Art, Past and Present* (1940); Sloane (1951); Boime (1986)

Académie Julian Started in 1873 by Rodolphe Julian in an old dance hall in the Passage des Panoramas, by the 1880s it had three branches and a student population of some 600. Julian, described by George MOORE as 'a typical Meridional; dark eyes, crafty and watchful, a seductively mendacious manner and a sensual mind', was himself a painter, who exhibited at the SALON DES REFUSÉS. He supervised the running of the studios, setting the pose for the model for a week at a time. He also arranged for weekly tuition sessions by well-known painters such as Bouguereau. The fees were 40 francs a month.

Although its primary intention had been to prepare students for the ECOLE DES BEAUX-ARTS, the Académie Julian developed characteristics that made it especially attractive to enterprising young artists: the teaching was flexible, and there were no restrictions; it was open every day except Sunday, from eight in the morning until nightfall – other teaching institutions were closed in the afternoon; there were no entry requirements, and it was much frequented by foreigners, who were excluded from the official educational system. Amongst those who studied there were George MOORE, William Rothenstein and the GERMAN Expressionist Lovis Corinth. Although not a student there himself, GAUGUIN was closely connected with many who were, whom he met in nearby cafés. *See also* ATELIER SYSTEM

□ Lethève (1972); C. Fehrer, 'New Light on the Académie Julian', in *Gazette des Beaux-Arts* (May–June 1984); Milner (1988)

Académie Suisse More a convenient place to paint and draw than an *académie* as such, it had been founded by a retired model, and provided no teaching or supervision, but a plenitude of models and accommodation. Situated on the Quai des Orfèvres, it was frequented by CÉZANNE, PISSARRO, MONET and GUILLAUMIN. *See also* ATELIER SYSTEM, BONVIN, GUILLEMET, PIETTE

□ Rewald (1973); Rewald (1984); Boime (1986)

Aix-en-Provence Described in the 18th c. by the traveller Charles de Brosses as the most beautiful city in France, Aix was the birthplace of ZOLA, CÉZANNE, Paul ALEXIS, and many other writers and painters of distinction. Rich in private collections and possessing in the Musée Granet (founded by a pupil of David) an impressive public art gallery, which greatly influenced the young Cézanne, it had a flourishing art school, a number of art dealers, and an active exhibiting society. The surrounding

Pissarro's drawing of a male nude was executed when he was at the **Académie Suisse** 1855–60.

Early 20th-c. photograph of Mont Sainte-Victoire, which dominates **Aix-en-Provence**.

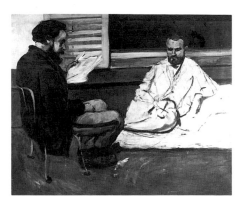

Cézanne's portrait of **Alexis** reading to Zola was painted in 1869 when the writer was about 22.

countryside was a rich source of inspiration to Cézanne, RENOIR and other artists; the area is most notable, of course, for the famous Mont Sainte-Victoire, a fact drawn to the attention of those who use the autoroute by extensive sign-posting. *See also* EMPERAIRE, GUIGOU, MARION, OLLER Y CESTERO [45]
□ Zeldin (1973); M. and P.-J. Chabert, *Aix-en-Provence au XIXe siècle* (1983); Rewald (1986)

Alexis, Paul (1847–1901) Writer, playwright and art critic, he was born in AIX-EN-PROVENCE and was a friend of both ZOLA and CÉZANNE, who painted a joint portrait of the two writers (1869; Museu de Arte Moderna, São Paulo, Brazil). A frequenter of the CAFÉ GUERBOIS, where he was a witness of a duel between MANET and DURANTY in 1870, he later became an habitué of the Nouvelle-Athènes, and in the issue of *L'Avenir* for 5 May 1873 he defended the idea of an artistic corporation as it was being propounded by the Impressionists. Two days later MONET wrote to the paper assuring Alexis of his support. At the fifth IMPRESSIONIST EXHIBITION in 1880 ZANDOMENEGHI submitted a strange portrait of him standing against a wall, to which were affixed numerous birdcages, and SEURAT also did a pastel portrait of him (1888; present whereabouts unknown).

An impassioned defender of Impressionism, he saw it as the visual equivalent of the spirit of REALISM, which he championed so vigorously in its literary context, mainly by producing and contributing to *Les Soirées de Médan* (1874). This was a collection of six stories by ZOLA, Guy de Maupassant, HUYSMANS and others, supposed to have been recounted at Zola's house at MÉDAN, and was considered a manifesto of the Realist spirit in LITERATURE. *See* NIEUWERKERKE
□ P. Alexis, *Emile Zola; Notes d'un ami* (1882); *Dictionnaire de biographie française*; D. Le Blond-Zola, 'Paul Alexis', in *Mercure de France* (1 March 1939)

Algiers Ever since Napoleon's incursion into Egypt, Africa had fascinated the imagination of the French, and their conquest of Algeria had made that country one of their main sources of pride and inspiration, variously typified by the paintings of DELACROIX. Its capital became an African Paris, visited by a host of writers and artists. MONET did his military service there, and found it 'really charming', adding significantly 'the impressions of light and colour I received there contained the germ of all my future researches'. RENOIR went there for the first time in 1881 and returned on several occasions. Among the works he produced as a consequence, the most remarkable is *Fantasia, Algiers* (1881; Musée d'Orsay). *See also* CORDEY, LEBOURG [125]

☐ C.A. Julien, *Histoire d'Algérie; la conquête et les débuts de la colonisation* (1964); Rewald (1973); *The Orientalists*, Royal Academy of Arts, London, exhibition catalogue (1984)

Ambre, Emilie (1854–98) A famous soprano who made her reputation singing the roles of Violetta in Verdi's *La Traviata* and Manon in Massenet's opera of that name. She met MANET in the summer of 1879 at Bellevue, where they were both undergoing hydrotherapy treatment. She was already an admirer of his works, and through the good offices of Edouard de Beauplan, her manager, took the painter's *Execution of the Emperor Maximilian* (1868; Kunsthalle Mannheim, lithograph in British Museum, London) on her tour of America later in the year, where it was exhibited in Boston and New York. It was probably in gratitude for this that in 1880 Manet painted her as Carmen in Bizet's opera (Philadelphia Museum of Art), a role for mezzo-soprano which she had performed in New Orleans, but not in the unsuccessful première of the opera in Paris in 1875. It was at its revival in 1883 that she scored her real triumph, helping to give the work a permanent place in the repertoire. Two years later she wrote an autobiographical novel, *Une Diva. See also* MUSIC [215]

☐ A. Tabarant, *Manet et ses oeuvres* (1947); K. Adler, *Manet* (1986)

André, Albert (1888–1943) As a young man he became a close friend and assistant of RENOIR, with whom he stayed for a considerable period at Cagnes in the early years of the 20th c. In 1901 he painted a portrait of Renoir at the latter's studio in Paris, wearing his ever-present hat, and accompanied by his servant and model Gabrielle, with his son Coco on her knee, and

Manet's portrait of Emilie **Ambre** in the role of Carmen, 1880.

Renoir's wife Aline, with their son Jean dressed as a clown. He remained close to the painter for the rest of his life, helping him in all kinds of ways and virtually becoming a member of the RENOIR FAMILY. In 1923 André published a book about Renoir which contains valuable accounts of his conversation and technique. In 1931, in collaboration with Michel Elder, he produced a two-volume work, *L'Atelier de Renoir*, reproducing in chronological order all the paintings found in the artist's studio after his death.

☐ A. André, 'Propos inédits de et sur Renoir' in *Les Nouvelles littéraires* (26 August 1933), 'Les Modèles de Renoir' in *Les Lettres françaises* (20–27 August and 27 August–3 Sept. 1953)

Andrée, Ellen (1857–*c*. 1915) An intelligent, witty and successful actress, who commenced her career as an artist's model and was one of the habitués of the Nouvelle-Athènes, where she became friendly with most of the Impressionists. She features in MANET's *La Parisienne* (1876; Nationalmuseum, Stockholm), *Au Café* (1878; Winterthur, Collection Oskar Reinhart) and *La Jeune Femme blonde aux yeux bleus* (1878; Musée d'Orsay), and most famously perhaps in

Degas painted Ellen **Andrée** seated beside Marcellin Desboutin in *L'Absinthe* of 1876.

DEGAS' *L'Absinthe* (1876; Musée d'Orsay), RENOIR's *Déjeuner des canotiers* (1881; Phillips Collection, Washington, D.C.), as well as in the works of more conventional Salon painters such as Alfred STEVENS, and in a famous nude by Henri GERVEX, which was refused admission to the SALON of 1878 for reasons of 'decency'. By the 1870s she had taken up the stage and was one of the stars of the Folies-Bergère. In 1887 she married the painter Henri Dumont and had a considerable success on the legitimate stage, especially at the Théâtre Libre, centre of the REALIST movement in drama. *[162]*
□ F.F., 'Des peintres et leurs modèles' in *Bulletin de la vie artistique* (May 1921); *Degas*, Grand Palais, Paris, exhibition catalogue (1988)

Angèle A girl who worked in a florist's shop in MONTMARTRE and whom RENOIR often used as a model. She appears in *Sleeping Girl with a Cat* (1880; Sterling and Francine Clark Art Institute, Williamstown, Mass.), *In the Summer* (1869; Nationalgalerie, Berlin) and in *Déjeuner des canotiers* (1881; Phillips Collection, Washington, D.C.), where she is seen drinking wine at a table with two men, one in profile, the other seen from the back. *[77, 162]*

Antecedents The oversimplifications that have resulted from the dramatization of Impressionism as a revolutionary movement in the history of painting have tended to obscure the fact that in certain ways it was part of a natural artistic evolution, and that the basic principles and attitudes it expressed were implicit in a European tradition which could be traced back at least as far as the Renaissance. Both in technique and in approach, there were presentiments of Impressionism in the works of artists such as Giorgione, Velazquez, El Greco, Frans Hals and Watteau, not to mention DELACROIX. It is interesting in this context to note the works which the Impressionists copied in the Louvre during their early student careers: MANET chose Delacroix, Titian, Velazquez and Tintoretto; DEGAS, Holbein, Delacroix, Velazquez, Poussin and the Italian primitives; MORISOT, Veronese, Velazquez and also works by COROT, which the artist lent her. There was therefore, right from the start, a degree of eclecticism, with each artist tending to find in the art of the past what he or she wanted. Just as Manet, on his visits to HOLLAND, became enraptured by the paintings of Frans Hals, and CÉZANNE found in Ribera a source of inspiration, so a seeming accident like the revaluation of Watteau and Fragonard in the 1860s, spearheaded by the GONCOURTS, brought technical and inspirational impetus to several Impressionists, especially RENOIR. The preoccupation with SPAIN that marked French culture during the first half of the century made the REALISM of Velazquez, Murillo, Ribera and Goya especially attractive, and the flickering brushwork of El Greco provided one of the many precedents for the lively handling of

Antecedents: Frans Hals, *Banquet of the Officers of the St Hadrian Militia Company*, 1627.

Constable's lyrical observation of light and atmosphere is well illustrated by *Dedham Mill*, c. 1815.

paint that became characteristic of the Impressionist movement. At a different level, the discovery of the art of JAPAN and an awakened interest in popular prints, such as the Images d'Epinal, added new elements to the historical palimpsest which was absorbed into Impressionism.

Perhaps the most widely noted influence is that of Constable, Turner and the English watercolourists (*see* ENGLAND). The most frequently quoted reference to this is from a letter by PISSARRO to DEWHURST, printed in the latter's book *Impressionist Painting* (London, 1904): 'Monet and I were very enthusiastic about the London landscapes. . . . We worked from nature. We also visited the museums. The watercolours and paintings of Turner and of Constable, the canvases of Old Crome, have certainly had an influence on us. We admired Gainsborough, Lawrence, Reynolds, etc., but we were struck chiefly by the landscape painters, who shared more in our aim with regard to *plein-air*, light and fugitive effects. Watts, Rossetti interested us among the modern men.' The French had been exposed to Constable since at least 1824, when his *View on the Stour* (1819) and his *Haywain* (1820; both in the National Gallery, London) won gold medals at the SALON. This had been due very largely to two dealers, Edouard Schroth and John ARROWSMITH, both of whom were close friends of Jean-Marie-Fortuné Ruel, father of DURAND-RUEL; when in 1841 the Englishman went bankrupt, he was helped by Durand-Ruel to re-establish himself, and it was in Schroth's gallery that Delacroix first saw the works of Bonington. Arrowsmith opened a brasserie in Paris, frequented by Théodore ROUSSEAU and his friends, which contained a 'Salon Constable', where the artist's paintings were on view; Ruel bought several from him, and it was

through this kind of contact that artists such as Corot, COURBET, DAUBIGNY and others of that generation first got to know his works. Delacroix had noted in his *Journal* on 23 September 1846, 'Constable says that the superiority of the green in his fields is made up of a multitude of different greens. The reason why the green of most landscapes lacks intensity and life is that they usually treat it in one single tint. What he says here about the green of meadows can be applied to all other hues.' Here was clearly the kind of painterly thinking that would have been of especial significance to the Impressionists, and though Constable's oil sketches, on the back of which he noted the date and time at which they were painted – as Monet did with many of his works – were not generally known in France until the late 1870s, there was an awareness of his concern with the transient effects of light and atmosphere.

Turner's influence is a little less clear. SIGNAC, in his book on the development of French painting in the 19th c., *D'Eugène Delacroix au néo-impressionnisme* (Paris, 1899), emphasized very strongly the influence of his 'placing a number of strokes of different colours, one beside the other, and reproducing at a distance the desired effect'. But this was perhaps special pleading, as it approximated so closely to a vindication of Signac's own theories. MONET seems to have been the most concerned of the group with Turner's work and techniques, though this interest only dates from the 1880s, when he was visiting London quite frequently. Despite superficial affinities to Turner in a work such as the famous *Impression: Sunrise* of 1872 (Musée Marmottan, Paris) his work shows no similarities with either his handling or colour range. He was certainly impressed by Turner's resolute PLEIN-AIR approach to painting and was also aware, in developing his 'series' paintings, of the fact that the English painter had produced pictures of the same place at differing times of day (e.g. the two views of Tabley House shown at the Royal Academy in 1809, and the three watercolours of differing light effects on Mount Rigi in his set of Swiss views of 1841–42).

It seems certain that most of the English influence on the Impressionists had been filtered through the sensibilities of the generation of BOUDIN and Daubigny. In any case their enthusiasm was not maintained. Monet confessed to the art dealer René Gimpel in 1918, 'Once I liked Turner very much, but now I like him less – he did not lay out his colour carefully enough, and he used too much of it.' Even Pissarro qualified his earlier remarks by adding 'Turner and Constable, while they taught us something, showed us in their works that they had no understanding of the *analysis of colour*, which in Turner's painting is simply used as an effect; a mere absence of light.' *See also* BARBIZON, GERMANY, IMPRESSIONISM, ITALY *[114]*

□ Sloane (1951); Champa (1973); Rewald (1973)

Argenteuil Before 1840 Argenteuil, a small village in the neighbourhood of PARIS, had depended on agriculture and the manufacture of plaster-of-Paris. The coming of the RAILWAY, which brought it within 15 minutes' distance of the Gare Saint-Lazare and the exploding population of Paris, changed all this. The Seine widens at Argenteuil, making it an ideal boating centre, and the renting of villas at the waterside soon became a major part of its economy. MONET rented a house there in 1872, where he first gave vent to a passion for gardening; he had been encouraged in this by CAILLEBOTTE, who considered it, along with boat-building, his main passion next to art. He was often joined by RENOIR, who in 1873 painted him working in the garden (The Wadsworth Atheneum, Hartford, Conn.). SISLEY was another visitor, and both he and Monet painted the boulevard Héloïse in the town. MANET also came there, and painted, amongst other things, Monet working in the floating studio he had created with the help of Caillebotte (1874; Bayerische Staatsgemäldesammlungen, Munich) and a portrait of the Monet family in their garden (1874; Metropolitan Museum, New York), which is identical in treatment and siting with one by Renoir (1874; National Gallery of Art, Washington). It was there, too, that Monet painted his first railway pictures, including several of the bridge across the river.

Argenteuil was one of the most significant places in the early history of Impressionism. In its relaxed atmosphere, marked by the presence of the Parisian petit-bourgeois seeking their weekend pleasures, the painters who worked together exerted on each other an influence that welded them together; using similar techniques on identical subjects, they adopted common attitudes to PLEIN-AIR painting and to that depiction of light which gives validity to the concept of Impressionism as a coherent movement. *See also* TECHNIQUE *[56, 168]*

The incursion of industry into the rural area around the Seine is reflected in Monet's *Unloading Coal, Argenteuil* (1875), while the photograph (*top*) shows a more unspoilt scene.

□ A. Martin, *Tout autour de Paris, promenades et excursions dans le département de la Seine* (1894); P.H. Tucker, *Monet at Argenteuil* (1982); Clark (1984); Herbert (1988)

Arnaud, Jules Arsène *see* CLARETIE, JULES

Arosa, Gustave (*c.*1835–*c.*1900) A successful banker who collected contemporary art and was especially enamoured of the paintings of PISSARRO, to whom he was exceptionally helpful. He was the godfather of Paul GAUGUIN, for whom he found a job in the financial world on the latter's return to Paris in 1871. His wife Margaret was an amateur painter, and encouraged the young Gauguin in his interest in painting. *See also* PATRONS AND COLLECTORS

□ Rewald (1973)

Arrowsmith, John (1798–1873) A member of a well-known English family of map-printers, he was a close friend of Constable, whom he

persuaded to exhibit at the SALON of 1824; together with Edouard Schroth he was largely responsible for popularizing Constable's works in France. He opened a brasserie in the rue Saint-Marc, which contained a 'Salon Constable', adorned with paintings by the artist, which was frequented by Théodore ROUSSEAU and his friends. One of Arrowsmith's close friends was Jean-Marie-Fortuné Ruel, father of DURAND-RUEL, who bought several works by Constable from him, thus establishing a direct link between Impressionism and this particular aspect of the English tradition. His sister married Daguerre. *See* ENGLAND
□ Venturi (1939)

L'Artiste An illustrated monthly magazine, founded in the 1840s, which had the same standing in France as the *Magazine of Art* in England. Although generally conservative in its outlook, and originally hostile to the Impressionists, it changed its attitude when Arsène HOUSSAYE was appointed as one of its directors and became generally supportive, especially of MONET. It is significant, however, that when in 1877 Houssaye asked Georges RIVIÈRE to write an article about the third IMPRESSIONIST EXHIBITION, he stipulated that to avoid irritating the public Rivière should avoid mentioning PISSARRO and CÉZANNE. *See also* CASTAGNARY, RASHDALL *[111]*
□ Rewald (1973); G. Ballas, 'Paul Cézanne et la revue "L'Artiste"', in *Gazette des Beaux-Arts* 98 (Dec. 1981)

Astruc, Zacharie (1833–1907) Sculptor, painter and art critic, he participated in the first IMPRESSIONIST EXHIBITION and also in the Exposition Universelle of 1900. His defence of living art was consistent and whole-hearted; he had been a defender of COURBET, and was one of the first to recognize the talent of PISSARRO and MANET. To celebrate the SALON DES REFUSÉS, he brought out a daily paper for its duration, in which he lauded the participating artists, describing Manet as 'one of the greatest artistic characters of his time'. In 1865 he hailed the genius of MONET and was responsible for introducing him to Manet. He wrote the introduction to the catalogue of the one-man exhibition that Manet arranged in a pavilion outside the Exposition Universelle of 1867. He appears seated beside Manet in FANTIN-LATOUR's *A Studio in the Batignolles Quarter* (1879; Musée d'Orsay), and was painted by BAZILLE (*c.* 1869;

Engraving by Manet of Lola de Valence, for the publication of songs written by **Astruc**, 1862.

Collection Frédéric Bazille, Montpellier) and by Manet (1866; Kunsthalle, Bremen). Astruc himself executed a bust of Manet and by the 1880s was receiving recognition as a sculptor, his most popular work being the *Mask Pedlar* (1883) in the Luxembourg Gardens. *See also* SCULPTURE *[86]*
□ *Dictionnaire de biographie française*; Hamilton (1954)

Atelier system Throughout most of the 19th c. the basic foundation of art teaching in PARIS was the atelier system, which basically consisted in a would-be painter working in an older painter's studio, in a position that was midway between that of an apprentice and a pupil. Largely abandoned in England and even in the French provinces by 1850, it provided the background against which all the Impressionists had their first real experience of art, and was given a degree of vitality and even official standing by its frequently close relationship to the Academy, from which most of its practitioners came. Virtually all those who entered an atelier did so in the hope of winning the Prix de

Rome, the first rung on the ladder of artistic success.

Starting by copying engravings, students progressed to drawing from plaster casts, usually of antique statues, the emphasis in this phase being on the manipulation of light and shade to represent volume. Then came confrontation with the living model, a point at which the student passed from being subject to initiation rites and all the humiliating horseplay which throughout history has, in most cultures, been characteristic of the apprenticeship process. At this point problems often arose because the earlier stages of training emphasized component parts at the expense of the whole, and there was the consequent difficulty of achieving compositional unity. It was to these life drawings that the master of the studio usually addressed himself, concentrating for the most part on proportional or anatomical mistakes and indicating corrections with a pencil or the indentation of a fingernail.

Then, drawing hopefully having been mastered, the student proceeded to the use of oil paint, commencing with the copying of old masters, usually at the Louvre, and then moving on to the painting of heads from life. It was at this stage that the didactic activities of the master would usually make their appearance, when he painted an *ébauche*, or sketch, of a head before the assembled students. Great emphasis was placed on the use of a limited range of colours, heavily diluted to secure a rapid notation of general effects, beginning with local highlights, then proceeding to middle tones and ending with the deepest shadows; the student was warned especially to set down the individual tones carefully beside each other, and not to allow them to mix on the canvas. The sketch was then allowed to dry and gradually worked up into a smoothly finished painting. The mastery of technical skills was considered all-important, and the success of any master of an atelier was measured in terms of how effective he was in communicating them. Drawing techniques were taught in a more or less standard way; it was with painting that the traditions of an atelier varied, and these variations had most influence on pupils.

COUTURE, who was the teacher of MANET and PUVIS DE CHAVANNES, opened his studio in 1847 on the groundswell of his successful *Romains de la décadence* (Musée d'Orsay) and claimed in his prospectus that he 'opposes the spurious classical school which reproduces the works of

A group of students in Cormon's **atelier**, including Toulouse-Lautrec and Emile Bernard, c. 1883.

bygone times in a banal and imperfect fashion. He is even more hostile to that abominable school known under the rubric of "Romantic", and views with disfavour the tendencies towards petty commercialism of art.' He was to go on teaching for the rest of his life and developed a cult following. Having made six unsuccessful attempts to win the Prix de Rome, he was averse to the whole educational system of ACADEMIC ART and placed great emphasis on the sketch as the most vital element in the creation of a painting. In his *Méthodes et entretiens d'atelier* (1867) he wrote 'Originality is a question of conveying one's impressions accurately . . . we must get into the way of catching nature on the wing'. Landscape played an important part in his teaching, and he took his students out to the fields, and sometimes on trips to the Normandy coast. Although Manet's criticism of Couture's atelier is well known – 'When I arrive I feel as though I were entering a tomb. Everything that meets the eye is ridiculous. The light is wrong; the shadows are wrong' – many of his early works show the influence of his teacher, with whom, incidentally, he stayed for six years. Two of PISSARRO's closest friends in the early 1860s, OLLER Y CESTERO and Ludovic PIETTE, whose technique at this time was much more experimental than his own, had been pupils of Couture, and CÉZANNE always kept a reproduction of *Les Romains de la décadence* in his studio.

RENOIR, MONET, SISLEY, BAZILLE and WHISTLER attended GLEYRE's atelier. He, too, was an opponent of official art education, and attracted little attention or patronage from officialdom. Regarded as an original, if not an eccentric, he strongly emphasized originality in his teaching

Atelier system: A paintbrush duel at the Ecole des Beaux-Arts, from *Bohemian Paris*, 1899.

Cézanne painted this view of Dr Gachet's house at **Auvers-sur-Oise** in 1873.

and advised, 'Do not draw on anyone's resources but your own.' Bazille, who wrote that Gleyre had taught him his métier, added that as a consequence of his teaching, 'I shall at least be able to boast that I have not copied anyone.' Gleyre's method of teaching allowed students a great deal of latitude, and in a letter to his parents Bazille recorded that 'M. Gleyre comes twice a week and has a word with each pupil, correcting his drawing or painting. Every now and again he assigns the subject of a composition, which everyone carries out as best he can.' In 1894 Georges du Maurier described in his novel *Trilby* (1894) the kind of timetable that operated during his student days there: 'We drew and painted from the male model every day but Sunday, from eight till twelve and for two hours in the afternoon, except on Saturdays, when the afternoon was dedicated to a much-needed cleaning of the Augean stables. One week the model was male, the next female and so on, alternating throughout the year. A stove, a model throne, stools, boxes, some fifty strongly built low chairs with backs, a couple of score easels and many drawing boards completed the *mobilier*. The bare walls were adorned with endless caricatures in charcoal and white chalk and also the scrapings of many palettes – a polychromous decoration not

unpleasing.' There are countless descriptions of the boisterous atmosphere that prevailed in these ateliers, but this was indicative of another merit of the atelier system: the constant interchange of ideas about art and techniques amongst the students themselves. As Du Maurier put it, 'All were animated by a certain *esprit de corps*, working very happily and genuinely together, and always willing to help each other with sincere artistic counsel, if it was asked for seriously, though it was not always couched in terms very flattering to one's self-love.' There can be no doubt that the nursery of Impressionism was the studio of Gleyre. *See also* ACADÉMIE JULIAN, ACADÉMIE SUISSE, CORMON, ECOLE DES BEAUX-ARTS, TECHNIQUE *[15, 64, 79]*
□ L. Ormond, *George du Maurier* (1969); Lethève (1972); Boime (1986)

Auvers-sur-Oise Like ARGENTEUIL, this little village on the banks of the river Oise was a leading centre of Impressionism, where its practitioners came into close and creative contact with each other. It had become a popular place for artists in the late 1850s when Daumier (who died in the neighbourhood), DAUBIGNY and COROT worked there. Berthe MORISOT came there frequently to visit her sister, and DR GACHET bought a house in the

De Balleroy is the last standing figure on the right of Fantin-Latour's *Hommage à Delacroix* (1864), which includes, from left to right, Cordier, Duranty, Legros, Fantin-Latour, Whistler, Champfleury, Manet, Bracquemond and Baudelaire.

village shortly after the outbreak of the FRANCO-PRUSSIAN WAR, where he entertained his Impressionist friends. CÉZANNE painted several pictures of the place, including one of the doctor's house (*c.* 1873; Collection of Mrs Mary Fosburgh, New York), as did RENOIR, GUILLAUMIN and SISLEY. Some of VAN GOGH's last works were of scenes in the neighbourhood. *See also* MURER, PONTOISE *[93]*
□ Rewald (1984); Herbert (1988)

B

Baille, Baptiste (1841–1918) A childhood friend of CÉZANNE and ZOLA, he became a professor at the Ecole Polytechnique and assistant mayor of the XIth *arrondissement* of Paris. Zola dedicated his first novel, *La Confession de Claude* (1865), to both him and Cézanne, and Baille appeared as one of the characters in Zola's *L'Oeuvre* (1886).
□ Rewald (1984); Rewald (1986)

Balleroy, Comte Albert de (1828–73) A close friend of MANET, who rented a studio with him in the rue Lavoisier, he was very much part of the fashionable world which Manet frequented in the 1860s; in *La Musique aux Tuileries* (1862; National Gallery, London) he is shown standing beside Manet. Predominantly an animal-painter, renowned for the brilliance of his technique, he exhibited regularly at the SALON between 1853 and his death, and was also well known for his etchings. He was a friend of FANTIN-LATOUR, who painted him, again standing beside Manet, in *Hommage à Delacroix* (1864; Musée d'Orsay). *[90]*
□ A. Tabarant, *Manet et ses oeuvres* (1947); K. Adler, *Manet* (1986)

Banville, Théodore de (1823–91) Writer, poet and critic, he was a friend of many of the artists of the period and was especially enthusiastic about the works of Daumier.
□ C. Baudelaire, 'Théodore de Banville', in *Oeuvres Complètes*, ed. C. Pichois (1975–76); U. Finke (ed.), *French Nineteenth-Century Painting and Literature* (1972)

Barbizon A small village in the forest of Fontainebleau, which had been known as a centre for artists since the middle of the 18th c. It

Photograph of a snow-covered street in **Barbizon**, in the forest of Fontainebleau, *c.* 1875.

achieved great prominence in the 1830s, when it gave its name to a whole school of landscape painters, now counted amongst the precursors of Impressionism, who worked and painted there. The principal members were Théodore ROUSSEAU, Constant Troyon and MILLET; COROT was also closely connected with them. Enamoured of light and feeling, they were opposed to ACADEMIC traditions, but unlike the Impressionists, they only sketched out-of-doors and completed their paintings in the studio. Influenced by English art, they tended to express a Romantic aversion to urban life.

Inevitably, the Impressionists came to a village frequented by those whom they admired; it was in the neighbourhood of Barbizon that MONET painted his *Déjeuner sur l'herbe* (1866; Pushkin Museum, Moscow) and at about the same time RENOIR painted a group of his friends around a table in the famous CABARET DE LA MÈRE ANTHONY in the village of Marlotte (1866; Nationalmuseum Stockholm). The inn of Mère Ganne, which the GONCOURTS described in *Manette Salomon* (1866), was also very popular. *See also* ANTECEDENTS, BELGIUM, DAUBIGNY, DIAZ, ENGLAND, PHOTOGRAPHY, PLEIN-AIRISME, POLITICS, PONTOISE *[37, 61, 68, 74, 139, 190]*
□ J. Gasquet, 'Le Paradis de Renoir', in *L'Amour de l'art* (February 1921); J. Bouret *The Barbizon School* (1973); Champa (1973); Clark (1973a)

Barnes, Alfred (1872–1951) One of the great American collectors of Impressionist paintings, he had made a fortune from a purgative preparation, Argyrol. He bought parts of the collection of the Prince de WAGRAM and was an assiduous client of DURAND-RUEL immediately before the Great War. His important collection of works by RENOIR was acquired in the early 1920s, when many of them came on to the market as a result of the artist's death. In 1924 he presented his collection to the Barnes Foundation at Merion near Philadelphia, Penn. *See also* PATRONS AND COLLECTORS, USA
□ Venturi (1939); Cooper (1954); *Barnes Collection*, Philadelphia, catalogue (n.d.)

Bartholomé, Paul Albert (1848–1928) Commencing his artistic career as a painter, somewhat in the style of MANET, with a penchant for subjects from everyday life, he devoted the best part of his later life to SCULPTURE, dealing mostly with themes of death and mortality, consequent upon the comparatively early loss of his wife. From the end of the 1870s he became very friendly with DEGAS and gave him a great deal of help with his sculpture, especially in the preparation of the wax models for casting. Their correspondence is of inestimable value in understanding the latter's work and character. Bartholomé's own most famous work was a huge monument to the dead in the cemetery of Père-Lachaise. After Degas' death he supervised the casting of all his sculptures, edited by Hébrard from 1919 onwards. *[70]*

Batignolles The building and rebuilding of PARIS that took place from the mid-19th c. under the aegis of Baron Haussmann spawned new districts and areas, as well as the great boulevards with which his name is connected. One of these, which became popular with artists and writers, was that which stretched

Caillebotte's *Rue de Paris, temps de pluie* (1877) depicts an area of the **Batignolles** quarter.

A photograph of the Place de Clichy in **Batignolles**, taken in 1900, reveals the lively Paris cityscape which so appealed to the Impressionists.

from the neighbourhood of the Gare Saint-Lazare to the industrialized suburb of Batignolles, which, like its neighbour MONTMARTRE, had been absorbed into greater Paris. Its main thoroughfare was the boulevard des Batignolles, formed in 1863, but the surrounding streets and squares became a virtual alternative Left Bank. BAUDELAIRE lived in the rue d'Amsterdam, which ran north from the Gare Saint-Lazare to the boulevard, and two doors away was Alphonse DAUDET. MANET had a studio here in 1879, though earlier he had lived at 34 boulevard des Batignolles and then in the rue de St-Pétersbourg, the setting for FANTIN-LATOUR's *A Studio in the Batignolles Quarter* (1870; Musée d'Orsay). CAILLEBOTTE, who lived with his parents on the nearby rue Mirmonsil, took the intersection of the rue de St-Pétersbourg and the Place de Clichy as the subject of one of Impressionism's most memorable townscapes, *Rue de Paris, temps de pluie* (1877; Art Institute of Chicago). RENOIR and BAZILLE lived at 9 rue de la Condamine. Manet himself did several paintings of the rue Mosnier, a new street that ran northwards from just opposite his studio window on the rue de St Pétersbourg, and

PISSARRO several times painted the Place du Havre, outside the station, from a room in the Hôtel Garnier. In the rue de Rome at number 89, MALLARMÉ held his famous evenings, thus ensuring the continuance of DEGAS' interest in the area.

But Batignolles has a greater significance in the history of Impressionism than as a popular area for its practitioners; it was the first name given to that group of artists who made up the movement and who came generally to be described by contemporary critics as the Batignolles group. This came about very largely because by c. 1866 Manet had begun to frequent the CAFÉ GUERBOIS at 11 Grande rue des Batignolles, which by 1869 was established as a regular meeting place – Thursday was the favourite day. MONET remembered these occasions vividly in his old age: 'Nothing could have been more interesting than these meetings and the discussions which went with them. There was a constant clash of opinions. They kept our wits sharpened, they supplied us with reserves of enthusiasm that inspired us for weeks and weeks until we accomplished what we had thought of. From these discussions we emerged with a stronger will, more clearly defined ideas, and our thoughts clearer and more distinct.' Those who took part in the meetings were Manet, Pissarro, Monet, SISLEY, Bazille, Degas, Renoir, BRACQUEMOND, Alfred STEVENS, Fantin-Latour and GUILLEMET, as well as fringe figures such as ZOLA, SILVESTRE, ASTRUC, DURANTY and NADAR. CÉZANNE made an occasional appearance but did not participate much in the discussions. If IMPRESSIONISM had a birthplace, the Batignolles area was undoubtedly it. [86]

□ J. Hillairet, *Dictionnaire historique des rues de Paris* (2nd ed., 1964); Milner (1988)

Baudelaire, Charles Pierre (1821–67) Born of an aristocratic Catholic family, he settled down in Paris in 1843 with his Mauritian mistress Jeanne Duval and began a career as a poet and writer. His influence on succeeding generations was formidable, largely because he substituted for the rather slack rhetoric of the earlier Romanticists a more rigorous self-analysis, combined with a quest for intense sensation which led him, on the one hand, to dependence on opium and alcohol but, on the other, to the production of some of the most powerful verse in the French language.

Deeply interested in art, a friend of DELACROIX, Daumier and others, as well as an habitué of the BRASSERIE DES MARTYRS and other artistic haunts, he produced in 1845 and 1846 reviews of the annual SALONS that struck a new note in art criticism. Although reflecting the influence of his 18th-c. predecessor in the genre, Denis Diderot (1713–84), and the kind of sensibility expressed by Stendhal (1783–1842), his own visual awareness gave his writings on art a vitality and spontaneity which compensated for their occasional lapses of judgment. His was the first consistent attempt to elevate subjective judgment to the level of a final criterion, uncontaminated by aesthetic ground-rules or ideological canons of taste. Initially preoccupied with the dichotomy between the art of Ingres and that of Delacroix, he devoted some of his most powerful passages to the defence and praise of the latter, showing an antipathy to realistic techniques that owed not a little to his own poetic experience. His dislike did not extend to REALISM itself, however. He admired COURBET's vitality and, in *Le Peintre de la vie moderne* (1863), devoted to the work of Constantin GUYS, he outlined a theory of contemporary realism in art which could act as an apologia for one aspect of Impressionism: 'The past is interesting not only because of the beauty which the artists of the past – whose present it was – have extracted from it, but because of its historical value. The same applies to the present. The pleasure which we derive from the presentation of the present derives from the beauty which it may possess, as well as from its essential quality as the present. Modernity is the transitory, the fugitive, the contingent, which make up one half of art, the other being the eternal and the immutable. This transitory, fugitive element, which is constantly changing, must not be despised or neglected. If you do so you tumble into the emptiness of an abstract and undefinable beauty.'

It has been forcibly suggested that it was these sentiments which persuaded MANET, who had once painted himself and his wife in the costumes of the Rubens period, and who at this time was concentrating on picturesque Spanish subjects, to opt entirely for subjects from contemporary life. Manet had met Baudelaire in 1858 and they became close friends, Manet producing two etchings of the poet – one informal, the other resembling a title page – as well as a rough oil sketch of his funeral (1867; Metropolitan Museum, New York). Four years after Manet had produced it, the more formal etching was used as the frontispiece to the first biography of the poet, Charles Asselineau's *Charles Baudelaire; sa vie et son oeuvre*. In the *Revue anecdotique* of 2 April 1862 Baudelaire published, anonymously, an article entitled 'L'eau-forte est à la mode', which he then reproduced in a much more extended form as 'Peintres et Aqua-fortistes' in *Le Boulevard* on 14 September in the same year. He praised BRACQUEMOND, JONGKIND, MILLET, DAUBIGNY, as well as Legros and Manet; of the latter he said, 'M. Manet is the painter of *The Spanish Singer* [1860; Metropolitan Museum, New York], which created a stir at the last Salon. At the next Salon we are promised several pictures by him [e.g. *Mlle Victorine in the Costume of an Espada* Metropolitan Museum, New York] spiced with the strongest Spanish flavour – which suggest that the genius of SPAIN has come to take its abode in France.' (Two years later in a letter to the critic Théophile Thoré, Baudelaire denied that Manet relied on the Spanish school, and even suggested that at this point he had seen no Spanish paintings, which was palpably untrue.) In his review of the Salon of 1859,

One of **Bayard**'s innovative negatives, c. 1840, which explored the artistic potential of the camera.

Baudelaire had already praised the work of LEGROS, and he now declared: 'MM. Manet and Legros combine a vigorous taste for reality, modern reality – already a good sign – with an imagination which is both abundant and lively, without which, it must be emphasized, even the finest gifts are no more than servants without a master, agents without a government.'

Baudelaire did not live long enough to be able to take up an attitude to the concept of a school of Impressionists, but there was hardly one of those who participated in the movement who did not at one point or another find in his writings justification for their attitudes, or sanctions for their choice of subject. *See also* BATIGNOLLES, GAUTIER, JAPANESE ART, LITERATURE, PRINTS *[23, 90, 138]*
□ Hamilton (1954); C. Baudelaire, *Art in Paris 1845–1862*, ed. J. Mayne (1965); U. Finke (ed.), *French Nineteenth-Century Painting and Literature* (1972); Clark (1973a)

Baudot, Jeanne (1877–1957) Daughter of a doctor who was a friend of Paul Gallimard, owner of the Théâtre des Variétés and a collector of RENOIR's works, who introduced the Baudot family to the painter in 1893. At the age of 17 she joined Julie Manet and the two GOBILLARD girls as part of a group to whom Renoir gave painting lessons – based on copying works from the Louvre. He maintained a correspondence with Jeanne, and she was one of the consolations of his old age.
□ J. Baudot, *Renoir, ses amis, ses modèles* (1949); Roberts and Roberts (1987)

Bayard, Hippolyte (1801–87) One of the pioneers of PHOTOGRAPHY, he was notable for his realization of that close link between art and the camera which was to play so important a role in the evolution of the Impressionist vision. He perfected a photographic technique which he described as 'photogenic drawing', exhibiting examples of the results at an exhibition of paintings held in 1839. His main contribution lay in his preference for paper, as opposed to metal, as a support for the photographic print, which naturally brought it closer to 'pure' art. His photographs were remarkable for their artistic and even painterly qualities, especially his landscapes and still lifes. His achievement was recognized by the Académie des Beaux-Arts, which allowed them to be shown in the Salon of 1850.
□ Lo Duca, *Bayard* (1943); A. Scharf, *Art and Photography* (1974)

Bazille, Frédéric (1841–70) One of the dominant figures in the early history of Impressionism and an artist of considerable power and originality. His career was cut short by his death in the FRANCO-PRUSSIAN WAR in a minor skirmish at Beaune-la-Rolande on 28 November 1870. He came from a well-to-do family of wine-producers in the Hérault, whom he portrayed on the terrace of the family home near Montpellier in 1868 (Musée d'Orsay), and he was first introduced to the paintings of DELACROIX and COURBET by a family friend, the collector Alfred BRUYAS. Bazille came to Paris as a medical student, but his real interest was in painting, and he attended the studio lessons of GLEYRE, where he met LEPIC, RENOIR, SISLEY and MONET. He went painting with Monet at Chailly, and produced a vivid portrait of him lying in bed after an accident (1866; Musée d'Orsay). Bazille had previously accompanied him to HONFLEUR, where he met BOUDIN and JONGKIND. From 1865 to 1866 he shared a studio with Monet in the rue Furstenberg (where Delacroix had lived), and in the following year, one with Renoir in the rue Visconti near the ECOLE DES BEAUX-ARTS, in both cases assuming the main financial responsibility.

In 1867 he wrote to his parents telling them of a project – the first known record of the conception of a 'movement' – to rent a large studio, 'where we'll exhibit as many of our works as we wish. . . . Courbet, COROT, DIAZ, DAUBIGNY and others have promised to send us pictures, and very much approve of our idea.

27

In 1870 **Bazille** painted the interior of his studio in the rue de la Condamine. He is the tall figure with a palette in his hand.

With these people and Monet, who is stronger than all of them, we are sure to succeed.' A regular attender at the social gatherings of the CAFÉ GUERBOIS, he himself took a large studio in the rue de la Condamine off the boulevard de Clichy in 1868, which he generously lent to his friends, and where he entertained musicians and writers as well as painters. In his painting of the studio (1870; Musée d'Orsay) he shows the musician MAÎTRE at the piano, ZOLA leaning over the staircase speaking to Renoir, who is seated on a table; and MANET, smoking his inevitable pipe, looking at a painting on the easel, with Monet behind him; the figure of Bazille himself was painted in by Manet. Clear-minded, practical, widely read and explorative in his tastes – it was he who introduced Renoir to the as yet largely unrecognized genius of Wagner – he would almost certainly have been one of the dominant figures in the movement that was to come into being four years after his death. *See also* MUSIC, PHOTOGRAPHY, PLEIN-AIRISME, POR-TRAITURE, SOCIAL BACKGROUND *[86, 131, 205]*

□ G. Poulain, *Bazille et ses amis* (1932); F. Daulte, *Frédéric Bazille et son temps* (1952); *Frédéric Bazille*, Musée Fabre, Montpellier, exhibition catalogue (Oct. 1959)

Belgium Created a nation in 1831, Belgium was a French enclave within a Flemish country, a Catholic state within a Protestant environ-ment, and throughout the 19th c. its connec-tions with Paris were intimate. It was a place for French refugees of all kinds, from BAUDELAIRE to Boulanger, and, especially during the FRANCO-PRUSSIAN WAR and the disturbances that followed it, Brussels was crowded with French artists, such as BOUDIN and DIAZ (who attracted a considerable body of patrons there), and dealers, such as DURAND-RUEL, who opened a gallery in the Place des Martyrs. He had rented the premises from a well-known Belgian pho-tographer, Ghemar, and built up an impressive list of customers, including the Prime Minister Van Praet, and Pierre Allard, the director of the Mint. The Belgians had always been quick to detect the new tendencies in French painting. COURBET commanded a following there, especially – for some obscure reason – in Antwerp, and the BARBIZON painters had a strong influence on a whole group of Belgian artists, including Hippolyte Boulenger (1837–74) and Alphonse Asselbergs (1839–1916), all of whom worked in and around Tervueren near Brussels. The influence of the Impressionists,

Belgium: van Rysselberghe's poster for the sixth exhibition of Les Vingt.

Boulenger's *Avenue of Elms at Tervueren* (1871) shows the early influence of Barbizon in **Belgium**.

however, became increasingly apparent in the work of the seascape painter Louis Artan (1837–90) and of Alfred Verwee (1838–95); together they founded the Société Libre des Beaux-Arts, which became a centre for 'new' art.

The Belgians seem to have had a particular penchant for such organizations, for the creation of Les Vingt in 1883 was to mark another stage in the impact of Impressionism, involving as it did extensive exposure of the works of the French Impressionists. The group got its name from the fact that it was originally composed of 20 artists, but it was given its dynamism and significance by the activities of Octave MAUS, who arranged annual exhibitions that included works not only by members but by invited artists from other countries. These were always very popular and controversial events and, though the bias of the group was anti-official, they were usually held in official buildings. The French Impressionists played a prominent, if not a dominant, role, and amongst those who exhibited were RENOIR, MONET, SISLEY, PISSARRO and GAUGUIN. DEGAS, however, who had visited Brussels in 1869 and had not only sold three paintings but had been offered a contract by Alfred STEVENS (though nothing came of it),

refused to participate. In 1886 Renoir sent eight works, including *Madame Charpentier and her Children* (1878; Metropolitan Museum, New York), Monet exhibited ten, and, in following years, Pissarro and CÉZANNE sent considerable numbers of paintings. Later BRACQUEMOND, Rodin, VAN GOGH, WHISTLER and the Pointillists were also exhibitors. In 1893 Les Vingt was disbanded, but Octave Maus created a similar institution – Le Libre Esthétique – which continued until the German invasion and which, though it tended to be dominated by the POST-IMPRESSIONISTS, still gave a good deal of exposure to the earlier generation, especially Renoir.

The effect of all this was to attract a considerable number of Belgian artists to Impressionism. The most consistent of these was Emile Claus (1849–1924), who had a large body of followers and was one of the founders of Les Vingt. He won his original fame as an exponent of realistic genre painting in the style of Jules Bastien-Lepage but, as a result of the Impressionist works he had seen in the Les Vingt exhibitions and of the writings of the critic Camille Lemmonnier in the pages of the influential magazine *L'Art libre*, he turned to

Impressionist techniques and approaches, being especially dependent on Monet. There were others, however, such as Theo van Rysselberghe (1862–1926), who, having felt the initial impact of Impressionism, were seduced by SEURAT into modified forms of Pointillism. Even the highly original, and eccentric, James Ensor (1860–1949) experienced the liberating effects of the movement, and his graphic works in particular for long reflected Impressionistic techniques. See also JOYANT [47]
□ M.O. Maus, Trente ans de lutter pour l'art 1884–1914 (1926); Le Groupe des XX et son temps, Musées Royaux, Brussels, exhibition catalogue (1962); Flemish Art, ed. H. Liebers (1985)

Béliard, Edouard (1835–1902) A student of GLEYRE, Béliard came into early contact with CÉZANNE, SISLEY, MONET, ZOLA and the circle of the CAFÉ GUERBOIS. He stayed frequently with PISSARRO at PONTOISE in the early 1870s and was a member of the inaugural committee which set about forming the Impressionist group, being especially active in helping RENOIR to manage the financial side. He exhibited in the first IMPRESSIONIST EXHIBITION and in 1875 joined the short-lived UNION, promoted by Pissarro. Zola always spoke kindly of his works and, according to the novelist's notebooks, Béliard helped him considerably not only with art matters, but also concerning things musical. His impact on posterity has been negligible.
□ E. Zola, Correspondance, in Oeuvres Complètes, ed. M. Le Blond (1928); Rewald (1973)

Bellelli family DEGAS had a great and, in some ways, typically Italian sense of family loyalty, painting numerous portraits of his brothers, his relatives and those connected with him. The most spectacular of these is the portrait of his father's sister, the Baroness Gennaro Bellelli, with her husband and her two daughters, Giulia and Giovanna; though Neapolitan, the family were living in exile in Florence when the portrait was painted (1858–59; Musée d'Orsay). At the same time Degas did a drawing of Enrichetta Dembowska, the ten-year-old daughter of Enrichetta Bellelli, Gennaro's sister-in-law (Private collection, San Francisco), who had married Baron Ercole Federico Dembowski, a famous astronomer. Degas also painted the two Bellelli daughters some seven years later (Los Angeles County Museum of Art). See also ITALY
□ R. Raimondi, Degas e la sua famiglia in Napoli,

1793–1917 (1958); Degas, Grand Palais, Paris, exhibition catalogue (1988)

Bellio, Georges de (1835–94) A devoted friend and PATRON of many of the Impressionists, he was a doctor of Romanian origin, who from a very early stage in his life had been an avid collector of paintings. One of his great merits was that, whether from a desire to be helpful or from shrewd commercial instincts, he invariably bought paintings that were slow to 'move', several of which he lent to the IMPRESSIONIST EXHIBITION of 1877. Amongst the many important works he acquired were MONET's Impression: Sunrise (1872; Musée Marmottan), RENOIR's Dancing at the Moulin de la Galette (1876; Whitney Collection, New York) and The Swing (1876; Musée d'Orsay). Like his colleague DR GACHET, he was a homeopath and tended many of the Impressionists and their models. [53, 114]
□ R. Niculesco 'Georges de Bellio, l'ami des Impressionnistes', in Paragone (1970); Rewald (1973)

Bérard, Paul (1823–1905) A banker and diplomat who had a large estate at Wargemont, near Dieppe, and became one of RENOIR's most reliable PATRONS. On his death, no less than 18 works by the artist were part of the collection that was sold off by Georges PETIT; one of them, The Afternoon of the Children at Wargemont (1884; Nationalgalerie, Staatliche Museen, Preussicher Kulturbesitz, Berlin), fetched 14,000 francs. Renoir kept up a regular corres-

Gennaro **Bellelli**, his wife and daughters, portrayed by Degas at Florence, 1858–59.

Renoir, *The Afternoon of the Children at Wargemont*, 1884, showing the daughters of his patron **Bérard**.

pondence with Bérard, and when in 1900 he was awarded the Legion of Honour, he asked that 'M. Paul Bérard, *chevalier* of the Legion of Honour of 20 rue Pigalle, Paris, represent me, and deliver to me at Grasse the insignia of the Legion of Honour'. He also accompanied him on a trip to HOLLAND, mainly to see the museums and art galleries there. In addition to the portraits of the Bérard family he produced at Wargemont, Renoir also painted a number of landscapes in the grounds of the château.
□ M. Bérard, *Renoir à Wargemont* (1939); F. Daulte, 'Renoir et la famille Bérard', in *L'Oeil* (Feb. 1974); *Renoir*, Hayward Gallery, London, exhibition catalogue (1985)

Bernard, Emile (1868–1941) A painter and critic of singular distinction who played an important part in the later development of the

Bernard, *The Bridge at Asnières*, 1887: a Post-Impressionist response to industrial themes.

movement, especially in relation to the works of GAUGUIN and CÉZANNE. He studied painting under CORMON, and quickly developed a style that combined elements of Symbolism with the effects that were being produced by Sérusier, DENIS and Gauguin himself. None of his later works achieved the same excellence as these early ones, but his impassioned articles about Cézanne, whom he visited at AIX, and about VAN GOGH, whose first exhibition he arranged in Paris in 1893, went far to establish the reputation of these artists. *See also* POST-IMPRESSIONISM *[21]*
□ E. Bernard, *Souvenirs* (1939), *Lettres de Paul Gauguin à Emile Bernard* (1954); M. Roskill, *Van Gogh, Gauguin and the Impressionist Circle* (1970)

Besnard, Paul Albert (1849–1934) In 1874 he won the Prix de Rome, after being a pupil of Cabanel at the ECOLE DES BEAUX-ARTS. Despite the ACADEMIC bent of his art, he was greatly influenced by the Impressionists and their followers. He painted nudes in the style of RENOIR, portraits in the style of SARGENT, and decorative paintings in the style of PUVIS DE CHAVANNES. In London, where he lived for three years between 1881 and 1883, he took up etching under the influence of LEGROS. He became an influential critic in Paris, and honours rained on him: in 1913 he became director of the French School at Rome, and in 1922 of the Ecole des Beaux-Arts. A member of the INSTITUT, he received the Grand Cross of the Legion of Honour, and was the first artist to be accorded a state funeral in the Louvre.
□ C. Mauclair, *Albert Besnard, l'homme et l'oeuvre* (1914)

Blanc, Charles (1813–82) Art historian, critic and engraver, he started his career as a writer on contemporary art in the columns of L'ARTISTE and in 1845 brought out the first (and only) volume of a projected encyclopaedic work that was to be devoted to the artists of the 19th c. In 1848 he was made Director of Fine Arts, but on the accession of NAPOLEON III he returned to private life. In 1859 he founded the prestigious *Gazette des Beaux-Arts*. On the advent of the Thiers government in 1870 he was again made Director of Fine Arts and held the post for three years, later becoming Professor of Aesthetics and Art History at the Collège de France. His writings on art were very influential, despite their conservative tendency, and he had a considerable impact on the young SEURAT. *See also* MANTZ

□ C. Blanc. *Grammaire des arts du dessin* (1867), *Les Artistes de mon temps* (1876); *Dictionnaire de biographie française*

Blanche, Jacques-Emile (1861–1942) More remarkable, perhaps, for his brisk social life and his fund of anecdotes than for his slight, though real, gifts as a painter, predominantly of portraits, he cultivated his contacts with the Impressionists and recorded them in the various autobiographical works he produced. A pupil of Henri GERVEX, who was a friend of RENOIR, Blanche was also in contact with DEGAS and had an overwhelming admiration for MANET. A dedicated Anglophile, he helped to strengthen the links between Impressionism and its English disciples. *See also* HALÉVY

□ J.-E. Blanche, *Propos de peintres de David à Degas* (1919), *Portraits of a Lifetime* (1937), *More Portraits of a Lifetime* (1939)

Bonvin, François (1817–87) A genre painter who supported himself as an official of the Préfecture de Police and studied painting in his spare time at the ACADÉMIE SUISSE. A close friend

Bonvin's *Servant Drawing Water* (1861) reflects the influence of the Dutch school and Courbet.

and supporter of COURBET, he held progressive views which led him to promote all new movements in art. When in 1857 painters such as WHISTLER and FANTIN-LATOUR were rejected by the SALON, he arranged an exhibition of their work in his own studio. This made a considerable impact and could be seen as one of the earliest foci of rebellion against the official system. He went to London in 1871, thus strengthening his links with painters such as MONET, DAUBIGNY and LEGROS, who were also there at the time. Giving up his job to become a full-time artist, he had only a moderate success, and his last years were blighted by virtual blindness. *See also* BRASSERIE DES MARTYRS

□ U. Thieme and F. Becker, *Allgemeines Lexicon der bildenden Künstler* (1950); G. Norman, *Nineteenth-Century Painters and Painting* (1977)

Boudin, Eugène (1824–98) 'My eyes were really opened, and I finally understood nature. I learned at the same time to love it', wrote MONET after meeting Boudin in Le Havre in the late 1850s; for him, as for other Impressionists, the influence of this painter, who spent virtually the whole of his life working on the Normandy coast, was seminal. The son of a local stationer and bookseller, Boudin was self-taught and at the age of 20 he opened his own shop, oriented towards framing and print- and picture-selling, which specialized in the works of the numerous painters who visited and worked in Le Havre, drawn there by the newly opened railway. Among his clients were COUTURE and Constant Troyon, whose romanticized pictures of rural landscapes appealed to him and whose style he imitated.

Then MILLET came to Le Havre *c.* 1845, where he was compelled to support himself doing portraits of the local citizens at 30 francs a time – and Boudin showed him his paintings. Millet gave him a great deal of fruitful advice, and the young man decided to devote all his energies to painting. He went to Paris in 1859 and spent much time copying in the Louvre; two of the works he did there were bought by a local art society and, on the recommendation of Troyon and Couture, he was awarded a scholarship to study at the ECOLE DES BEAUX-ARTS. While there, however, he started to produce pictures painted in the open air of the countryside surrounding PARIS; he later pointed out to the young Monet, 'Everything that is painted on the spot has always a strength, a power, a vividness of touch that one doesn't find again in

Boudin's painting of the Empress Eugénie and her suite at the popular resort of Trouville, 1863, has an informality of approach and freshness of observation which explain his appeal to the Impressionists.

one's studio.' This alone would have been a major contribution to the genius of Impressionism, but throughout the whole of his career Boudin's concern with atmosphere, with the nature of light, with the transience of visual sensation, was to make him a constant source of inspiration to painters of the younger generation. He became the father-figure of a whole group of painters, including JONGKIND, who were to make the Normandy coast the subject of their creative attention, and who were centred on HONFLEUR and Le Havre. Another aspect of Boudin's work which brought him close to the Impressionists was his belief that ordinary urban, middle-class people were just as worthy of the artist's attention as were picturesque peasants.

Although he participated in the first IMPRESSIONIST EXHIBITION, he held himself aloof from art politics generally, though the fact that his dealers were usually those who marketed the work of the Impressionists meant that his works were often exhibited with theirs. In 1905, for instance, an exhibition of 'Impressionist Paintings' at the Grafton Galleries in London included 38 of his works, one of which was bought by the National Gallery. His success at the SALONS and elsewhere in later life was clouded by ill-health and depression. *See also*

ANTECEDENTS, DRAWING, PASTELS, PLEIN-AIRISME
□ Rewald (1973); R. Schmitt, *Eugène Boudin* (3 vols.; 1973)

Bougival One of the popular Parisian resorts on the Seine which, despite the presence along its banks of sawmills, docking facilities and chalk quarries, still offered the semblance of a rural retreat. The area had first been developed by Louis XIV and contained a number of châteaux, whilst more recently, celebrities such as Alexandre Dumas, the politician Odilon Barrot, and the Pereire brothers, bankers whose RAILWAYS served the area, had built houses for themselves there. A new bridge had been built in 1858 to span the two branches of the Seine between Bougival and Croissy, and three islands in the river provided space for establishments such as LA GRENOUILLÈRE.

In the 1830s a number of artists had come to live in the area, and Souvent's inn at Bougival was frequented by painters such as COROT, Célestin Nanteuil, Ferdinand Heilbuth and others. The GONCOURTS on a visit there in 1855 commented, 'Bougival is the homeland of landscape, its very studio, where every patch of ground reminds you of an exhibition, and wherever you go you hear people saying "this was painted by so-and-so; that drawn by

Monet, *The Seine at Bougival*, 1869: the rural charm of **Bougival** attracted many visitors.

somebody else".' MONET took up residence in the hamlet of Saint-Michel just above Bougival in the late spring of 1869 and was joined by RENOIR, who stayed at nearby LOUVECIENNES, where PISSARRO was living. All three painted the area (e.g. Monet's *The Seine at Bougival; Evening* 1869; Smith College Museum of Art; Pissarro's *The Road to Versailles at Louveciennes* 1870; William and Francine Clark Art Institute, Williamstown, Mass.; Renoir's *La Grenouillère* 1869; Oscar Reinhart Collection, Winterthur), and it was here that the most specifically recognizable Impressionist paintings were produced some five years before the first exhibition. SISLEY lived at Louveciennes and nearby Marly between 1870 and 1877, and it was he who produced the most extensive body of paintings of the area (e.g. *Floods at Port-Marly* 1876; Musée d'Orsay).

Manet's lively view of the imminent departure of the Folkestone boat from **Boulogne** in 1869.

Between 1881 and 1884 Berthe MORISOT and her family spent some time there, and painted views of the district, including a portrait of her husband and daughter in the garden of the villa which they rented (1881; Private collection). *[56, 103, 130]*
□ Clark (1984); Herbert (1988)

Boulogne The Channel ports became increasingly popular during the century as holiday resorts, made easy of access from Paris by the growing network of RAILWAYS which served them. They appealed to artists partly because of their picturesque quality, partly because they offered a fascinating view of contemporary society. Both these qualities MANET found in Boulogne, which he first visited in the summer of 1864, when he produced several seascapes. Five years later he took his family there for several months, and created a number of works recording the specific qualities of the place, notably *The Departure of the Folkestone Boat* (1869; Philadelphia Museum of Art), a theme later dealt with by SICKERT. He also produced several beach scenes, and a view of the harbour at night. DEGAS did a number of PASTELS there in the same year, and his *Beach Scene* (1869; National Gallery, London) seems to have been painted in the neighbourhood.
□ Herbert (1988)

Boussod and Valadon Etienne Boussod was the successor of GOUPIL, whose granddaughter he had married. Together with Pierre Valadon, he started the firm cumbersomely known as 'Goupil-Boussod et Valadon Successeurs'. They operated from a luxurious gallery in the Place de l'Opéra, with a branch at 19 boulevard MONTMARTRE and a printing works for producing reproductions at 9 rue Chaptal. One of the main activities of the firm was selling SALON paintings, but from 1879 onwards the Montmartre branch was virtually under the control of THÉO VAN GOGH, who was very conversant with the activities of DURAND-RUEL and of his rival Georges PETIT, and who was absolutely convinced of the importance of the Impressionists.

By the mid-1880s the firm was quite deeply entrenched in the buying and selling of works by MONET, SISLEY, RENOIR and PISSARRO. The proprietors were not in fact greatly pleased with this activity, which was entirely sustained by Van Gogh on his own initiative, and brought in negligible profits in comparison

The logo of **Boussod**, **Valadon**, & Cie.

with those made at the Opéra branch. In 1888 they came to a permanent arrangement with Monet, who was growing discontented with Durand-Ruel: they were to have first refusal of his works, paying him a flat fee of 1000 francs for each and dividing equally the profit made on each sale. Two years later, Théo van Gogh left the firm and was replaced by Maurice JOYANT, who had gone to school with Toulouse-Lautrec, and who carried the interest of the firm into the new generation of painters such as GAUGUIN. Boussod complained to Joyant that Théo van Gogh had 'accumulated appalling things by modern artists, which had brought the firm into disrepute'. In fact, when Berthe MORISOT had an exhibition there in 1892 it was extremely successful. [103]

□ Rewald (1973); J. Rewald, *Studies in Post-Impressionism* (1986)

Bracquemond, Félix (1833–1914) and **Marie** (1841–1916) A pupil of GUICHARD, who was a pupil of Ingres, Félix Bracquemond made his early reputation as a lithographer and etcher, the techniques of which he taught MANET, and in 1863 his engraving of Erasmus figured in the SALON DES REFUSÉS. Although his paintings attracted considerable approval at the SALON, his friendship with Manet and other Impressionists led him to participate in the IMPRESSIONIST EXHIBITIONS of 1874, 1879 and 1880; but as a painter he was never really in sympathy with their ideas or techniques. In 1871 he was appointed art director of the Sèvres porcelain factory and shortly afterwards moved to the same position at the Haviland factory in Limoges. In 1886 he published *Du Dessin et de la couleur*, which was largely concerned with

engraving. It was in this medium that his real achievements lay, and the 200 or so plates that he produced are among the most innovative of the century. He greatly helped PISSARRO with his experiments in the medium. In 1879 he planned with DEGAS, Pissarro and CASSATT the publication of a journal, *Le Jour et la nuit*, backed by Caillebotte, dedicated to graphic art; but nothing came of it, largely because Degas lost interest.

The paintings of his wife Marie were both a good deal closer to the general ideas of Impressionism and more interesting than his, a fact of which he seems to have been conscious; their son Pierre, one of her staunchest supporters, noted that he was jealous of her achievement, seldom showed her works to visiting artists and resented any criticisms she might venture about his paintings. She was something of a recluse, and many of her finest works (e.g. *On the Terrace at Sèvres*, 1880; Musée du Petit Palais, Geneva) were painted in her own garden. She was a vocal as well as an enthusiastic supporter of Impressionist doctrines and she exhibited at the exhibitions of 1879, 1880 and 1886. *See also* CAFÉ GUERBOIS, ILLUSTRATION, JAPANESE ART, PRINTS [23]

□ H.G.E. Degas, *Letters* (1947); M. Eidelberg, 'Braquemond, Delâtre, and the Discovery of Japanese Prints', *Burlington Magazine* (April 1981); T. Garb, *Women Impressionists* (1986)

Brasserie des Martyrs A café that achieved a reputation as the headquarters of REALISM and a meeting place for all those who, for political or aesthetic reasons, were opposed to the artistic establishment. Dominated in the 1850s and 1860s by COURBET, its smoke-ridden atmosphere of heated debate and mild alcoholism was caricatured by one of its habitués, Jules CHAMPFLEURY, in a novel *Les Amis de la nature*, published in 1859. BAUDELAIRE, CASTAGNARY and BONVIN were regular customers, and so too, for a time, was MONET, who came to the Brasserie to meet Courbet, at that time his idol. Despite the fact that many of the clientele of the Brasserie were early supporters of MANET, he did not visit the Brasserie much, and other CAFÉS became more favoured by the Impressionists. *See also* DELVAU, DESNOYERS, GACHET

□ F. Maillard, *Les Derniers Bohèmes* (1874); Rewald (1973); R. Courtine, *La Vie parisienne; cafés et restaurants des boulevards, 1814–1914* (1984)

Bonjour, Monsieur Courbet, 1854, shows the painter meeting **Bruyas** near Montpellier.

Bruyas, Alfred (1801–73) Living in Montpellier, he was known chiefly as one of COURBET's great patrons and features in that artist's *The Artist's Studio* (1855; Musée d'Orsay) and, more remarkably, in *Bonjour, M. Courbet* (1854; Musée Fabre, Montpellier), where the two of them are shown meeting on the road to Montpellier. It was he who inspired DR GACHET with an enthusiasm for contemporary art when he was a medical student in that city, and he also encouraged the young BAZILLE, who lived nearby and with whose parents he was friendly. MONET attempted, in 1864 when he was going through a parlous time, to get Bazille to persuade Bruyas to buy three of his paintings, but the effort was unsuccessful. On his death he bequeathed his collection to the Musée Fabre in Montpellier. [62]
□ G. Poulain, *Bazille et ses amis* (1932); P. Borel, *Lettres de Gustave Courbet à Alfred Bruyas* (1951); *Frédéric Bazille and Early Impressionism*, Art Institute of Chicago, exhibition catalogue (1978)

Bürger, Wilhelm (Théophile Thoré) (1824–69) He was one of the first critics to approve of the works of the Impressionists, before they were known as such. A friend of BAUDELAIRE, he was an ardent supporter of COURBET and ROUSSEAU. It was probably through Baudelaire that he came to be interested in the works of MANET, who, in gratitude for his support, gave him the painting *Peony Stems and Pruning Shears* (1864; Musée d'Orsay). Commenting on RENOIR's *Lise* (1867; Folkwang Museum, Essen), he noted, astutely for his time, 'The dress of white gauze is in full light, but with a slight greenish cast from the reflection of the foliage. The head and neck are held in a delicate half-shadow under the shade of a parasol. The effect is so natural and so true that one might very well find it false, because one is used to nature represented in conventional colours, but does not colour depend on the environment which surrounds it?' [213]
□ T. Thoré (Bürger), *Salons* (1870); E. Moreau-Nélaton, *Manet raconté par lui et par ses amis* (1926); Hamilton (1954); P. Grate, *Deux Critiques d'art de l'époque romantique: Blanche et Thoré* (1959)

Burty, Philippe (1830–90) Critic and man of letters, he was one of the staunchest supporters of Impressionism, basing his stance on a general support for REALISM in all its aspects. In 1874 he was virtually the first to realize the implications of the IMPRESSIONIST EXHIBITION, about which he wrote a favourable review in *La République française*. In the following year it was he who wrote the introduction to the catalogue of the ill-fated sale of works by the Impressionists at the HÔTEL DROUOT on 24 March.

He started his career as an 'ornamental painter' at the Gobelins factory, and in 1859 joined the *Gazette des Beaux-Arts* as editor of the sales and *curiosités* section. In 1861 he produced catalogues of the lithographs of Charlet, Vernet and Géricault, and was one of the authors of a catalogue of drawings by DELACROIX. In 1876 he published a volume on the etchings of Jules de GONCOURT, and nine years before his death he was made an Inspector of Fine Arts. He was an early admirer and collector of JAPANESE ART. He also wrote about photography and in 1880 published a novel, *Grave Imprudence*, based on the lives of his Impressionist friends. *See also* SOCIÉTÉ ANONYME
□ P. Burty, *Grave Imprudence* (1880); E. Zola, *Correspondance*, in *Oeuvres Complètes*, ed. M. Le Blond (1928); Rewald (1973)

C

Cabaner (Jean de Cabannes) (1832–81) A musician and philosopher who moved exten-

sively in Impressionist circles. His portrait was painted by MANET in 1880 (Musée d'Orsay) and he also appeared in RENOIR's *The Artist's Studio* (1876; Santamarina Collection, Buenos Aires), where he is the second figure from the right, seated beside PISSARRO. He introduced the unsociable CÉZANNE to the delights of the Nouvelle-Athènes, and was himself a frequent guest at the dinners given for the Impressionists by MURER in the 1870s. Cézanne gave him the *Bathers* of 1873 (Barnes Foundation, Merrion, Pa.). When Cabaner died of tuberculosis, Cézanne wrote to ZOLA asking him, unsuccessfully, to write a preface to the catalogue for the sale of Cabaner's collection.
□ A. Tabarant, *Manet et ses oeuvres* (1947); Rewald (1984)

Cabaret de la mère Anthony Situated at Marlotte in the forest of Fontainebleau, in the 1860s it was much patronized by artists, including COURBET, PISSARRO, SISLEY and MONET; they covered the walls with caricatures, which can

Renoir, Sisley, Le Coeur and possibly Pissarro in the **Cabaret de la Mère Anthony**, 1866.

be seen in RENOIR's painting of 1866 (Nationalmuseum, Stockholm). The village had achieved fame in artistic circles largely because of Henri Murger, author of *Scènes de la vie de Bohème* (1847–49), who stayed there for lengthy periods in the 1850s, choosing Père Anthony's – as it was then called – for his headquarters. The GONCOURTS also stayed there during the same period and wrote: 'Here we live a family life. The sound of love-making can be heard through the walls. We borrow soap from one another and throw ourselves upon meagre meals with huge appetites. Even the women get their shoes wet without grumbling.'

In a letter written to VOLLARD some 30 years after he had painted it, Renoir described the scene he had chosen: '*The Inn of Mother Anthony* is one of my pictures which I remember with most pleasure. It is not that I find the picture itself particularly exciting, but it does remind me of good old Mother Anthony and her inn at Marlotte. That really was a village inn! I took the main bar, which doubled as a dining room, as the subject of my study. The old woman in a headscarf is Mother Anthony herself, and the splendid girl serving the drinks is her barmaid Nana. The white poodle is Toto, who had a wooden leg. I had some of my friends, including Sisley and LE COEUR, pose round the table. The motifs that make up the background were borrowed scenes painted on the wall, they were unpretentious and often successful paintings by the regulars. I myself drew a sketch of Murger on the wall, and copied it in the upper left-hand corner of the painting.' *See also* BARBIZON
□ J. Meier-Graefe, *Auguste Renoir* (1912); J. Gasquet, 'Le Paradis de Renoir', *L'Amour de l'art* (Feb. 1921)

Cafés One of the most characteristic and significant features of Parisian social life in the 19th c., they played an important role in society at all levels. They commenced proliferating in the 1850s, the growth in their numbers stimulated by Baron Haussmann's rebuilding of the Right Bank of PARIS under the Second Empire. The spacious streets and boulevards allowed the development of one of their most familiar features, the *terrasse*, with its indication to the passing world of the nature of the café's clientele, its outward-looking character (as opposed to the inward-looking quality of the English pub) and its invitingness.

Types of waiter and waitress to be found in French **cafés**, from *Harper's Monthly Magazine*, 1889.

By the end of the century there were some 24,000 cafés in the greater Paris area and each tended to have its own particular quality. Sometimes this was regional – particular cafés would cater for people from certain areas, parts of that rural population which migrated to Paris in such large numbers; others might attract people from certain political groups or, most significantly, from certain professions. In this latter category, especially as far as writing, the arts and journalism were concerned, cafés had very largely come to take the place occupied by salons in the 18th c. as places for the discussion of ideas, new attitudes and new techniques – a phenomenon persisting into the 20th c. in the part played at differing times by the Dôme, the Coupole and the Flore. Each, too, tended to have its presiding genius, surrounded by his devotees and disciples.

Impressionism was virtually born in a café, and the successive stages of its development were planned in them. That assiduous observer of the Impressionists, the young Anglo-Irish writer George MOORE described one café, the

Nouvelle-Athènes, thus: 'He who would know something of my life must know something about the academy of fine arts. Not the official stupidity you read of in the daily papers, but the real French academy, the café.' The following are the most important of the cafés in the history of Impressionism:

Café Guerbois This was situated at 11 rue des Batignolles, in an area, now the avenue de Clichy, where many artists had studios and which, at one point, gave its name to that group of painters who became the Impressionists. MANET first started using the café in 1866, after abandoning the Café de Bade, which had a reputation for being the haunt of dandies and the *bon ton*. Very soon the Café-Guerbois became the favoured meeting place of all his admirers and friends: the writers ZOLA, DURANTY, DURET, Armand SILVESTRE (who later wrote an enthralling account of its golden age in his *Au Pays des souvenirs*, 1892), the musician Edmond MAÎTRE, and the photographer NADAR, as well as BAZILLE, MONET, DEGAS, Félix BRACQUEMOND, RENOIR, Alfred STEVENS, Constantin GUYS, and, less frequently, PISSARRO, CÉZANNE and SISLEY. Thursday was their most popular day for meeting and, as Monet later noted, 'Nothing could have been more stimulating than the regular discussions which we used to have there, with their constant clashes of opinion. They kept our wits sharpened, and supplied us with a stock of enthusiasm which lasted us for weeks, and kept us going until the final realization of an idea was accomplished. From them we emerged with a stronger determination, and with our thoughts clearer and more sharply defined.' (*Le Temps*, 27 November 1900)

Nouvelle-Athènes In about 1875, as a result of one of those shifts in fashion so typical of such situations, there was a move away from the Café Guerbois to the Nouvelle-Athènes in the Place Pigalle, which had already achieved a reputation under NAPOLEON III as a centre for dissidents, attracting people such as COURBET, CLEMENCEAU, Gambetta and CASTAGNARY. It was there that in 1876 Degas painted the actress Ellen ANDRÉE and the painter Marcellin DESBOUTIN, seated on a *banc* against the wall, at a marble-topped table with their famous drink in front of them (*L'Absinthe*; Musée d'Orsay). Desboutin was the most regular customer, along with Manet and Degas, who brought

The Nouvelle-Athènes in Montmartre, c. 1890: one of the most popular Parisian **cafés**.

many of his own disciples, including FORAIN, ZANDOMENEGHI and RAFFAËLLI. CAILLEBOTTE complained to Pissarro in 1881 that Degas 'has introduced disunity into our midst and spends all his time haranguing everybody in the Nouvelle-Athènes'. Among the less frequent attenders was Cézanne, and in 1878 Duranty wrote to Zola 'Cézanne has appeared recently at the little café on the Place Pigalle. He was attired in one of his out-of-date costumes, a blue overall, white linen jacket, completely covered with smudges of paint and brushmarks and wearing a battered old hat.' GAUGUIN also became an habitué. George MOORE has given a vivid and convincing description of life at the Nouvelle-Athènes in his *Reminiscences of the Impressionists* (1906).

As time went by and they got older, frequently living away from Paris, the Impressionists were less assiduous in their visits to either the Guerbois or the Nouvelle-Athènes, but between 1891 and 1894 a custom grew up of holding dinners at the Café Riche in the boulevard des Italiens. These were attended by Pissarro, Sisley, Renoir, Caillebotte, Duret and MALLARMÉ. Another popular venue was the small but flourishing restaurant in the boulevard Voltaire owned by Eugène MURER, who used to give his painter friends dinner on Wednesday evenings, the most frequent guests being GUILLAUMIN, Renoir, Sisley, Père TANGUY, Pissarro, Monet and DR GACHET. When he opened a hotel in Rouen, he also offered hospitality there to Pissarro and Monet. FANTIN-LATOUR and his friends were dedicated to the

Café Taranne, also frequented by Flaubert; while the Café Fleurus, decorated with panels by COROT, was patronized by students from the nearby Studio Gleyre. *See also* BRASSERIE DES MARTYRS, GUIGOU, GUILLEMET *[17, 138]*

□ A. Delvau, *Histoire anecdotique des cafés et cabarets de Paris* (1862); Zeldin (1973); Clark (1984); R. Courtine, *La Vie parisienne; cafés et restaurants des boulevards 1814–1914* (1984); Denvir (1987); Herbert (1988)

Cafés-concert This particularly French phenomenon, which involved various forms of popular entertainment taking place in a café, had first appeared in Paris in the 1830s, and reached the apogee of its popularity in the last two decades of the century. Cafés-concert appealed to the Impressionists as centres of that urban life which they so liked to depict. Those in the Champs-Elysées, such as the Alcazar d'Eté and the Ambassadeurs, were especially popular, as was the Folies-Bergère, the bar of which was the subject of a painting by MANET. He also recorded life in the well-known Cabaret de Reichshoffen on the boulevard de Rochechouart in *Café-Concert* (1878; Walters

Jules Chéret's poster of 1879 for L'Horloge, a **café-concert** on the Champs-Elysées.

Manet's *Serveuse de bocks*, 1878, shows the Cabaret de Reichshoffen, a popular **café-concert**.

Art Gallery, Baltimore) and *Corner in a Café-Concert* (1878; National Gallery, London). The entertainment offered consisted basically of singing and comic acts, and some of the performers became public figures. Emma Valadon, whose stage name was Thérésa, was reputed to be making 50,000 francs per year by 1875. She was especially admired by DEGAS, who painted her several times. Between 1877 and 1878 Degas produced a number of prints in various media devoted to the Café des Ambassadeurs, featuring the well-known singer Emilie Bécat. The theme of the café-concert also became one of Toulouse-Lautrec's preoccupations, though his treatment of it lies beyond the confines of Impressionism as such. *See also* DANCING, MUSIC

□ *See* CAFÉS, *above*; M. Constantin, *Histoire des cafés-concert et des cafés de Paris* (1872)

Caillebotte, Gustave (1848–94) A painter of great power and originality who produced some of the most memorable urban images of his century. He was 14 years younger than DEGAS, and still a law student when MONET and

Caillebotte's *The Floor Strippers* of 1875 was probably painted in the family home in the Batignolles area. It is typical of his taste for unusual perspectives and scenes from modern life.

RENOIR started discussing the idea of a group exhibition. Yet he did more than almost anybody else to foster and support the movement, affording its members financial help by buying their paintings at artificially elevated prices, by making direct gifts of money, and by such devices as buying his own paintings at the auction held in 1877 to raise funds for future exhibitions. Wealthy, and gifted in many ways, he was an enthusiastic gardener, communicating his enthusiasm to Monet, and also the designer of a series of racing yachts, some of which were adorned with fanciful silk sails. He contributed greatly to the success of the various IMPRESSIONIST EXHIBITIONS, not only financially, but by his powers of organization and diplomacy.

Initially his own paintings were close to those of Degas, but they were marked by an even stronger preference for unposed gestures and unusual viewpoints, exemplified at their most dazzling in the remarkable painting *Pont de l'Europe* (1876; Musée du Petit Palais, Geneva), with its startling PERSPECTIVE and sense of photographic immediacy. Even in so straightforward a picture as the *Partie de bateau* of 1877 (Private collection), his close-up image of the oarsman in his top hat is entirely unexpected. Caillebotte was very much preoccupied with urban vistas, which he always perceived in a very individual way, usually depicting them from some elevated viewpoint.

Caillebotte's reputation as a painter has been largely overshadowed by his controversial legacy to the French nation of his remarkable collection of paintings by his fellow Impressionists. Rightly prescient of an early death, he drew up a will in 1876, in which, after making provision for financing the next Impressionist exhibition, he left his collection of paintings to the nation, with the proviso that they be shown first in the LUXEMBOURG and eventually in the Louvre. When he died, 18 years later, this collection consisted of 3 Manets, 16 Monets, 8 Renoirs, 13 Pissarros, 7 Degas, 8 Sisleys, 5 Cézannes, and his own *Floor Strippers* of 1875 (Musée d'Orsay). Renoir was named as executor. After a good deal of delays, caused rather by bureaucratic inefficiency than ill-will, the bequest was accepted, and formed the core of the Jeu de Paume collection; most of the works have now been transferred to the Musée d'Orsay. See also ARGENTEUIL, BATIGNOLLES, CAFÉS, PATRONS AND COLLECTORS, PHOTO-GRAPHY, REALISM, SOCIAL BACKGROUND *[24, 160]*

□ M. Berhaut, *Caillebotte; sa vie et son oeuvre* (1978), 'Le legs Caillebotte; Vérités et contre-vérités', in *Bulletin de la Société de l'histoire de l'art français* (1983); J.K.T. Varnedoe, *Gustave Caillebotte* (1987)

Callias, Nina de (1844–84) The estranged wife of the editor of *Figaro*, Nina de Callias (*née* Marie-Anne Gaillard) was also known as Nina de Villard. Pianist, composer and poet, she presided over one of the most spectacular and exotic salons in Paris at 82 rue des Moines. Amongst her regular guests were MALLARMÉ, Anatole France, Verlaine, César Franck and MANET, who painted a portrait of her (1873–74; Musée d'Orsay) reclining against a background of oriental fans. Famous for the vigour of her sexual life, her fondness for alcohol and her alternating moods of hilarity and depression, she came to an early end. *[224]*
□ *Dictionnaire de biographie française*; A. Tabarant, *Manet et ses oeuvres* (1947); K. Adler, *Manet* (1986)

Cals, Adolphe-Félix (1810–80) Trained initially as an engraver, he secured admission to the ECOLE DES BEAUX-ARTS, where he worked under Léon Cogniet, a great believer in the value of the freely painted sketch. Choosing peasant life and landscape as his themes, he came into contact with BOUDIN and JONGKIND, mainly through his liking for HONFLEUR as a painting ground. Through them he met MONET and other Impressionists, with whose ideas he largely concurred, and he took part in four of their exhibitions, being the oldest participator. He died in Honfleur, and there are several of his works in the museum there, as well as in the Louvre, and at Rheims.
□ A. Alexandre, *A.F. Cals, ou le bonheur de peindre* (1900); E. Bénézit, *Dictionnaire des peintres, sculpteurs, dessinateurs et graveurs* (1966)

Carolus-Duran, Emile-Auguste (1838–1917) was to many Impressionists, especially DEGAS, the very epitome of the successful society artist who had abandoned his early idealism. At the beginning of his career, Carolus-Duran was very close to MANET, with whose early style his own had some affinities, especially in its debt to Velazquez and other Spanish artists. In fact, George MOORE said that Manet was in despair at not being able to paint portraits like his. A skilled portrait painter as well as a sculptor, he was co-founder with

Carolus-Duran in the uniform of a member of the Institut, adorned with academic decorations.

Self-portrait of Mary **Cassatt**, painted *c.* 1880.

Meissonier and PUVIS DE CHAVANNES of the Société Nationale des Beaux-Arts, and in 1905 became director of the French School in Rome. In 1867 he painted a portrait of MONET (Musée Marmottan) and in 1877 produced an etching of Manet. He was one of the main contributors to the fund that MONET organized to buy Manet's *Olympia* for the nation. *See also* SARGENT

Cassatt, Mary (1844–1926) The daughter of an affluent Pittsburgh businessman, whose French ancestry had endowed him with a passion for that country, she studied art at the Pennsylvania Academy of Fine Arts in Philadelphia, and then travelled extensively in Europe, finally settling in Paris in 1874. In that year she had a work accepted at the SALON and in 1877 made the acquaintance of DEGAS, with whom she was to be on close terms throughout his life. His art and ideas had a considerable influence on her own work; he introduced her to the Impressionists and she participated in the exhibitions of 1879, 1880, 1881 and 1886, refusing to do so in 1882 when Degas did not.

She was a great practical support to the movement as a whole, both by providing direct financial help and by promoting the works of Impressionists in the USA, largely through her brother Alexander. By persuading him to buy works by MANET, MONET, MORISOT, RENOIR, Degas and PISSARRO, she made him the first important collector of such works in America. She also advised and encouraged her friends the HAVEMEYERS to build up their important collection of works by Impressionists and other contemporary French artists.

Her own works, on the occasions when they were shown in various mixed exhibitions in the USA, were very favourably received by the critics and contributed not a little to the acceptance of Impressionism there. Despite her admiration for Degas, she was no slavish imitator of his style, retaining her own very personal idiom throughout her career. From him, and other Impressionists, she acquired an interest in the rehabilitation of the pictorial qualities of everyday life, inclining towards the domestic and the intimate rather than the social and the urban (*Lady at the Teatable*, 1885; Metropolitan Museum, New York), with a special emphasis on the mother and child theme in the 1890s (*The Bath*, 1891; Art Institute of Chicago). She also derived from Degas and

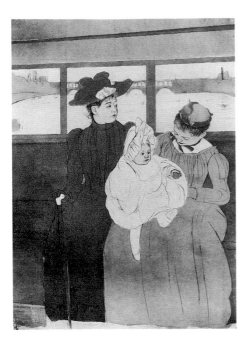

Cassatt, *The Tramway*, 1891: a drypoint etching showing clear influence of Japanese prints.

others a sense of immediate observation, with an emphasis on gestural significance. Her earlier works were marked by a certain lyrical effulgence and gentle, golden lighting, but by the 1890s, largely as a consequence of the exhibition of JAPANESE prints held in Paris at the beginning of that decade, her draughtsmanship became more emphatic, her colours clearer and more boldly defined. The exhibition also confirmed her predilection for print-making techniques, and her work in this area must count amongst the most impressive of her generation. She lived in France all her life, though her love of her adopted countrymen did not increase with age, and her latter days were clouded with bitterness. *See also* PASTELS, PEINTURE CLAIRE, PRINTS, SOCIAL BACKGROUND

□ L.W. Havemeyer, *Sixteen to Sixty; Memoirs of a Collector* (1961); F.A. Sweet, *Miss Mary Cassatt; Impressionist from Pennsylvania* (1966); A.D. Breeskin, *Mary Cassatt, a catalogue raisonné of the Oils, Pastels, Watercolours and Drawings* (1970); G. Pollock *Mary Cassatt* (1980)

Castagnary, Jules (1830–88) A friend of BAUDELAIRE, an art critic and politician, he first came to attention as an ardent defender of COURBET, whose reputation he was still defending in 1883, with the publication of his *Plaidoyer pour un ami mort*. He was acutely conscious of the transition taking place in contemporary art from REALISM to Naturalism, an idea that he first formulated in a stimulating article in L'ARTISTE, which could be read as an apologia for Impressionism: 'The Naturalist school affirms that art is the expression of life in all its forms and degrees and that its sole purpose is to reproduce nature, this leading it to its greatest power and intensity; it is truth being put on the same level as science.' His works were collected in two publications, *Les Artistes au XIXe siècle* (1864) and *Salons* (1892). He became Minister of Religion under Gambetta in 1879, and eight years later, Minister of Fine Art. *See also* BRASSERIE DES MARTYRS, CAFÉS, JAPANESE ART, JONGKIND, PISSARRO, SALON DES REFUSÉS
□ *Dictionnaire de biographie française*; Rewald (1973)

Cézanne, Paul (1839–1906) Son of a prominent citizen of AIX-EN-PROVENCE, who had started as a hat-maker and went on to become a prosperous banker and one of the pillars of the local social order, Cézanne benefited enormously from a childhood spent in one of the leading cultural centres of France, with a well-endowed museum, numerous collections and every facility for studying art. One of his earliest and closest friends was Émile ZOLA, whose father had built a nearby aqueduct. It was to Zola that Cézanne turned when he came up to Paris in 1861 to study at the ACADÉMIE SUISSE. Thanks to his contact with the writer, and to his studies at the Académie, he met first of all PISSARRO, who was to be one of the dominant figures in his creative career and whom he saw as his 'master', and then the whole circle of the CAFÉ GUERBOIS. His own artistic ideals at this time were more than a little confused; DELACROIX, COURBET, Daumier, Meissonier and a medley of Italian and Spanish 17th-c. artists all exerted some influence, and this was melded by a powerful, often erotic, fervour which owed not a little to his Provençal heritage. His relations with his father were often stormy, and complicated by the fact that in 1869 he started to have an affair with Hortense FIQUET. In 1872 they had a son, whose existence Cézanne hid from his father, and he only married Hortense after his father's death.

Between 1872 and 1874 he was in especially close contact with Pissarro, who was then living

Cézanne starting out on an open-air painting expedition in Auvers, *c.* 1874.

at Saint-Ouen near PONTOISE. Inevitably he took part in the first IMPRESSIONIST EXHIBITION and in that of 1877. Reactions to his work were mixed, even among his friends. MANET said to GUILLEMET, one of Cézanne's most fervent admirers, 'How can you abide such foul painting?'; and even Zola, who dedicated *Mon Salon* to him in 1866, drew a very clear line between affection for Cézanne as a man, and his reactions to him as a painter. This distinction became painfully apparent in *L'Oeuvre*, published in 1886, which contained a character, obviously based on Cézanne, who was depicted as a frustrated artistic failure; and this led to a complete break between the two.

The image which Cézanne projected of a farouche, uncultured, aggressive peasant attracted attention and something of a cult following amongst the habitués of such places as the Café Guerbois – but it had little foundation in fact. Julie Manet's reactions on first meeting him in a hotel in GIVERNY (they were both visiting MONET) are typical: 'He looks like a cut-throat, with large red eyeballs standing out from his head in a most ferocious manner, a rather fierce-looking pointed beard, and a way of talking that makes the dishes rattle.'

I found out later on that, far from being fierce or a cut-throat, he has the gentlest nature possible. In spite of his total disregard for the dictionary of manners, he shows a politeness which no other man here would have shown. He is one of the most liberal artists I have ever seen.' Cézanne was in effect very 'liberal'. Virgil, Hugo, de Musset, BAUDELAIRE, Flaubert and Stendhal were his favourite authors and he was devoted to the MUSIC of Beethoven and Wagner. For most of his life a cynical atheist in the traditions of French radicalism, by the 1890s he had 'gone back' to the church and, though never fervently pious, had become the kind of Catholic who constituted the backbone of the Provençal bourgeoisie.

His art reflected perfectly the kind of dichotomies implicit in his personality: a struggle between the untamed and the disciplined. His frequently quoted ambition to remake Poussin after nature and to convert Impressionism into something solid and enduring 'like the Old Masters' expresses perfectly the dynamism of his work, which in fact contained the seeds that, as it were, destroyed Impressionism. It is significant that it appealed at a very early stage to those artists who themselves found the 'looseness' of Impressionism so unsatisfying. In 1883 SIGNAC bought one of Cézanne's works and in the following year GAUGUIN purchased two. He was a welcome exhibitor with Les Vingt in Brussels (*see* BELGIUM) and (despite the disapproval of the Kaiser) his works were well received in Berlin. In 1897 the astute VOLLARD bought up the contents of a studio at Corbeil which Cézanne had abandoned, and the artist's

The dark violence of *The Murder* (1870) is typical of **Cézanne**'s earlier works.

Cézanne's *Mont Sainte-Victoire* (1886–88) is one of many versions he painted of the same scene. It was given by the artist to Joachim Gasquet, and bought by Samuel Courtauld in 1925.

name started to appear in all the leading Symbolist magazines. A kind of contemporary apotheosis came in 1901 when Maurice DENIS (who had never met him) exhibited at the SALON a large painting, *Hommage à Cézanne* (Musée d'Orsay), which included amongst his devotees Bonnard, Redon, Vuillard, Vollard and Denis himself. Significantly, the work was bought by the current white hope of French literature, André Gide.

Cézanne himself would probably have preferred the Legion of Honour, for he had a child-like craving for official recognition, and a passion to escape from the imaginary opprobrium of being a rich dilettante. It was his ideal of achieving a blend of freedom and control, and evolving a new visual grammar, that made him probably the most influential figure in the development of 20th-c. painting, the forbear of Cubism, and much else besides. Treating his figures like still lifes (e.g. *The Card Players*, 1891; Metropolitan Museum, New York), he developed remarkable techniques for rendering space and three-dimensional qualities by pre-senting different angles of vision, articulating planes and harmonies of colour, and by approaching pictorial problems as though they

were geometrical ones – 'treating nature', in his own words, 'in terms of the cylinder, the sphere and the cone'. To achieve this simple-seeming, but actually very complex and sophisticated, syntax of expression, he returned time and time again to similar themes, in oils, drawings and watercolours – card players, the mountain of Sainte Victoire, just outside Aix, and still lifes, which in his hands attained the kind of classic monumentality that had previously only been achieved by Chardin (e.g. the watercolour *Still Life with Apples, a Bottle and a Milk Pot*, 1902; Dallas Museum of Art).

For the English-speaking world, any under-standing of the work of Cézanne is complicated by the extent to which it became involved in the art polemics of the first half of the 20th c., when writers such as Roger Fry and Clive Bell used his works as the basis of an apologia for POST-IMPRESSIONISM; their emphasis on 'plasti-city' and similar ideological notions – Bell said that Cézanne was 'the Christopher Columbus of a whole new continent of form' – has detracted from the real nature of his work. It is true that he was a precursor; it is true that he pushed Impressionism into new and adventur-ous paths – so, too, did SEURAT and Signac. But

his achievement was a personal one, and it was only made possible by his experience of main-line Impressionism. *See also* DEWHURST, DRAWING, EMPERAIRE, GACHET, GASQUET, ILLUSTRATION, INDÉPENDANTS, MARION, MÉDAN, PERSPECTIVE, PHOTOGRAPHY, PLEIN-AIRISME, POLITICS, PORTRAITURE, PRINTS, SOCIAL BACKGROUND *[15, 22, 57, 84, 88, 164, 175, 218–19]*
□ P.N. Doran (ed.), *Conversations avec Cézanne* (1978); Rewald (1984); Rewald (1986); L. Gowing, *Cézanne, the early years*, Royal Academy, London, exhibition catalogue (1988)

Champfleury, Jules Husson (1821–89) A critic and man of letters who was a staunch defender of the doctrines of REALISM; even though at various times he quarrelled with most of its protagonists, he was a member of the group surrounding COURBET at the BRASSERIE DES MARTYRS. His researches into the works of the 17th-c. Le Nain brothers created a revival of interest in their paintings, and he was also the author of several novels. He became director of the porcelain factory at Sèvres. Through his friend the pâtissier Eugène MURER he came into contact with many of the Impressionists,

A *Charivari* cartoon by Cham (1874) shows the Turks using Impressionist paintings in battle.

whose work he collected. *[23, 62]*
□ J.H. Champfleury, *Souvenirs et portraits de jeunesse* (1872); U. Finke (ed.), *French Nineteenth-century Painting and Literature* (1972); Clark (1973b)

Charivari, Le A satirical magazine founded in 1832 by an enterprising republican journalist, Charles Philipon (1800–62), who made it an important vehicle of political propaganda and social comment (*Punch*'s subtitle was 'Or the London Charivari'). Utilizing the new technique of lithography as well as developments that had taken place in engraving processes, he employed some 20 artists to illustrate its pages. It was in *Charivari* that Daumier presented his famous character Robert Macaire, the prototype of the spivish speculator, and that Grandville (1803–47) displayed his imaginative humanized animals. *Charivari* was very concerned with the arts, but tended to be slightly reactionary in this sphere. Its critic Louis LEROY was fairly hostile, and it was in a satirical piece about the first IMPRESSIONIST EXHIBITION that he gave the movement its name (*see* IMPRESSIONISM). One of the magazine's leading caricaturists Cham (Amédée de Noé, 1819–79) was especially vitriolic about the movement. *See also* NADAR, SALON *[115, 127]*
□ E. de Bechtel, *Freedom of the Press; Philipon*

The front cover of **Champfleury**'s *Les Chats*, published in 1869, features a lithograph by Manet.

Madame **Charpentier** and her children Paul (at her knee) and Georgette, painted by Renoir in 1878. Proust compared it with 'Titian at his best'.

versus Louis Philippe (1952); C. Bellanger *et al., Histoire générale de la presse française*, vol. 2 (1969); Zeldin (1973)

Charpentier, Georges (1846–1905) At the age of 25 he inherited a successful publishing house, the reputation of which he further enhanced, not only by his shrewd business acumen, but by his ability to pick successful authors, amongst whom are to be included Flaubert, ZOLA, Maupassant, DAUDET and the GONCOURTS. In 1872 he married Marguerite Lemonnier (1848–1904), who reinforced the interest in art that he had inherited from his father, Gervais – a supporter of the Romantics. The Charpentiers lived first in the Place Saint-Germain-l'Auxerrois and later at 11 rue de Grenelle, and Madame Charpentier's salon became famous as a meeting place for writers, artists and left-wing politicians. Both of them were enthusiastic patrons and supporters of the Impressionists, and it was largely on their behalf that they founded the magazine LA VIE MODERNE and ran an art gallery on its premises. They were particularly close to RENOIR, and in 1878 he painted the portrait of Madame Charpentier with her two children (Metropolitan Museum, New York) which, when it was exhibited at the SALON in the following year, enhanced the painter's reputation amongst the general public. Proust described the painting at some length in *Le Temps retrouvé* in a way that demonstrates both his visual sensibility and his snobbery. One of the most valuable things that the Charpentiers did, primarily for Renoir, but to a lesser extent for the other Impressionists, was to introduce them into a stratum of society likely to afford them patronage and support. *See also* PATRONS AND COLLECTORS, PORTRAITURE □ M. Florisoone, 'Renoir et la famille Charpentier', in *L'Amour de l'art* (Feb. 1938); M. Robida, *Le Salon Charpentier et les impressionnistes* (1958)

Chatou A small village on the banks of the Seine, greatly used by Parisians for weekend excursions, and one of the places about which it was said 'wherever there was a wretched square of grass with half a dozen rachitic trees, there the proprietor made haste to establish a ball or a café-restaurant' (V. Fournel, *Paris dans sa splendeur*, 1867). RENOIR worked there between 1879 and 1881, and a small island facing the village provided the scene for his *Déjeuner des canotiers* (1881; Phillips Collection, Washington, D.C.) and *Oarsmen at Chatou* (1879; National Gallery of Art, Washington, D.C.). MONET also painted there in the late 1860s. *See also* LA GRENOUILLÈRE, RESTAURANT FOURNAISE [162]

Renoir's picture of oarsmen was painted from a small island opposite **Chatou** in 1879.

□ J. Catinat, *Douze grandes heures de Chatou et la naissance du Vésinet* (1967); Clark (1984); Herbert (1988)

Chennevières-Pointel, Charles-Philippe, Marquis de (1820–99) A government official who was successively an Inspector of Museums, Curator of the LUXEMBOURG and Director of Fine Arts. He was responsible for commissioning the paintings for the decoration of the Panthéon. He wrote a number of books, including *Essais sur l'organisation des arts en province* (1850) and *Portraits inédits des artistes français* (1853). *See also* SALON DES REFUSÉS
□ *Dictionnaire de biographie française*

Chesneau, Ernest (1833–98) An active and assiduous art critic who played an important part in the French art world of the Second Empire – he was Inspector of Fine Arts from 1869 – partly through his friendship with NIEUWERKERKE. A friend and admirer of John Ruskin, he was deeply concerned with the relationship between art and society, and published various books on this theme. He was one of the first to recognize the merits of MANET, and immediately picked up the connection between the *Déjeuner sur l'herbe* (1863; Musée d'Orsay) and Raphael. Initially hostile to the Impressionists, he later modified his hostility and built up a close relationship with Manet. *See also* SALON
□ Hamilton (1954); Boime (1986)

Chevreul, Eugène (1786–1889) A French chemist who made significant discoveries about the nature of COLOUR and our perception of it. At the age of 27 he became professor of chemistry and director of dyeing at the Gobelins tapestry factory, having published in 1823 a book on animal fats that won considerable acclaim. But his real fame depended on two later publications, *De La Loi du contraste simultané des couleurs et de l'assortiment des objets colorés* (1839) and *Des Couleurs et de leur application aux arts industriels à l'aide des cercles chromatiques* (1864). His theories about divisionism and the optical combination of colours had a great influence on many painters from DELACROIX onwards, even though earlier artists such as Watteau had employed the technique without understanding its theoretical basis. SIGNAC, who made Chevreul's theory the foundation of his own style, summed it up admirably: 'Divisionism is a method of securing the utmost luminosity, colour and harmony by (a) the use of all the colours of the spectrum and all degrees of these colours without any mixing; (b) the separation of local colours from the colour of light, reflections etc.; (c) the balance of these factors and the establishment of these relations in accordance with laws of contrast, tone and radiation; and (d) the use of a technique of dots of a size determined by the size of the picture.' *See also* SEURAT
□ M.-E. Chevreul, *De La Loi du contraste simultané des couleurs et de l'assortiment des objets colorés* (1839), trans. C. Martel as *The Principles of Harmony and Contrast of Colours* (1854); R. Rood, *Professor Rood's Theories on Colour and Impressionism* (1906); P. Signac, *D'Eugène Delacroix au néo-impressionnisme* (1899)

Colour

(See entry on p. 59)
The Impressionists' most innovative and enduring achievement lies above all else in their use of colour. This was influenced by several factors: scientific investigations into the nature of perception and the qualities of light and colour by Bunsen and Kirchoff, Chevreul and Rood; the invention of new artificial pigments, which broadened the available palette range; the increasing vogue for working *en plein air*, which replaced the subdued tone of studio paintings with more intense, light-suffused hues; and perhaps even the cultural shock of exposure to the bright colours of oriental art. Whether they result from the empirical observations of Monet or from the more theoretical experiments of Pissarro in his Pointillist phase, all Impressionist paintings represent the desire to discover a pictorial equivalent to the rich intensity of visual experience.

The reflective and refractive properties of water made it
the perfect vehicle for the Impressionists' interest in light
and colour. In Renoir's The Seine at Asnières
(c. 1879) the traditional academic concern with line,
perspective and chiaroscuro shading is completely
abandoned in an attempt to capture the sensation of
open-air perception. Shadows, earth colours and black
are banished in favour of pure, prismatic hues and an
extensive use of white. Rather than being applied in a
series of thin, superimposed layers, in the conventional
manner, opaque paint is applied directly with a loaded
brush to create a more immediate effect. The vibrant
contrast of the complementary colours orange and blue
provides the central focus of the image, the rich orange
of the boat's reflection almost overpowering the blue of
the river. Where pure colours are applied wet in wet
with repeated short brushstrokes – as in the foreground
reflections – they mingle to create optical mixtures,
while in the distance a soft haze is created by scrubbing
colour wet over dry with a stiff brush. The variety of
Renoir's brushwork enlivens the paint surface, evoking
a vivid sense of shimmering sunlight and summer heat,
while the puff of smoke from a train on the horizon
adds a touch of modern life to the rustic scene, and
mirrors the modernity of Renoir's technique.

Overleaf: In his Gare Saint-Lazare series of 1876–78
Monet created powerful images of Paris in the age of
the Industrial Revolution. Yet his central preoccupation
in these works was not the subject-matter, but the
challenge of capturing on canvas the elusive effects of
amorphous steam-clouds rising into the station vault.
Inspired partly by Chevreul's investigations into the
properties of colour, Monet studied how colour and
light are affected by moisture in the air, and, especially,
how the effect of a colour varies according to its
context. Exploiting his restricted palette of twelve
colours to the full, he creates a series of subtle
modulations across the canvas, playing blue against
white, against purple-black, and against pinkish grey;
the dark body of the engine in the centre stands out
sharply against the white of steam and daylight, but this
is counterbalanced by the play of white steam against
dark roof in the top right-hand corner. These dispersed
touches of white, blue and red, the balancing of light
and dark areas, tie the image together visually, and the
relatively austere use of colour is animated by the
spontaneity of the brushwork. The bold strokes that
economically delineate the station structure contrast
vividly with the broken, almost scribbled handling of
the steam. Though partly the result of Monet's need to
work rapidly, the brushmarks aptly convey the sketchy,
insubstantial nature of the steam as against the emphatic
solidity of the machines.

Women in the Garden *(1866–67) was Monet's first radical gesture towards plein-air painting. He later said of this period, 'I fell in love with the rayon [ray of light] and the reflet [reflection]', and the image clearly shows his fascination with coloured shadows – the* white dress of the woman in the foreground is dappled with blue reflected from the sky – and with the tendency of the eye to perceive reality as a pattern of coloured patches. The influence of photography is also evident in the arbitrary, informal poses of the figures.

Renoir's desire to depict light as it is truly perceived led him, in such works as The Swing (1876), to create compositions in which pools of light and shade give the effect of an almost decorative curtain falling over the blurred contours of his forms. Attuned to the carefully graduated tones of Salon paintings, in which light was firmly tied to the definition of form, critics found Renoir's technique disturbing: G. Vassy in L'Evénement complained that the patches of light resembled 'spots of grease on the models' clothes'.

'What does the frame, the motif, matter if the effect is varied?': one of the Impressionists' greatest achievements was to show how, once liberated from form, light and colour could be studied for their own sake, as independent elements within a painting. These concerns found their purest expression in Monet's 'series' pictures of the 1890s, in which a single, static motif – haystacks or poplars – acted as a focus for the ever-changing effects of light and atmosphere. Based on relatively simple colour contrasts, the Rouen cathedral compositions chart the play of sunlight, from dawn to dusk, over the neutral grey stone of the Gothic structure; Rouen cathedral: sunset (1894), for example, sets a warm, burnt orange against a cool grey-blue. The underlying pattern of the façade and the tangible atmospheric enveloppe provide an overall unity to the image, in which solid forms threaten to disintegrate beneath Monet's almost expressionistic impasto brushwork. The use of non-descriptive colour and brushstrokes seems to point towards the development of a purely abstract art, but Monet's aim in these works was still to represent the essence of perceived reality, 'to fix my sensations'.

In common with the Realist writers of the nineteenth century, painters longed to discover a precise method of creating an accurate representation of reality – a quasi-scientific system that would lend greater credibility to their opposition to the long-established conventions of the academic tradition. When Pissarro met Seurat and Signac in 1885, he was powerfully convinced by their experimental Divisionist theories of painting, describing their approach as 'a modern synthesis by methods based on science'. The technique was essentially derived from the discovery that light can be divided into its constituent prismatic parts, and it was believed that by applying tiny, regular strokes of pure hues, which would blend in the eye of the viewer rather than being mixed on the palette, the artist would be able to create a more convincing reflection of the nature of perception. Pissarro's Femme dans un clos (1887), painted at Eragny, indeed conveys vividly the sense of dazzling midday heat and light, the uniform dabs of sharp lime green, bright blue and warm yellow dissolving the outlines of the forms.

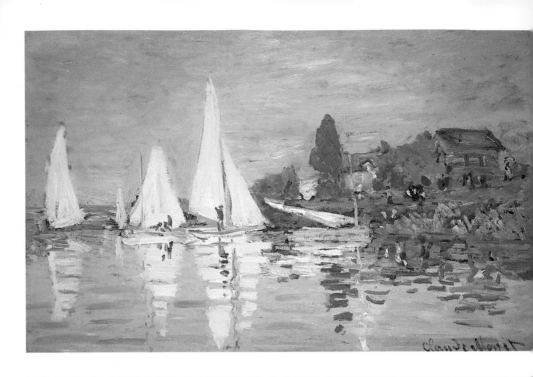

Chintreuil, Antoine (1814–73) A follower of COROT, with whose works his own are often confused, he specialized in landscapes devoted to the countryside around Paris. He was an early influence on PISSARRO, who met him in 1861, and was one of the signatories of a letter to NAPOLEON III praising him for initiating the SALON DES REFUSÉS. DURANTY, in his *Nouvelle Peinture* of 1876, included him as one of the precursors of Impressionism.

☐ C.H. La Fizelière, *La Vie et l'oeuvre de Chintreuil* (1874); L. Saint-Michel, *L'Univers de Corot* (1974)

Chocquet, Victor (1821–91) An official in the Customs Service who had private means, Chocquet was a born collector. He started off by accumulating bric-à-brac, and then moved on to paintings and drawings, showing an early interest in the works of DELACROIX. In 1875 he attended the Impressionist sale at the HÔTEL DROUOT and, though he did not buy anything, he was deeply impressed by the works of RENOIR, seeing an affinity between his style and that of Delacroix; he immediately commissioned him to paint portraits of himself and his wife (*Victor Chocquet*, Fogg Art Museum, Cambridge, and *Madame Chocquet*, Staatsgalerie, Stuttgart). They got on famously together, and Renoir gradually introduced him to the work of his friends, taking him first to the shop of Père TANGUY to show him the works of

Cézanne's portrait of **Chocquet** was exhibited at the 1877 Impressionist exhibition.

CÉZANNE. Chocquet commissioned a portrait from him, and Cézanne actually produced two, one analogous to that of Renoir (1876–77; Collection of Lord Rothschild, London), the other showing him in slippered ease, seated in an armchair (*c.* 1877; Columbus Gallery of Fine Arts, Ohio). Henceforth, Chocquet became an Impressionist addict, intent on proselytizing as well as buying. When he attended their exhibitions, DURET recounted, 'People amused themselves by teasing him on his favourite subject. He was always ready for them, invariably finding the right words as far as his friends were concerned. He was above all else indefatigable on the subject of Cézanne, whom he counted as one of the greatest of painters. Many visitors were amused by this zeal, which they saw as a mild form of insanity.' Chocquet's already large collection was further increased as he became richer and installed himself in a large house in the rue Monsigny. After his death, his collection was sold at the Hôtel Drouot, and included 32 works by Cézanne, 11 by Renoir, 11 by MONET, 5 by MANET and one each by PISSARRO and SISLEY, as well as works by Delacroix, COROT, COURBET and Daumier. *See also* PATRONS AND COLLECTORS [177]

Quite apart from the fact that they were attracted by the spontaneous effect and anti-academic implications of the loosely executed sketch, the Impressionists' preference for working in the open air meant that they were forced to adopt short-hand techniques in order to capture the fleeting effects of nature. Monet's Regatta at Argenteuil (1874) shows how the thick, creamy consistency of commercially prepared tube paints could be used to cover the entire canvas with a single layer of opaque pigment, creating an immediate effect. Bold slabs of pure, unmodulated colour break up the flatness of the picture surface, while the pale ground, left uncovered in places, increases the sense of intense luminosity. Sisley's more lyrical version is reflected, in the Floods at Port-Marly (1876), in his more fluid use of paint and the looseness of his brushwork. The frontal positioning of the building, with its solid black doorway, and the insistent verticals of the trees stress the flatness of the picture surface, but this is played against the receding diagonal of the trees at the centre, and the broken, unblended brushwork in the water and sky, which create a sense of movement, depth and texture.

□ J Joëts, 'Les Impressionnistes et Chocquet; lettres inédits', in *L'Amour de l'art* (April 1935); Rewald (1984); Rewald (1985)

Claretie, Jules (Jules Arsène Arnaud) (1840–1913) Novelist, historian and art critic who was also keenly interested in the theatre; he was made administrator of the Comédie Française in 1885, and was later elected to the Academy. As the art critic of *Le Temps*, he had considerable influence and was generally hostile to the Impressionists, relying very much on internal information about the various feuds and rivalries that beset them to undermine their standing, especially in the 1880s.
□ Sloane (1951); Hamilton (1954)

Clemenceau, Georges (1841–1929) Known as 'the Tiger', he was one of the dominant figures of the Third Republic and was largely responsible for France's success in the First World War. A militant republican, he made his name first as a journalist and as leader of the radical Left; he was founder and editor of *Justice*, leading with ZOLA the campaign for the rehabilitation of Colonel Dreyfus (*see* POLITICS).

Degas took this photograph of himself and Zoé **Closier** in the 1890s.

Clemenceau, as seen by Manet, 1879. The portrait did not appeal to the politician.

Defeated at the polls in 1920, he retired into morose solitude. He was a man of many interests, with a great enthusiasm for art and literature. In 1879 his successor on the Conseil Municipal of Paris, Gustave Manet, introduced Clemenceau to his brother Edouard, who painted two portraits of him (*Clemenceau at the Tribune*, Kimbell Art Museum, Fort Worth, and *Clemenceau*, Musée d'Orsay). But his real favourites were Rodin, and MONET, whom he visited frequently at GIVERNY. He wrote a very perceptive article about Monet's views of Rouen cathedral in *Justice* in May 1895, and was largely responsible for ensuring that the artist's *Nymphéas* were hung in the Orangerie. *See also* CAFÉS [54]
□ G. Clemenceau, *Claude Monet, les Nymphéas* (1928); J. Martet, *Clemenceau peint par lui-même* (1929)

Closier, Zoé (*c.* 1850–*c.* 1920) In 1882 she became DEGAS' housekeeper, cook, factotum and, eventually, nurse. Her cooking was reputedly appalling, a fact which she attributed to Degas' tendency to spend money on old master drawings rather than on food. She was invaluable to him in many ways, reading to him and, above all, deterring unwelcome visitors.
□ *Degas*, Grand Palais, Paris, exhibition catalogue (1988)

Colour It was in their use of colour that the Impressionists made their most significant contribution to the development of Western art, and one which, by destroying old concepts of colour as a merely descriptive adjunct to form, was to allow it to be used for a variety of independent purposes. Originally, their approach had been influenced by the discoveries of CHEVREUL, especially that relating to simultaneous contrast, which pointed out that if two strips of the same plain colour, but of different shades, are placed side by side, then the part of the lighter strip nearer the darker strip will appear lighter than it actually is, and vice versa. Similarly, Chevreul demonstrated how every colour tends to tint neighbouring colours with its own complementary colour. In terms of the awareness of the spectator, he described the first phenomenon as *mixed contrast*, the second as *successive contrast*.

Preoccupied as they were with depicting actual visual experience in a perceptual rather than a conceptual way, the Impressionists seized upon these notions, of which they had already become at least partially aware through their own observations, but modified them according to their own sensibilities. Above all else they were excited by the idea that colour was not a fixed and isolated constituent, its nature predetermined by the label on the tube from which it emerged. As Jacques Lassaigne put it (*Impressionism*, 1969), 'Henceforward Impressionism was able to go beyond the accepted conventions of studio painting, contrived lighting and the rest. It could suggest shapes and distances by vibrations and colour contrasts, considering the subject matter in its luminous atmosphere and in the changes of lighting. A landscape bathed in light is made up of a thousand vibrant clashes, of prismatic decompositions, of irregular strokes, which from a distance meld with one another to create life.' Colour had become an independent element in the creation of a work of art, capable not only of performing compositional tasks, but of adumbrating emotion and feeling.

No single formula can be devised to define the actual use of colour by all the Impressionists. With some there were considerable variations within the course of their careers. RENOIR's early works had a greenish-blue tonality, his later ones a vibrant red-tinted accent. But all of them, with the possible exception of DEGAS, gave a great deal of time and effort to producing colour effects of great technical complexity.

MONET was especially active in this respect. In the *Gare Saint-Lazare* (1877, National Gallery), for instance, it would seem that he used a certain amount of black to darken the shadows, especially in the intense blackness of the engine. A recent analysis, carried out by the scientific staff of the National Gallery, however, reveals that this is not the case. The dark colour is made up of a dark purple, laid on side by side with an intense deep blue. In the roof of the station the shadows are depicted by the same combination, with the warmer colour predominating to the right, the cooler to the left. At the other end of the chromatic scale the steam and smoke are painted mainly in lead white, tinted with small quantities of blue, green and red pigment.

A similar analysis of Renoir's *The Seine at Asnières* (1879) in the same gallery, shows the Impressionist palette at its most typical – and most complex. In painting this work Renoir used the following colours: lead white, cobalt blue, chrome yellow, lemon yellow, chrome orange, vermilion and crimson lake, which he applied in unmixed dabs, sometimes over quite a large area. The only mixing of colours occurs where one pigment is introduced to make some minor change to the dominant one (e.g. the use of a tiny amount of viridian to modify the colour of the foliage, which is predominantly yellowish-green). As the picture was painted wet in wet, the brushstrokes merge and patches of colour intermingle with the streaks left by the brush. However, the actual creation of colour takes place in the eye of the spectator rather than on the artist's palette. Though Renoir has mixed thin paint for the background to produce softer, more graduated tones, the major part of the picture surface is covered with thick brushstrokes applied in superimposed strokes of pure colour.

In emancipating colour from its purely descriptive functions, even though originally they had been endeavouring to achieve a higher degree of objective realism, the Impressionists had initiated a revolution in art, which would lead through GAUGUIN and VAN GOGH to the figurative Expressionism of painters such as Ensor and the Blaue Reiter, to the Abstract Expressionism of Pollock and the New York School, and eventually to the single colour paintings of Rothko. Feeling had asserted its primacy over form, and through colour the visual REALISM of the Impressionists led to the last renaissance of Romanticism. *See also* FLOCHETAGE, PEINTURE CLAIRE, TECHNIQUE *[49–56]*

□ A. Callen, *Techniques of the Impressionists* (1982); A. Roy, 'The Palettes of Impressionist Paintings in the National Gallery', *National Gallery Technical Bulletin*, vol. 9 (1985)

Cordey, Frédéric (1854–1911) A rather undistinguished painter who, having with a group of friends left the ECOLE DES BEAUX-ARTS in a mood of revolt against its teachings, met RENOIR – then living in MONTMARTRE – and became a virtual disciple. Thanks to this contact, he exhibited four works at the 1877 IMPRESSIONIST EXHIBITION. In 1881 he was in ALGIERS with Renoir, but his painting career never made any headway and he lapsed into a kind of modified academicism.

□ Rewald (1973); B.E. White, *Renoir, His Life, Art and Letters* (1984)

Cormon, Fernand (1845–1924) Professor of painting at the ECOLE DES BEAUX-ARTS, he had first achieved wide fame in 1880 with his *Cain* (Musée du Luxembourg), which was the sensation of the SALON of that year. Known for his portraits as well as his history paintings, he ran an ATELIER and counted amongst his pupils GAUGUIN, VAN GOGH, Toulouse-Lautrec and Emile BERNARD. Cormon's teaching methods depended very much on making his students copy pictures from the Louvre, and Van Gogh was totally disillusioned by his experience with him. Inevitably Cormon became a favourite butt of the main-line Impressionists, who saw in him the very epitome of the reactionary ACADEMIC artist. In fact this was not true. He was especially impressed by the work of Toulouse-Lautrec, who reported home in 1883 that Cormon had approved of some works of his 'of a highly Impressionistic bent', and a year later he invited the young artist to assist him in illustrating the Imprimerie Nationale edition of the works of Victor Hugo, though the work Lautrec did for *La Légende des siècles* was not actually used. [21]

□ J. Rewald, *Post-Impressionism* (1956); Rewald (1973); Milner (1988)

Corot, Camille (1796–1875) No painter of his generation had a greater influence on the Impressionists, in whose activities and experiments he took a lively interest; he offered advice and counsel to PISSARRO, MORISOT and others, who responded warmly not only to his artistic achievements, but to his obvious integrity and generosity of spirit. The son of a Norman textile merchant, he started his career in his

A corner of **Cormon**'s studio, showing sketches for his famous 'stone-age' paintings.

A photograph of **Corot** on a brochure for the 'Fête de Corot' held at Ville d'Avray in 1903.

The Cart; Souvenir de Marcoussis, 1865: **Corot**'s exact study of light and landscape was to have great impact on the Impressionists, but his lyrical vision also appealed to more conservative tastes.

father's firm, but the strength of his desire to become an artist persuaded his family to allow him to become a student of Jean-Victor Bertin, who gave him a neo-classical training. Despite this ACADEMIC background, he felt drawn to landscape painting and spent most of his spare time in the forest of Fontainebleau, on the banks of the Seine and on the Channel coast.

His first stay in ITALY between 1825 and 1828 had a decisive influence on his development. He was entranced by its light, and found in its landscape a source of inspiration which looked back towards the tradition of Claude and Poussin, renovated by a sense of lyricism that found nourishment in the bucolic poetry of Virgil, to which he was passionately devoted. On his return to France he continued to paint those landscapes that had previously attracted him, but he greatly extended his areas of interest, visiting Burgundy, the Auvergne and the Morvan. He was indeed one of the most peripatetic painters of his age, covering most of the French provinces (e.g. *Chartres*, 1830, and

The Belfry at Douai, 1870; both in the Musée d'Orsay). He also visited Italy again, painting views of Venice and elsewhere (*The Grand Canal and S. Maria della Salute*, Pushkin Museum of Fine Arts, Moscow). Corot gradually became widely recognized; BAUDELAIRE wrote in praise of him, and NAPOLEON III bought one of his works, *Souvenir de Marcoussis* (1865; Musée d'Orsay) for his private collection. He served on the jury of the SALON from 1864 and always had his pictures accepted there.

Pissarro had been in close contact with Corot since the commencement of his career as a painter, and most of his early work shows Corot's influence quite strongly; indeed, when he sent two pictures to the Salon in 1864 he described himself as 'the pupil of A. Melbye and Corot'. Paradoxically, the one and only piece of advice that Corot ever gave to anybody was not to imitate others, though to Pissarro he added the rider 'Except for this; above all else study tonal values. We don't see in the same way; you see green, and I see grey and silver. But this is no

Commonly known as *The Artist's Studio*, **Courbet**'s enormous painting, which includes portraits of Baudelaire, Champfleury and Bruyas, was exhibited in 1855 in the 'Pavillon du Réalisme' near the Salon.

reason at all for you not to work at values, for that is the basis of everything, and in whatever way one may feel and express oneself, one cannot do good painting without it.' RENOIR and MONET were equally impressed by Corot's work, though the former held back from personal contact, largely out of shyness, giving as his reason the fact that Corot was 'always surrounded by idiots'. It was probably the charm of Berthe MORISOT that impelled Corot to a closer relationship with her and her sister Edma, with whom he frequently dined, but to whom he also gave the advice not to copy 'papa Corot'. As he grew older his own work tended to come closer to the explorations of the habitués of the CAFÉ GUERBOIS, and paintings such as his *Sens Cathedral* (1874; Musée d'Orsay) show how great was the debt they owed him. *See also* ANTECEDENTS, AUVERS-SUR-OISE, CHINTREUIL, IMPRESSIONISM, VILLE D'AVRAY *[204]*
□ E. Moreau-Nélaton, *Corot, raconté par lui-même* (1924); J. Leymarie, *Corot* (1962); *Corot*, Orangerie, Paris, exhibition catalogue (1975)

Courbet, Gustave (1819–77) Born into a family of rich vine-growers, his early years in Ornans (Franche-Comté) gave him a life-long devotion to that area, from which he drew much of his material. In 1839 he went to PARIS to fulfil his long-held desire to become an artist, and was seduced by the painters of SPAIN, whose works were then becoming so accessible. Escaping from the initial appeal of Romanticism, he became the accepted leader of the REALIST group, a position confirmed by the two works which he exhibited at the SALON of 1850: *The Stone Breakers* and *The Burial at Ornans* (Musée d'Orsay). One of the main beliefs which actuated him was that, in his own words, 'Painting is an art of sight and should therefore concern itself with things seen; it should eschew both the historical scenes of the classical school, and poetic subjects chosen from Goethe and Shakespeare of the kind chosen by the Romantics.' He saw in the events of ordinary life – an encounter by the roadside, peasants winnowing grain or girls sleeping, far from gracefully, in the grass – themes in themselves worthy of being recorded without the addition of any intellectual or sentimental gloss. In some ways his work combined the clear-eyed gravity of the Spanish painters with the ability of their Dutch and Flemish contemporaries to record the actualities of daily existence.

Such an approach was very much in the air. It was to be seen in the works of English painters, such as Luke Fildes and Ford Madox Brown; in the writings of ZOLA and the GONCOURTS, and in a mildly sentimentalized form in the paintings of contemporary artists such as MILLET. But it implied a new attitude to the social dimensions of life and their political implications. What differentiated Courbet from most others who shared his aesthetic ideals was the fact that, by the almost physical force of his personality, and by his deeply held political convictions as a socialist – he was a friend and disciple of Pierre Joseph Proudhon – which were thrown into relief by the nature of the political regime then operating in France, he became a symbolic figure, who epitomized the artist as rebel against both the artistic and the political establishment. He therefore helped to create the climate of opinion and the entrenched attitudes that were to mark the emergence of Impressionism.

Courbet's paintings anticipated the iconography of the Impressionists in that they were unheroic, unhistorical and entirely unconcerned either with religious symbolism or patriotic propaganda. They rejected, in fact, nearly all the themes that had exercised most French painters during the previous century, and qualified him for the description which BAUDELAIRE, one of his admirers, applied to GUYS: 'a painter of modern life'. One of the first to appreciate the significance and vitality of the kind of popular imagery associated with the printing centre of Epinal, he avoided the least suspicion of emotion, and the only rhetoric in his work was of a gestural variety. His most ambitiously spectacular work, which reflected the vitality of his egomania, as well as more admirable qualities, was *The Artist's Studio* (Musée d'Orsay), painted in 1854–55. It was subtitled 'Allegory of Realism', and, apart from its determined avoidance of any suggestion of the semi-erotic glamour usually attached to subjects of this kind, it involved a complicated metaphor of the forces of reaction and enlightenment placed to the left and the right of the artist. Inevitably, it was rejected at the Salon, and Courbet exhibited it, in what could be seen as an appeal to 'the people', and as a precedent for the Impressionists' own 'alternative exhibitions', in a temporary building on the avenue Montaigne.

From then onwards, however, he tended to concentrate on landscapes and sylvan hunting scenes, with which he had a considerable popular success, not only in France, but especially in HOLLAND and GERMANY; and eventually he experienced the pleasure of being able to reject the offer of the Legion of Honour. With the fall of the Second Empire he became involved in the Commune, and was made virtually its Minister of Fine Arts. When the government forces retook Paris, he was held responsible for the destruction of the Vendôme column, and briefly put into prison, where he continued painting and was visited by MONET, BOUDIN and Amand Gautier. He was condemned to pay personally for the restoration of the column and, probably with the connivance of the authorities, fled to Switzerland, where he died in 1877.

Apart from the fact that Courbet provided the Impressionists with a notion of contemporary realism and served as a prototype of the artist as innovator in conflict with traditionalism, he exerted, especially in the 1860s, a stylistic influence which, although it was later melded with their own individual developments and experiments, would always be perceptible in their work in the form of a

SOUVENIRS DE LA COMMUNE.

L'homme qui était un jour appelé à démolir la Colonne devait commencer par être casseur de pierres.

A comment on **Courbet**'s imprisonment for the destruction of the Vendôme Column.

freedom of handling, a sense of surface vibrancy and a boldness of composition. Even the somewhat austere visual effect of DEGAS succumbed to the older artist's self-confidence, notably in *Mlle Fiocre in the Ballet 'La Source'* (1867; Brooklyn Museum, New York), in which the rocks of the stage-set take on the textured solidity of one of Courbet's quarry paintings. Monet's work, until at least 1869, was dominated by the influence of Courbet, with whom he was in clost contact; and CÉZANNE, who praised his 'unlimited talent, for which no difficulties exist', found in his realism an antidote to the rather baroque fantasies that were preoccupying him. PISSARRO's *The Hermitage at Pontoise* (c.1867; Guggenheim Museum, New York) typifies in its treatment of trees and foliage, its high sloping horizon, its handling of the stone and tiles of the cottages, and in the breadth of its composition, the kind of hold that Courbet's work had on artists of that generation. RENOIR's figures of women reflect the *Demoiselles au bord de la Seine* (1856; Ville de Paris); Monet's paintings at Etretat echo Courbet's at the same place; SISLEY's *View of Montmartre* (1869; Musée de Grenoble) has the breadth of handling and of concept that Courbet had made seem so enviable to his admirers.

Until 1870 MANET and Courbet were thought by many to be rivals for the leadership of a new movement in painting. A variety of factors, not all of them connected with the older painter's misfortunes, decided otherwise, but traces of the legacy of the master of Ornans persisted into the beginnings of the 20th c. *See also* BONVIN, BRASSERIE DES MARTYRS, BRUYAS, CAFÉS, CASTAGNARY, ETRETAT, POLITICS *[36, 171, 204]*

☐ P. Courthion, *Courbet raconté par lui et par ses amis*, 2 vols. (1948, 1950); G. Mack, *Gustave Courbet* (1951); Clark (1973b)

Couture, Thomas (1815–79) A history and portrait painter who first achieved renown with his *Romains de la décadence* (1847; Musée d'Orsay). He was a highly successful teacher, his most famous pupil being MANET, of whom he said that he would be no more than the Daumier of his generation. He was also the teacher of PUVIS DE CHAVANNES, the Americans W.M. Hunt and John La Farge, and the German Anselm Feuerbach. He wrote two interesting books on painting, one devoted to techniques and practice, the other to landscape. Although he was, and often still is, taken as the prototype of the unimaginative ACADEMIC painter, in fact he laid strong emphasis on

The combination of academic realism and French eroticism which characterizes **Couture**'s *Romains de la décadence* of 1847 goes far to explain its immense popularity.

spontaneity and would not examine a student's painting if it had been retouched. His own work was marked by strong tonal contrasts and a freedom of handling. He was very sensitive to the attacks made on him by younger artists, and towards the end of his life retired to the country, where he led virtually the life of a peasant. *See also* ATELIER SYSTEM, PLEIN-AIRISME
□ T. Couture, *Thomas Couture, 1815–79; sa vie, son oeuvre, ses idées etc.* (1932); A. Boime, 'Thomas Couture and the evolution of painting in nineteenth-century France', in *Art Bulletin* (1969); M. Fried, 'Thomas Couture and the theatricalisation of French painting in the nineteenth century,' in *Artforum* (June 1970)

Critics and criticism Although there had been a certain amount of art criticism in the 18th c. – Diderot, for instance, had written annual reviews of the SALON – it was not until the 19th c. that the art critic emerged as a formidable manipulator of taste and an important influence on the history of art. This had been brought about by a number of technical innovations: the application of steam power to printing, the invention of the rotary press, the growth of a fast and cheap postal service, and the development of various reproductive processes which facilitated illustrations. Though these underpinned the phenomenon, other factors lent additional significance. In the first place a new type of PATRONAGE had grown up, exercised for the most part by men whose fortunes were of recent growth, created by one of the many diverse effects of the Industrial Revolution. On the whole, they lacked the acquired tastes of their 18th-c. predecessors, and they looked for guidance in an art world that was steadily becoming at once more diffuse and more complex. At the same time, more people were becoming interested in art. The Salons, which annually exhibited some 6000 paintings by about 2000 artists, attracted visitors whose numbers rose from some 150,000 in the 1840s to 562,000 in 1887. Nearly a million visited the fine art section of the Exposition Universelle of 1855. There was therefore a vast potential market for writings about art, which was catered for by a wide range of papers and periodicals; popular newspapers, such as *Figaro* and *Le Petit Parisien*, and specialist magazines, such as the *Gazette des Beaux-Arts* or L'ARTISTE, gave employment to well over a hundred writers of varying status, interests and ability, all of whom would have described themselves

In his portrait of Zola (1867–68) Manet surrounds the **critic** with symbols of his tastes and activities.

as art critics. In 1881 there were 19 magazines devoted to the fine arts, by 1901 no less than 45. The position was further complicated by the growing commercialization of the art world, and the emergence of highly professional art dealers, creating almost inevitably a sub-world of venality and corruption amongst journalists, which could range from direct bribery to devices such as lavish advertising or an agreement to purchase a certain number of copies of any publication that provided favourable reviews.

The influence that critics exercised is not as straightforward as it might at first appear. In 1883 Monet noted 'Nothing can be achieved today without the press. It is not so much that artistically one should pay attention to it. It is the commercial aspect which counts, for even intelligent connoisseurs are sensitive to the least noise made by the press.' This, of course, was true, though it is not always easy to decide to what extent critics made taste or followed it. One thing is certain, that without the support of critics such as ZOLA, SILVESTRE, DURANTY and RIVIÈRE, the Impressionists would not have had the success that they achieved in little more than 20 years. The fact that the very concept of

IMPRESSIONISM was in fact the almost accidental invention of an art critic, Louis LEROY, writing in CHARIVARI, is in itself significant. Faced with the problems of producing interesting and, preferably, amusing copy, critics had to simplify, to dramatize, to resort to anecdote and exaggeration. To entice their readers they created oppositional situations, in which the Impressionists were portrayed as more farouche, more anarchistical, more iconoclastic, the 'academic' artists as more intolerant, more hidebound, more establishmentarian than either side really was. But the mere suggestion of these antitheses helped to bring them into existence, and it might be said, with only a touch of exaggeration, that it was because of the critics that Impressionism was the first significant art movement to be allotted the role of the avant-garde, fighting a high-principled battle against the forces of reaction.

It is in part this scenario that has led subsequent generations to exaggerate the degree of critical hostility which the Impressionists had to endure. Much of this was expressed, of course, in papers such as *Figaro* or *Charivari* with large circulations, and there was as much political as aesthetic motivation for it (*see* POLITICS). MANET was not alone in his constant courting of unfriendly critics; he even commenced a portrait of one of the most hostile of them, Albert WOLFF of *Figaro*, in a not entirely unsuccessful attempt to persuade him to moderate his venom. By the mid-1870s, however, a whole group of critics had recognized the changes which the Impressionists were making to the nature of painting, and there were others, such as the painter-critic Eugène Fromentin, who, whilst criticizing them for their lack of 'science', admitted that they possessed 'keenly observed powers of observation, delicate sensibilities and the most exceptional faculties'. Paul MANTZ, a renowned art historian and editor of the *Gazette des Beaux-Arts*, spoke in its columns in 1878 of the Impressionist as 'A free and sincere artist who, breaking with the traditions of the Ecole des Beaux-Arts and the dictates of polite taste, experiences, in the simplicity of his heart, the absolute enchantment which is distilled by nature and expresses it as simply and freely as possible, in what might be described as the intensity of the impression he has received.' By 1879, partly as a result of RENOIR's success at the Salon, even the most hostile papers and magazines, such as *L'Artiste*, had started to show

Daumier's caricature shows the omnipotent **critic** being saluted by cringing artists.

some tolerance and understanding, even though they attributed this change of heart to the supposed fact that it was the Impressionists who were becoming more conformist.

The problem was that by this time Impressionism as an integrated movement was breaking up, and the critics began to make their own individual preferences clear. Armand Silvestre saw PISSARRO as the real guardian of the main Impressionist tradition; Philippe BURTY and Charles EPHRUSSI could not stand his paintings, though both applauded Renoir and felt that MONET was losing his independence. HUYSMANS, whose aesthetic sensibilities were moulded by his literary tastes, lauded DEGAS, as well as such artists as FORAIN and RAFFAËLLI, largely because of their REALISM, and deprecated the works of Monet and Pissarro. Only in ENGLAND and the USA would critics continue to praise or condemn Impressionism as a unitary phenomenon. In 1888 Zola, who had acted as godfather to the movement, pronounced what he saw as its epitaph: 'The group's life is finished. The great tragedy is that no single member of the group has ever managed to unite in his own work the entirety of that new approach, elements of which are dispersed through all their paintings. They have not produced a comprehensive genius.' *See also* BAUDELAIRE, BESNARD, BLANC, BURGER, CASTAGNARY, CHESNEAU, CLARETIE, DELVAU,

DEWHURST, DURET, FÉNÉON, FOURCAUD, GAU-
TIER, GEFFROY, HAMERTON, HOUSSAYE, JAMES,
LAFENESTRE, MACCOLL, MALLARMÉ, MARTELLI,
MAUCLAIR, MIRBEAU, MOORE, RUTTER, STEVENS,
STEVENSON, VALABRÈGUE, LA VIE MODERNE, WED-
MORE [15, 88, 120, 127, 132, 136, 230]
□ Sloane (1951); Hamilton (1954); L. Venturi,
Histoire de la critique d'art (1969); Denvir (1987)

D

Degas' painting (1873–76) of a **dancing** class at the Opéra, conducted by choreographer Jules Perrot.

Dancing In 1867 the American Henry Tuckerman wrote about PARIS, 'Dancing there is a function of life, a normal phase of national development; it is what racing and boxing are in Britain, and speechifying in the United States. Balls in Paris are representative and share the distinctions of society; the middle class, the ruling powers and the fanatics of all ranks may find appropriate gyrations in their respective spheres' (*Papers about Paris*, New York). It was just because of this intimate connection with the life and spirit of the times that the Impressionists found in dancing one of their favourite themes.

At the top of the dancing hierarchy was the ballet at the Opéra, which was housed in a building in the rue Le Peletier until 1875, when it was moved into Charles Garnier's master-piece. Employing as it did a staff of 650, the Opéra was an integral part of the fashionable life of Paris, though artistically, it could not be thought of as experiencing a golden age – at least, as far as the ballet was concerned. This was the world which fascinated DEGAS and which constituted one of the most important elements in his art, covering every medium and providing an incessant stimulus to his imagination. The dancers whom he portrayed presented very varying types of people. Until about the 1870s ballet dancers were mostly drawn from the lower classes, for the middle classes saw great moral dangers for their daughters in the *coulisses* of the Opéra. Gradually, however, as the whole organization of the opera and ballet became more 'official', the status of the dancers altered and they began to be recruited from the offspring of the staff, musicians and instructors. This is typified by Degas' portrait of the Mante family, which portrays Mme Mante, whose

husband was a bassoonist in the Opéra orchestra, and her two daughters, Suzanne and Blanche, both of whom entered the ballet at the age of seven and had successful careers in ballet.

Next on the scale came social dances; the most popular were the masked balls held at the Opéra every Saturday night from December until Shrove Tuesday, one of which was painted by MANET in 1873–74 (National Gallery of Art, Washington). Admission cost ten francs, so these balls were not in any way 'select'; they lasted from midnight until five in the morning

Dancing at the Bal de l'Assommoir on the Elysée Montmartre, from *Le Monde illustré*, 1879.

and were considered happy hunting-grounds for Casanovas, anxious to pick up a dancer or member of the Opéra chorus.

Then came the *bals publics*, which visitors found such an idiosyncratic aspect of Parisian life, and which varied in nature from the near-orgiastic to events specially designed for family relaxation. In 1876 RENOIR started attending dances at the Moulin de la Galette in MONT-MARTRE, an area which at that time had not achieved the cultural chic that it was later to assume. The actual *moulin*, one of three that gave the hill its characteristic profile, was used to grind iris roots for a perfumier, and the dancing area was an enclosed courtyard, adjacent to a café owned by the Debray family. Renoir's *Dance at the Moulin de la Galette* (1876; Musée d'Orsay) not only conveys the atmosphere of the place, but, by his selection of the participants – four painters, a civil servant, two journalists, several models (one of whom also features in *The Swing* of 1876; Musée d'Orsay), and a host of ordinary people whom he asked to pose – gives a realistic picture of urban pleasures in the Paris of his day. The women were not prostitutes but working-class girls, who typify the kind of people who attended these *bals*. Toulouse-Lautrec was to continue this concern with public entertainment, though his was a more sophisticated world. *See also* CAFÉS-CONCERT, MUSIC, PERROT *[39, 40, 159, 187]*

□ I. Guest, *The Ballet of the Second Empire* (1974); F. Gasnault, *Guinguettes et lorettes, Bals publics et danse sociale à Paris entre 1830 et 1870* (1986); Herbert (1988)

Daubigny, Charles François (1817–78) The pupil of his father Edmé-François, he attended the studio of Paul Delaroche, went to Rome, and on his return became a picture restorer at the Louvre. His own style of painting evolved in the direction of the BARBIZON School (although he did not live or work in that locality) and he was an enthusiastic practitioner of out-of-doors painting, very much concerned with atmospheric effects. He first attracted public attention and praise at the SALON of 1848 with a series of landscapes of the Morvan (*Valley of the Cousin*, Musée d'Orsay), and he maintained his popularity, despite the fact that his brushwork became increasingly free and spontaneous. Although Dutch influence was

Daubigny's *Evening* clearly demonstrates the Dutch influence on his work and that interest in atmospheric effects which so appealed to the Impressionists.

evident in his works, as, indeed, was that of Constable, his style was never derivative, and it is obvious that his work would have appealed to the younger generation of artists which was to produce Impressionism.

From the begining, MONET was one of his devoted admirers; the two first met at TROU-VILLE in 1865, and in 1868 Daubigny was largely instrumental in getting works by Monet, as well as by MANET, PISSARRO, BAZILLE, MORISOT, RENOIR and SISLEY, admitted to the Salon, in which he was serving as a jury member. It was also Daubigny who first introduced Monet to his dealer Paul DURAND-RUEL, in January 1871 when they were all in London; who persuaded him to go to HOLLAND in 1872; and who bought his *Canal in Zaandam* (Collection of Mr & Mrs Clifford, New York). It is not without interest, too, that Monet's famous floating studio, in which he was painted by Manet (1874; Bayerische Staatsgalerie, Munich), was based on a similar *botin* that Daubigny, who was particularly attracted to river scenes, had used some two decades earlier.

There can be little doubt that of all the older artists who presided over the genesis of Impressionism, Daubigny was one of the most helpful and, stylistically, one of the most influential. *See also* ANTECEDENTS, HÔTEL DROUOT, PLEIN-AIRISME *[168]*
□ E. Morceau-Nélaton, *Daubigny raconté par lui-même* (1925); M. Fidell-Beaufort and J. Bailly-Herzberg, *Daubigny; the life and work* (1975)

Daudet, Alphonse (1840–97) Considered in his day to be, with Maupassant, the leading exponent of REALISM in literature, he was an extremely prolific and successful novelist, playwright and journalist, whose novels dealt with a wide range of subjects, from the home life of the Bonapartes and the history of the Académie Française to the Salvation Army and the country life of Provence. His most famous works are the *Lettres de mon moulin* (1866) and *Tartarin de Tarascon* (1872).

Daudet's natural inclination to Realism and his social contacts led him into touch with the Impressionists. His publisher CHARPENTIER was a close friend and patron of RENOIR, who used to visit Daudet at his home in Champrosey, and his friendship with DEGAS was reinforced by their common interest in the lives of ordinary people. He was a frequent visitor to the Nouvelle-Athènes, bought several paintings from the Impressionists and was a prominent buyer at the otherwise disastrous HOSCHEDÉ sale in 1878. *See also* BATIGNOLLES

Davies Collection Between 1908 and 1924 Margaret and Gwendoline Davies, the daughters of an affluent coal and railways contractor, amassed at Gregynog Hall, Montgomeryshire, in Wales, a collection of paintings which, in its wealth of works by the Impressionists, rivalled that of Sir Hugh LANE. They had begun by collecting artists of the BARBIZON School, but by 1912 they were moving on to MONET, some of whose Venetian works they had seen in Paris at an exhibition at Bernheim-Jeune's gallery. They were advised in their purchases by David Croal Thomson, who had worked for Henry Wallis, the English partner of DURAND-RUEL. Their collection included 3 MANETS, 3 RENOIRS, 2 paintings and 6 drawings by PISSARRO, 9 paintings by Monet, 3 CÉZANNE oils and 3 watercolours, 1 MORISOT, 1 SISLEY, and two bronze statuettes by DEGAS. The whole collection was bequeathed to the National Museum of Wales. *[54]*
□ J. Ingamells, *The Davies Collection of French Art* (1966)

Degas, Hilaire-Germain-Edgar (1834–1917) The son of an upper middle-class banking family with aristocratic Neapolitan connections, Degas early expressed a wish to become an artist, and as this aroused no parental opposition, he entered the ECOLE DES BEAUX-ARTS at the age of 21. After a year there, however, he went to ITALY, staying first in Naples, before visiting other Italian cities, and eventually spending three years in Rome. By this time he had acquired a passion for Italian painting which was never to leave him and which was to give his paintings a clarity and linear elegance that set him somewhat apart from many of those with whom his own artistic career would be associated. In Italy he painted a number of portraits, mainly of his relations (*see* BELLELLI), in which he expressed for the first time his own attitude to PORTRAITURE: 'to depict people in familiar and typical attitudes, above all to give to their faces the same choice of expression as one gives to their bodies'. Apart from these, he started producing what were, in effect, 'ACADEMIC' paintings of classical and historical subjects, dealt with in a style that had suggestions of Mantegna, of Bellini and of Ingres. But even in the most traditional of these, there was a sense of REALISM and a clarity of

A photograph of **Degas** taken in Bartholomé's garden at Auteuil, *c.* 1915.

observation which gave them a character all their own. It is significant, for instance, that in *Young Spartans Exercising* (1860–62; National Gallery, London), which was not publicly exhibited until the fifth Impressionist show of 1880, the models are not based on classical statues but on 'children from Montmartre'.

In 1862 Degas met MANET, whilst making an etching of a Velazquez in the Louvre, and was introduced by him to the circle of the CAFÉ GUERBOIS. The most immediately apparent consequence of this contact was that he abandoned 'history' painting and applied himself to contemporary Parisian life, painting race-courses – his first in 1862 – and going on, in a style that attracted the limited approval of the GONCOURT brothers, to evolve that imagery of CAFÉS, ballet, theatre, working girls, brothels and the slightly seamier sides of Parisian life with which his name is associated. Horses were a special preoccupation. Influenced by the researches of Eadweard Muybridge and others (*see* PHOTOGRAPHY), by 1869 he had produced his first statue of a horse, using a medium which he was later to develop with great skill and sophistication (*see* SCULPTURE). In 1872 he visited the USA, where his family had business interests, producing the memorable *Cotton Office, New Orleans* (Musée des Beaux-Arts, Pau) the following year. In 1874 he participated

in the first IMPRESSIONIST EXHIBITION with ten paintings, including *The Dancing Class* and *The Ballet Rehearsal* (both Musée d'Orsay). He contributed other paintings of horse-racers and dancers, as well as straightforward landscape-format paintings such as *Beach Scene* (National Gallery, London) and *Woman Seated at a Café* (Musée d'Orsay). To the 1879 and 1880 shows he contributed oils, pastels and painted fans, and in 1881 the figure of a ballet-dancer in wax.

The role of Degas as an Impressionist is not an easy one to define. On a personal level he had many of the characteristics of Manet: especially a certain aloofness and reluctance to be too deeply compromised. He was, moreover, on the social plane, a rather prickly person, often intent on pressing for his own friends and connections to be included in the group shows or, alternatively, taking exception to friends of the other Impressionists. More than his colleagues, he was absorbed in the human figure, and only marginally concerned with nature and landscape; more than the other Impressionists he was interested in draughtsmanship and line, rather than in COLOUR and flickering brush-work. 'Even when working from nature, one

Degas' *Little Dancer aged 14* (1878–81) is one of an edition of about 20 cast by Hébrard in 1918.

has to compose', he once said, and though most of his works suggest spontaneity, it was a spontaneity arrived at after a good deal of preliminary work; his sketches and preliminary drawings throw invaluable light on the whole creative process.

His concern with different media and his constant technical explorations led him into a wide variety of works. He was a dedicated photographer, and relied on its productions for compositional devices, unusual viewpoints and 'awkward' poses. Influenced by JAPANESE prints, he also experimented with print-making himself – in which he had the help of PISSARRO and CASSATT – and explored various combinations of watercolour and gouache, and, increasingly as he became older, PASTELS. It was indeed in the series of large-scale pastels which he produced from the 1890s onwards that he came closest to what might be called 'mainstream Impressionism', using bold, simplified colours applied with a certain degree of abandon.

Leading a bachelor life, but greatly loved by his acquaintances and friends, Degas devoted his whole personal fortune to making good the debts of the family business. He was violently anti-Dreyfus (see POLITICS) and, indeed, anti-Semitic; despite close professional links with Pissarro, he always referred to him as 'that Israelite' – and yet, to quote a notorious phrase, 'some of his best friends were Jews' (see HALÉVY). His work was accepted more readily and more quickly than that of most of his colleagues, especially by the English. This popularity was no mere chance. Nobody had succeeded as well as he in melding the new vitality that Impressionism had brought to art with the precise disciplines and controlled emotions that had been part of the French pictorial tradition since at least the time of Poussin. On the other hand Degas was no timid devotee of compromise. His sculpture is outstandingly innovative, and some of his later pastels reach out to the chromatic and compositional fervours of Expressionism. *See also* BARTHOLOMÉ, CLOSIER, COURBET, DANCING, DOBIGNY, DRAWING, ENGLAND, FAURE, ILLUSTRATION, LECOQ DE BOISBAUDRAN, MARTELLI, MIRBEAU, MUSIC, PATRONS AND COLLECTORS, PERSPECTIVE, PHOTOGRAPHY, PRICES, PRINTS, ROUART, SOCIAL BACKGROUND, TILLOT, TISSOT, VALERNES *[17, 30, 58, 67, 74, 106, 119, 126, 128, 136, 149, 157, 158, 173, 198, 212, 222, 223]*

□ T. Reff, *Degas; the artist's mind* (1976), *The Notebooks of Edgar Degas*, 2 vols. (1985); Adriani (1985); Rewald (1985), *Studies in Post-Impressionism* (1986); *Degas*, Grand Palais, Paris, exhibition catalogue (1988)

Delacroix,   Ferdinand-Victor-Eugène (1798–1863) The son of a Napoleonic general (or, according to some sources, a bastard of Talleyrand), he entered the studio of Pierre Guérin in 1816, but relied more for his art education on copying old masters in the Louvre, being especially attracted by Rubens and the Venetians. It was there that he met Bonington and became interested in British art, an interest that was further stimulated by the sight of Constable's *Haywain* (exhibited in the SALON of 1824) and by a trip to ENGLAND in 1825.

By this date he had already established a reputation as the most advanced exponent of the Romantic approach to art; his first major work, *Dante and Virgil in Hell* (Louvre), had received considerable critical acclaim when it was exhibited at the Salon of 1822, and was bought by the State. Inevitably, he was cast in the role of one of the protagonists in that struggle between the Classicists and the Romantics, which had first become evident in the contrast between Poussin and Claude. His work – with its emphasis on colour rather than on line, his whirling compositions with their sense of barely suppressed passion, his choice of farouche subjects – was diametrically opposed to the tradition which in his own time was expressed by Ingres, who had inherited it from David: a preference for draughtsmanship and hard, clear outlines, and restrained, formalized emotions.

Delacroix's sense of uninhibited colour and his sensitivity to the exotic were further enhanced in 1832, when the Comte de Mornay took the painter with him on an official trip to ALGIERS, Morocco and southern Spain. From this Delacroix brought back seven albums of watercolours, drawings and sketches, which were to provide the material for close on a hundred paintings, such as *The Sultan of Morocco and his Entourage* (1845; Musée des Augustins, Toulouse) and *Women of Algiers* (1834; Louvre).

In terms of the traditional stylistic phases of European art he was endeavouring to combine the baroque with the classical, investing the combination with a contemporary sensibility that projected him into the role of one of the

Delacroix, *The Sultan of Morocco and his Entourage*, 1845.

founding fathers of what is still called 'modern' art. This process was greatly emphasized by the constant and informed support of BAUDELAIRE, whose critical writings might almost be said to centre on the works of Delacroix. At the Exposition Universelle of 1855 he was represented by 36 paintings, and official honours showered on him – however belatedly. He himself said 'I am a rebel, not a revolutionary', and his influence on the Impressionists was profound and decisive. It can be seen at its most obvious in the works of RENOIR, but in a more pervasive sense his use of pure COLOUR and of vibrating adjacent tones, his liberation of technique from the mechanical and the obsessive, helped to create the kind of atmosphere which made the development of Impressionism possible. In 1854 MANET, accompanied by Antonin PROUST, went to Delacroix's studio in the rue Furstenberg to ask permission to copy his *Dante and Virgil in Hell*; it was a significant moment in the history of art. *See also* ANTECEDENTS, FLOCHETAGE, IMPRESSIONISM, PHOTOGRAPHY *[23]*
□E. Delacroix, *Correspondance générale*, ed. A. Joubin, 5 vols. (1936–38); H. Wellington (ed.), *The Journal of Eugène Delacroix* (1980); L. Johnson, *The Paintings of Eugène Delacroix, a critical catalogue*, 2 vols. (1981)

Delvau, Alfred (1825–67) Writer and art critic, he was much involved in the social life of

the Impressionists and, in a book he wrote about PARIS, he gave an extensive account of the meetings at the BRASSERIE DES MARTYRS.
□ A. Delvau, *Histoire anecdotique des cafés et cabarets de Paris* (1862)

Denis, Maurice (1870–1943) Painter and writer on art, whose career started with his making what has become one of the classic statements about 'modern' art: 'Remember that a picture, before being a battle charger, a nude woman or a story, is essentially a flat surface covered with colours arranged in a certain pattern.' A member of the group of painters centred around Bonnard and Vuillard, he became increasingly obsessed with religious art of a vapidly decorative kind. In 1901, before Denis had even met the painter, he produced a large painting entitled *Hommage à Cézanne*, which showed Vuillard, Roussel, VOLLARD, Bonnard and others standing around one of the master's still lifes. It was bought by André Gide and is now in the Musée d'Orsay.
□ S. Barazzetti-Demoulin, *Maurice Denis* (1945); M. Denis, *Journal* (1957); *Maurice Denis*, Orangerie, Paris, exhibition catalogue (1970)

Dépeaux, Félix-François (1853–1920) A rich Norman businessman from Rouen with offices in Paris, who was a client of DURAND-RUEL from 1892 until family complications forced him to sell his extensive collection of paintings in 1906. It included 46 SISLEYS, an important group by RENOIR, including *Summer* (1868; Staatliche Museen Preussischer Kulturbesitz, Berlin) and *Dance at Bougival* (1882; Museum of Fine Arts, Boston), and works by MONET, PISSARRO, GAUGUIN and Toulouse-Lautrec. Not all his collection was sold, however; he gave some important works to the museum at Rouen, and after his death a large number of paintings by GUILLAUMIN belonging to him came on the market. *See also* PATRONS AND COLLECTORS
□ S. Monneret, *L'Impressionnisme et son époque*, vol. 2 (1979); *Renoir*, Hayward Gallery, London, exhibition catalogue (1985)

Desboutin, Marcellin (1823–1902) Painter, engraver and author – he had a play put on by the Théâtre Français – he originally studied law but then took up painting and attended the ECOLE DES BEAUX-ARTS. An indefatigable, professional Bohemian, he was of putative aristocratic background and claimed to have gambled away a castle in Italy. He was one of the liveliest members of the CAFÉ GUERBOIS circle, and led the move away from there to the Nouvelle-Athènes. MANET painted a portrait of him in 1875 (Museu de Arte, São Paulo), explaining afterwards to Antonin PROUST, 'I make no claim to have summed up an epoch, but to have painted the most remarkable type in that part of the city. I painted Desboutin with as much feeling as I painted Baudelaire.'

In entitling the portrait *The Artist*, Manet was in fact underlining one of Desboutin's main characteristics. He was typical of a whole group of not particularly successful painters, who were always on the fringe of the Impressionist movement – he exhibited at the 1876 exhibition – but who, through a lack of determination or an excessive preoccupation with café life and other distractions, never achieved the reputation of the movement's leading figures. Desboutin features in what seems to be a role characteristic of his personality in DEGAS' *L'Absinthe* of 1876 (Musée d'Orsay). He was happier as an etcher than a painter in oils, and his portraits of Manet, Degas and DURANTY in this medium are convincing in presentation and incisive in technique. *See also* PORTRAITURE *[17]*
□ R. Pickvance, 'L'Absinthe en Angleterre', in *Apollo* LXXVII (15 May 1963), B. Duplaix, *Marcellin Desboutin, Prince de Bohème* (1985)

Desnoyers, Fernand (1826–69) An habitué of the BRASSERIE DES MARTYRS, a resolute champion of COURBET and of the REALIST movement generally, he was one of the first to hail MANET as rising star in the art world. He was both poet and journalist, and his most popular work was the *Chansons parisiens* of 1853. In 1863 he was one of the most vehement protagonists of the SALON DES REFUSÉS.
□ Hamilton (1954)

Deudon, Charles (1832–1914) A lawyer and financier who had interests in the well-known Paris shop 'Old England'. He was a friend of MONET, PISSARRO and MANET, as well as of RENOIR, whom he met through DURET and whom he visited at CHATOU in 1881, when the artist was painting his *Déjeuner des canotiers*. He was mainly responsible for persuading Renoir to continue exhibiting at the SALON. Amongst his collection were Monet's *Gare Saint-Lazare* (1877; Fogg Art Museum, Cambridge, Mass.) and Manet's *The Plum* (1878; National Gallery of Art, Washington, D.C.), which he bought directly from the artist for 3500 francs. In 1899,

after he had retired to Nice, he was pestered by dealers anxious to buy from him and was offered any price he cared to name for *The Plum*; he suggested an inhibiting 100,000 francs. In the event, on his death his collection was acquired by the dealer Paul Rosenberg. *See also* EPHRUSSI *[138, 162]*
□ Venturi (1939); B.E. White, *Renoir, His Life, Art and Letters* (1984); *Renoir*, Hayward Gallery, London, exhibition catalogue (1985)

Dewhurst, Wynford (1868–1927) After studying painting in Paris in the 1890s, he returned to ENGLAND, where he wrote extensively about art. In 1904 he published *Impressionist Painting; its Genesis and Development*, consisting of articles that he had written for the *Artist*, the *Studio* and *Pall Mall Magazine*. Based largely on his contacts with MONET and with PISSARRO, who criticized it bitterly despite the contribution he had made to its composition, it was the first serious book on the subject to be published in English and was clearly well-intentioned. His interpretation of the term 'Impressionist' was generous to the point of fatuity, and it is doubtful whether he really understood the underlying dynamism of the movement. He did, however, contribute greatly to enhancing the popularity of Monet in the English-speaking world, and paid some attention to CÉZANNE, though his judgment was not flattering: 'His landscapes are crude and hazy, weak in colour, and many admirers of Impressionism find them entirely uninteresting. . . . His figure compositions have been called "clumsy and brutal". Probably his best work is to be found in his studies of still life, yet even in this direction one cannot help noticing that his draughtsmanship is defective.'
□ Cooper (1954); Flint (1984)

Diaz de la Peña, Narcisse Virgile (1807–76) Born in Bordeaux, the son of a Spanish refugee, and brought up by a Protestant clergyman, he was apprenticed first to a printer and then to a potter, but was inexorably drawn to painting. He had a rapid success as an ACADEMIC painter, but meeting MILLET and through him Théodore ROUSSEAU, he became enamoured of the BARBIZON style of painting and rapidly established himself as one of its leading members, producing pictures with a heavy impasto, an almost melodramatic sense of nature, and an emphasis on dramatic lighting – qualities which can be seen at their most typical in *Landscape* (1870;

Heavy brushwork and sensitive notation of light and shade characterize **Diaz**' *Woodland Scene*, 1867.

Fitzwilliam Museum, Cambridge). RENOIR said that his meeting with Diaz led him to lighten his palette, and Diaz also had a great influence on artists such as Adolphe Monticelli. Lame from birth, he was loved for the warmth of his personality and often bought paintings by his younger contemporaries as a means of helping them.

□ E. Moreau-Nélaton, *Millet raconté par lui-même* (1924); G. Pillement, *Les Pré-Impressionnistes* (1973); Rewald (1973)

Dobigny, Emma (Marie-Emma Thuilleux) (1851–1925) A model who posed for COROT, TISSOT, PUVIS DE CHAVANNES, and DEGAS, who was especially fond of her; his most moving portrait, painted on wood in 1869, is now in a Swiss private collection. In the same year he also painted her in *Bouderie* (Metropolitan Museum, New York), leaning on a desk (behind which sits DURANTY), and probably as *La Femme en peignoir rouge* (1870; National Gallery of Art, Washington, D.C.). It would seem from the obvious affection he lavished on her portraits that his feelings towards her went beyond the merely professional, and in a note, quoted in the catalogue for the Musée d'Orsay exhibition of 1988, he says 'Little Dobigny is coming to sit for me – and perhaps afterwards?'

□ P.A. Lemoisne, *Degas et ses oeuvres*, vol. 2 (1946); *Degas*, Grand Palais, Paris, exhibition catalogue (1988)

Doria, Comte Armand (1824–96) A collector who, according to his friend DEGAS, had the features and manners of a Tintoretto. He started with works by artists such as COROT, Daumier and JONGKIND, but soon progressed to the

Impressionists. At their first exhibition he bought CÉZANNE's *Maison du pendu* for 300 francs, and at the auction of his pictures after his death there were no fewer than ten RENOIRS offered for sale, a fact no doubt partly due to his connection by marriage to the CHARPENTIER family.

Drawing The Impressionists were born into an art world which was dominated by a belief in the central importance of draughtsmanship; at every level of education, from the *lycée* to the ECOLE DES BEAUX-ARTS, it was insisted on as the syntax of visual expression. According to the accepted view, Impressionism, both at the time when it was being evolved, and subsequently, was seen as a painterly technique, involving loose, broken brushwork, heavy reliance on sophisticated chromatic effects, and explorative forms of composition. In fact, however, quite apart from the revolutions which DEGAS effected in the use of PASTEL, and CÉZANNE in the use of watercolour drawing, a cardinal element in the Impressionist canon was the meticulous observation of life and nature. To achieve this, constant recording of observation was necessary, and, almost without exception, the Impressionists were intent on drawing in notebooks and on sheets of paper, recording actions,

Degas, *La Femme en peignoir rouge*, 1870: possibly a portrait of Emma **Dobigny**.

Drawing: Pissarro's draughtsmanship is at once precise and relaxed, and this sketch is closely related to the many paintings of Pontoise which he did in the late 1860s.

landscape motifs, and other material which could only be expressed in the form of drawing. The notebooks of Degas, preserved almost in their entirety, record a whole lifetime given to meticulous observation; MANET's *croquis*, MONET's notes on potentially attractive views, PISSARRO's sketches of labourers in the fields, SISLEY's fluent outlines of river scenes, and BOUDIN's analysis of figures walking on a seaside promenade, all emphasize the fact, not that they had rejected drawing, but that they had conferred on it a new freedom; they used it, not to construct eventual paintings – as the Ecole des Beaux-Arts practitioners did – but to explore pictorial possibilities and to experiment with potentials of composition.

They did have precedents for this. The controversies produced by the SALON DES REFUSÉS in 1863 had drawn from Viollet-le-Duc, architect, historian and aesthetician, an attack on too rigid an adherence to the ACADEMIC tradition of life-drawing, in the course of which he said 'Beyond the confines of the life-class in the academy there is a real sun, real trees, real mountains and real people going about their business, and not posing for the artist.' At the time that he was giving vent to these opinions, there appeared a second edition of LECOQ DE BOISBAUDRAN's *L'Education de la mémoire pittoresque*, which emphasized the importance of drawing from memory rather than adhering slavishly to what was before the eye, and related observation to imaginative interpretation. The impact of this particular work on the Impressionists, especially on Manet, Degas and Pissarro, was considerable and evident. There had therefore appeared generally a new, more inspirational approach to drawing, which was reflected in the work of the Impressionists more quickly than in that of more conventional artists.

There were, of course, obvious differences in the approach to drawing adopted by individual members of the group – differences that tended to increase as time went by and each artist developed further along his own line of visual exploration. There was initially the bias towards either landscape or figure painting, each tending to call for a specific approach to drawing. Then there was the more fundamental distinction between an artist such as Degas – still, even in his most free style of draughtsmanship, showing the influence of Ingres and something of the Ecole des Beaux-Arts tradition – and, at the other end of the spectrum, artists such as RENOIR and Monet, whose art depended very largely on the spontaneous brushstroke. But even here there were ambiguities. When EDMOND RENOIR wrote a piece about his brother in *La Vie moderne*, he specifically praised the spontaneity of *The Two Little Circus Girls* (1879; The Art Institute of Chicago); yet we know that the artist did a preliminary drawing for the work and many of his other drawings are outstanding.

In a letter to one of his patrons and friends, the Duc de Trevises, in 1920, Monet wrote, 'Drawing . . . what do you mean by that? Drawings in black on white? Yes, I had to do some like everybody else when I was young. Since then I have been asked to do drawings of my paintings for various magazines, but I have never liked to isolate drawing from colour.' He did, in fact, produce about a dozen of these drawings intended purely to give the reader some vague idea of what the original oil-colours were like, and they have little independent value or significance. Very much the same could be said about the plans for paintings – it is hard to describe them otherwise – which survive in eight sketchbooks in the Musée Marmottan in Paris.

By the end of the 1870s there was a gradual change perceptible in the Impressionists' attitude to drawing. The 1879 exhibition contained a greater proportion of drawings – some 79 – than any of the earlier ones, including a large number by Pissarro, who was partly forced into this medium because smaller works were easier to sell – a factor which undoubtedly influenced others. There was a new interest, among less affluent patrons, in watercolours and other *bons-bons*, as Diego MARTELLI described them. In fact, in that same year, the Société d'Aquarellistes Français was founded for the express purpose of improving the standard of watercolour drawings, and stimulating the market for them. Another factor was the improvement in mechanical reproduction processes, which encouraged the growth of magazines such as *Le Salon illustré*. These featured drawings by artists of their major exhibited works, an excellent means of publicity and a stimulus to the production of drawings as works in their own right. The Impressionists benefited through the fact that this was the period when LA VIE MODERNE (George CHARPENTIER's magazine which was so favourable to them) was being published. Degas, CASSATT, Monet and Sisley all had drawings printed in it. So, too, did Renoir,

Manet's squared-up **drawing** (pre-1862) hints at the academic probity which underlies his painting.

who in 1879 even offered to produce weekly fashion drawings for the periodical. Pissarro, usually the most enthusiastic about any new venture, would not participate because he felt that the quality of the paper used would not allow of accurate reproduction.

Drawing played an important part in the art of the Impressionists, but it was not a dominant one. It is impossible to hit on any single generalization that would cover the specific nature of 'Impressionist drawing'. It could variously, and at different times, be an instrument of observation, a means of analysing movement or choosing appropriate vantage points, and a way of trying out compositional structures. It could vary from person to person, from medium to medium. Within the artistic career of one artist there could be considerable variations. Degas, for instance, gradually abandoned the use of pencil for black chalk, which by its very physical structure could hold and refract light. What the Impressionists did achieve in their drawings was what the GON-COURTS had stipulated as an ideal in their novel

Manette Salomon (1867): 'There must be found a line that would render human life precisely, embrace from close at hand the individual, the particular, a living, human, inward line – a drawing more real than all other drawing – a more human drawing.' *See also* EMPERAIRE, ILLUSTRATION, SEURAT [15, 80, 106, 185]
□ F. Daulte, *Le Dessin français de Manet à Cézanne* (1954); Lloyd and Thomson (1986)

Durand, Charles *see* CAROLUS-DURAN, EMILE-AUGUSTE

Durand-Ruel, Paul (1831–1922) The son of a picture dealer, Jean-Marie-Fortuné (who had been a supporter of DELACROIX and who was amongst the first to deal in works by COROT, DAUBIGNY, COURBET and others), Paul took control of the family business in 1865. His first real contact with the Impressionists was in 1871, when he met PISSARRO at the gallery he had opened in London (*see* ENGLAND) and introduced him to MONET. On returning to Paris, Durand-Ruel decided that, whilst continuing to sell works by the BARBIZON School and others, he would nail his colours to the mast of what was to become Impressionism; without him its course would have been very different.

The first major public demonstration of his commitment came with an exhibition held in London in 1872, at which he showed 13 works by MANET, 9 by Pissarro, 6 by SISLEY, 4 by Monet, 3 by DEGAS and 1 by RENOIR. Three years previously he had stated his policy as a dealer in the pages of a magazine he edited, the *Revue de l'art et de la curiosité* (December 1869):

The salon in **Durand-Ruel**'s house at 35 rue de Rome, showing Renoir's *Girl with a Cat* (1880).

'A true picture dealer should also be an enlightened patron; he should, if necessary, sacrifice his immediate interest to his artistic convictions and oppose rather than support the interest of speculators.' This philosophy led him to support through thick and thin – both financially and morally – the artists in whom he believed.

He was, of course, not unmotivated by self-interest, and in being one of the first art dealers to exploit the system of providing regular income in return for a lien on what his artists produced, he did himself no disservice. Nor must it be thought that his relationship with the Impressionists was always a happy one. They were continually complaining, selling works through other dealers on the sly and, in the case of Monet and Degas, were often downright hostile. Sometimes, too, his influence was indirect, even inadvertent. In 1874, for instance, badly hit by the recession of that year, he had to close his London gallery, and was forced to stop buying new works. It was this, as much as anything else, that induced his artists, as an attempt at self-help, to organize their first joint exhibition.

Infinitely resourceful in the cultivation of potential patrons, Durand-Ruel had a keen sense of public relations, issuing a variety of publications; these included a three-volume catalogue of the most important works in his collection (1874) with 300 reproductions, which not only gave considerable emphasis to the works by Impressionists but included an essay on them by Armand SILVESTRE. His energy was boundless; he continued arranging exhibitions in London even after the closure of his gallery and, after holding two exhibitions in New York, opened a gallery there in 1888 (*see* USA). Impressionism would have happened without him; but the fact that it achieved the position it did in such a comparatively short time was due more to him than to anyone else. *See also* BELGIUM, BOUSSOD AND VALADON, GERMANY, HÔTEL DROUOT, PATRONS AND COLLECTORS, PETIT, PRICES, SOCIETY OF FRENCH ARTISTS, SPAIN, VENTURI [177]
□ Venturi (1939); Rewald (1973); D. Wildenstein, *Monet; biographie et catalogue*, 4 vols. (1974–85)

Duranty, Louis Edmond (1833–80) One of the main theorists and practitioners of literary REALISM, he was the founder and manager of the short-lived but influential magazine *Réalisme*, and was closely linked to the GONCOURTS. He wrote a string of novels, which, though not very successful, merited the approval of ZOLA, who praised the purity and integrity of their literary form. In a posthumous work *Le Pays des arts* (1881) he portrayed MANET, DEGAS, CÉZANNE and FANTIN-LATOUR, as well as making the hero, Louis Martin, defend the theories and practice of Impressionism. But Duranty's real achievement lies in the role he played in defending and popularizing Impressionism. A critic of the *Gazette des Beaux-Arts* and of the *Beaux-Arts illustrés*, he was an habitué of the CAFÉ GUERBOIS, and was especially attracted by the ideas of Degas – sometimes to the discomfiture of MONET and RENOIR.

In 1876 he published *La Nouvelle Peinture*, subtitled 'A propos du groupe d'artistes qui expose dans les Galeries Durand-Ruel'. Although it was the first publication entirely devoted to Impressionism, the word was never actually mentioned. True to his literary pre-occupations, Duranty emphasized the extent to which they confronted modern life, but he also paid adequate attention to the technical innovations they were practising, adding that 'The most erudite physicist could not quarrel with their analysis of light.' He was especially impressive in his treatment of DRAWING, showing in this the influence of Degas. The latter's ideas were also reflected in certain provisos he made, counselling a degree of caution – advice that irritated many of the group. In March 1879 Degas painted a portrait of Duranty in his study (Collection of Mr and Mrs Julian Eisenstein, Washington, D.C.; pastel study in Burrell Collection, Glasgow). *See also* CHINTREUIL, CRITICS, LITERATURE *[23]*

□ O. Reutersvärd, 'Duranty and his "Nouvelle Peinture"', in *Konsthistorisk Tidskrift* (1949)

Duret, Théodore (1838–1927) A man of great gifts, blessed by fortune with a long life, Comte de Brie, President of the Winegrowers' Society of Charente, owner of a cognac distillery, politician, journalist and art critic, Duret had remarkable portraits of himself painted by MANET (1868; Musée des Beaux-Arts, Paris), WHISTLER (1883; Metropolitan Museum, New York) and Vuillard. He was related to COURBET, and met Manet for the first time by chance in Madrid in 1865; their acquaintance soon ripened into friendship. In 1868 Duret, together with ZOLA and others, started a paper, *La Tribune française*. An ardent republican, he

Whistler painted **Duret** in 1883 with a cloak over his arm, dressed for the theatre.

supported Courbet in his destruction of the Vendôme Column, and when the government of Thiers came to power he undertook a long and tactful tour of the Far East. Elegant and dandified, Duret was a great Anglophile; Whistler and George MOORE had been amongst his earliest friends, and he made an annual visit to London.

The debt that the Impressionists owed him was great. A frequenter of the CAFÉ GUERBOIS and the Nouvelle-Athènes, he was intimately involved in their discussions, and supported them in his writings with perspicacity and in his patronage with generosity. Amongst other things, he was partly responsible for spreading amongst them an appreciation of JAPANESE art, especially through prints that he had acquired in the course of his journey to the Orient. In 1878 he published *Les Peintres impressionnistes*, which combined a short but illuminating general account of the movement with biographical notes on MONET, SISLEY, MORISOT, RENOIR and PISSARRO. Seven years later there appeared a collection of his reviews of the SALONS and his introductions to the catalogues of various exhibitions, entitled *Critique d'avant-garde*.

In 1894 he suffered considerable business losses as a result of the failure of the grape harvest, and was forced to sell the larger part of his collection at the HÔTEL DROUOT, where it fetched 160,000 francs – a record price for paintings of that nature. He soon started building up another collection, however, extending his interests to include GAUGUIN, Toulouse-Lautrec and the Nabis. His later writings include comprehensive studies of Whistler and Manet, and a history of Impressionism (1906), as well as shorter studies of Courbet, VAN GOGH and Renoir.

□ T. Duret, *Les Peintres impressionnistes* (1878), *Critique d'avant-garde* (1885); Hamilton (1954); Rewald (1973)

E

Ecole des Beaux-Arts The lynch-pin of the French system of art education, the Ecole des Beaux-Arts was of significance – whether positive or negative – even for those of the Impressionists who had not been students there. Founded in 1648 as part of the system of state-controlled patronage of the arts inaugurated by Colbert, it moved into new premises in the rue Bonaparte in 1838, and these were extended in 1862. One of its main features was a large, glass-covered court replete with life-size Graeco-Roman statues, which served as models for the basic DRAWING courses that were the foundation of the whole curriculum. In fact, before 1863 drawing alone was taught, although there were periodic competitions in painting for advanced

students. The entire approach to art was based on obtaining mastery of the human form; students began by learning to draw component parts of the human anatomy and then united them into studies of the whole body, amassing groups of bodies to form 'compositions'. Those who had been grounded in this visual grammar found it very difficult to escape from its influence, though this was by no means invariably a bad thing. It was his training at the Ecole des Beaux-Arts that underpinned DEGAS' whole artistic output, even though he adapted it to his own needs and ideas.

In its more advanced stages the training at the Ecole centred around a series of competitions, culminating in the Prix de Rome, which was theoretically open to all Frenchmen over 15 and under 30 but which, because its students were exempt from the preliminary trials, was actually confined to the Ecole des Beaux-Arts. There were ten candidates admitted for painting and eight each for sculpture and architecture; each candidate had to produce a single sketch within a day. The final test consisted of producing within a month a canvas 1.5 m (4′11″) by 1.2 m (3′11″), on a theme chosen by the members of the Fine Arts section of the

The central court of the **Ecole des Beaux-Arts** in 1929, filled with casts of classical sculpture.

INSTITUT DE FRANCE from subjects in ancient history or the bible. Candidates had 36 hours in which to prepare a detailed sketch indicating the main lines of the composition with sufficient clarity, so that nothing could be changed in the final painting; this was sealed and put in safe keeping. They then had 70 days in which to produce in their rooms at the Ecole the final painting; they were not allowed to use models, engravings or tracings brought in from outside. The eventual winner went on to the French Academy at Rome, where he was free to work on his own, studying at leisure, without the supervision of a professor, drawing and painting both landscape and monuments, and permitted, within certain limitations, to travel around ITALY.

In 1863 the Ecole set up an ATELIER teaching system, based on that which had been operating outside it for some time, and featuring artists such as Gustave MOREAU and Léon Bonnat as tutors. The ateliers were largely under the control of a *massier*, who set the poses of the living model and managed the general discipline of each studio, which the nominal professor visited only once or twice a week. *See also* ACADEMIC ART, CORMON, FOURCAUD, GÉRÔME, GLEYRE, GUICHARD, TECHNIQUE
□ E. Müntz, *Guide de l'Ecole nationale des Beaux-Arts* (1889); Harrison and White (1965); Boime (1986)

Emperaire, Achille (1829–1910) He was a schoolfriend of CÉZANNE, with whom he was to remain on consistently friendly terms for most of his life, and who painted in 1866 a memorable portrait of him (Musée d'Orsay), which reveals Emperaire's physical deformities: a

Nude with Faun, one of **Emperaire's** curiously erotic and technically interesting drawings.

dwarf-like body and a large head. He made constant and unsuccessful attempts early in life to establish himself as a painter in Paris, but was forced to return to his native AIX, where he partly supported himself by selling 'pornographic' drawings to students at the university. In fact his drawings are of great interest, showing the use of black and white merged to form subtle nuances of grey and to model volume. His draughtsmanship is strongly reminiscent of that of Odilon Redon and, indeed, of SEURAT. Few of his paintings survive, but those that do (e.g. in the Musée Granet at Aix) show a heavy impasto style, which is reminiscent of that adopted by Monticelli and also by various of his contemporaries at Aix.
□ V. Nicollas, *Achille Emperaire* (1953); Rewald (1985)

England
The Impressionists in England
Although it is possible to exaggerate the contribution which English artists such as Turner, Constable and others made to the evolution of Impressionism (*see* ANTECEDENTS), there can be no doubt that, like many of their fellow painters in France ever since the beginnings of Romanticism, the Impressionists looked across the Channel, at least on a cultural plane, with affection and respect. MANET was the first to visit London, in 1868, mainly in the belief that an earlier arrival, LEGROS, together with WHISTLER, had created favourable ground for the reception of contemporary French painting. He was wrong. Then, between October 1870 and June 1871, during the FRANCO-PRUSSIAN WAR and the subsequent troubles in Paris, MONET, PISSARRO and SISLEY arrived, painting several views of London. Monet continued to be a frequent visitor; his son Michel studied there in the 1890s, and he himself stayed three or four times between 1899 and 1904, taking rooms at the Savoy Hotel, whilst he was painting his great series of views of the Thames. Pissarro was also in London at about the same time, and painted views of Kensington Gardens, Hyde Park, Charing Cross Bridge and Hampton Court. When his son Lucien, who lived in London, was ill in 1897, he came over again and did a series of paintings of Bedford Park. Sisley painted a view of Charing Cross Bridge in 1871 and three years later returned in the company of the singer FAURE, producing a series of views of Hampton Court. He was back again in 1881,

England: Monet painted this view of Hyde Park in 1871 during his stay in London to avoid the troubles of the Franco-Prussian War.

working in the Isle of Wight, which had been a favourite resort of Berthe MORISOT and her family in the mid-1870s, and in 1897 he spent several months in Wales. RENOIR visited London in 1895 with the publisher Paul Gallimard, having two years earlier stayed in Guernsey.

Between 1870 and 1875 DURAND-RUEL, who had also fled to England during the Franco-Prussian War, held a series of exhibitions in a gallery he had rented at 168 New Bond Street. They were supposed to represent a partly fictional organization, the SOCIETY OF FRENCH ARTISTS, but were in effect a selection of his own Paris stock, with a few additions. They covered a wide range of artists from Ingres onwards, with a few English painters such as Burne-Jones, but also included works by the, to him, newly discovered innovators – Monet, Manet, Pissarro, Sisley and DEGAS. When he returned to Paris at the end of hostilities, Durand-Ruel left the gallery in the charge of Charles W. Deschamps. At the end of 1875 financial problems forced him to close the gallery, but this was not the end of his dealing activities in London. In 1882 he showed a few paintings at a gallery he had rented in King Street, St James's, and in the spring of 1883 a much larger and more extensively advertised exhibition took place at Dowdeswell's Galleries, 133 New Bond Street. This included 7 works by Degas, 3 by Manet, 7 by Monet, 2 by CASSATT, 3 by Morisot, 9 by Renoir and 8 by Sisley. Unlike

his earlier exhibitions, this one attracted a good deal of attention in the press and elsewhere, and can be taken to represent the first serious impact of the movement on English critics and collectors.

English reactions to Impressionism

English reactions to the works of the Impressionists were far less favourable than those in the USA. The first British collector to buy works by the Impressionists was Henry Hill of Brighton, who used the title of Captain, but was described by Durand-Ruel as a tailor. He acquired no less than seven works by Degas to add to a collection that was predominantly composed of fashionable English painters such as Orchardson. Another early collector was Samuel Barlow, a botanist and owner of a bleach factory in Lancaster, who in the early 1880s acquired four paintings by Pissarro. On the advice of Legros, the Greek businessman Constantine Alexander Ionides (1833–1900) bought Degas' *Orchestre de Robert le Diable* (1876; Victoria and Albert Museum) some time before 1884. Between 1885 and 1899 SICKERT bought a number of works by Degas, and a Mr Burke, about whom nothing is known, acquired works by Degas, Sisley and Pissarro in the 1890s. At about the same time Hill's pictures came up for sale at Christie's, and fetched prices around the £50 – £60 mark, though Degas' *L'Absinthe*, or *Au café* (1876; Musée d'Orsay),

Sisley, *The Bridge at Hampton Court*, 1874: born in Paris of English parents, Sisley was a frequent visitor to **England**.

was bought for £180 by Alexander Reid of Glasgow, who was later to do so much for VAN GOGH. The painting was later acquired by Arthur Studd, a fellow student in Paris with William Rothenstein and Roger Fry, who himself in 1892 paid £200 for one of Monet's *Haystacks*. It is significant that, whereas the Americans were very keen on Monet, from quite an early stage, the English were almost exclusively dedicated to the stylistically more conventional Degas.

There were other people, such as George MOORE, Whistler and SARGENT, who possessed works by Impressionists, but this was largely an accident of friendship rather than a deliberate collecting policy. Although primarily concerned with marketing his own works, Whistler was not unmindful of his old friends, and when he founded the International Society in 1898 he persuaded Renoir, Cézanne, Sisley and Pissarro to exhibit. Included in the first exhibition were three works by Degas, which had been bought some time earlier, probably on Whistler's advice, by the publisher Thomas Fisher Unwin. Another outlet was the New English Art Club (*see below*), which in 1892 and 1893 showed works by Degas and Monet.

In all, between 1870 and 1900, works by one or more of the Impressionists were exhibited in London on 16 occasions. In *The Courtauld Collection* (London, 1954), Douglas Cooper estimated that up to 1905, when Durand-Ruel held an important exhibition of Impressionist works in London (at which he sold some ten paintings, mostly to non-English collectors), English buyers had acquired 25 paintings by Degas, 6 by Manet, 4 by Monet, and about 20 divided between Pissarro, Renoir and Sisley. An attempt to present the National Gallery with a work by Monet in 1905 was a failure, whilst even the critic D.S. MACCOLL, during his tenure of office as Director of the Tate Gallery from 1906 to 1911, made no attempt to buy one. The situation was redeemed, slightly later, by the activities of Sir Hugh LANE and Samuel Courtauld.

The reactions of English critics were predictable. Art magazines such as the *Magazine of Art* and *Portfolio*, as well as national newspapers such as *The Times*, gave quite a large amount of space to Parisian exhibitions and French art generally, but they tended to concentrate on its more acceptable and academic forms, with painters such as Rosa Bonheur, Ernest Meissonier and even, at times, MILLET receiving favourable attention. Philip HAMERTON set the tone when, reviewing the SALON DES REFUSÉS, he referred to Manet as 'some wretched Frenchman' and to the *Déjeuner sur l'herbe* as 'leading to the inference that the nude when painted by vulgar men is invariably indecent' (*Fine Arts' Quarterly*, October 1863). Reviewing Durand-Ruel's 1883 exhibition of Impressionists at Dowdeswell's Galleries, for the *Morning Post*, he praised it for 'having provided the London season with a new sensation which, besides its novelty, has the pleasant recommendation of also being mirth-provoking . . . it is something for Londoners to have in their midst a source of comic entertainment, which Parisians heartily enjoy.'

Nevertheless, there were some serious attempts to come to grips with this new kind of art, though many were limited by a widely held English belief that landscape was inferior to figure painting. The critic of the *St James's Gazette* put it clearly when, after praising the landscapes of Monet and Renoir, he went on to add the proviso that 'the real strength of the school lies in the figure pictures of such men as Manet and Degas' (25 April 1883). Those who were prepared to look at the paintings with a comparatively unprejudiced eye invariably praised Monet: 'How remarkable in all his paintings is the expression of nature' (*The Academy*, 23 April 1883); though the same writer blamed him for choosing unworthy stretches of landscape, condemning the Seine at Argenteuil as 'a very common river'.

By the time Durand-Ruel arranged another exhibition in London 22 years later, the British public had been exposed to a barrage of writing favourable to the Impressionists, ranging from Wynford DEWHURST's *Impressionist Painting; its Genesis and Development* (1904) to the more sophisticated special pleading of D.S. MacColl, Sickert and Frank RUTTER, as well as to the less accurate but better written prose of George Moore. The result was that the exhibition attracted a great deal of publicity and drew large crowds – up to 3000 a day – including the Princess Louise, herself a critic and sculptor, and Mr and Mrs Joseph Chamberlain. Only ten paintings, however, were sold, and Frank Rutter later summed up the situation in 1933 when he wrote in *Art in My Time*, 'Except for a few hundred artists, art students and enthusiasts, the Impressionist exhibition made very little impression on London or England. The general public was hardly aware of its existence and it received nothing like the public attention that was given five years later to the Post-Impressionist exhibition.'

Impressionism and English painting
The appointment of Legros to the Slade School of Art in 1876 opened up a channel of communication between English art students and what was going on in Paris, and this was institutionalized by the foundation of the New English Art Club in 1886. It had originally been intended to call this 'The Society of Anglo-French Artists', and its goal was 'to vindicate the soundness of engrafting English feeling and sentiment on what is known as French technique'. In fact, this 'technique' could involve a whole gamut of devices, not all of which had anything to do with Impressionism as such, and which owed more to Bastien-Lepage and the BARBIZON School than to Monet or Renoir. Indeed, George Clausen, one of the most active members of the Club, expressed a typically English point of view when he said 'One cannot help feeling that some Impressionist work is, in spite of its beauty, disgusting and violent, and it is questionable if, after all, this method is as true to nature as the older convention of painting, where the effect is less brilliant but more restful.'

There was within the New English Art Club a group of artists – Sickert, Wilson Steer and Spencer Gore being the most prominent, though there were others, such as Sargent, Laura Knight and even at times Augustus John – who showed that Impressionism had influenced them in their sense of colour, the vivacity of their brushwork and their quest for a certain immediacy of observation. But their allegiance was only slight. There was a constant belief, expressed by painters themselves and repeatedly echoed by the more conservative critics, that the English, by choosing 'nicer' subjects, in a decorous setting, painted with a light palette and preferably out-of-doors, were far better than the French, who 'took things to extremes'.

Dame Laura Knight's *The Beach* (1908) shows the diluted influence of Impressionism in **England**.

Pissarro's studio at **Eragny**, *c.* 1890, where he first came to live in 1884.

There was in reality no such thing as Impressionism in England. On the other hand there was an 'Impressionistic' school, which was to have a vital influence on the official scene for at least the first three decades of the 20th c., becoming a semi-official art style, which eventually dominated the most representative elements in English art life: the Slade School of Art, the New English Art Club and the Royal Academy. Here, Impressionism was never an avant-garde movement; the high explorative ground of British painting was occupied by various forms of POST-IMPRESSIONISM, Futurism and, marginally, by Surrealism and eventually Abstraction. *See also* ARROWSMITH, BLANCHE, DURET, FANTIN-LATOUR, MAUCLAIR, STEVENSON, TISSOT, WEDMORE
□ A. Thornton, *Fifty Years of the New English Art Club 1886–1935* (1935); Cooper (1954); D. Barr, *English Art 1870–1940* (1978); Flint (1984); K. McConkey, *British Impressionism* (1989)

Ephrussi, Charles (1845–1905) is the top-hatted figure in the background of RENOIR's *Déjeuner des canotiers* (1881; Phillips Collection, Washington, D.C.). His interest in art started with the collection of JAPANESE prints, but he soon moved to the works of Impressionists, buying paintings by MANET, MONET, MORISOT, SISLEY, PISSARRO and Renoir. He was soon on intimate terms with Renoir, arranging for his entries to be sent to the SALON, and publicizing his works to a larger audience. He was editor of the prestigious *Gazette des Beaux-Arts* and a close friend of the financier and collector Charles DEUDON. Marcel Proust was for some time his secretary. [162]

□P. Kolb and J. Adhémar, 'Charles Ephrussi etc.', in *Gazette des Beaux-Arts* (Jan. 1984)

Eragny A village on the banks of the Epte, some 30 kms (18½ miles) south of Dieppe. PISSARRO first came to live there in 1884, and his family's devotion to the place is shown by the fact that when, ten years later, they established a fine art press in London, they gave it the name of the Eragny Press (*see* PISSARRO, LUCIEN). It became Pissarro's main centre for work during the last ten years of his life, and he painted its surrounding landscape on many occasions – e.g. *Springtime in Eragny*, 1886; Memorial Art Gallery, Memphis, USA.
□ Rewald (1942); Rewald (1973)

L'Estaque A small fishing village near Marseilles, which CÉZANNE first got to know in 1870

Mountains at **L'Estaque**, 1886–90: the vibrant South inspired Cézanne for many years.

Monet painted the pierced cliff at **Etretat** on several occasions. This version dates from *c.* 1885.

when he was living there with Hortense FIQUET. It was here that he re-established his original passion for landscape, which he had momentarily abandoned in Paris. He was strongly attracted by the village – 'like a playing card; red roofs against a blue sea', he wrote to PISSARRO in 1876 (*L'Estaque*, 1876; The Bernard Foundation, New York) – and he returned to the place on several occasions. Many of his friends stayed there with him, including ZOLA and RENOIR, who, when he first went there in 1882, was equally entranced (*Crags at L'Estaque*, 1882; Museum of Fine Arts, Boston).

Etretat A thriving fishing village, 26 kms (16 miles) east of Le Havre, which had been popular with DELACROIX, and which COURBET had made into one of his favourite painting sites. They were especially attracted by the arch-like rock formations that characterize the three promontories which jut out into the sea around the village.

Perhaps because of the Courbet connection, MONET was also very much attracted by the place, though there was the additional fact that the singer FAURE, a great patron of the Impressionists, had a villa there, which he lent to the painter in 1885. Other Parisian notables who had 'secondary residences' in Etretat were

Offenbach, Michelet and Maupassant, who in 1885 watched Monet at work there. A year later, in an article for *Gil Blas*, he recorded the experience: 'At Etretat I often followed Monet about. He was not so much a painter as a hunter. He stalked on ahead, followed by his children and Madame HOSCHEDÉ, who carried his canvases, sometimes as many as five or six, representing the subject at different times of day and with different effects. He took them up and put them aside in turn, according to the changes in the sky. Face to face with his subject, the painter lay in wait for the sun and shadows, capturing in a few brushstrokes the ray that fell or the cloud that passed. I have seen him seize a glittering shower of light on the white cliff and fix it in a flood of yellow tone which strangely rendered the surprising and fugitive effect of that elusive and dazzling brilliance. On another occasion he took a downpour beating down on the sea into his hands, and dashed it on the canvas – and succeeded in really painting the rain as it seemed to the eye.' The last-named painting is probably *Etretat; Rainy Weather* (1885; Nasjonalgalleriet, Oslo).
□ M. Belloncle, 'Les Peintres d'Etretat', in *Jardin des Arts* (March 1967); Herbert (1988)

Exposition Universelle *see* FRANCE

F

Faivre, Jules Abel (1867–1945) A pupil and friend of RENOIR, who helped him in giving lessons to Julie Manet and Jeanne BAUDOT, and who accompanied him on his trip to HOLLAND. He later became well-known as a contributor to magazines such as *Le Rire* and *L'Assiette au beurre*.
□B.E. White, *Renoir, His Life, Art and Letters* (1984); Roberts and Roberts (1987)

Fantin-Latour, Ignace-Henri-Jean-Théodore (1836–1904) Born in Grenoble and trained as an artist first by his father and later by LECOQ DE BOISBAUDRAN and at the ECOLE DES BEAUX-ARTS, he very quickly became involved with all the younger generation of forward-thinking artists, including MANET, WHISTLER,

Fantin-Latour painted this group portrait of what was virtually the 'Batignolles group' in Manet's studio, in 1870. From left to right, Scholderer, Manet, Renoir, Astruc (seated), Zola, Maître, Bazille and Monet.

MONET, RENOIR, and their literary equivalents, BAUDELAIRE, ZOLA and MALLARMÉ. The memorials to these contacts are the well-known group paintings *Hommage à Delacroix* (1863; Musée d'Orsay), which included Baudelaire, LEGROS, BRACQUEMOND, DURANTY, BALLEROY and Fantin himself, and *Studio in the Batignolles Quarter* (Musée d'Orsay), in which appeared Zola, ASTRUC, BAZILLE, Monet, Manet and Renoir, and which was exhibited at the Salon of 1870. Despite his closeness to the Impressionists and his sympathetic response to what they were doing, his work was almost entirely uninfluenced by their stylistic innovations. In the 1870s and 1880s he pursued a kind of photographic REALISM that owed something to the traditions of the Ecole des Beaux-Arts, and something to COURBET. His many flower and still-life paintings, however, did possess a greater lightness and freshness of handling, which made them very popular amongst the English. He spent a lot of time in London from the early 1860s, being very intimate with

Whistler, Legros and Rossetti, whom he had wanted to include in the *Hommage à Delacroix* painting.

Later, Fantin turned towards a more imaginative kind of work, based very frequently on musical themes from the works of composers such as Wagner, Berlioz and Schumann, which was in sympathy with the Symbolist tendencies then current in both painting and literature and had affinities with the works of MOREAU and Redon. *See also* BATIGNOLLES, ILLUSTRATION, MORISOT, SCHOLDERER [23]
□ V. Fantin-Latour, *Catalogue de l'oeuvre complète de Fantin-Latour* (1911); J. and E. Pennell, *The Whistler Journal* (1921); *Fantin-Latour*, Grand Palais, Paris, exhibition catalogue (1982)

Faure, Jean-Baptiste (1830–1914) Probably the most interesting and catholic collector of works by the Impressionists, as well as being their patron and friend, Faure made his début at the Paris Opéra in 1861 as a baritone, and became almost immediately widely popular. A successful teacher of singing, who published several books on the subject, he was also a prolific composer of songs, one of which, *Les Rameaux*, can still be heard on French concert platforms.

He showed an early interest in art and collecting, and struck up a mutually advantageous friendship with DURAND-RUEL, from whom he purchased works by DELACROIX and COROT. The two spent a lot of time together in London in 1870–71; the singer was very popular in ENGLAND and retained a house there, offering accommodation to SISLEY for four months in 1874. He became deeply interested in the group of new artists whom Durand-Ruel was beginning to promote and in 1873 he bought an important group of MANETS: *Lola de Valence* (1862; Musée d'Orsay) for 2500 francs; *Luncheon in the Studio* (1868; Bayerische Staatsgemäldesammlungen, Munich) and *Le Bon Bock* (1873; Philadelphia Museum of Art) for a total of 6000 francs. These were generous PRICES, made possible by the fact that Faure was reputed to be earning in excess of 100,000 francs a year.

In the same year he also bought DEGAS' *Aux Courses en Provence* (1869; Boston Museum of Fine Arts) for 1300 francs. This marked the beginning of a close relationship between the two, in the course of which Faure built up the most important collection of works by Degas – eleven of them – in France. The first of these was the *Examen de danse* (Payne Collection), which he commissioned for 5000 francs in 1872, and which Degas finished in 1874. In the same year, at the painter's request, he bought back from Durand-Ruel for 8000 francs six paintings with which Degas was not satisfied. He handed them over to the painter, together with 1500 francs, on condition that he would receive, when they were finished, four large paintings on which Degas was working. Two of these, including *L'Orchestre de Robert le Diable* (Victoria and Albert Museum), were finished in 1876, but Degas did not complete the transaction until 1887, and then only as a consequence of legal action against him. The relations between the two had become completely soured. In the 1890s Faure sold to Durand-Ruel, at a handsome profit, all the works by Degas that he had acquired, and when in 1902 he published *Notice sur la collection J.-B. Faure, suivi du catalogue des tableaux formant cette collection*, Degas was the only important Impressionist unrepresented. Nothing like this

spoiled his relationship with the other Impressionists.

One of Faure's biggest successes had been as Hamlet in Thomas' opera of the same name. The hundredth performance had been scheduled to take place on the night of 28 October 1873, but on the previous night the opera house on the rue Le Peletier was burned down and it had to be transferred elsewhere. Three years later Faure retired from the official Opéra and commissioned Manet to paint him as Hamlet (Folkwang Museum, Essen). He was not altogether satisfied with the painting, which was also received coldly by the critics when it was exhibited at the Salon; one of them described it as 'a wooden head on which is stuck a false beard, with an open mouth crying ridiculously and big eyes looking like two unlit gaslights'. Faure continued to collect works by Manet, however, buying them either directly from the painter or through Durand-Ruel, and eventually accumulated 68 of them. In April 1878, in a momentary lack of confidence, he sent 42 of his pictures for sale at the HÔTEL DROUOT, but he had to buy most of them back himself, *Le Bon Bock* being withdrawn at 10,000 francs.

During this period Faure was also buying MONETS on a lavish scale. His holdings of RENOIR were slightly less extensive but he had some 30 works by SISLEY and a number by PISSARRO. Faure belatedly received the Legion of Honour in 1881, at the same time as Manet, through the good offices of their mutual friend Antonin PROUST. *See also* ETRETAT, MUSIC, PORTRAITURE [126, 174]

□ Venturi (1939); A. Callen, 'Faure and Manet', in *Gazette des Beaux-Arts* (March 1974); *Degas*, Grand Palais, Paris, exhibition catalogue (1988)

Fénéon, Félix (1861–1944) Writer, art critic and active anarchist, he published a brochure entitled *The Impressionists in 1886*, in which he put forward the view that the vital impulse of the movement was dead and that its mantle had been assumed by the 'Divisionists' SEURAT and SIGNAC. He went on to promote their works in the pages of the Symbolist magazine *La Revue blanche*, to which he became a regular contributor, and in the offices of which he organized the first retrospective exhibition of Seurat's work in 1900; he also edited the first *catalogue raisonné* of his works. Despite his advocacy of the POST-IMPRESSIONISTS, he never ceased to praise their predecessors, emphasizing always the extent to which they had progressed from the initial

A caricature of Félix **Fénéon** by Toulouse-Lautrec, c. 1896.

discoveries of MANET, and underlining the notion that art has an organic growth pattern of its own. Perhaps his most memorable remark, however, had nothing to do with art. In the course of being interrogated in a trial at which he was accused of being involved in an anarchist plot and planting a bomb in a Paris café, he was told by the judge that he had been seen skulking behind a lamp post, and asked, 'Where exactly is *behind* a lamp post?'

□ F. Fénéon, *Oeuvres plus que complètes*, 2 vols. (1970); J. Halpérin, *Félix Fénéon, Aesthete and Anarchist in Fin-de-Siècle Paris* (1988)

Fiquet, Hortense (1850–1918) Working as an artists' model in Paris, she met Paul CÉZANNE in 1869, and shortly afterwards they started living together; when war broke out they moved to L'ESTAQUE near Marseilles. Cézanne was very anxious to hide the liaison from his parents, even though in 1872 on their return to Paris, they had a son, to whom they gave Cézanne's father's Christian name. When in 1878 Cézanne's father did find out, he cut his son's allowance. Eight years later the couple married and went to live in AIX, their fortunes greatly improved by the death of the painter's father six months after the event.

Hortense does not seem to have liked provincial life, and the relationship between the two was never a happy one. Although he painted her many times (e.g. *Mme Cézanne in the Conservatory*, 1890; Metropolitan Museum, New York), she seems to have had little appreciation of his artistic gifts, and told Matisse after Cézanne's death, 'You must realize that

Cézanne didn't really know what he was doing. He had no idea how to finish his pictures. Now RENOIR and MONET – they *did* know their craft as painters.'

□ Rewald (1973); Rewald (1986)

Flochetage The use of flakes (*floches*), or large spots of colour, to break up and give dynamism to matter, COLOUR and form, had been used intermittently by painters such as Rubens and Watteau, and was popularized by DELACROIX. It became very much part of the Impressionists' TECHNIQUE, and was pushed to its extreme limits by the Pointillists. [*49, 55, 56*]

□ S. Monneret, *L'Impressionnisme et son époque* (1978); A. Callen, *Techniques of the Impressionists* (1982)

Flornoy, Louis (1846–1904) Deputy mayor of Nantes, he was one of the city's leading citizens. A merchant, shipowner and chairman of the local Chamber of Commerce, he was a typical example of the enlightened art collector of the period. When he sold his collection to DURAND-RUEL, shortly before he died, it included works by RENOIR, SISLEY, COURBET, COROT, DAUBIGNY, BOUDIN and PISSARRO.

Cézanne's portrait of **Fiquet** was painted in the conservatory of their home near Aix in 1890.

PSST...! Images par FORAIN CARAN D'ACHE

L'Affaire Dreyfus

— Eh bien, père Salomon, où en sommes-nous?

Forain's caricature (1898) in *Psst. . !* reflects the anti-Semitism kindled by the Dreyfus affair.

Fontainebleau *see* BARBIZON

Forain, Jean-Louis (1852–1931) A recorder of life in the tradition of Daumier, he was an habitué of the Nouvelle-Athènes, and a close friend of most of the Impressionists. It is a commentary on the nature of the movement that he participated in the exhibitions of 1879, 1880, 1881 and 1886, even though his work — apart from an interest in contemporary scenes that brought him close to DEGAS — had very little in common with mainstream Impressionism; apart from anything else, he worked in a sombre palette, slightly reminiscent of that of Daumier (*Le Tribunal*, Tate Gallery, London).

His major achievement was in his drawings and caricatures, with their incisive line, their wit, and their ability to delineate character. Although most of his work in this vein was originally social in intent, at the time of the Dreyfus affair he became increasingly involved in political themes, and with Caran d'Ache founded a weekly, *Psst*, for the expression of these opinions. Later in life he returned to a greater concern with oil paintings. *See also* IMPRESSIONIST EXHIBITIONS, POLITICS

□ C. Dodgson, *Forain* (1936); J. Pujet, *La Vie extraordinaire de Forain* (1957)

Fourcaud, Louis de (1853–1914) Journalist and critic who contributed to the *Gazette des Beaux-Arts* and *Figaro*. He was one of the earlier supporters of Impressionism – and also of the MUSIC of Wagner. In 1893 he succeeded Hippolyte Taine as professor of aesthetics and art history at the ECOLE DES BEAUX-ARTS.
□ *Dictionnaire de biographie française*

France Most of the Impressionists were born under the so-called constitutional monarchy of Louis-Philippe, which was replaced in 1848 by the Second Republic, based on the concept of universal suffrage. Three years later a coup d'état established the President Louis-Napoleon as virtual dictator, a role he signalized in the following year by becoming Emperor under the title of NAPOLEON III.

Beginning on a repressive note, the Second Empire became mildly liberal as time went by, and it inaugurated a period of considerable wealth, spectacular, if occasionally vulgar, social ostentation, and the creation of massive public works. PARIS was largely remodelled, and the same process of renovation was carried out in provincial cities; churches and public buildings were built on an impressive scale, and private enterprise equalled and sometimes surpassed – though in a more dubious and adventurous way – the activities of the state. It was a world which Winterhalter painted, which ZOLA described, and which the GONCOURT brothers chronicled. Patronage was

France: reading the papers in the gardens of the Palais-Royal; engraving of a Parisian scene, 1864.

lavished on the arts by a state anxious to preserve its own prestige, but reluctant to encourage any art form that might imperil what were seen as 'the foundations of society'. There were indeed marked analogies between the Second Empire and the reign of Louis XIV. The problem was that Napoleon III was an adventurer who lacked both the flair and the self-confidence that such a role demands; too nice to be a villain, he was too shifty to be a hero. Virtually tricked into a disastrous war with Prussia in 1870, he was defeated in the most humiliating way in a matter of weeks, and fled to England, where he died a year later. As a result of the war, France lost Alsace and Lorraine with a population of nearly 1½ million, important mining enterprises and industries, and the city of Strasbourg, and had to pay an indemnity to the Germans of 5 billion francs. Peace was made by the newly elected President Adolphe Thiers in February 1871, and a month later revolution broke out in Paris, which had endured a five-month siege by the Prussians. The government moved to Versailles, and a self-governing Commune was proclaimed in the capital, which for two months was ravaged by fighting as 30,000 Communards struggled with 130,000 government troops. In the final assault and the blood-letting that followed, nearly 20,000 Parisians were killed.

The curious thing is that the Third Republic, which was to survive until 1940 through 107 different governments, had a far more felicitous career than these sombre beginnings would have seemed to promise, and the period up to the outbreak of the First World War appears in history as *la belle époque*. By 1874 France had already paid the German indemnity and balanced its budget. The wounds of the Commune were healed by a general amnesty in 1880, when Marshal Mac-Mahon was succeeded as President by the eminently democratic lawyer Jules Grévy. Between 1870 and 1900 the national income doubled, industrial production tripled, and foreign trade increased by three-quarters. A new iron vein was discovered in the east of the country, greater in potential than any that had been sequestrated by the Germans. The French overseas empire, already established in ALGIERS and Tunisia, was

France: Manet's *Musique aux Tuileries* (1862) is a perfect image of the glittering social life of Paris under the Second Empire. It features, among others, Manet, de Balleroy, Astruc, Fantin-Latour and Baudelaire.

France: the boulevard des Capucines, where the first Impressionist exhibition was held, *c.* 1890. The busy life of this Parisian thoroughfare is captured in paintings by Monet.

extended to Central Africa and Indo-China, and a series of great international exhibitions proved, to the delight of its inhabitants and the surprise or chagrin of the rest of the world, that Paris had become the virtual capital of Europe. There were, of course, hiccoughs; occasional financial slumps; scandals of a financial or sexual kind; the danger of a right-wing coup d'état under General Boulanger in 1889, and the divisive trauma of the Dreyfus affair, which dragged on from 1893 until 1906. But on the whole, the picture was one of a reasonably prosperous and well-ordered society.

The apparently confused and confusing pattern of political events between the reign of Louis-Philippe and the end of the century did little to alter two fundamental facts: that the country was, during this period, reaping the fruits of the Industrial Revolution, and that real power was firmly in the hands of the urban and rural bourgeoisie. RAILWAYS spread over the country at an amazing speed; in 1850 there were 3083 kms (1914 miles) of track; in 1900, 13,059 kms (8110 miles); infant mortality dropped from 179 per thousand in 1861 to 126 in 1900; the number of houses rose from 7 million in 1847 to 9½ million in 1900. There were constant improvements in education at all levels, culminating in 1897 with the establishment of a network of provincial universities. The ECOLE DES BEAUX-ARTS was reconstituted in the 1870s,

and art classes became an essential part of education at all pre-graduate levels Art education was greatly improved by the activities of men such as F.L. Ravaisson-Mollien (1813–1900), whose *De l'Enseignement de l'art dans les lycées* of 1854 became the accepted guide, until the beginning of the next century. Gaston Quénioux, who was professor at the Ecole des Arts Décoratifs in Paris, introduced another system of teaching art, in which the emphasis was on the recording of personal impressions, rather than on technical skill. The surviving drawings that CÉZANNE and Zola produced during their early days in AIX-EN-PROVENCE indicate the level of achievement already reached by young students in the 1850s.

As elsewhere in the western world, science and technology played an increasingly important role in human affairs. France was a pioneer of technical education, and in the Ecole Normale Supérieure had a teaching institute that was for long unequalled in Europe. Paris was the first city in Europe to be lit by electricity; Charles Tellier (1828–1913) introduced the concept of food-refrigeration; Alphonse Beau de Rochas (1815–93) developed the principle of the internal combustion machine; Charles Cros (1842–88), who was also a poet, was one of the pioneers of colour PHOTOGRAPHY; and it was in France that reinforced concrete was first used, the first aerial photographs were taken, and the first public telephone system inaugurated in 1878.

The process of urbanization maintained its momentum throughout the century, but it was to Paris rather than the important provincial cities that people moved; the capital's population more than trebled between 1840 and 1900, attracting provincials, country people and foreigners to a city that rapidly adapted itself to provide for their needs and leisure. This migration is strikingly proved by the Impressionists themselves. RENOIR was born in Limoges, MONET in Le Havre, Cézanne in AIX, PISSARRO in the Virgin Islands and MORISOT in Bourges; DEGAS' parents were Italian, SISLEY's English. Only MANET could be thought of as a native Parisian. The whole economy of the country became city-orientated. Industrialization meant cheaper goods, and mass-production changed the appearance and accessibility of clothes, furniture, crockery and books. Sewing machines made their appearance and so, towards the end of the period, did typewriters and central heating. To cope with increasing demands, new marketing techniques were evolved. Georges Dufayel, originally a photographer, started a hire-purchase business, which by 1880 had nearly 2 million clients. Large department stores opened (Monet's friend and patron HOSCHEDÉ was the director of one), and it was the same pressures that brought about these phenomena which stimulated the rapid growth of the art trade during the period. *See also* POLITICS, SOCIAL BACKGROUND

□ Clark (1973a); Zeldin (1973); M. Crubellier, *Histoire culturelle de la France XIX–XX siècles* (1974); J.M. Merriman, *French Cities in the Nineteenth Century* (1982)

Franco-Prussian War Precipitated by a combination of the political ineptitude of NAPOLEON III and the Macchiavellian policies of Bismarck, the Franco-Prussian War of 1870 was one of the most traumatic events in French history. Defeated in the field, her capital besieged and occupied, FRANCE was forced to cede Alsace-Lorraine and to pay an enormous indemnity to the conquerors. Moreover, as a consequence of the war, the emergence and suppression of the Commune in PARIS resulted in acts of brutality by both Communards and government on a scale to compare with the worst excesses of the Revolution.

Inevitably, the effects on the Impressionists were significant. BAZILLE was killed in action on

Pilotell's cartoon reflects opposition to the treaty agreed at the end of the **Franco-Prussian War**.

28 November; RENOIR was offered a job on the staff of his patron, Prince Bibesco, but refused and was sent as a cavalry orderly to a barracks near Tarbes; CÉZANNE evaded military service altogether; MANET became a staff officer in the National Guard with Meissonier as his commanding officer, in a unit that also included PUVIS DE CHAVANNES, CAROLUS-DURAN, TISSOT and BRACQUEMOND. PISSARRO and his family first took refuge in Brittany and then, with his mother and his own family, joined his half-sister, who lived in London; MONET, leaving his wife and child behind, also went there, as did DAUBIGNY, BONVIN, FANTIN-LATOUR and others; DURAND-RUEL opened a gallery in New Bond Street. BOUDIN and DIAZ went to Brussels. DEGAS remained in Paris, enlisted in the infantry, and was posted to the fortifications of the city; in his unit he met Henri ROUART, who became one of his closest friends. SISLEY, although British, stayed on at LOUVECIENNES, but as a consequence of the war the family fortune was lost and his life was henceforward

Franco-Prussian War: the rue Royale after the defeat of the Commune in 1871.

dogged by poverty. COURBET was hopelessly compromised by the role he played in the Commune, spent six months in prison, was financially ruined, and fled to Switzerland, where he died in 1877.

Strangely enough, in their attempt to expunge the humiliations of the war, the French seemed in its aftermath to make super-human efforts to establish their capital as the centre of European culture. The *belle époque* between the suppression of the Commune and the outbreak of war in 1914 was a golden age in which Impressionism found an ideal context for its development and eventual success. *See also* ENGLAND, GERMANY, POLITICS *[130, 170]*

□ C. Seignebos, *Le Déclin de l'Empire et l'établissement de la 3ᵉ République, 1859–1875* (1921); Zeldin (1973); M. Howard, *The Franco-Prussian War: The German invasion of France* (1981)

G

Gachet, Dr Paul (1828–1909) Perhaps one of the most fascinating figures in the history of Impressionism, he was a doctor who specialized in homœopathy, a psychiatrist, an engraver, a Darwinian, a Socialist and a consistently helpful and generous patron and friend to all those artists with whom he came into contact. As a young student in Paris he had frequented the BRASSERIE DES MARTYRS, and after concluding his medical studies at Montpellier he became a frequenter of the seminal CAFÉ GUERBOIS. He bought a house at AUVERS-SUR-OISE and, in his studio there, became an enthusiastic engraver, partly as a consequence of his earlier contacts with Daumier, Charles Méryon and Rodolphe Bresdin, artists whose styles were reflected in his own. He signed his works 'Paul van Ryssel', deriving the surname from his native village near Lille.

It was in this studio that several of the Impressionists took up etching; CÉZANNE produced there an etching of GUILLAUMIN, as well as painting a number of flower pieces arranged in Delft vases for him by the doctor's wife. On the recommendation of PISSARRO, Gachet took VINCENT VAN GOGH into his house in 1890, and it

Dr Gachet's house in Auvers-sur-Oise, where Van Gogh stayed in 1890.

was in Auvers that he committed suicide. Gachet's great collection of paintings by all the major figures of the movement was given to the state by his son and is now in the Musée d'Orsay. *See also* BRUYAS, PRINTS, VÉTHEUIL *[22]*

□ P. Gachet, *Deux Amis des impressionnistes, Le Docteur Gachet et Murer* (1956), *Lettres Impressionnistes* (1957); R. Delage, 'Chabrier et ses amis impressionnistes', in *L'Oeil* (Dec. 1973)

Gaillard, Marie-Anne *see* CALLIAS, NINA DE

Gangnat, Maurice (1856–1924) An engineer educated at the Ecole des Arts et Manufacture and once a business associate of Alfred Natanson, the founder of the important avant-garde magazine, *La Revue blanche*. He retired from business early and began to build up a collection of paintings, starting with a Vuillard from Bernheim-Jeune in 1905 and following it in the succeeding year with works by RENOIR, CÉZANNE and JONGKIND. He then met Renoir personally at the home of their mutual friend, the publisher Paul Gallimard, and became a close friend, being frequently invited to Renoir's home at Cagnes-sur-Mer.

Between then and the painter's death, he accumulated over 150 of his works, mostly small, informal paintings; he also commissioned seven works, including a portrait of his son Philippe (1906; Private collection), one of himself (1916; Private collection), and the *Dancing Figures* (1909; National Gallery, London). Renoir said of Gangnat 'He has an eye'. After his father's death, Philippe Gangnat presented *Gabrielle with Roses* (1911; Musée d'Orsay) to the French nation before the sale of the collection in 1925. *[220]*
□ E. Faure, 'A propos d'une collection célèbre; La Collection Gangnat', in *La Renaissance de l'art français* (April 1925); *Renoir*, Hayward Gallery, London, exhibition catalogue (1985)

Gasquet, Joachim (1873–1921) The son of Henri Gasquet, a childhood friend of CÉZANNE, he was a poet who wrote exuberant verse in Provençal. He first met the painter in April 1869, and they struck up a close friendship that lasted until 1904, when they quarrelled with that bitterness that Cézanne always managed to introduce into his relationships with others. During their period of friendship, however, they corresponded regularly; Cézanne painted a portrait of Gasquet in 1896 (Gallery of Modern Art, Warsaw) and gave him a painting of Mont Sainte-Victoire. In the winter of 1912–13, Gasquet wrote a book on Cézanne, the first edition of which appeared shortly before his death, the second posthumously. It contained a fascinating series of 'conversations' with the painter, which, though they may not be a literal transcript, are very revealing.
□ J. Gasquet, *Cézanne* (1921); Rewald (1984); Rewald (1986)

Gaudibert, Louis-Joachim (1812–78) A businessman and amateur painter, who lived in a château at Montivilliers near Le Havre and became a generous patron of MONET. In 1868 he acquired several of the artist's seascapes when they were seized by creditors, and provided Monet with an allowance in 1868 and 1869. He also commissioned several portraits from him, which Monet executed in a fairly conventional style, exemplified especially in the portrait of Gaudibert's daughter-in-law, Marguerite-Eugénie-Mathilde (Musée d'Orsay).
□ J. House, *Monet; Nature into Art* (1986)

Gaugain, Paul-Octave, Abbé (1850–1904) Born of working-class parents, he became a priest and a teacher, being headmaster of the Cours Saint-Augustin in the boulevard Haussmann. Eventually he returned to his native village of Boulon, near Caen, where he became mayor. He was a regular client of DURAND-RUEL, but also bought directly from the Impressionists themselves, including from PISSARRO and RENOIR, thus circumventing the commission they should have paid to Durand-Ruel. This led, on one occasion, to a hilarious imbroglio with Renoir; abashed to discover that some of his paintings were coming up in a sale of works belonging to the Abbé, Renoir apologized profusely to Durand-Ruel, who did not admit that he had already bought the collection for 101,000 francs. It consisted entirely of paintings by the Impressionists – an unusual thing at the time – and contained works of a very high quality.
□ *Renoir*, Hayward Gallery, London, exhibition catalogue (1985)

Gauguin, Paul (1848–1903) Although his main achievements were to lie elsewhere, Gauguin was, to use a fanciful metaphor, nursed in the bosom of Impressionism. His attitudes to art were deeply influenced by his experience of its first exhibition, and he himself

Gauguin's *Portrait of Marie Lagadu*, 1890, was clearly influenced by Cézanne.

participated in those of 1880, 1881 and 1882. The son of a French journalist and a Peruvian Creole, whose mother had been a writer and a follower of Saint-Simon, he was brought up in Lima, joined the merchant navy in 1865, and in 1872 began a successful career as a stockbroker in Paris.

In 1874 he saw the first IMPRESSIONIST EXHIBITION, which completely entranced him and confirmed his desire to become a painter. He spent some 17,000 francs on works by MANET, MONET, SISLEY, PISSARRO, RENOIR and GUILLAUMIN. Pissarro took a special interest in his attempts at painting, emphasizing that he should 'look for the nature that suits your temperament', and in 1876 Gauguin had a landscape in the style of Pissarro accepted at the SALON. In the meantime Pissarro had introduced him to CÉZANNE, for whose works he conceived a great respect – so much so that the older man began to fear that he would steal his 'sensations'. All three worked together for some time at PONTOISE, where Pissarro and Gauguin drew pencil sketches of each other (Cabinet des Dessins, Louvre).

In 1883–84 the bank that employed him got into difficulties and Gauguin was able to paint every day. He settled for a while in Rouen, partly because Paris was too expensive for a man with five children, partly because he thought it would be full of wealthy patrons who might buy his works. Rouen proved a disappointment, and he joined his wife Mette and children, who had gone back to Denmark, where she had been born. His experience of Denmark was not a happy one and, having returned to Paris, he went to paint in Pont-Aven, a well-known resort for artists.

Here, he stopped working exclusively out-of-doors, as Pissarro had taught him, and generally began to adopt a more independent line. His meeting with VAN GOGH, the influence of SEURAT, the doctrines of SIGNAC, and a rediscovery of the merits of DEGAS – especially in his pastels – all combined with his own streak of megalomania to produce a style that had little in common with the thoughtful lyricism of the work of his erstwhile mentor Pissarro. Monet confessed to a liking for his *Jacob Wrestling with the Angel* (1888; National Gallery of Scotland), which he saw at the exhibition Gauguin organized in 1891 to finance his projected excursion to places where he could live on 'ecstasy, calmness and art'; the proceeds amounted to 10,000 francs, some of it coming from Degas, who bought several paintings. There were still evident in these new works traces of pure Impressionism, and of the very clear influence of Cézanne (as in the *Portrait of Marie Lagadu*, 1890; Art Institute of Chicago) – a fact pointed up by a Cézanne still life owned by Gauguin which is shown behind her – but basically this period marked the parting of the ways between Gauguin and Impressionism. *See also* AROSA, CORMON, INDÉPENDANTS, LUXEMBOURG, MIRBEAU, POST-IMPRESSIONISM, PRINTS, SCANDINAVIA, SCHUFFENECKER [132, 197]
□ M. Roskill, *Van Gogh, Gauguin and the Impressionist Circle* (1970); J. Rewald, *Post-Impressionism* (1978); *Gauguin*, Grand Palais, Paris, exhibition catalogue (1989)

Gautier, Théophile (1811–72) Although he started his career as a painter, Gautier soon found his real vocation as a poet, critic and novelist. An ardent defender of Victor Hugo at a time when he was considered an anarchical and disruptive force in LITERATURE, he published in 1835 his most famous work *Mademoiselle de Maupin*. This contained the first definitive statement of the theory of 'art for art's sake', which was to have an important influence on subsequent aesthetic theories.

Progressive in his social thinking, Gautier saw RAILWAYS as positive signs of progress, balloons as a means of obtaining easy communication, so removing the threat of war, and the machine as a means of relieving man of distasteful work. He was endowed with remarkable verbal facility; articles and books flowed from his pen, dealing not only with literature but with music and the visual arts. He was an indefatigable traveller, writing about his experiences in SPAIN, Russia, Greece and Turkey in books which also contained pertinent and stimulating comments about art and architecture. Always supportive of new tendencies, he was one of the first to recognize the genius of Wagner and Berlioz. In 1861 he had warm praise for MANET's works in the SALON, and the artist featured him in *Musique aux Tuileries* (1862; National Gallery, London). He was, however, very critical of *Olympia* (1863–65; Musée d'Orsay). Later in life, he had indulgent things to say not only about Manet but also about MONET and RENOIR. Much of his critical thinking was influenced by BAUDELAIRE, who dedicated his collection of poems *Les Fleurs du Mal* to him. [90, 134]
□ T. Gautier, *L'Art moderne* (1856); Hamilton

(1954); U. Finke (ed.), *French Nineteenth-Century Painting and Literature* (1972)

Geffroy, Gustave (1855–1926) A radical journalist who commenced his career on CLEMENCEAU's paper *Justice*. His literary activities later took many forms; he wrote extensively about current social and political injustices and published a number of novels with a strongly REALIST bent. His interest in painting and especially in Impressionism was kindled by a visit he paid to MANET's studio in 1876, as a consequence of which he came into contact with all the other artists of the group, as well as Rodin, and maintained an on-going correspondence with most of them. His closest connection was with MONET, whom he first met at Belle-Ile in 1886 and about whom, some 30 years later, he wrote a book – *Claude Monet, sa vie, son temps, son oeuvre* (1924) – which is still valuable in many ways.

All his writings about Impressionism are significant and amongst the most intelligently perceptive of his time. His articles about contemporary art were collected in the eight volumes of *La Vie artistique*, published between 1892 and 1903, the third volume, entitled *Histoire de l'impressionnisme*, being the most comprehensive book about the movement that had so far appeared. It consisted of a historical opening section followed by individual chapters devoted to each artist. He also wrote introductions to the catalogues of one-person exhibitions by PISSARRO, Monet, Rodin and MORISOT, as well as to that of the sale of the BURTY collection. He ended his career as the director of the Gobelins tapestry factory.

□ D. Wildenstein, *Monet, biographie et catalogue raisonné*, 4 vols. (1974–85)

Germany The Germans seem to have felt an instinctive and natural empathy with Impressionism, almost from the beginning. An interest in contemporary French painting had been stimulated by the International Art Exhibition in Munich in 1869, where the works of COURBET had made a great impact, and where a circle of artists around Wilhelm Leibl (1844–1900) began to move in very much the same direction as those French artists who were following Courbet. Leibl had settled in Paris for a short period before the outbreak of the FRANCO-PRUSSIAN WAR, and had won a gold medal at the SALON in 1869, while several Germans actually attended the ACADÉMIE JULIAN. But it was Berlin, slightly more adventurous and cosmopolitan than the Bavarian capital, that was to provide the most successful shop window for Impressionism.

In 1882 Georg Brandes (1842–1927), the polymath Danish author of *Main Currents of Nineteenth-Century Literature* (6 vols; 1901–05), who spent a great deal of his time there (and whose brother married Mette Gauguin's sister Ingeborg, previously married to the Swedish painter Fritz Thaulow), wrote an interesting account of the impact of Impressionism on German opinion, in an article later incorporated into an extensive book about Berlin, which he published in 1885. It was occasioned by an exhibition of some ten Impressionist paintings bought by a 'wealthy Russian gentleman', possibly Carl Bernstein, a cousin of RENOIR's friend EPHRUSSI, who had been buying extensively from DURAND-RUEL. In the following year Durand-Ruel put on an Impressionist show at the Gurlitt Galleries, billed as being 'from the collection of a well-known German collector'. Brandes decided that 'The first reaction among German painters was one of astonishment, almost consternation, on the part of the youngest and most impressionable artists. Some did not know whether to take this seriously; one naively asked the owner whether he had actually paid for this mess of paint. However, even those who at the beginning had been among the most amazed and dismayed, came back after several days and asked to see the pictures once more. The impression had not left them a moment's peace and they will, I think, in the end include some of the new ideas in their work.' They did. Even Adolf Menzel, the

Germany: Lovis Corinth, *Emperor's Day in Hamburg*, 1911.

Germany: *Terrace of the Restaurant Jacob*, 1902. The contemporary subject-matter, loose brushwork and outdoor lighting of this work explain why Liebermann is often described as a German Impressionist.

father-figure of late 19th-c. German painting, who was admired by DEGAS, and of whom MANET once said 'He is a great artist, but a bad painter', saw merits in MONET and admired the work of MORISOT.

By the end of the 1880s artists such as Lesser Ury (1861–1931) were painting palette-knife versions of Impressionism, which had become completely identified with the German avant-garde, centred first around the Munich Secession in 1892 and then around the Berlin Secession seven years later. Three outstanding painters of the period, Max Liebermann (1847–1935), Lovis Corinth (1858–1925) and Max Slevogt (1868–1932), were known as the 'Triumvirate of German Impressionism'. The description is somewhat reckless. Liebermann and Corinth had both worked in Paris for some time, and were influenced by COROT, Courbet and others, as well as by the Impressionists. To all three, Impressionism was at most a key to that liberation of light, colour and atmosphere that was to lead them into different, perhaps more Germanic, paths. As in so many cases where one attempts to evaluate Impressionism

in any country outside France, in Germany the word was used to describe almost any explorative art form, and its influence was so diffused in the spheres of both technique and visual apprehension as to preclude the concept of a 'school'. Influence, however, there was, and again this is true of most countries, but it was the influence of emancipation rather than of precedent. The whole magnificent episode of German Expressionism in the first quarter of the 20th c. was made possible by the impact of Impressionism.

The influence of the critics was seminal in this context. One of the first in the field had been Julius Meier-Graefe, who in 1883 had published a laudatory piece about Renoir. (This may have stimulated the patronage of Dr Franz Thurneyssen, a Munich industrialist who built up an important collection of Impressionist works. In 1910 he invited the whole Renoir family to stay with him at Wessling, where the painter produced the portrait of his wife now in the Albright-Knox Art Gallery, Buffalo.) Meier-Graefe's writings about Impressionism were copious, informed, invariably favourable and often enthusiastic. In 1902 he published *Manet und sein Kreis*, which contained sections on Monet, PISSARRO, CÉZANNE and RENOIR, followed in 1904 by *Der moderne Impressionismus*, largely devoted to Toulouse-Lautrec, GAUGUIN and POST-IMPRESSIONISM. But Meier-Graefe's most substantial contribution to the dissemination and comprehension of Impressionism was his widely acclaimed and popular *Entwicklungsgeschichte der modernen Kunst* (2 vols.; 1908). He gave not only Impressionism, but its constituent members, an, as it were, 'official' place in the history of art.

Another important figure was that of Paul Cassirer, critic, dealer and publisher, who was also involved in the magazine *Pan*, mouthpiece of the avant-garde, and who acted as Durand-Ruel's agent in Berlin. Influential in Berlin before the First World War was the French writer Jules Laforgue, who had been Ephrussi's secretary at the *Gazette des Beaux-Arts* before establishing himself in Germany. He became an habitué of the Bernstein salon, and encouraged the critic Max Klinger in his defence of the principles and practice of Impressionism. More directly important was Hugo von Tschudi, who was appointed Director of the National Gallery in Berlin in 1896, and who was himself an impassioned collector, his tastes being largely influenced by Max Liebermann. His first gesture, on assuming his post, was to buy for the gallery Manet's *Dans la serre* (1879) and, later, works by Pissarro (1897), Monet (1899) and Renoir (1906). Other German museums followed suit; Bremen acquired a Degas in 1903, a Monet in 1906, a Manet in 1908, a Pissarro in 1909 and a VAN GOGH in 1911; the Städel Institute in Frankfurt acquired a Sisley in 1899, a Van Gogh in 1908, a Renoir in 1910 and a Degas and a Manet in 1912. When in 1909 von Tschudi was sacked from his Berlin post and moved to the Neue Pinakothek in Munich, he bought, or was responsible for the presentation to the gallery of works by Cézanne, Renoir, GUILLAUMIN, Manet, Monet and Pissarro. Other important German collectors of this period include the painter Max Liebermann, who started collecting Impressionists in the early 1890s, Oscar Schmitz, Graf Harry Kessler and Paul von Mendelssohn-Bartholdy. It could be said that Germany came second to the USA in the warmth of its reactions to the new movement. The artistic influence was, on the whole, transitional and stylistically ephemeral, but German collectors and museums had accumulated by the 1930s an outstanding body of Impressionist works. *See also* WOLFF *[89, 92, 170]*

□ J. Meier-Graefe, *Manet und sein Kreis* (1902); W. Uhde, *Von Bismarck bis Picasso* (1938); U. Finke, *German Painting from Romanticism to Expressionism* (1974)

Gérôme, Jean-Léon (1824–1904) Painter, sculptor and engraver, he represented the apogee of French official art during a large part of the 19th c. Entering the studio of Delaroche at the age of 18, he then became a student of GLEYRE and visited Italy with him. Henceforward his career was crowned with popular and official success. At each of the Expositions Universelles, in 1855 and 1867, he rose one rank in the Legion of Honour and in 1865 he was nominated professor at the ECOLE DES BEAUX-ARTS, and elected to the INSTITUT DE FRANCE. He was extremely versatile, starting as a portrait painter in the style of Ingres and then, after a visit to Egypt and Turkey, turned to oriental subjects to accompany the numerous classical themes he had already undertaken. He was bitterly opposed to the Impressionists, and when the acceptance of the CAILLEBOTTE bequest was being discussed he said 'The state must have sunk very low to accept such rubbish.' He

Gérôme's bust of Sarah Bernhardt suggests the nature of his versatility and popularity.

Monet standing on the wisteria-covered Japanese bridge which spanned his waterlily pond at **Giverny**, with Mme Hoschedé and her daughter Blanche, *c.* 1920.

produced remarkable SCULPTURE in tinted marble, sometimes adorned with jewellery.

☐ F.F. Hering, *Gérôme; His Life and Works* (1892); M. Gerald, 'Gérôme and Manet', in *Gazette des Beaux-Arts* (Sep. 1967); *Jean-Léon Gérôme*, Dayton Art Institute, Ohio, exhibition catalogue (1972)

Gervex, Henri (1852–1929) A successful painter of historical and mythological scenes (for instance, those in the Hôtel de Ville and the Opéra-Comique), he became famous for his painting of a surgeon giving a demonstration of an operation, which started off a whole spate of works on similar Realist themes. He was a friend of both MANET and RENOIR. *See also* BLANCHE *[192]*

☐ *Equivoques; peintures françaises du XIXe siècle*, Musée des Arts Décoratifs, Paris, exhibition catalogue (1973); A. Celebonovic̀, *The Heyday of Salon Painting* (1974)

Gill (Louis-Alexandre Gosset de Guignes) (1840–85) A well-known painter, who frequently exhibited at the SALON, especially in the mid-1870s. He wrote semi-serious art reviews for a variety of journals, including *La Lune* and *Le Journal pour rire*, and produced a celebrated caricature of Manet's portrait of ZOLA.

☐ E. Bénézit, *Dictionnaire des peintres, sculpteurs, dessinateurs et graveurs* (1966)

Giverny Few places have been so completely identified with an artist as the little village of Giverny, close to the Seine, some 30 kms (18½ miles) from Rouen, is with MONET. He acquired a house there with the HOSCHEDÉS in 1883, and for the rest of his life it provided the source of most of his imagery, the neighbouring landscape inspiring the famous paintings of poplars (e.g. that in the Philadelphia Museum of Art, painted in 1891) and haystacks (e.g. *Two Haystacks*, Art Institute of Chicago, painted in the same year). Above all else, it was at Giverny that Monet and his wife cultivated with argumentative affection and complete dedication the garden, which centred around a waterlily pond; created by slightly diverting the Epte, an adjoining tributary of the Seine, it was traversed by a JAPANESE-style bridge, and became the subject of many of his most significant paintings. Restored to their original state, the house and garden are now open to the public. *See also* ROBINSON *[141]*

☐ J.P. Hoschedé, *Claude Monet, ce mal-connu*, 2 vols. (1960); *Monet's Years at Giverny*, Metropolitan Museum, New York, exhibition catalogue (1978); C.F. Stuckey (ed.), *Monet; A Retrospective* (1985)

Gleyre, Charles (1808–74) Born in Switzerland, he settled in Paris in 1838 and became an instructor at the ECOLE DES BEAUX-ARTS. His

Gleyre's *Les Illusions perdues*, c. 1843, combines a
Romantic subject with classical composition.

Théo van Gogh, c. 1888, only shortly
before his death, aged 34.

own paintings, such as his most famous *Les
Illusions perdues* (1843; Louvre) are of little
significance, melding suggestions of Romanticism with Classicist compositional ideas, but he
was a very active and apparently able teacher.
He opened a school which had a direct and, as
far as the students were concerned, fruitful
relationship with the Ecole des Beaux-Arts.
There was considerable freedom in the school,
the fees were modest, and live models were
always available. Amongst those who worked
there were WHISTLER, MONET, RENOIR, SISLEY and
BAZILLE. In 1863, however, on the urging of
Monet – 'Let's get away from here. The place is
unhealthy; it lacks sincerity' – the future
Impressionists left, mainly to pursue their
creative activities in the forest of Fontainebleau.
Shortly afterwards the school closed. *See also*
ATELIER SYSTEM, BÉLIARD, GÉRÔME, LEPIC,
PLEIN-AIRISME

□ J.P. Crespelle, *Les Maîtres de la belle-époque*
(1966); *Le Musée du Luxembourg en 1874*, Grand
Palais, Paris, exhibition catalogue (1974);
Boime (1986)

Gobillard, Yves (1838–93) was one of Berthe
MORISOT's two sisters. Although she studied
painting, she did not persist with it, especially
after her marriage in 1863 to Théodore Gobillard, a tax official, by whom she had three
children. DEGAS did a memorable portrait of her
in 1869 (Metropolitan Museum, New York).
□ *The Correspondence of Berthe Morisot*, ed. D.
Rouart (1957); *Degas*, Grand Palais, Paris,
exhibition catalogue (1988)

Gogh, Théo van (1857–91) The younger
brother of Vincent, he joined the firm of
GOUPIL-BOUSSOD-VALADON in 1878 and, after
being put in charge of its stand at the Exposition
Universelle, he was made manager of the

Montmartre branch, where Adolphe Goupil
had started his career. Knowing the work of the
Impressionists and being a frequent visitor to
the DURAND-RUEL gallery, he was soon engaged
in a struggle to persuade his employers to buy
their works.

In 1884 he bought a PISSARRO for 125 francs,
which he sold for a profit of 25 francs. At first he
proceeded cautiously, and succeeded in selling
one painting each by Pissarro, SISLEY, MONET
and RENOIR. After 1886, however, when his
brother Vincent arrived in Paris and strengthened his judgment, he became much more
active in dealing in the work of the Impressionists, despite the reluctance of his seniors. He
was assisted in this by the fact that Durand-Ruel
was going through a period of retrenchment
and his painters were anxious to find other
outlets. He was hampered in his efforts by the
fact that the usual customers of the gallery were
not partial to these new forms of painting, so he
had to build up a new body of clients, some of
whom, such as VOLLARD, were dealers themselves. At the same time, too, Théo was
expanding his interests to include artists such as
Odilon Redon, GAUGUIN and others. In the
course of his activities – he died in HOLLAND on

Vincent van Gogh's *Montmartre* (1886) was painted soon after his arrival in Paris.

25 January 1891 – he acquired and sold one work by CÉZANNE, 23 by DEGAS, 18 by Gauguin, 5 by MANET, 24 by Monet, 23 by Pissarro, 4 by Renoir and 7 by Sisley.
□ *The Complete Letters of Vincent van Gogh* (1958); J. Rewald, *Studies in Post-Impressionism* (1986)

Gogh, Vincent van (1853–90) The son of a pastor, he was born at Groot-Zundert in HOLLAND, and at the age of 16 started working at the GOUPIL art gallery in The Hague. When he was 20 he was moved to the London branch of the firm, where he stayed until 1875; he then went as a lay-preacher to work amongst the miners of the Borinage in Belgium, but in 1881 he returned to his parental home and decided to become an artist. His interest in art had always been strong, and his earlier letters show his admiration for painters such as MILLET, and for the works of the English artists Frank Holland and Hubert von Herkomer, whose illustrations in *The Graphic* and other magazines were often concerned with the lives of the poor, a subject with which he was deeply concerned.

For some months he studied at the Antwerp Academy, where he painted a number of works showing the life of peasants in a style that could, rather ambitiously, be described as realistic. It was during this period, in a letter to his brother Theo, written in April 1883, that he makes his first reference to the Impressionists: 'There is a school, I believe, of Impressionists, but I know very little about it.' This somewhat remarkable gap in his artistic knowledge was plugged in February 1886 when he left Antwerp for the more liberated atmosphere of Paris. There he presented himself at the atelier of Félix COR-MON, a liberal teacher, who included amongst his pupils Toulouse-Lautrec, Anquetin (whose works greatly impressed Van Gogh), GAUGUIN, who introduced him to PISSARRO (whom Van Gogh surprisingly saw as the heir to Millet), and Emile BERNARD. His initial reactions to the Impressionists were, as he later explained, less than favourable. In a letter to his sister written in June 1888 he explained, 'One has heard much about the Impressionists, one expects much and . . . when one sees them for the first time, one is very much disappointed and thinks they are ugly, sloppily and badly painted, badly drawn, of a poor colour; everything that is miserable. That was my first impression when I came to Paris.'

In actual fact, Impressionism, along with the influence of JAPANESE prints, provided Van Gogh with just the kind of liberating influence which he needed. From Impressionism he discovered a new attitude to COLOUR, substituting for his older, monochromatic palette brighter and simpler shades; it gave his brushwork a freedom and vigour that it was to maintain throughout the rest of his brief career. This had already become apparent in works such as *The Windmill on Montmartre* (1887; Collection Mrs Charles Engelhard, Newark, USA), and his connection with Pissarro – who was generous with advice, and who at this time was going through his Pointillist phase – was reflected in the *Interior of a Paris Restaurant* (1887; Rijksmuseum, Kröller-Müller, Otterlo), with its emphatically Signac-like technique. But Van Gogh was never an Impressionist in any real meaning of the word, certainly much less so than Gauguin, who in his early days was very close to the movement. Van Gogh made use of the technical discoveries of the Impressionists, but directed these towards the expression of feeling, rather than to the depiction of external phenomena, and though he shared with them an interest in contemporary life, it was touched with something of that idealistic fervour that he had retained from his early admiration for Millet. Pissarro, though possibly being wise after the event, said some time after Van Gogh's suicide on 27 July 1890 that he had always thought he would either go mad, or leave the Impressionists far behind. In the event he did both. *See also* ENGLAND, TANGUY [210]

□ *The Complete Letters of Vincent van Gogh*, 3 vols. (1958); *Verzamelde Brieven van Vincent van Gogh*, ed. J. van Gogh-Bonger, 4 vols. (1952–54); J. Rewald, *Post-Impressionism* (1956); M. Roskill, *Van Gogh, Gauguin and the Impressionist Circle* (1970)

Goncourt, Edmond (1822–96) and **Jules de** (1830–70) Mirrors of taste as well as creators of it, the Goncourt brothers were basically novelists and critics, but their fame depends to a much greater extent on their *Journal*, which is one of the most revealing and detailed pictures of a society ever written. Their novels were resolutely REALIST, dealing with affairs of contemporary life, often of a 'low' character, and thus reflecting, to a certain extent, one of the major concerns of the Impressionists. Although they were outmatched by ZOLA, some of their works achieved considerable popularity – especially *Manette Salomon* (1866), which gives a convincing account of art life in Paris.

Inevitably, the closest analogy between their work and that of the Impressionists was with DEGAS, a relationship of which both were conscious. Degas had a greater appreciation of their writings than he did of Zola's, which he found coarse in comparison with the rather detached attitude that the Goncourts took towards their subject-matter; in a letter to Ludovic HALÉVY, he ironically described his work as *style Goncourt*. In recording his first visit to Degas' studio in 1874, Edmond wrote 'Of all the men I have met, he is the one most likely to capture in his account of contemporary life the real essence of that life. But will he ever achieve a complete realization of his intentions? I doubt it.'

The Goncourts, especially Edmond, had acute visual sensibilities and they were at least partially responsible for rekindling interest in the art of the 18th c., which had been undergoing a period of deep unpopularity during the period of excessive Romantic tastes. Their writings, such as *L'Art du dix-huitième siècle* (1859), encouraged collectors, including the Marquess of Hertford, who bought paintings by Watteau, Lancret, Boucher and others that are now housed in London's Wallace Collection. Edmond became deeply interested in JAPANESE art and published books on Utamaro (1891) and Hokusai (1896), which contributed to the general vogue for all things Japanese. *See also* BOUGIVAL, DURANTY, GUYS, ILLUSTRATION, CABARET DE LA MÈRE ANTHONY, LITERATURE, NIEUWERKERKE [128]

□ E. and J. de Goncourt, *Journal, mémoires de la vie littéraire*, ed. R. Ricatte (1956); U. Finke (ed.), *French Nineteenth-Century Painting and Literature* (1972)

Gonzalès, Eva (1849–83) The daughter of a fashionable novelist, she started to study painting under the academician Chaplin, but in 1867 met MANET and became his only pupil, to the chagrin of MORISOT. Although deeply influenced by his style, her early works were cautious enough to gain admission to the SALON – in 1870 she had a study of a boy soldier accepted, although Manet's version of the same

Manet's portrait of his only pupil, Eva **Gonzalès**, 1870.

subject had been rejected four years earlier. (It was at this period that he painted the portrait of her now in the National Gallery, London.) She very rapidly, however, acquired her own, freer, more personal style, with a penchant for a certain kind of social realism, as for example *The Milliner* (*c.* 1877; Art Institute of Chicago), and her works were lauded by ZOLA and CASTAGNARY. In 1878 she married the engraver Henri Guérard, and died of an embolism resulting from childbirth a short while after Manet, to whom her personal and artistic loyalty had never faltered. *See also* LUXEMBOURG

□ *Eva Gonzalès*, Bernheim-Jeune Gallery, Paris (1914); C. Roger-Marx, *Eva Gonzalès* (1950)

Goupil, Adolphe (1806–93) At the age of 21, after originally wanting to become an artist, Adolphe Goupil opened a small shop in the boulevard MONTMARTRE, specializing in the sale of reproductions of works of art, which he produced on his own presses in a variety of

La Grenouillère, the popular bathing-place near Croissy, from *Le Journal amusant* (1873).

media: engraving, aquatint, lithography and mezzotint. Amongst the works he reproduced were many by contemporary artists, and as he bought some of these he gradually evolved into an art dealer. In the 1860s he was joined by Vincent van Gogh – uncle of the painter – who had a gallery of his own in The Hague. This became part of the Goupil empire, which by now included two galleries in Paris and branches in New York (later bought out by its manager Michael Knoedler, who gave his name to it), London, Brussels and Berlin. The gallery's range of interests was wide, covering works by ACADEMIC painters such as his son-in-law GÉRÔME, Cabanel and Meissonier, as well as by members of the BARBIZON School. VINCENT VAN GOGH, who had joined his uncle's gallery in The Hague in 1869 at the age of 16, was sent to the London branch of Goupil in the Strand in 1873. Two years later he was transferred to Paris, where his unsuitability for the job soon became apparent, and he was sacked in 1876. By this time, however, the firm had been taken over by Etienne Boussod, who had married Goupil's granddaughter, and Pierre Valadon. It came to be known as BOUSSOD AND VALADON, though it was often referred to as Goupil's. *[35]*

□ H. Lauzac, *Goupil* (1864); *The Complete Letters of Vincent van Gogh* (1958); J. Rewald, *Studies in Post-Impressionism* (1986)

La Grenouillère ('The Froggery') A restaurant and bathing place on a small branch of the Seine at Croissy. It was an extremely popular area because the RAILWAY-line from PARIS to Saint-Germain, the first to be opened in France, had a station at nearby CHATOU. Both MONET and RENOIR painted several views of it in 1869 (Monet: *La Grenouillère*, Metropolitan

The façade of **Goupil**'s gallery in the Place de l'Opéra, where Van Gogh was briefly employed.

Museum, New York; Renoir: *La Grenouillère*, Oskar Reinhardt Collection, Winterthur, Switzerland). Several successful academic painters had houses nearby, and the place was extensively written about, sometimes approvingly, sometimes not so, during the 1860s. It was thought of as a very 'contemporary' subject, and its popularity was confirmed in the year that Monet and Renoir painted it, when it was visited by the Emperor NAPOLEON III and Eugénie, his wife. *See also* BOUGIVAL

□ C.P., 'La Grenouillère', in *L'Illustration* (28 August 1869); R. Gordon and A. Forge, *Monet* (1986); Herbert (1988)

Groupe des Artistes Indépendants *see* INDÉPENDANTS

Guichard, Joseph-Benoît (1806–80) A successful painter in a predominantly ACADEMIC tradition, who had been a pupil of Ingres. He was deeply interested in those sketching procedures which many of his colleagues in the ECOLE DES BEAUX-ARTS saw as essential preliminaries to the creation of a 'finished' painting and which the Impressionists were to elevate into autonomous works of art. A popular teacher, he counted amongst his pupils BRACQUEMOND and MORISOT. In 1862 he published a pamphlet about COURBET, attacking his emphasis on 'fashionable terms such as values, localities, *taches* and impressions' which would lead students to abandon serious study for the seductively easy technique these terms seemed to imply. He was a close friend of COROT, to whom he recommended Berthe Morisot and her sister when he felt that he himself could not teach them adequately. In 1874 Madame Morisot asked him to visit the first IMPRESSIONIST EXHIBITION at NADAR's old studio, at which her daughter was exhibiting, and to report back. 'When I entered,' he replied, 'I became distraught at seeing the works of your daughter in these pernicious surroundings. I said to myself "One doesn't live without impunity amongst madmen. MANET was right in opposing her participation." After an honest and critical examination of the paintings here one certainly finds some excellent fragments, but they all have *cross-eyed* minds.' (J. Baudot, *Renoir, ses amis et ses modèles*, 1949, p. 57). Bracquemond, however, remained devoted to Guichard, and when in 1885 he published a book on drawing, he dedicated it to his old master.

□ F. Bracquemond, *Du Dessin et de la couleur*

Guigou's *The Washerwoman* employs dramatic lighting and rich impasto.

(1885); *The Correspondence of Berthe Morisot*, ed. D. Rouart (1957); Boime (1986)

Guigou, Paul (1837–71) Like CÉZANNE a native of AIX-EN-PROVENCE, where he went to university, he worked for some years in Marseilles, where he met Monticelli and visited the numerous exhibitions then held in the city. It was through these that he conceived an admiration for the paintings of the BARBIZON School, which confirmed his own ambitions to become an artist. After several visits to Paris, where he was impressed by COURBET's work, he met Paul GACHET, whom he had known in Marseilles, and decided to settle there. Gachet introduced him to the CAFÉ GUERBOIS, and he became friendly with MONET, PISSARRO and SISLEY, as well as BURTY and DURET. He developed a style marked by its freshness and richness of impasto and he had several works accepted by the SALON. Having served in the FRANCO-PRUSSIAN WAR he died suddenly on being demobilized.

Guillaumin, Armand (1841–1927) The longest surviving Impressionist, the most loyal, and probably the least known, Guillaumin was born in Paris of a family that had recently moved there from central France, where as a boy he spent much of his time. At the age of 15 he started working in his uncle's shop, whilst studying drawing in the evenings. In 1860 he obtained a job on the Paris–Orleans railway, continuing to paint in his spare time. In 1861 he entered the ACADÉMIE SUISSE and met CÉZANNE and PISSARRO, with whom he was to remain on close terms for the rest of his life. They spent some time together at PONTOISE, and Cézanne was greatly impressed by a view of the Seine that Guillaumin painted in 1871 (Museum of Fine Arts, Boston). At this time all three were frequent visitors to GACHET's house at AUVERS, and it was there that Cézanne did a portrait-etching of Guillaumin. Cézanne also copied a painting by him of the Seine at Bercy (1876–78; Kunsthalle, Hamburg).

Guillaumin exhibited at the SALON DES REFUSÉS and at most of the IMPRESSIONIST EXHIBITIONS. DEGAS and MONET were not particularly impressed by his works, which were marked by a passion for colour that, towards the end of his life, brought him close to the Fauves. His prospects improved when he was taken up by the dealer Auguste Portier, who had commenced his career with DURAND RUEL, and he was assured of financial stability when he won a large prize in the Loterie Nationale in 1891. He became friendly with VAN GOGH, with whose work his own has certain affinities (1895; *View of Agay*, Musée d'Orsay), and in 1904 he spent some time in HOLLAND. The vigour of his brushwork, and the obvious lyrical zest that informs his landscapes bring him close to VAN GOGH, and clearly influenced the young Matisse. *See also* DÉPEAUX, INDÉPENDANTS
□ G. Lecomte, *Guillaumin* (1926); Rewald (1985)

Guillemet, Antoine (1843–1918) A pupil of COROT, he became friendly with CÉZANNE and PISSARRO, whom he met at the ACADÉMIE SUISSE, and in 1866 he stayed with the former in AIX. It was he who introduced Cézanne to MANET, with whom he was to remain on friendly terms, and who painted him standing beside Berthe MORISOT in *The Balcony* (1869; Musée d'Orsay). Close to all the Impressionists, whose meetings at the CAFÉ GUERBOIS he regularly attended, he did not get involved in the movement from a painterly viewpoint, persisting in his own mildly conservative style, which won approval

Guillemet with Morisot (left) and the violinist Jenny Clause in Manet's *The Balcony*, 1869.

at the SALON, and where he was able to use his influence to assist his less amenable friends. One of his typical works, *Bercy in December* (1874), now hangs in the Assemblée Nationale in Paris.
□ E. Bénézit, *Dictionnaire des peintres, sculpteurs, dessinateurs et graveurs* (1966)

Guys, Constantin (1805–92) Made initially memorable by one of BAUDELAIRE's most famous pieces of art criticism, 'The Painter of Modern Life', Guys spent his early life in the army and travelled widely, going to Greece to fight in its War of Independence, and covering the Crimean War for the *Illustrated London News*. Despite his martial air and interests, he was mostly preoccupied with the life of Parisian society, which he recorded in drawings and watercolours marked by a brisk liveliness of line, an economy of expression, and a REALISM that won the approval of artists as disparate as COURBET and DEGAS. Thackeray greatly admired his works, as did NADAR and the GONCOURTS, in whose *Journal* he figures prominently. MANET possessed several of his wash drawings, and in 1880 drew a pastel portrait of him (Shelburne Museum, Shelburne, Vermont). His drawings of contemporary life were

Guys, *The Champs-Elysées* (detail): a lively Parisian scene, by the 'Painter of Modern Life'.

not financially successful, however; he had difficulty in eking out a living and had to give English lessons to supplement his income. His problems were complicated by the fact that in 1885 he became deaf as the result of an accident, and he died in abject poverty.

In emphasizing his modernity and concern with contemporary life – 'this transitory, fugitive element, the metamorphoses of which are so frequent, and which should not be despised, because without it you inevitably tumble into the emptiness of an abstract and indefinable beauty' – Baudelaire pinpointed the contribution that Guys made to the ideology of Impressionism. *See also* CAFÉ GUERBOIS, ILLUSTRATION

□ E. d'Euguy, *Au Temps de Baudelaire, Guys et Nadar* (1945); C. Hall, *Constantin Guys* (1945); C. Baudelaire, *The Painter of Modern Life and Other Essays*, ed. J. Mayne (1964)

H

Halévy, Ludovic (1833–1908) Novelist and dramatist, Halévy was most famous as the librettist of many of Offenbach's works and of Bizet's *Carmen*. Although brought up as a Catholic, he belonged to a well-known Jewish family, and this led in 1898 to a break with DEGAS, who had been his friend since their schooldays at the Lycée Louis-le-Grand, but

who was resolutely anti-Dreyfus and, indeed, fundamentally anti-Semitic. Nevertheless, when Halévy, in collaboration with Meilhac, had written a comedy, *La Cigale* (1877), which presented a satirical picture of the Impressionists, Degas, with typical ambivalence, offered to help and sketched the décor for a scene in a studio. Some five years later he also produced a series of monotypes and related drawings intended to illustrate Halévy's very successful novel, *La Famille Cardinal*, which had appeared in 1880. The illustrations were not published, however, partly because Halévy preferred a more popular artist, and partly because, by making Halévy the model for one of the protagonists, Degas had emphasized the autobiographical element in the story. Degas often stayed with Halévy at Dieppe, where they associated with SICKERT and Jacques-Emile BLANCHE. In 1879 Degas painted a portrait of him in pastel and tempera standing with one of his friends, the dilettante Albert Boulanger-Cavé in the wings of a theatre – possibly the Opéra (Musée d'Orsay). Degas also took innumerable photographs of the Halévy family, whose home life he seems greatly to have

Degas, *Ludovic* **Halévy** *finds Madame Cardinal in an opera box*: monotype with pastel, *c.* 1880.

appreciated. Halévy's sister, Geneviève, married Bizet and, after his death, the light-opera composer Oscar Straus. *See also* HECHT, ILLUSTRATION, LITERATURE

Hamerton, Philip Gilbert (1834–94) An English painter, CRITIC and essayist who published several novels, books of essays and an enthralling account of his life on the isle of Innistrynich on Loch Awe (1862). He became art critic of the influential *Saturday Review* and in 1869 established, with Robert Seeley the publisher, the *Portfolio*, which became one of the most lively art journals of its time and which he continued to edit until his death. Having written a hostile article on the SALON DES REFUSÉS in 1863, he published in 1892 *The Present State of the Fine Arts in France*, a collection of articles on the subject that had previously appeared in the *Portfolio*. In these he attacked the Impressionists generally for 'their resolute refusal of concession to all established views about taste'. He also attacked PISSARRO for ruining the view of a cathedral by allowing the picture to be dominated by a factory chimney, but had kind words to say about DEGAS. *See also* ENGLAND, SALON, REALISM
□ *Dictionary of National Biography*; Cooper (1954); Flint (1984)

Havemeyer, Henry Osborne (1847–1907) A large, domineering American businessman who was head of the American Sugar Refining Company and who by 1888 had established a reputation as a patron of the Metropolitan Museum in New York. His tastes in art had originally been excessively traditionalist, but in the 1880s he was converted first to COURBET and then to the Impressionists by his adored second wife Louisine (*née* Waldron-Elder), who had been a childhood friend of Mary CASSATT in Philadelphia. Cassatt acted as an intermediary in diverting part of the Havemeyer fortune into the culturally admirable channel of supporting the Impressionists, and the movement owes a great deal to that combined operation. Through Cassatt, the Havemeyers also became interested in Spanish painting and acquired some remarkable Goyas and El Grecos. Thanks to the alliance between these two remarkable women – after the death of her husband Louisine became an ardent suffragette – the Havemeyer Collection in the Metropolitan is now one of the greatest in the world. *See also* USA

□ L.W. Havemeyer, *Sixteen to Sixty; Memoirs of a Collector* (1961); F. Weitzenhoffer, *The Havemeyers* (1986)

Hecht, Albert (1842–94) A collector and a close friend of DEGAS, who portrayed him in *The Ballet of Robert le Diable* (1871; Metropolitan Museum, New York) as the character in the foreground, with raised opera-glasses, looking over his shoulder. Devoted to the opera, Hecht was a member of the HALÉVY circle. A banker by profession, he was an admirer especially of the works of MANET, who depicted him in the foreground of *The Masked Ball at the Opéra* (1873–74; National Gallery of Art, Washington). His brother Henri was also a collector and devotee of the opera.

Holland MANET was the first of the Impressionists to have close contact with Holland, visiting it in his early twenties either with, or to see, a young Dutch girl, Suzanne LEENHOFF, with whom he was in love. She was the daughter of an organist and herself an admirable pianist, specializing in modern music, especially that of Schumann, who was then comparatively unknown in France. She became Manet's mistress

Holland: Manet's *Surprised Nymph*, 1860, was probably inspired by Rembrandt's *Bathsheba*.

Holland: Monet's view of the Zuiderkerk in Amsterdam, looking up the Groenburgwal, 1872.

of Frans Hals, and there are many hints at similar influences picked up from the Rijksmuseum: the 1867 portrait of Suzanne at the piano (Musée d'Orsay), for instance, relates to Gabriel Metsu's *Woman Playing the Clavichord*, and *The Surprised Nymph* of 1860 (Museo Nacional de Bellas Artes, Buenos Aires) to Rembrandt's *Bathsheba* in the Louvre.

In 1871 MONET visited Holland at the suggestion of DAUBIGNY, who had spent some time there and was deeply influenced by the experience. One of the pictures that Monet produced during his stay of several months, *Mill in Zaandam* (Earl of Jersey, Jersey), is close in subject-matter and style to a painting of Dordrecht that Daubigny painted at the same time (Detroit Institute of Arts). Both paintings are marked by a darkness of colour and heaviness of texture that may also have been partly attributable to the influence of the Dutch-born JONGKIND, for whose works Monet had a particularly warm admiration.

The Dutch themselves had always been very receptive to French art, and they showed an early and enthusiastic interest in the works of

and then, in 1863, a year after his father's death, his wife. Manet visited Holland on several occasions and was entranced by many aspects of Dutch painting. The most striking evidence of this is *Le Bon Bock* (1873; Philadelphia Museum of Art), with its obvious references to the work

Holland: G.H. Breitner's *Paleissmat, Amsterdam* (*c.* 1896). The similarity with street scenes by Caillebotte and Degas – in the dramatic use of perspective and the photographic immediacy – is striking.

Honfleur *c.* 1880: a photograph of the Channel resort, known as the 'Barbizon of Normandy'.

COURBET, COROT and the BARBIZON School. This is especially evident in the paintings of G.H. Breitner (1857–1923), who also used a kind of visual realism which, in its indebtedness to the arbitrary viewpoints of the camera, comes close to the urban scenes of CAILLEBOTTE. The fact that the Impressionists were so actively concerned with the depiction of light and atmosphere especially recommended them to the country-men of Van Goyen and Ruisdael, and by the 1890s a whole group of painters, the Hague School, taking as their subject the coast and the polders around The Hague, used Impressionist techniques to recreate the mysterious light and atmosphere of that landscape. Typical of them were Jacob Maris (1837–99), Jan Hendrick Weissenbruch (1824–1903) and P.J.C. Gabriel (1828–1903). But, like other Dutch painters who came close to Impressionism, they were far too preoccupied with the Romantic notion of individual expression and feeling to follow with any rigour the basically pragmatic explo-ration of vision that was at the heart of the movement; and the whole Dutch school veered, happily in the long run, towards the more self-indulgent gratifications of Expres-sionism. *See also* ANTECEDENTS, ASTRUC *[68, 174]*
□ P. Haesaerts, *Histoire de la peinture moderne en Flandre* (n.d.)

Honfleur This Channel resort and the country-side around it became so popular as a haunt for painters that it was known as the 'BARBIZON of Normandy'. BAZILLE, who stayed there in 1864, wrote enthusiastically to his parents, 'As soon as we arrived in Honfleur, we looked for land-

scape motifs. They were easy to find because the country is heaven. One could not see richer meadows, or more beautiful trees. . . . The sea, or rather the Seine broadening out, gives a delightful horizon to the masses of green. We are staying in Honfleur itself, at a baker's who has rented us two small rooms; we eat at the Saint-Siméon farm, situated on the cliffs a little above Honfleur. It's there that we work and spend our days.' BOUDIN, COURBET, DIAZ, JONG-KIND and COROT also stayed at this farm, and MONET, who was living nearby, was a frequent visitor. Honfleur and nearby SAINTE-ADRESSE feature constantly in Impressionist paintings of the 1860s and early 1870s.
□ G. Désert, *La Vie quotidienne sur les plages normandes du Second Empire aux années folles* (1983); Herbert (1988)

Hoschedé, Ernest (1838–90) and **Alice** (1841–1911) A director of one of those large department stores that became such a feature of Parisian life during the period of the Second Empire, Hoschedé was an avid and informed collector of works by the Impressionists, attending their social gatherings and often inviting them to his imposing residence at Mongeron near Paris. He and his wife were especially fond of MONET, who spent most of 1876 there, painting in return some decorative panels and landscapes. But, like a character from a ZOLA novel, Hoschedé's financial deal-ings were often foolhardy, if not dubious, and in 1874 he sold – quite successfully – at the HÔTEL DROUOT, a selection of works by PIS-SARRO, SISLEY, DEGAS and Monet. Four years later he became bankrupt, and his entire collection was auctioned. It consisted of 6 works by MANET, 16 by Monet, 13 by Sisley and 9 by Pissarro, and DURANTY described the sale as a disaster.

The Hoschedés then decided to share Monet's home at GIVERNY and established themselves there with their six children. The position became increasingly ambiguous after the death of Monet's wife Camille in 1879, and may, at least in part, have been responsible for Monet's lack of contact with his fellow Impres-sionists during the 1880s – a suggestion put forward in a scurrilous article in *Le Gaullois* in January 1880. Hoschedé left Giverny to pursue what has been described as 'an impecunious bachelor life' in Paris. In 1882 he published *Impressions de mon voyage au Salon*, the cover of which was illustrated by a painting by Manet,

Ernest Hoschedé

Impressions de mon Voyage
Au Salon de 1882

Jeanne (par Édouard Manet)
En vente chez Tolmer et Cⁱᵉ
Et chez tous les libraires
PRIX : 1 fr. 50

Hoschedé's *Impressions de mon voyage au Salon de 1882*, with Manet's portrait of Jeanne.

for which the artist had prepared a drawing for black and white reproduction processes.

On Hoschedé's death in 1891, Alice and Monet married and lived a prosperously respectable life. She was a dominant woman who argued with the painter about the layout of his garden and forced him to take her to endless wrestling matches, a sport to which she was passionately addicted. Her daughter Blanche married Monet's son Jean. Alice died in 1911 and, after the death of Jean in 1914, Blanche returned to Giverny to look after Monet in his old age. *See also* FRANCE *[99]*
□ J.P. Hoschedé, *Claude Monet, ce mal-connu*, 2 vols. (1960)

Hôtel Drouot Named after one of Napoleon's generals, whose home it had originally been, this was the main auction house of Paris, run by the state and mostly devoted to the sale of works of art. It provided a general guide to the level of PRICES that an artist could command, and its major occasions were the sales that took place on an artist's or collector's death, or on bankruptcy.

To the Impressionists, sales of this kind were major events when their own works were involved, acting as barometers of popularity and giving clues to their dealers as to what prices to charge. One of their most traumatic experiences was in 1878. First, the singer FAURE, speculating on possible gain, put up for sale some of his own collection, but the response was so bad that he had to buy back most of the pictures himself. MANET's *Pulcinello* was sold for 2000 francs, but his *Bon Bock* was withdrawn at 10,000 francs, and *Masked Ball at the Opéra* at 6000. Three months later HOSCHEDÉ was forced by a court judgment to sell the very significant collection he had built up over the past decade. This was a disaster: the 6 works by Manet fetched on average 400 francs each; 12 MONETS ranged from 62 francs to 250, and the 13 SISLEYS, 21 francs to 200. A typical reaction to the sale was recorded by PISSARRO, who wrote to Sisley 'I discovered a possible patron the other day, but the Hoschedé sale has ruined the whole thing for me. He can now get them cheap at the Hôtel Drouot'; and, indeed, Pissarro was forced to reduce the price of his works to between 50 and 100 francs.

What could happen on the death of an artist was shown in April 1883 when DURAND-RUEL and Georges PETIT were entrusted with putting up for sale the works that Manet had left. A

A woodcut by Daumier showing a public sale at the **Hôtel Drouot**, 1863.

total of 159 paintings, pastels and drawings fetched only 116,637 francs, and even that was largely achieved because family friends such as CAILLEBOTTE and Emmanuel Chabrier paid prices above the average. The highest individual price was 5850 francs for *The Bar at the Folies-Bergère*, and certain works had to be withdrawn (*Christ Mocked by the Soldiers* and *The Aged Musician*, for instance) because no offers were made for them.

The most disastrous contact the Impressionists had with the Hôtel Drouot, however, had occurred some years earlier, in 1875, when RENOIR convinced Monet and Sisley that the best way to raise money quickly would be to follow the unusual and, in this case, effective precedent set by DAUBIGNY the previous year, when he had arranged a successful auction of his own works. They were joined in the venture by Berthe MORISOT, and the auction took place on 24 March; the catalogue carried a perceptive and illuminating introduction by Philippe BURTY, in which he compared the pictures to 'little fragments of the mirror of universal life', and declared that 'the momentary, colourful and subtle reflections we see in them deserve our attention and respect'. There were in the sale 21 works by Sisley, 20 each by Monet and Renoir, and 12 by Morisot, including 7 PASTELS and watercolours. Remembering the SALON DES REFUSÉS and the publicity that had subsequently accrued to the Impressionists' exhibition, the public turned up in large numbers to jeer, howling derisively at each bid, and at one point the auctioneer had to call the police. 'We had good fun with the purple landscapes, red flowers, black rivers, yellow and green women and blue children which the pontiffs of the new art present to the public', commented *Paris-Journal* the next day. The prices fetched were less than satisfactory. Half of the Renoirs did not even reach 100 francs each, and several had to be bought back by him. Sisley's 21 works brought in a total of 2500 francs, and Monet reached an average of 233 francs a picture. The net result of the sale, including the works bought back by artists, was about 11,500 francs.

As is the case with all auction prices, those reached at the Hôtel Drouot were influenced by taste and, to a lesser extent, by the general economic situation. By 1900, for instance, works by Pissarro were reaching 10,000 francs, those by Sisley 15,000 francs – and on one occasion 43,000 francs (Tavernier sale, 6 March) – and by 1912 Manet's *The Music Lesson*, which

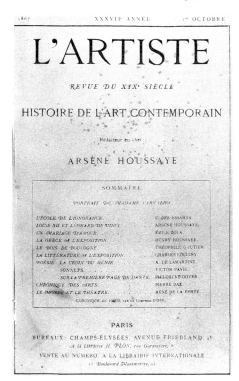

Cover of *L'Artiste*, 1867, listing contributions from Zola, **Houssaye**, Lamartine and Gautier.

19 years earlier had cost ROUART 4400 francs, sold for 120,000 francs. *See also* DURET, TANGUY

Houssaye, Arsène (1825–1896) Writer and art CRITIC, he was an inspector in the Department of Fine Arts and director of the influential journal L'ARTISTE, in the pages of which he offered a certain degree of encouragement and support to the Impressionists. In 1867 he bought MONET's *The Cradle, Camille and Jean* (Mr & Mrs Paul Mellon Collection, New York) at an exhibition in Le Havre, and was persuaded to buy a work by RENOIR, as well as attempting, unsuccessfully, to acquire WHISTLER's *White Girl* at the SALON DES REFUSÉS. In 1877 he commissioned Georges RIVIÈRE to write a lengthy article on the Impressionists for *L'Artiste*, but insisted that, to avoid offending his readers, he should mention neither PISSARRO, seen as an anarchist, nor CÉZANNE, seen as a madman. *[229]*

□ G. Ballas, 'Paul Cézanne et la revue "L'Artiste"', in *Gazette des Beaux-Arts* (Dec. 1981)

Huysmans, Joris-Karl (1848–1907) was a French novelist of Dutch extraction who spent most of his life in Paris. His early works were in the REALIST tradition, but his fame rests largely on *A Rebours* and *Là-bas*, both written and published by the 1890s, which became virtual bibles of the so-called 'decadent' movement, lauding as they did the pursuit of every kind of possible experience, every form of sensual self-indulgence. He was a prolific writer on many subjects and a percipient art CRITIC, who did much to support and publicize the Impressionists. His *L'Art moderne* (1883) was a collection of his articles on the SALONS and the IMPRESSIONIST EXHIBITIONS, and his book *Certains* (1889), a collection of miscellaneous articles and reviews, contains, amongst other pieces about art, an especially astute study of CÉZANNE. He was one of the first to applaud the works of CASSATT, but in his early comments on the Impressionists was apt to criticize those who did not choose 'modern' subjects; he therefore inclined to the DEGAS camp, though he himself deplored the outbreaks of internecine warfare that spasmodically agitated the movement. He even objected to the fact that the girls in RENOIR's *Déjeuner des canotiers* (1881; Phillips Collection, Washington) were not 'fresh and Parisian enough' and looked more like 'prostitutes imported from London'.

Huysmans' approach to art was literary rather than visual, and it took him some considerable time fully to appreciate the visual aims and technical innovations of the Impressionists; but he was always on the side of the new and the innovative, being especially quick, for instance, to appreciate and analyse the idiosyncratic art of Odilon Redon, which indeed had affinities with his own. *See also* LITERATURE, MOREAU, RAFFAËLLI [128, 162]

□ J.-K. Huysmans, *Oeuvres complètes* (1928), esp. vol. VI; U. Finke, *French Nineteenth-Century Painting and Literature* (1972)

I

Illustration Primarily concerned with painting, as the medium in which their innovations found form, the Impressionists did not devote much time or attention to the field of illustration. This reluctance was fortified by the fact that, in France especially, the immense demand for illustrations, created by the spectacular growth in the number of papers, magazines and books, had fostered the evolution of specialists in this field, men such as Gavarni, Doré and Constantin GUYS. In a conversation with GASQUET, CÉZANNE emphasized another aspect of the problem: 'When one writes underneath a figure what it thinks and what it does, that is an admission that its thoughts or its actions have not been translated into line and colour. . . . Painting is first and foremost a matter of the visual. The content of our art is what our eyes think.' On the other hand, there were temptations to turn to illustration, either because of literary likes and connections, or for financial reasons.

The rediscovery of etching in the middle of the century was, of course, a powerful incentive (*see* PRINTS). It was BRACQUEMOND who made the medium popular amongst the younger artists. In 1852 the publisher Alphonse Cadart, who was an important influence in the etching revival, published Bracquemond's series *Huit sujets tirés des fables de La Fontaine*, and when, seven years later, the GONCOURT brothers published their book on the art of the 18th c., it was illustrated with their own etchings. In 1862 BAUDELAIRE published an article entitled 'L'Eau-forte à la mode', in which he praised at great length the etchings of LEGROS and mentioned MANET's etching *The Spanish Singer* of 1860–61 (part of an album also published by Cadart).

Manet had, indeed, been influenced by popular illustrations in his painting, in which there are frequent echoes from such successful publications as the *Magasin pittoresque* and *Les Français peints par eux-mêmes*. In 1869 he produced a lithograph of the execution of the Emperor Maximilian, but its publication was forbidden by the government because, according to ZOLA, who published a bitter attack on this piece of censorship, the uniforms of the soldiers gave the impression that they were French. In 1875 Manet produced six lithographs for MALLARMÉ's translation of Edgar Allan Poe's *The Raven*, and a year later four small wood-engravings for the same author's *L'Après-midi d'un faune*.

DEGAS, who might seem the most likely to have indulged in illustration, does not seem to have been greatly attracted by the idea, though

Illustration: Manet's lithograph for Edgar Allan Poe's *The Raven*, published in 1875.

apparently he did submit one to the *Illustrated London News* on the recommendation of Legros. This was accepted but not published. Between 1880 and 1883 he produced a series of monotypes to illustrate HALÉVY's *La Famille Cardinal*, but they were not published either.

RENOIR's main incursion into the field of illustration was in the pages of LA VIE MODERNE, the magazine edited by his brother Edmond. Some of these drawings, which appeared on the title-pages, were of writers and artists such as Théodore de BANVILLE and Leon Riesener, but others were of a more general nature; in December 1883 he illustrated in the magazine a story by Edmond, 'L'Etiquette', and in the same year produced an illustration for a feature article on 'La Pêche à travers Paris'. Occasionally he also produced drawings of various paintings for the magazine: Manet's *Fifer* (1866; Musée d'Orsay) on 12 January 1884 (to coincide with the painter's memorial exhibition held at the ECOLE DES BEAUX-ARTS), and two variations on his own *Dance in the Country* in 1883, the year in which it was painted. Unlike PISSARRO, who was very finicky about how his works were reproduced, Renoir was quite keen to do illustrations of almost any kind, conscious as he was of the publicity value of such exercises. In

1879 he wrote to Madame CHARPENTIER, the driving force behind the magazine, saying that Madame BÉRARD had suggested that a fashion page should appear each week: 'I would take it upon myself to make very exact drawings as soon as I return to Paris. In this manner you would attract the whole female audience, who are not always interested in the sketches of Meissonier and others. An arrangement might be worked out with milliners and dressmakers. . . . I would go to their shops to make the drawings from the model at different angles.' Nothing came of the idea, but the fact that he seriously considered it throws light on his amenability and also demonstrates that interest in dress which characterizes so many of his paintings.

It was not until VOLLARD appeared that book-illustration began to play an important role in modern French art, and in his *Peintres-graveurs* albums there appeared works by Renoir, FANTIN-LATOUR and VALADON. Pissarro also did sketches for woodcuts engraved by his son LUCIEN. *See also* DRAWING, LITERATURE *[46, 106, 110, 178]*

□ U. Finke, 'French painters as book illustrators', in *French Nineteenth-Century Painting and Literature*, ed. U. Finke (1972); J. Isaacson, 'Impressionism and Journalistic Illustration', *Arts Magazine* (June 1982)

Impressionism As a named movement, Impressionism was almost a fluke. The word by which it is known was neither invented by those who participated in it, nor, when it was reluctantly accepted by them, greatly approved of. It conveyed little of their real, sometimes divergent artistic aims, and though the word had frequently been used in artistic parlance in the past – by Constable, by DELACROIX and by COROT – in its application to the processes of painting, its significance to the general public in 1874 was, initially at least, a pejorative one, suggesting superficiality, perfunctory handling and unconsidered subjectiveness.

The name was first used by Louis LEROY in an article, published in CHARIVARI on 25 April 1874, headed 'Exhibition of the Impressionists'. In the course of the piece he made much play with the word, first using it with reference to works by MONET, PISSARRO and SISLEY, and then going on, for instance, to comment: 'Now take Mlle MORISOT! That young lady is not interested in reproducing trifling details. When she has a hand to paint, she makes as many brushstrokes

It was Monet's view of Le Havre, *Impression; Sunrise* (1872), which led the critic Leroy to coin the term **Impressionism**.

lengthwise as there are fingers, and the business is done. Stupid people who are finicky about the drawing of a hand don't understand a thing about Impressionism, and great Manet would chase them out of his republic.'

The reference to Manet is significant, indicating a realization amongst the art-conscious public that there was a more or less coherent group of painters who – though they had issued no manifesto, published no programme, and had described themselves in the exhibition held at NADAR's old studio as a *Société anonyme des artistes, peintres, sculpteurs, graveurs, etc.* – shared certain things in common, including a leader, forced into that role presumably because of the publicity engendered by his *Déjeuner sur l'herbe* of 1863. The existence of such a group had been indicated by the fact that they were from time to time known as the 'BATIGNOLLES group', or even as 'the JAPANESE', on the assumption that, because there was a craze for things Japanese amongst the artistically 'advanced', all art styles that did not conform to the ACADEMIC were influenced by that cultural tradition.

Despite the reluctance of both RENOIR and DEGAS to approve of the concept of a group, and despite the fact that ZOLA (possibly more accurately) continued to call them *naturalistes*, Leroy's word stuck, and within a year it was even appearing in the USA, in an article written by Henry JAMES, as part of the accepted language of the art world. Nor was it without a kind of implicit approval within the group. MONET had selected for the exhibition of 1874 a painting of Le Havre, with the sun appearing through the mists outlining the masts of ships and the general view of the harbour. He later recorded, 'I was asked to give a title for the catalogue. I couldn't very well just call it "View of Le Havre", so I said, put *Impression*.' Leroy, therefore, although he gave the name wide exposure, did have some justification from within the ranks of the exhibitors. So far, indeed, was the name eventually accepted, that by the time of the third exhibition in 1877 they were calling themselves 'Impressionists' (though in the fourth exhibition of 1879 they took the name 'Indépendants').

One thing is certain, that the creation of a group name polarized attitudes amongst themselves, and amongst the general public, which came to use the word Impressionist almost as a synonym for 'modern'. In fact, when a play about the movement by Ludovic HALÉVY was produced in London, the word 'Impressionists' was translated as 'followers of Whistler'. The very word imposed a fictitious stylistic unity on a group of very disparate artists. The first exhibition included 30 painters, including some, such as BOUDIN, LATOUCHE, Léopold Robert and Gustave Colin, who could by no stretch of the imagination be thought of as Impressionists; and the second exhibition swept into the net such outsiders as MILLET and LEGROS. Then, of course, there is the anomaly of Manet, and his relationship to the 'republic' that Leroy and public opinion generally saw him as leading. He never participated in any of the group exhibitions, and his own styles of painting were at best intermittently Impressionistic. If the word had not existed it would have had to have been invented, but once it had been, it created almost as many problems as it solved. *See also* IMPRESSIONIST EXHIBITIONS, SOCIÉTÉ ANONYME DES ARTISTES [127, 183]

☐ *See general bibliography, p. 232.*

Impressionist exhibitions There were eight 'Impressionist' exhibitions, though none of them bore that title. According to VENTURI's

— Pour en apprécier le mérite, ces tableaux doivent être vus de loin.
— Certainement, et c'est pour cela que je m'en éloigne.

A comment from *Charivari* on the first **Impressionist exhibition**. The elderly character tells the young lady that 'To appreciate these paintings you should view them from a distance.' Making for the exit she replies 'That's why I'm going as far away as I possibly can!'

Archives de l'Impressionnisme, 2 vols. (1939 and 1968), the catalogues recorded the following exhibitors and details:

1874 Société anonyme des artistes, peintres, sculpteurs, graveurs, etc. 35 boulevard des Capucines: 15 April – 15 May. Open 10 a.m.–6 p.m. and 8–10 p.m. Works by: ASTRUC (Zacharie); Attendu (Antoine-Ferdinand); BÉLIARD (E.); BOUDIN (Eugène); BRACQUEMOND (Félix); Brandon (Edouard); Bureau (Pierre-Isidore); CALS (Adolphe-Félix); CÉZANNE (Paul); Colin (Gustave); Desbras (Louis); DEGAS (Edgar); GUILLAUMIN (Jean-Baptiste); LATOUCHE (Louis); LEPIC (Ludovic-Napoléon); Lépine (Stanislas); Levert (Jean-Baptiste-Léopold); Mayer (Alfred); De Molins (Auguste); MONET (Claude); Mlle MORISOT (Berthe); Mulot-Durivage; DE NITTIS (Joseph): Ottin (Auguste-Louis-Marie); Ottin (Léon-Auguste); PISSARRO (Camille); RENOIR (Pierre-Auguste); ROUART (Stanislas-Henri); Robert (Léopold); SISLEY (Alfred).

1876 2e. Exposition de peinture 11 rue Peletier: April. Open 10 a.m.–5 p.m. CAILLEBOTTE (Gustave); Degas (Edgar); Monnet [sic] (Claude); Morisot (Berthe); Pissarro (Camille); Renoir (Pierre-Auguste); BAZILLE (Frédéric); Sysley [sic]; Béliard (E.); Beneau (Pierre-Isidore); Cals (Félix-Adolphe); DESBOUTIN; François (Jacques); LEGROS (Alph.); Levert; Lepic; MILLET (J.-B.): Ottin *fils* (Léon-Auguste); Rouart (Stanislas-Henri); TILLOT (Charles).

1877 3e. Exposition de peinture, par MM. Caillebotte, Cals, Cézanne, CORDEY, Degas, Guillaumin, Jacques-François, LAMY, Levert, Maureau, C. Monet, B. Morisot, PIETTE, Pissarro, Renoir, Rouart, Sisley, Tillot. April. Open 10 a.m.–5 p.m. 6 rue Le Peletier, Paris.

1879 4e. Exposition de peinture, par M. Bracquemond, Mme Bracquemond, M. Caillebotte, M. Cals, Mlle CASSATT, MM. Degas, FORAIN, LEBOURG, Monet, Pissarro, Feu Piette, Rouart, H. Somm, Tillot et ZANDOMENEGHI. From 10 April to 11 May. Open 10 a.m.–6 p.m. 28 avenue de l'Opéra, Paris.

1880 5e. Exposition de peinture, par Mme Bracquemond, M. Bracquemond, M. Caillebotte, Mlle Cassatt, MM. Degas, Forain, GAUGUIN, Guillaumin, Lebourg, Levert, Mme Berthe Morisot, MM. Pissarro, RAFFAËLLI, Rouart, Tillot, Eug. Vidal, VIGNON, Zandomeneghi. From 1 to 30 April. Open 10 a.m.–6 p.m. 10 rue des Pyramides, on the corner of the rue Saint-Honoré, Paris.

1881 6e. Exposition de peinture, par Mlle Mary

Cassatt, MM. Degas, Forain, Gauguin, Guillaumin, Mme Berthe Morisot, MM. Pissarro, Raffaëlli, Rouart, Tillot, Eug. Vidal, Vignon, Zandomeneghi. From 2 April to 1 May. Open 10 a.m.–6 p.m. 35 boulevard des Capucines, Paris.

1882 7e. Exposition des artistes indépendants, 251 rue Saint-Honoré (Salons du Panorama de Reichshoffen): March. Caillebotte, Gauguin, Guillaumin, Monet, Morisot, Pissarro, Renoir, Sisley, Vignon.

1886 8e. Exposition de peinture, par Mme Marie Bracquemond, Mlle Mary Cassatt, MM. Degas, Forain, Gauguin, Guillaumin, Mme Berthe Morisot, MM. C. Pissarro, Lucien Pissarro, Odilon Redon, Rouart, SCHUFFE-NECKER, Seurat, Signac, Tillot, Vignon, Zandomeneghi. 1 rue Laffitte (corner of the boulevard des Italiens). From 15 May to 15 June. Open 10 a.m.–6 p.m.

In all eight exhibitions, the main figures of the movement exhibited the following total number of works (the figures in brackets indicate works that were 'on loan', either genuinely or from a dealer such as DURAND-RUEL): Cézanne 18 (1); Degas 113 (40); Monet 118 (55); Morisot 65 (2); Pissarro 170 (41); Renoir 45 (11); Sisley 56 (19).

It is impossible to give a complete picture of attendance figures at all the exhibitions. The first attracted the modest total of 3500 over a complete month, but in 1876 Caillebotte boasted that 500 people a day were visiting the exhibition in the rue Le Peletier. In 1879 admission fees and so forth brought in a total of 10,500 francs, enabling the exhibitors to receive a share-out of 439 francs each. *See also* CRITICS, L'IMPRESSIONNISTE, INDÉPENDANTS, SOCIÉTÉ ANONYME DES ARTISTES, L'UNION *[206]*
□ Venturi, vol. 2 (1939); Denvir (1987)

L'Impressionniste Right from the beginnings of the Impressionist movement there had been talk of publishing a paper or magazine to expound the views of the group, and on the occasion of the third exhibition in 1877 RENOIR took up the project more vigorously, partly as a consequence of the very hostile attacks by Albert WOLFF in *Figaro*. He succeeded in persuading Georges RIVIÈRE to start a weekly journal, *L'Impressionniste; journal d'art,* which appeared on Thursdays and ran for four issues from the 6 until the 28 April. It was mostly written by Rivière himself, with obvious help

Front page of *L' Impressionniste*, with an article praising the 1877 Impressionist exhibition.

from Renoir, and was so patently a propaganda publication that its impact must have been minimal.

The first issue contained a letter to the editor of *Figaro*, bitterly attacking Wolff, and in that of 14 April another onslaught was directed against such diverse publications as *Le Sportsman* and *La Petite République française*, whilst the *Petit Parisien* was praised for its sympathetic review by a writer with the unlikely name of 'M. Flor O'Squarr'. One issue contained a very spirited and convincing defence of CÉZANNE, and Renoir got an even larger share of the laudatory bouquets that were handed out to all of the group. An unexpected amount of space was given to a letter and, subsequently (in the last issue), an article attacking contemporary architectural decoration, especially on the new buildings of the Louvre and the Opéra, and lavishing praise on Les Halles.

Rivière rather ineptly defined IMPRESSIONISM as an art form that contained no historical, biblical or oriental subject-matter, a notion which, though true enough, hardly got to the heart of the matter.

□ G. Rivière, *Renoir et ses amis* (1921); Venturi, vol. 2 (1939)

Indépendants The constant dissatisfaction with the SALON that exercised the French art world and brought about the SALON DES REFUSÉS, found expression again in 1884, when a large body of artists whose works had been rejected got together to found the Groupe des Artistes Indépendants, for the purpose of exhibiting their works and creating an alternative outlet. The group was amorphous in composition and even in its ideals. Anybody who wished to exhibit could do so by payment of a fee, and when they held their first exhibition in an empty barracks in the Jardin des Tuileries, many of the participants had not even submitted their works to the Salon. Amongst them were SEURAT, SIGNAC, and Odilon Redon, who later played an important part in the administration of the group. This was, in fact, originally farcical. There were no accounts; members of the executive committee fought each other; the local police were constantly being called in to settle fights in the exhibition hall, or to arrest members for assault. By 9 June things had got so bad that a meeting of all the members was called with Redon in the chair.

A new body was legally constituted two days later, with the title La Société des Artistes Indépendants, with the aim of 'the suppression of juries, and allowing artists freely to present their works for the judgment of public opinion'. It was to survive and become one of the constituent elements of the French art world. At its first exhibition in December 1884, GUILLAUMIN, as well as Seurat, Signac and GAUGUIN's friend SCHUFFENECKER, took part. By 1890 it had become the main showcase for the work of Gauguin, CÉZANNE and all the varying strands of POST-IMPRESSIONISM, including the works of the Douanier Rousseau. In 1891 the exhibition contained a small memorial show, arranged by Signac, to VAN GOGH, who had killed himself in July. The name of the group must not be confused with that which, on DEGAS' suggestion, the Impressionists had first used to describe themselves. *See also* SOCIÉTÉ ANONYME DES ARTISTES

□ Rewald (1973); J. Rewald, *Post-Impressionism* (1956)

Institut de France The combination of the five academies created by Richelieu in the 17th c., consisting of the Académie Française

Renoir's *Pont des Arts, Paris*, 1867, shows the dome of the **Institut de France**.

(entrusted with the maintenance of the purity of the French language and the creation of an as yet uncompleted dictionary), and the academies of 'Inscriptions et Belles Lettres', of Science, of Fine Arts, and of Moral and Political Science. In 1795 the academies were reorganized, and their individual titles changed to 'Institut', as it was felt that the older name had royalist connotations. With the restoration, however, the name of Académie was re-applied to the constituent parts, and the body as a whole came to be known as the Institut.

By the middle of the 19th c. the Beaux-Arts section consisted of 40 members with a perpetual secretary; its main functions were to look after the Schools of Fine Art in Paris and Rome, and 'to amend and correct those matters that fall within its province; it cautions or requests help from the governmental authority to which it owes many benefits in the world of art'. Whereas under the *ancien régime* the main purpose of the fine arts academy had been to enhance the status of the artist and secure support for his work, by the 19th c. the emphasis had changed to teaching, with all the imposition of stylistic uniformity that this implied (*see* ACADEMIC ART). *See also* BESNARD, ECOLE DES BEAUX-ARTS, GÉRÔME

□ Boime (1986)

Italy The most obvious link between the Impressionists and Italy was DEGAS, who was a member of an Italian family which had a *palazzo* in Naples and a country residence near Capo di Monte. His father's sister married Gennaro BELLELLI, who had been forced to leave Naples in 1849 as a consequence of his involvement in the revolt against the Bourbons, in which Degas' cousin, Gustavo Morbilli, had been shot. The painter had an almost tribal loyalty to

Italy: Silvestro Lega's *The Pergola* of 1868 is reminiscent of Bazille's *The Artist's Family on a Terrace near Montpellier*, painted in the same year.

his relatives, and painted many of their portraits (e.g. *Monsieur et Madame Edmondo Morbilli*, 1865; Boston Museum of Fine Arts, *The Bellelli Family*, 1858; Musée d'Orsay, *La Duchesse de Montejasi*, 1868; Cleveland Museum of Art – she was his aunt). But it was not just family loyalty that drew him to Italy. He spent a good deal of time there. At the beginning of his career as an artist he lived in Italy from 1856 to 1859, working in Rome, Naples and Florence, as well as visiting other centres, such as Siena, Pisa and Venice. He was deeply influenced by Italian art of the 15th c., copying the works of Mantegna (there is a copy by him of the Mantegna *Crucifixion* from the Louvre in the Musée des Beaux-Arts at Tours), Sebastiano del Piombo and others. He was strongly supportive, too, of fellow Italian artists, and created considerable ill-feeling at the seventh Impressionist exhibition because he insisted on the inclusion of DE NITTIS, ZANDOMENEGHI and RAFFAËLLI (though the last-named was a French citizen).

MANET first went to Italy in 1853 with his brother Eugène, visiting Venice, Florence – where he copied works by Ghirlandaio, Fra Angelico and Filippo Lippi – and Rome. He returned again in 1857 in the company of a sculptor, Eugène-Cyrille Brunet, and at Florence he asked permission to copy Andrea del Sarto's frescoes in the cloisters of the Annunziata. In the summer of 1875 he went to Venice with TISSOT, and they stayed at the Palazzo Barbaro, which was (and still is) owned by the American Curtis family; the family also gave hospitality to Henry JAMES and to SARGENT, whose diploma painting in the Royal Academy shows the interior of the Palazzo. On the whole, Manet does not seem to have found this visit especially inspiring. He admired Carpaccio, as well as the Titians and Tintorettos of the Scuola di San Rocco but, according to the painter Charles Troché, who met him there, he was incapable of appreciating the Italian genius as such: 'These Italians bore after a time, with their allegories and their *Gerusalemme Liberata* and their *Orlando Furioso*, and all that noisy rubbish. A painter can say all he wants to with fruit or flowers, or even clouds.'

When MONET visited Venice in 1908 he was more concerned with painting than with seeing the sights, and he produced a number of especially incandescent views, notably *The Ducal Palace* (Brooklyn Museum), most of which he finished in his studio at GIVERNY.

The impact of Impressionism on Italian art is slightly complicated by the fact that, when Romanticism had lost its initial impact on Italian artists in the early 1850s, they started to move in directions that very roughly paralleled those of their French contemporaries. The Macchiaioli group, as their name implies (*macchia*, stain or blot), adopted a technique marked by its 'sketchiness' and use of patches of colour, and were self-consciously opposed to the academic tradition. They too specialized in painting out-of-doors, and works by artists such as Giovanni Fattori (1825–1908) or Giuseppe Abbati (1836–68) would not have looked out of place in the SALON DES REFUSÉS, or even in the Impressionist exhibitions. But by the 1870s this latent affinity had become more explicit. Silvestro Lega (1826–1900) reacted directly and immediately to the work of Manet and others, even though he had not travelled outside Italy. His portrait of Eleanora Tomassi (*c.*1884; Ojetti Collection, Florence) is very closely based on Manet's *Jeanne, Spring* (1882), which had a considerable success at the Salon; it was reproduced on the cover of Ernest HOSCHEDÉ's *Impressions de mon voyage au Salon* of 1882 and, in a more widely disseminated form, as an illustration to an article by Antonin PROUST in the *Gazette des Beaux-Arts* of June in the same year.

A powerful intermediary between Impressionism and Italian artists was Diego MARTELLI, who in 1879 gave a lecture on Manet and the Impressionists (subsequently published in pamphlet form) to the *Circolo filologico* in Livorno; ten years later he wrote a lengthy commemorative article on Manet in the journal *Fieramosca*. He also wrote extensively in the popular press, praising especially Monet and his own close friend Degas. In September 1878 Martelli persuaded PISSARRO and Degas to send pictures to Florence for the next exhibition of Promotrice, an annual event at which the Macchiaioli group had always been very much in evidence. The pictures were not very well received, however, even by the progressives, and eventually Martelli bought them himself (they are now in the Galleria d'Arte Moderna in the Pitti Palace in Florence).

Another influential Italian critic and painter, Adriano Cecioni (1838–86), in a series of essays mainly concerned with defending the Macchiaioli, published in book form in 1905, also vigorously expounded some of the basic doctrines of the Impressionists. But for many years Impressionism as such was coolly received in Italy. To Italian taste it was too amorphous in outline, too crude in its handling, too unclassical. When acceptance finally came in the early part of the 20th c. it was due, in part at least, to the Venice Biennale, inaugurated in 1895, which began to show an increasing number of Impressionist works, culminating in a one man RENOIR exhibition in 1910. *See also* ANTECEDENTS, VENTURI *[30, 110, 136, 153, 181, 230]*

□ R. Longhi, 'L'Impressionismo e il gusto degli italiani', intro. to Italian trans. of J. Rewald, *History of Impressionism* (1949); E.G. Holt, *The Art of All Nations 1850–1873; The Emerging Role of Exhibitions and Critics* (1981); N. Broude, *The Macchiaioli* (1987)

Italy: Degas' copy of Mantegna's *Crucifixion* (1456–59) in the Louvre, which he painted in 1868–69.

J

James, Henry (1843–1916) American writer and novelist, educated in New York, London,

Henry **James** on the steps of the Villa Borghese in Rome in 1899.

The cover of *Paris illustré* for May 1866 shows the popularity of things **Japanese** at an early date.

Paris and Geneva. He lived most of his life in ENGLAND and was naturalized in 1915. Interested in art, he contributed occasional articles to American papers on the subject. In 1877 he wrote an interesting piece on the third IMPRESSIONIST EXHIBITION for the *New York Tribune*. Although he rather rashly compared the Impressionists with the Pre-Raphaelites, he pointed out that 'The beautiful to them is what the supernatural is to the Positivists – a metaphysical notion which can only get one into a muddle and is to be severely left alone. Let it alone, they say, and it will come at its own pleasure; the painter's proper field is the actual and to give a vivid impression of how a thing looks at a particular moment is the essence of his mission.' James was very friendly with SARGENT, sharing with him the hospitality of the Curtis family at the Palazzo Barbaro in Venice (*see* ITALY), and doing much to further his career. *See also* IMPRESSIONISM

□ H. James, *The Painter's Eye*, ed. J.J. Sweeney (1956), *Letters*, ed. L. Edel, vols. 2, 3 and 4 (1978–84); M. Easton, *Writers and artists in Paris* (1964)

Japanese art 'Hiroshige is a marvellous Impressionist', wrote PISSARRO in 1893, and the influence of Japanese art on the Impressionists has long been recognized. The intermittent cultural and commercial contact between Europe and the Far East, which had been going on since classical times, had accelerated in the 18th c. and was rapidly promoted in the 19th c. by the invention of the steamship, which made contact quicker and easier, and by the forcible opening up of Japan by the Americans. Brightly coloured Japanese prints began to arrive in European ports in the 1850s – MONET bought his first at Le Havre in 1856, and by the 1860s La Porte chinoise and L'Empire chinoise in PARIS were two of the leading shops selling oriental wares of all kinds. Both were frequented by BAUDELAIRE, the GONCOURTS, ZOLA, BRACQUEMOND, TISSOT, WHISTLER and MANET. At this point it was contemporary prints that were available; works by artists such as Utamaro, Hiroshige and Hokusai were not generally imported until the mid-1870s.

Japanese influence existed on two levels. On the more superficial plane it provided a background to life and props for paintings: Whistler collected blue and white china and painted his mistress in a kimono; there is a Japanese painting in DEGAS' portrait of Tissot, and two

Japanese prints are featured in Manet's portrait of Zola. Monet had a large collection of prints – still to be seen at GIVERNY, where he decorated his dining room with white damask cloth covered with Japanese designs – and between 1875 and 1876 he painted *La Japonaise* (Museum of Fine Arts, Boston), in which the Japanese element is confined to the dress and the pose. He later described the picture as 'rubbish', and RENOIR was clearly also embarrassed by the oriental background he introduced into his portrait of *Madame Charpentier and her Children* (1878; Metropolitan Museum, New York).

On a creative and technical level, however, the Japanese impact was far more significant, though it would be more accurate to describe it as providing reinforcement for explorations and innovations to which most of the Impressionists had already addressed themselves, rather than as an 'influence'. A concern with depicting contemporary, often urban life; very close-up viewpoints; a dynamic tension between figures and space; the cutting off of figures and objects by the margins of the picture; the use of devices such as bridges to introduce the spectator into the pictorial space; the delicately skilful contrast between blank and worked-over spaces; the use of sinuously definitive lines: all these were aspects that the Impressionists found in the art of the Japanese, and all were aspects that either extended or confirmed their own innovations.

They were influenced in varying degrees, but the most clearly discernible reactions are in the compositions of Monet, and in the technical devices and choice of subject-matter in many of the works of Degas, who was especially susceptible to the world of courtesans, actors and dancers depicted in the transitory world of the masters of *Ukiyo-e*. It is also worth noting that many of the popular Japanese prints shared stylistic characteristics with those popular French prints, the *Images d'Epinal*, which had influenced COURBET and, through him, Manet. Although Japanese art had no discernible influence on Renoir or CÉZANNE, there was enough evidence of it in the work of their colleagues for the BATIGNOLLES group to be known as 'the Japanese of painting'. According to CASTAGNARY in an article he wrote for *Le Siècle* in April 1874, Monet reflected a general sentiment when he said 'Their refinement of taste has always pleased me, and I approve of their aesthetic doctrine which evokes the presence of something by a shadow; and the whole by means of a fragment.' *See also* ANTECEDENTS, BURTY, DURET, IMPRESSIONISM, PERSPECTIVE, PHOTOGRAPHY *[47, 65, 161, 210, 212, 223, 224]*
□ C.F. Ives, *The Great Wave: the influence of Japanese woodcuts on French prints* (1974); *Japonisme; Japanese influence on French art, 1854–1910*, Cleveland Museum of Art, Ohio, exhibition catalogue (1975); J. Dufwa, *Winds from the East. A Study in the Art of Manet, Degas, Monet and Whistler 1856–86* (1981); M. Eidelberg, 'Bracquemond, Delâtre and the Discovery of Japanese Prints', *Burlington Magazine* (April 1981)

Jongkind, Johann Barthold (1819–91) Born at Latrop near Rotterdam, he studied art at The Hague and was awarded a scholarship that allowed him to move to PARIS in 1843. Here he met Eugène-Gabriel Isabey, who had a considerable influence on him. Particularly attracted to painting the Dutch and French coasts, he was a frequent visitor to HONFLEUR, where he came into contact with BOUDIN, MONET and others. With Monet he established a lasting friendship which was of mutual benefit. He was also close to COURBET, COROT and Alfred STEVENS. He had his first work accepted at the SALON in 1848 and received a medal for his contribution to that of 1852. After several visits to HOLLAND, he finally settled in Paris in 1860, but was bedevilled by problems. Afflicted with a profound persecution neurosis, he was for some considerable time an alcoholic, and was nearly always on the verge of penury, though his artist friends were especially supportive of him, for he seems to have had a particularly engaging personality. He exhibited at the SALON DES REFUSÉS in 1863, and made visits to Honfleur in 1864 and 1865, when he was temporarily relieved of his psychological problems by a moustachioed harridan (according to the GONCOURTS), who looked after him with tender affection. His paintings also began to have a modest financial success, and in 1878 he moved to Côte-Saint-André near Grenoble, where he lived for the rest of his life, apart from occasional excursions to Paris and Provence. In 1889, however, he had a relapse into his old afflictions, and died in the asylum of Saint-Rambert near Grenoble.

CASTAGNARY said of him 'I love this fellow Jongkind; he is an artist to his fingertips. I find in him a rare and delicate sensibility. With him everything lies in the *impression*' (article in L'ARTISTE, 1863). There can be no doubt that he had a profound influence on many of the

Jongkind's seascape *La Ciotat* was painted in 1880. The influence of his work on Monet is clearly apparent.

Impressionists, especially Monet. Although he was not a PLEIN-AIRISTE, his sense of colour and atmosphere was transmitted spontaneously into his canvases and he had inherited from the Dutch school a feeling for light that he communicated to those of the Impressionists with whom he came into contact. He was concerned primarily with the appearance of things, not with their conceived reality (*The Coast of Sainte-Adresse*, 1862; Rijksmuseum, Amsterdam). *See also* LUXEMBOURG, MUSÉE DU
□ E. Moreau-Nélaton, *Jongkind raconté par lui-même* (1918); G. Besson, *J.B. Jongkind 1819–1891* (1945); V. Hefting, *Jongkind d'après sa correspondance* (1969)

Joyant, Maurice (1864–1930) A friend of Toulouse-Lautrec since childhood, he went to work as manager for the dealers BOUSSOD AND VALADON in 1891. He replaced THÉO VAN GOGH, who had developed the connection with the Impressionists and with such newcomers as GAUGUIN. The owners of the firm were anxious that he should break this tradition, but he refused to do so, lending works by MONET and others to the Belgian critic MAUS for the exhibitions of Les Vingt in Brussels (*see* BELGIUM) and arranging a very important retrospective exhibition of the works of MORISOT in

May 1892. The following year, however, largely because he was not allowed to replace Impressionist works that he had sold from the firm's diminishing stock, he left Boussod and Valadon and went into partnership with DEGAS' friend Michel MANZI. Joyant had a considerable private income and built up an important collection of works by the Impressionists and their immediate successors. After the death of Toulouse-Lautrec he was asked to catalogue his works and in 1926 produced what is still regarded as an authoritative book on that artist (*Henri de Toulouse-Lautrec*, 2 vols., Paris, 1926–27).

K

Khalil Bey (1831–79) Immensely rich, a spectacular gambler, an Egyptian-born liberal who wanted to impose some kind of democratic government on the Ottoman empire, Khalil Bey was a man of considerable culture. He was appointed Turkish commissioner to the Exposition Universelle held in Paris in 1855, and after acting as ambassador first to Athens and then St Petersburg, he returned to Paris in a private capacity, becoming one of its most colourful residents and building up an enormous but heterogeneous art collection.

He had been initiated into the art world by his mistress, Jeanne de Tourbey, Comtesse de Loynes, who was a friend of Sainte-Beuve, Flaubert, Renan and other leading French writers. Through them she got to know COURBET, whose works she recommended to the Bey; he bought the notorious *Les Dormeuses* (1866; Musée d'Orsay) and several important works by Ingres, DELACROIX and Chassériau, as well as a number of old masters, some of them of very dubious authenticity. He became one of the main patrons of DURAND-RUEL's gallery and was led into the purchase of works by ROUS-SEAU, COROT, DAUBIGNY and others. Gambling, however, led to his downfall, and in 1868 his collection was sold at auction. Théodore Rousseau's *Les Châtaigniers*, for which he had paid Durand-Ruel 14,000 francs, was bought by the dealer for 27,000 francs and later sold by him for 40,000 (in 1912 the Louvre paid 270,000 francs for it). He continued his career as a gambler and man-about-town, but eventually returned to the Middle East to pursue his political ideals, and died there of syphilis, apparently contracted in Russia.

□ F. Haskell, *Past and Present in Art and Taste* (1987)

L

Lafenestre, Georges (1837–1919) Poet and art critic, who was a regular contributor to the *Moniteur universel* from 1868, and whose collected art criticism, *La Peinture et la sculpture aux Salons de 1868 à 1872*, was published in 1881. Although critical of certain technical details of the works of the Impressionists, his judgments were, on the whole, favourable. From 1870 he was an official in the Ministry of Fine Arts; in 1886 he became assistant curator, and later curator, of paintings in the Louvre.

□ Venturi (1939); Hamilton (1954)

Laforgue, Jules (1860–87) A poet who was a

member of the group consisting of Verlaine, Rimbaud and Lautréamont. The writer Paul Bourget secured him a post as reader to the Kaiser's grandmother, and while in GERMANY he saw an exhibition of Impressionist paintings, about which he wrote a most illuminating study; it appeared in his posthumous works published in Paris in 1900.

□ J. Laforgue, *Oeuvres complètes* (1925); J.U. Halpérin, *Félix Fénéon; Aesthete and Anarchist in Fin-de-Siècle Paris* (1988)

Lamy (Franc-Lamy), Pierre (1855–1919) A friend of RENOIR, he started at the ECOLE DES BEAUX-ARTS as a pupil of Lehmann, but with others he staged a revolt, as a result of which they were expelled. They wrote to MANET, asking to become his pupils, a request he refused, partly because of the nature of his own personality, partly because he was anxious not to offend the establishment. The group then became regular visitors to Renoir's studio in the rue Cortot in MONTMARTRE. Renoir painted Lamy as the seated figure on the extreme right in the *Dance at the Moulin de la Galette* (1876; Musée d'Orsay). Lamy attended the Impressionists' dinners given by MURER, and participated in the 1877 exhibition, but by the 1880s had lost contact with the movement. [187]

□ E. Bénézit, *Dictionnaire des peintres, sculpteurs, dessinateurs et graveurs* (1966); Rewald (1973)

Lane, Sir Hugh Percy (1875–1915) One of the first of the few great British collectors of Impressionism, he started buying from DUR-AND-RUEL in 1905, intending to build up a collection of modern French art for a public art gallery in Dublin. His purchases included MANET's *Portrait of Eva Gonzalès* (1870) and *La Musique aux Tuileries* (1862); *Les Parapluies* (c.1884) by RENOIR and works by MONET, PISSARRO, BOUDIN, COROT, COURBET, Théodore ROUSSEAU and DEGAS (*Beach Scene*, 1869). He offered the whole collection of 39 works to the National Gallery in London on loan until the completion of the Dublin gallery, but they were relegated to the cellars until two years after his death on the *Lusitania* in 1915. The paintings were the subject of a contentious law suit between the National Galleries of London and Ireland, which dragged on for half a century. *See also* ENGLAND [90, 102]

□ R. Fry, 'The Sir Hugh Lane Pictures at the National Gallery', *Burlington Magazine* (April 1917); Cooper (1954)

Sargent's portrait of the collector Sir Hugh **Lane**, painted in 1906.

Latouche, Louis (1823–97) A paint-dealer who had a small shop on the corner of the rue Laffitte and the rue LaFayette, he was very interested in contemporary art. He became acquainted with MONET and others, whose paintings he would exhibit in the windows of his shop, and would sometimes sell. When in 1869 he showed Monet's *Terrace at Sainte-Adresse* (Metropolitan Museum, New York) it attracted crowds in front of the window. He also organized evening parties, over his shop, for people with interests similar to his own. Latouche was himself a painter; he exhibited at the IMPRESSIONIST EXHIBITIONS (at which he sometimes acted as a steward) and was deeply involved in the various organizing committees. In 1875 he also joined L'UNION, PISSARRO's attempt to create an alternative exhibiting body.
□ Venturi (1939); Rewald (1973)

Laurent, Méry (Anne-Rose Louviot) (1849–1900) Described as 'an indifferent actress, but a courtesan of genius', she was kept first by Marshal Canrobert, then passed to the enigmatic Dr Thomas W. Evans, one of the most influential characters in Second Empire society – a role he owed to the fact that he was dentist to the imperial family.

Méry was especially enamoured of writers, artists and musicians. She was the great love of MALLARMÉ, had an affair with François Coppée, and, towards the end of her life, was involved with the homosexual musician and composer Reynaldo Hahn, whom she made her executor. It was through him that she met Marcel Proust, who was enraptured and very largely based Odette Swann on her.

She was introduced to MANET by Alphonse Hirsch (whose daughter figures in *The Railroad*, 1872–73; National Gallery of Art, Washington) on the occasion of the exhibition he staged in his studio in 1876 to show the works that had been rejected by the SALON in that year. She expressed great pleasure in seeing the pictures, and the rapport between them was so immediate and profound that in gratitude Manet gave her one of the versions of *The Execution of the Emperor Maximilian* (1867; Ny Carlsberg Glyptotek, Copenhagen). George MOORE insinuated that she had an affair with the painter, but whether or not that was the case, they remained very close. During his last illness she constantly sent him flowers and delicacies and, after his death, put lilacs on his grave. She features in *Autumn* (1881; Musée des Beaux-Arts, Nancy), one of a set of four paintings representing the seasons, commissioned from Manet by Antonin PROUST. She also figures in *Woman in Furs; Portrait of Méry Laurent* (1882; Private collection). At the posthumous sale of Manet's works, Méry bought *Autumn* for 1500 francs, to join the other works by him she possessed, and on her death she bequeathed it to her native city of Nancy. She also bought works by GAUGUIN from the sale he organized before his departure to the East. *[215]*
□ G. Moore, *Modern Painting* (1898); J. Blanche, *Manet* (1924); K. Adler, *Manet* (1986)

Lebourg, Albert-Charles (1849–1928) After studying at the ECOLE DES BEAUX-ARTS and working in an architect's office at Rouen, he spent two years as a drawing master in ALGIERS. There, on his own initiative, he developed a painting style that had remarkable analogies with that of the Impressionists, and he exhibited with them in 1879 and 1880.
□ E. Bénézit, *Dictionnaire des peintres, sculpteurs, dessinateurs et graveurs* (1966); Rewald (1973)

Le Coeur, Jacques (1832–82) Son of a successful architect, and himself trained as an architect, he decided to become a painter and in 1865 met

Lebourg, *Port d'Alger*, 1876. He explored light and colour independently from the Impressionists.

RENOIR, with whom he was to have a close friendship. At this time Jacques' mistress was Clémence Tréhot, with whose 17-year-old sister Lise TRÉHOT Renoir was to fall in love. Over a period of eight years the Le Coeur family and the Tréhot sisters played an important part in the artist's life, acting as models (*Lise in a Hat*, 1867; Barnes Foundation, Merrion, Pa.; *Jules le Coeur in the Forest of Fontainebleau*, 1866; Museo de Arte Moderna, São Paulo) and providing him with contacts and hospitality.

In 1865 Jacques acquired a house and studio at Marlotte (*see* CABARET DE LA MÈRE ANTHONY), where Renoir frequently worked with him, and in the following year he had a painting accepted at the SALON. In the following year Jacques secured a commission for Renoir to paint two ceilings in the house that his brother Charles had designed for Prince Bibesco in the boulevard Latour-Maubourg. These have not survived, but they seem to have been painted in the styles of Fragonard and Tiepolo. Renoir also painted portraits of other members of the Le Coeur family. It was probably through them that he met the CHARPENTIERS, who were their relatives, and who were to become his enthusiastic patrons and supporters. The Le Coeurs also befriended SISLEY, whom they took on a holiday to Berck on the Channel coast in 1866. Renoir's connection with the Le Coeurs ceased rather suddenly in about 1874. There was a tradition in the Le Coeur family (recounted by Douglas Cooper), that it was because the painter had sent a love note to Jacques' 16-year-old niece, Christine. [37]

☐ D. Cooper, 'Renoir, Lise and the LeCoeur family', *Burlington Magazine* (May and Sept.–Oct. 1959)

Lecoq de Boisbaudran, Horace (1802–97) A teacher of DRAWING at the Municipal Art School in the rue de l'Ecole-de-Médecine in PARIS, he had a profound influence on the development of drawing techniques, which went beyond France. In addition to the then standard practice of drawing from casts and engravings, he introduced his students to two new methods. He encouraged the development of visual memory by making them draw objects that had been removed from their presence at the time when they were drawing them. He also took them on outings, where they were encouraged to draw out-of-doors in a more relaxed way than was possible in the studio. In 1847 he published *L'Education de la mémoire pittoresque*, which was later republished with a laudatory introduction by Rodin; in 1875 there followed his *Sommaire d'un méthode pour l'enseignement du dessin*, and in 1877 *L'Enseignement artistique*. Amongst his pupils, in addition to Rodin, were LEGROS – who transplanted his methods to the Slade School in London, where they influenced two generations of artists –, FANTIN-LATOUR and Dalou. His attitude to drawing clearly had an effect on many of the Impressionists, notably DEGAS. *See also* LHERMITTE

☐ H.L. Lecoq de Boisbaudran, *L'Education de la mémoire pittoresque et de la formation de l'artiste*, ed. L.D. Durand (1914); Boime (1986)

Leenhoff, Léon (1852–1925) Although passed off as the brother of MANET's wife Suzanne, he was almost certainly the son of Manet, who had been having an affair with the Dutch-born Suzanne since 1850. He did not marry her until October 1863, after the death of his father, from whom the boy's existence had been kept hidden. Léon featured in many of Manet's paintings: in the background of *La Pêche* (1861; Metropolitan Museum, New York), in *Reading* (1865–73; Musée d'Orsay) and *Luncheon in the Studio* (1868; Bayerische Staatsgemäldesammlungen, Munich). *See also* HOLLAND, MUSIC

☐ A. Tabarant, *Manet et ses oeuvres* (1947); 'Letters of Edouard Manet to his Wife during the Siege of Paris', ed. M. Curtiss, *Apollo* (June 1981)

Legros, Alphonse (1837–1911) After a penurious youth, when he studied under LECOQ DE

Manet's *Luncheon in the Studio* of 1868 portrays Léon **Leenhoff** - also shown in the photograph, right – in his putative father's studio. Faure is seated on the right of the painting.

BOISBAUDRAN, he had some considerable success at the SALON, and several of his works were bought by the state. In 1863, however, he participated in the SALON DES REFUSÉS, partly under the influence of his friend WHISTLER. He came to London in the same year and taught first at the South Kensington School of Fine Art and then at the Slade, where he exerted a great influence on those artists who were to become the nucleus of the New English Art Club (*see* ENGLAND). Although he could in no way be thought of as an Impressionist, on the invitation of DEGAS he participated in the second IMPRESSIONIST EXHIBITION and was an invaluable contact between Paris and London in the dissemination of Impressionist ideas. PISSARRO

was very dubious about his teaching methods, especially when LUCIEN, his son, was working under him. Legros' own paintings were rather sentimental genre scenes (*The Angelus*, 1859; Musée d'Orsay). *See also* ILLUSTRATION, PRINTS, SICKERT *[23]*

□ L. Bénédite, *Alphonse Legros* (1900); A. Salaman, *Legros* (1926)

Lepic, Vicomte Ludovic-Napoléon (1839–89) Painter and engraver, he participated in the first and second IMPRESSIONIST EXHIBITIONS, having met MONET and BAZILLE at the atelier GLEYRE, and became very friendly with DEGAS. CAILLEBOTTE, in a letter to PISSARRO in January 1881, commented 'Lepic, heaven knows, has no talent', and few of his works, which were mainly seascapes, seem to have survived. However, he used his not inconsiderable wealth and influence to promote the careers of his friends to the best of his ability – though he made strenuous efforts to have CÉZANNE excluded from the joint exhibitions.

□ Venturi (1939); E. Bénézit, *Dictionnaire des peintres, sculpteurs, dessinateurs et graveurs* (1966); *Degas*, Grand Palais, Paris, exhibition catalogue (1988)

Degas' *Place de la Concorde, c.* 1875 (now lost), showing **Lepic** and his daughters.

Lerolle, Henry (1852–1929) A conventional painter, who exhibited at the SALON, a keen amateur musician and a *littérateur*, Lerolle became acquainted with several of the Impressionists at Berthe MORISOT's Thursday dinners.

He became very friendly with both DEGAS and RENOIR, buying their works on an impressive scale and commissioning Renoir in 1896 to paint portraits of his two daughters, Yvonne and Christine. In one of these two works by Degas are featured; in the other, a work by Renoir and two by Degas appear. The two daughters later married the sons of Degas' friend Henri ROUART, and their brother, Ernest, married Julie Manet.
□ Roberts and Roberts (1987); *Degas*, Grand Palais, Paris, exhibition catalogue (1988)

Leroy, Louis (1812–85) Engraver, genre painter, art critic and popular playwright, it was he who coined the word 'Impressionist' in his review of the 1874 exhibition (*see* IMPRESSIONISM), which appeared in CHARIVARI, a periodical to which he contributed pieces illustrated by himself. He had already launched an attack on MANET's *Bullfighter* when it was shown in the SALON of 1864. *[114]*
□ Hamilton (1954); E. Bénézit, *Dictionnaire des peintres, sculpteurs, dessinateurs et graveurs* (1966); Rewald (1973)

Lhermitte, Léon (1844–1925) A pupil of LECOQ DE BOISBAUDRAN, he built up a reputation as a painter of peasant subjects and had a considerable influence on VAN GOGH; he was famous, too, for his decorative paintings. Using a sometimes vaguely Impressionist technique, he was invited to exhibit at the 1879 Impressionist exhibition, though he did not do so, and his great popularity, which extended to Britain, owed much to the belated recognition of MILLET. He was in fairly close contact with DEGAS in the period between 1879 and 1883.
□ G. Norman, *Nineteenth-Century Painters and Painting; a Dictionary* (1977)

Literature The sharing of a common historic experience should, and indeed often does, establish bonds between various art forms. The MUSIC of Beethoven, the writings of Goethe and the paintings of Turner have much in common. Never, however, had painting and literature been so closely linked as they were in France from the middle of the 19th c. onwards. The emergence of a self-aware avant-garde, sharing common enemies in both officialdom and the 'philistines', prompted alliances and fostered already latent shared attitudes and even techniques. This *entente* was further encouraged by such phenomena as the Parisian CAFÉS, like

— « IMPRESSION, *Soleil levant.* »
— *Impression*, j'en étais sûr. Je me disais aussi, puisque je suis impressionné, il doit y avoir de l'impression là-dedans... Et quelle liberté, quelle aisance dans la facture! Le papier peint à l'état embryonnaire est encore plus fait que cette marine-là !
— Cependant qu'auraient dit Michalon, Bidault, Boisselier et Berlin devant cette toile impressionnante?
— Ne me parlez pas de ces hideux croûtons ! hurla le père Vincent. En rentrant chez moi, je crèverai leurs devants de cheminée !
Le malheureux reniait ses dieux !
En vain je cherchai à ranimer sa raison expirante en lui montrant une *Levée d'étang*, de M. Rouart, à laquelle il manque peu de chose pour être tout à fait bien ; une étude de château à Sannois, de M. Ottin, très - lumineuse et très-fine ; mais l'horrible l'attirait. *La blanchisseuse*, si mal blanchie, de M. Degas, lui faisait pousser des cris d'admiration.
Sisley lui-même lui paraissait mièvre et précieux. Pour flatter sa manie et de peur de l'irriter, je cherchais ce qu'il y avait de passable dans les tableaux à impression et je reconnaissais sans trop de peine que le pain, les raisins et la chaise du *Déjeuner*, de M. Monet, étaient de bons morceaux de peinture. Mais il repoussait ces concessions.
— Non, non ! s'écriait-il. Monet faiblit là. Il sacrifie aux faux dieux de Meissonnier. Trop fait, trop fait, trop fait !... Parlez-moi de la *Moderne Olympia*, à la bonne heure !
Hélas ! allez la voir, celle-là ! Une femme pliée en deux à qui une négresse enlève le dernier voile pour l'offrir dans toute sa laideur aux regards charmés d'un fantoche brun. Vous vous souvenez de l'*Olympia*, de M. Manet? Eh bien, c'était un chef-d'œuvre de dessin, de correction, de fini, comparée à celle de M. Cézanne.
Enfin le vase déborda. Le cerveau cla-sique du père Vincent, attaqué de trop de côtés à la fois, se détraqua complètement. Il s'arrêta devant le gardien de Paris qui veille sur tous ces trésors, et, le prenant pour un portrait, se mit à m'en faire une critique très-accentuée.
— Est-il assez mauvais! fit il en haussant les épaules. De face il a deux yeux... et un nez... et une bouche !... Ce ne sont pas les impressionnistes qui auraient ainsi sacrifié au détail. Avec ce que le peintre a dépensé d'inutilités dans cette figure, Monet eût fait vingt gardiens de Paris !
— Si vous circulez un peu, vous, lui dit le *portrait*,
— Vous l'entendez ! il ne lui manque même pas la parole !... — Faut-il que le cuistre qui l'a pignoché ait passé du temps à le faire !
Et pour donner à son esthétique tout le sérieux convenable, le père Vincent se mit à danser du scalp devant le gardien ahuri, en criant d'une voix étranglée :
— Hugh !... Je suis l'impression qui marche, le couteau à palette vengeur, le *Boulevard des Capucines*, de Monet, la *Maison du pendu* et la *Moderne Olympia*, de M. Cézanne ! Hugh ! hugh ! hugh !

LOUIS LEROY.

Leroy's article in *Charivari*, 1874, which first gave the movement its name.

the Guerbois and the Nouvelle-Athènes, common meeting-grounds for artists, writers and journalists. The development of 'Bohemian' quarters further enhanced physical and social proximity. The BATIGNOLLES quarter, for instance, housed at various times BAUDELAIRE, MANET, RENOIR, DAUDET, CAILLEBOTTE, PISSARRO and Armand SILVESTRE.

Literature: Degas' *Miss La La au cirque Fernando* 1879, was described in a story by Huysmans.

EDMOND DE GONCOURT

MANETTE

SALOMON

PIÉCE EN NEUF TABLEAUX

PRÉCÉDÉE D'UN PROLOGUE

Tirée du Roman

D'EDMOND ET JULES DE GONCOURT

PARIS

G. CHARPENTIER ET E. FASQUELLE, ÉDITEURS

11, RUE DE GRENELLE, 11

1896

Tous droits réservés.

Literature: the title page of E. de Goncourt's play about the life of artists under the Second Empire.

Above all others in his bringing together of art and literature was Stéphane MALLARMÉ. The friend of Manet, about whom he wrote an article, 'The Impressionists and Edouard Manet', in the London magazine *Art Monthly Review and Photographic Folio* (30 September 1876), he himself translated WHISTLER's *Ten o'clock Lecture* into French, and Manet illustrated his translation of Poe's *The Raven*. His portrait was painted by Manet, Whistler, GAUGUIN and Edvard Munch. His Tuesday night salons in his flat at 89 rue de Rome brought together many painters and writers of differing allegiances, including the Impressionists (among them MORISOT, to whom he was especially attached), and others such as Strindberg, George MOORE, Redon and MOREAU.

DEGAS was, for a considerable period, a close friend of Mallarmé and took a remarkably fine photograph of him and Renoir in front of a mirror, which reflects the photographer himself, as well as Mallarmé's wife and daughter. The poet had written about Degas' work, 'He is a master of a new abstract form, if I may use a

word which he himself would reject in his daily conversation'; but Degas was too prickly in his social relations and, failing to understand Mallarmé's later work, gradually distanced himself from the poet. Paul Valéry, who was part of the Mallarmé circle, also had a great admiration for Degas: 'This man gives me infinite pleasure', he wrote to André Gide in 1886, 'and not only in his paintings. He has such an intelligent air.' He was anxious to dedicate one of his works to him, but Degas turned down the request. Degas' relationship to literature is extremely interesting and, though it cannot be taken as typical, it reflects the intimacy and the complexity of the connections between the Impressionists and contemporary writers. He himself wrote a number of sonnets, and was involved in active collaboration with Ludovic HALÉVY on *La Famille Cardinal* (1880) and the stage production of *La Cigale* in 1877. Degas' early works abound in literary themes, but they are mostly of a romantic or historical nature. By the 1870s he had become fascinated by realist writers such as DURANTY, ZOLA, the GONCOURTS and HUYS-

MANS, echoes of whose works are to be found in his own. On the other hand, however, although he knew Daudet and Maupassant well, he does not seem to have been influenced by their writings or attitudes in any way. In his choice of themes, and in his rather disdainful realism, Degas was closest to Edmond de Goncourt, and both of them were aware of the fact, seeing each other almost as rivals. In 1891, for instance, Goncourt wrote somewhat defensively about the painter in his *Journal*, 'He is enamoured of modernity, and within this context he has concentrated on washerwomen and dancers. I find this quite an admirable choice, especially since it was I who, in *Manette Salomon* [1867], have written about these two professions, as providing the most pictorial examples of woman in our age that an artist could think of.' If Goncourt saw Degas as a kind of plagiarist, there are examples of influences working the other way. There are several passages in the earlier novels of Huysmans which, though they purport to be descriptions of incidents or situations, are actually verbal transcriptions of paintings. In one of his *Croquis parisiens* of 1880, for instance, there is an account of an acrobatic act at the Folies-Bergère which is based entirely on Degas' *Miss La La au cirque Fernando* (1879; National Gallery, London).

The literary interests of all the Impressionists were very pronounced. Renoir, whose letters are marked by a strong sense of style, wrote in 1911 an extensive introduction to a new translation of Cennino Cennini's *Il Libro dell'Arte*, which contained wide-ranging reflections on many matters, including Catholicism, of which by that time he had become a warm defender. Monet had an extensive library at GIVERNY and amongst his favourite authors were Zola, Flaubert, Maupassant, Maeterlinck, Huysmans and Balzac. Flaubert, who lived near Giverny, was sensitive to many of the Impressionists' ideas, and it is significant that in *L'Education sentimentale* (1869) he has the artist Pellerin working on a painting entitled *The Republic, Progress or Civilization*, which shows Christ driving a railway engine through a virgin forest – a gesture towards the concept of making modern life a suitable theme for art. Monet first met Maupassant, who was a frequent visitor to Berthe Morisot's Thursday dinner parties, at ETRETAT in 1885, and the writer published a vivid account of Monet's painting a seascape in *Gil Blas* on 28 September 1886, in a piece entitled 'La Vie d'un paysagiste'. CÉZANNE's closest literary contact was with Zola, but his own correspondence reveals a person with a wider and deeper interest in literature than might be supposed. At school he wrote poetry extensively, and throughout his life his favourite books were the *Eclogues* of Virgil and Baudelaire's *Fleurs du mal*.

There were, of course, practical reasons why painters should cultivate writers. From the days when Baudelaire had defended Manet, to those when Mallarmé defended Degas, the Impressionists were able to find in writers of what one might call the avant-garde, protagonists of great importance. But it was not merely a matter of social contacts, physical propinquity or occasional stylistic affinities. Baudelaire encapsulated the common ground between writers and painters when he entitled his work on Constantin GUYS 'The Painter of Modern Life'. A whole host of factors had led the creative consciousness of Europe away from the escapism of the Romantic approach to a more objective, 'scientific' observation of the actual world, and to a preference for themes taken from the everyday life of ordinary people, rather than from the past, or from an idealized society. REALISM, or Naturalism, as it was variously called, was to be found in the Impressionists' concern with representing natural phenomena not as they were conceptualized in the mind, but as they were actually seen by the eye, and in their preoccupation with scenes of ordinary, rather than idyllic, life; these concerns were also at the heart of the writings of Duranty, the Goncourts, George Moore and above all Zola.

Zola's connection with the Impressionists and ardent support for them has long been accepted as an outstanding example of the correlation of art and literature. He himself emphasized this constantly; he used the words *impressionniste, naturaliste* and *actualiste* to mean the same thing, and wrote, 'The old masters of the future will be our brothers, who will have accomplished the task of bringing into art that movement which in literature has led to a precise analysis and a questing study of the present.' It was not quite as simple as Zola's quest for a persuasive ideology suggested, however. A concern with the present was not the dominant concern of Impressionism, and in some ways Zola did not really understand its specifically pictorial dynamism. Nor were the Impressionists united in their approval of his sometimes tediously statistical analysis of life in contemporary France. Degas said that Zola was like a giant who had accidentally got hold of a street directory. Their reserve was not without foundation. Shortly after the publication of *L'Oeuvre*, in a conversation with George Moore (*Impressions and Opinions*, 1891), Zola said, 'I cannot accept a man who shuts himself up all his life to draw ballet girls as ranking co-equal in dignity and power with Flaubert, Daudet and Goncourt.'

More complex is the relationship between literature and painting in the work of Marcel Proust, whose interest in the Impressionists was stimulated by his contacts with the Prince de WAGRAM. In February 1920, two-and-a-half years before his death, when asked, with other writers, to choose 12 paintings to represent French art in the Louvre, he included Manet's *Olympia*, an unnamed work by Renoir, and Monet's *Les Falaises d'Etretat*. There is no denying the almost hypnotic influence the last-named artist had on him. It is not merely that Monet provided many of the characteristics of Elstir the painter, to whom Proust devotes so much attention in *A la Recherche du temps perdu*, but that his own prose and his own apprehension of external reality are expressed in Impressionist modalities: he describes the impact of visual experience in an instinctual way before the intellect has had time to intervene, capturing the fleeting, significant moment, and recording time sequences according to the pattern that Monet exploited in the *Nymphéas* series. As he himself put it, the important thing is 'to show things in the sequence in which we perceive them, instead of first explaining them in terms of what caused them'. *See also* CHAMPFLEURY, CHARPENTIER, GAUTIER, GEFFROY, ILLUSTRATION, LAFORGUE, MAUCLAIR, MIRBEAU [*106, 113, 182, 231*]
□ M.E. Chernowitz, *Proust and Painting* (1943); J. Seznec, *Literature and the Visual Arts in Nineteenth-Century France* (1963); *French Nine-teenth-Century Painting and Literature*, ed. U. Finke (1972)

Louveciennes A village to the west of Paris between BOUGIVAL and Versailles, where PIS-SARRO lived 1869–70 and 1871–72. MONET also lived there for some time (*The Road to Versailles at Louveciennes; Snow Effect*, 1869–70; Nelson Harris Collection, Chicago), as did SISLEY (*Early Snow at Louveciennes*, c.1870; Museum of Fine Arts, Boston).
□ Clark (1984); Herbert (1988)

A view of **Louveciennes**, site of an unsuccessful French sortie from Paris during the 1871 siege.

Luxembourg, Musée du The repository of officially sponsored art, it played an important role in the history of 19th-c. French painting as the main museum of 'contemporary' art. Originally the home of Marie de' Medici, it became the seat of the House of Peers before being transformed into a national art gallery in 1818. By 1875 it had accumulated some 240 works, though a constant process of filtering went on; when an artist attained posthumous fame, his or her works were transferred to the Louvre (e.g., David's works were moved there in 1824), and other paintings were distributed amongst provincial museums and galleries.

This was especially true of works of which the administration did not really approve. In 1870, for instance, the Luxembourg acquired Eva GONZALÈS' *The Little Soldier* for 2000 francs, because her father, Emmanuel, was an important journalist, President of the Comité de la Société des Gens de Lettres, and was 'highly thought of' by the Minister of Fine Arts. The painting was almost immediately transferred to

View of the Palais du **Luxembourg** on the Left Bank in Paris.

the town of Villeneuve-sur-Lot, where it was consigned to a cellar in the Mairie, languishing there until the 1960s. A similar fate overtook JONGKIND's *Harbour at Honfleur*, which was acquired in 1851 and immediately transferred to the museum of Amiens. During the latter half of the century the most 'advanced' paintings owned by the Luxembourg were by MILLET, DAUBIGNY and COROT, who in 1875 had bequeathed two of his Italian landscapes to the museum.

The extent to which the museum was hamstrung by bureaucracy and political complications is exemplified by the débâcle of the CAILLEBOTTE bequest. The collection was left to the Luxembourg, but part of it was rejected for lack of space, the balance being shown in 1897 in a newly built annexe of the museum. In giving his *Nymphéas* series to the nation in 1920, MONET was very concerned that the pictures should not hang in the Luxembourg, and eventually in 1922 they were installed in the Orangerie of the Louvre, thanks to the intervention of CLEMENCEAU. In 1902 GAUGUIN, smarting under the rejection of his *D'où venons-nous? Que sommes-nous? Où allons-nous?*, described the Luxembourg as 'A vast prison and a kind of compulsory brothel. Kings are buried at Saint-Denis; painters in the Luxembourg. It is no more than a house of the past, which ought to be destroyed.' *See also* CHENNEVIÈRES-POINTEL, PARIS

□ *Le Musée du Luxembourg en 1874*, Grand Palais, Paris, exhibition catalogue (1974)

director first of the Tate Gallery and then of the Wallace Collection. His major publication was *Nineteenth-Century Art* (1902).

His preferences were clearly for the 'realists' of the group – MANET and DEGAS especially – and, though he helped to organize a fund for the purchase of a MONET for the National Gallery, he did nothing to acquire any Impressionist works during the time he ran the Tate Gallery. On the other hand, the consistent bias of his critical writing was towards an understanding and appreciation of contemporary, especially French, art.

□ D.S. MacColl, *Nineteenth-Century Art* (1902); Cooper (1954); *Dictionary of National Biography* (1970)

Maître, Edmond (1840–98) Writer and musician, he was deeply interested in art, largely through his friendship with BAZILLE, who portrayed him playing the piano in *The Artist's Studio, rue de la Condamine* (1870; Musée d'Orsay), and painted a portrait of him in 1867 (Madame Cardenal Collection, Bordeaux). He is also to be seen standing next to ZOLA in FANTIN-LATOUR's *A Studio in the Batignolles Quarter* (1870; Musée d'Orsay). Amongst his

M

Macchiaioli *see* ITALY

MacColl, D.S. (1859–1948) No other CRITIC of his generation did more to awaken an appreciation of Impressionism in ENGLAND than Dugald Sutherland MacColl. After an academic education at Edinburgh and Oxford, he studied painting at the Slade School of Art under Frederick Brown, and became a member of the New English Art Club. He was successively art critic of the *Spectator* and the *Saturday Review*, editor of the *Architectural Review*, and

Bazille's portrait of **Maître** is a fragment from a larger, lost work of 1867.

other friends were BAUDELAIRE, LECOQ DE BOISBAUDRAN and Verlaine. An habitué of the CAFÉ GUERBOIS, he also became very friendly with RENOIR, who shared with him a passion for Wagner and, indeed, for German music in general. *See also* MUSIC *[28, 86]*
□ A. Jullien, *Fantin-Latour* (1909); G. Poulain, *Bazille et ses amis* (1932)

Mallarmé, Stéphane (1842–98) One of those charismatic literary figures of the kind that France produces so abundantly, Mallarmé was a painter in words, whose very personal style was influenced by writers such as BAUDELAIRE, Poe and the Parnassians. His flat on the rue de Rome in BATIGNOLLES became a centre of Parisian cultural life, and his connections with artists were close and mutually fruitful. MANET painted his portrait (1876; Musée d'Orsay) and illustrated his translation of Poe's *The Raven* and *L'Après-midi d'un faune*. For his part, Mallarmé wrote brilliantly in defence of Manet, WHISTLER and MORISOT, and persuaded Octave MIRBEAU to champion the works of GAUGUIN. In 1876 he published an article on 'The Impressionists and Edouard Manet' in the short-lived London publication, *Art Monthly Review*. He used his

Gauguin's etching on copper of the poet Stéphane **Mallarmé**, 1891.

influence with Henry Roujon, the Director of Fine Arts, to ensure that the state bought Whistler's *Portrait of the Artist's Mother*, as well as a work by Morisot. He was on close terms with RENOIR and DEGAS, who took a memorable photograph of the former with the poet. *See also* CALLIAS, ILLUSTRATION, LAURENT, LITERATURE, PHOTOGRAPHY, RAFFAËLLI *[113]*
□ *Correspondance de Berthe Morisot*, ed. D. Rouart, (1950); S. Mallarmé, *Correspondance*, vol. 3, ed. H. Mondor and J.L. Austin (1969); J.A. Lloyd, 'Mallarmé and the visual arts', in *French Nineteenth-Century Painting and Literature*, ed. U. Finke (1972)

Manet, Edouard (1832–83) The virtually reluctant leader of the Impressionists, who never participated in their exhibitions, he was nearly 50 before he adopted a truly Impressionist technique, largely under the influence of MONET and MORISOT. The son of a magistrate, he clearly belonged to the ranks of the *haute bourgeoisie*, a fact underlined by his immaculately correct dress and behaviour, as well as by his early years as an eligible and frivolous bachelor given to the pursuit of 'high life'. Manet was, next to PISSARRO, the most radical, or at least the most politically sceptical, member of the group of artists with whom he was connected; and yet he was terribly hungry for official recognition, complaining bitterly to NIEUWERKERKE, whose successor as Director of Fine Arts had procured the Legion of Honour for him, 'It would have made my fortune once, but now it is too late to make up for 20 years of failure.' One of his earliest ambitions was to obtain a commission to decorate one of the ceilings of the newly renovated Hôtel de Ville, and, in the catalogue of the one-man exhibition he mounted in 1867, in connection with the Exposition Universelle of that year, Zacharie ASTRUC wrote (presumably at the artist's dictation), 'M. Manet has never wished to protest . . . he has no intention to overthrow old methods of painting or to create new ones. He has merely tried to be himself and nobody else.'

As much at home in a cosmopolitan restaurant such as Tortoni's as in the Bohemian milieu of the CAFÉ GUERBOIS, well-educated, intelligent, humorous and witty, Manet had little or no pretentiousness, and Jacques-Emile BLANCHE seems to have hit him off perfectly: 'He was no theoretician. His customary conversation about art was slightly ironical prattle. He spoke of it as an amateur Communard might have spoken

Photograph of **Manet** taken by Nadar c. 1869.

about the Revolution of 1789.' Financially independent, he was not harassed or motivated as Monet or Pissarro were, neither turning out works in such abundance as they, nor being over-attentive to dealers. Indeed, his persistent concern with getting his works into the SALON was dictated by a desire for recognition rather than to enhance his sales. Clearly, he possessed what a later generation would describe as charisma. Despite the rows he had with others, the worst that was ever said of him – by DEGAS – was that he was a bourgeois. Younger artists clustered naturally around him, and a number of students at the ECOLE DES BEAUX-ARTS invited him – in vain, of course – to take over Lehmann's atelier. A student song of the time went: '*Courbet, Manet, tous ceux qui ont génie / N'ont pas la Croix, ça dégoûte de la vie*' (Courbet, Manet and all those others who have genius do not get the cross of the Legion of Honour. It's enough to make one sick of life).

The juxtaposition of Manet's name with that of COURBET is in fact significant, because both were forced, the one willingly, the other less so,

into symbolic roles as leaders of artistic experiment and political intransigence. Having spent six years in the studio of COUTURE, whose influence on him was greater than is often acknowledged, Manet evolved a style that clearly owed a great deal to the old masters, especially the Spaniards Velazquez, Murillo and Ribéra, and sought to achieve a kind of objective realism, uncomplicated by emotion. (In fact, he only spent a little over a week in SPAIN, in 1865, and was dependent upon the impressive collection of Spanish paintings in the Louvre, which had been amassed by Napoleon and Louis-Philippe.) His first submission to the Salon, *The Absinthe Drinker* (Ny Carlsberg Glyptotek, Copenhagen), with its BAUDELAIREAN undertones, was rejected in 1859, but his more appealing *Spanish Singer* (Metropolitan Museum, New York) and *The Artist's Parents* (Private collection) were accepted at the Salon of 1861, at which he received an honourable mention. During this period he painted a number of Spanish subjects, based mostly on the members of a Spanish dancing troupe that was currently visiting Paris, and generally chose subjects of a picturesque type.

In 1863 he submitted the *Déjeuner sur l'herbe* to the Salon. It was rejected, but shown in the SALON DES REFUSÉS. The scandal that ensued is now part of the folklore of art history and it established Manet securely, and for him uncomfortably, in the position of leader of the anti-establishment faction in the French art world. The irony of the situation, typical in a way of Manet's whole career, was that the picture had no offensive or revolutionary intention. It was based, in fact, on a classical theme, with obvious references – noted at the time – to Giorgione, Raimondi and Raphael. The nude figure was far less sexually provocative than many academic paintings, such as, for instance, Cabanel's *Birth of Venus* (1863; Musée d'Orsay), admired and bought by NAPOLEON III. What horrified the establishment was the fact that Manet had transferred the situation out of the anodyne atmosphere of a fictitious, idyllic past into the world of 1863, and so proclaimed himself as a REALIST – a movement that in its literary and artistic idioms was widely regarded as aesthetically repulsive and politically suspect. The same paradox was apparent in the hostile reception given to his *Olympia* (1863; Musée d'Orsay), which was exhibited at the Salon of 1865, and which was in effect a translation into contemporary idiom of a theme – that of the

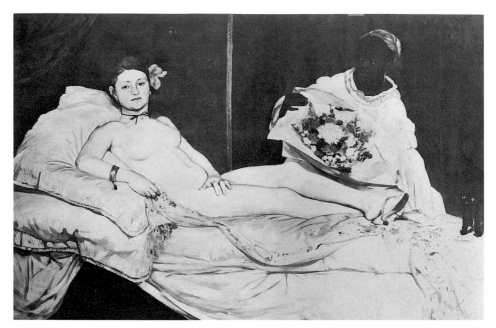

Manet's *Olympia* caused an uproar when it was exhibited at the 1865 Salon, his notoriety causing him to be seen as the unofficial leader of the avant-garde.

recumbent Venus – which was virtually a cliché amongst the painters of the late Renaissance.

Manet's work at this time was marked by considerable technical virtuosity (*see* PEINTURE CLAIRE), by an unemotional realism that owed much to the Spanish tradition, and by an interest in contemporary life; but also by certain more innovative characteristics that help to explain why his paintings had such a profound effect on Monet, RENOIR, SISLEY and BAZILLE when they saw them at the MARTINET Gallery. Manet presented many elements in his works in an apparently uncomposed and arbitrary way, reproducing tonal values as a pattern of light and shade, rather than as local colours.

By now, although his social life still had its *mondaine* quality, Manet was moving much more in the artistic world inhabited by people such as Monet and Renoir. In the late 1860s he met Berthe Morisot, who came from a social context similar to his own and by whose charm and creative intelligence he was greatly impressed. She served as his model on many occasions, notably for *The Balcony* (1869; Musée d'Orsay). They established a relationship that might be described as that of master

and pupil, except that the influence went both ways; and the connection was strengthened in 1874 when she married Manet's brother Eugène. By this time Manet was becoming reasonably successful, and the impulses that Morisot had been giving him towards PLEIN-AIR painting and a general lightening of his palette were emphasized in 1874, when he spent a good deal of time painting in and around ARGENTEUIL with Monet and Renoir. Works such as *Monet Working in his Studio-Boat* (Bayerische Staatsgemäldesammlungen, Munich) and *Argenteuil* (Musée des Beaux-Arts, Tournai) were, so to speak, fully-fledged Impressionist works; though the latter was accepted at the Salon of 1875, it was bitterly criticized, and his works were rejected there for the next few years.

His concern with contemporary life started to assume a slightly different accent in this period, partly as the result of an interest in Dutch genre painting, which had been strengthened by his marriage to the Dutch pianist Suzanne LEENHHOFF and his subsequent visits to HOLLAND. *Le Bon Bock* of 1873 (Philadelphia Museum of Art), a portrait of the engraver Emile Bellot, which was warmly received at the

Salon, clearly owed a great deal to Frans Hals. Bellot actually used the work in an engraved form on the mast-head of a paper, with the same title, which he published as a weekly publication for the brewing trade – and it was this world of cafés and cabarets that now began to attract Manet's interest. Two of his most important works, remarkable for the brilliance of their technique, the originality of their conception and their fluent manipulation of the innovative elements of Impressionism, were both concerned with creating a modern version of the tavern life that had so beguiled the Dutch masters of the 17th c. *Corner in a Café-Concert* (1878 or 1879; National Gallery, London) is a sparklingly painted view of the Brasserie de Reichshoffen; *A Bar at the Folies-Bergère* (Courtauld Institute, London) is his last masterpiece, a tribute on a magisterial scale to the PARIS of his time, typified in one of its most popular haunts 'that smells sweetly of the *maquillage* of purchased favours and the extremes of jaded corruption'. The great sweep of the composition is contrasted with the Chardin-like material intensity of the beer and champagne bottles, and with the lyricism of the still life created out of the flowers and oranges on the bar.

Already suffering from the disease, probably a kind of circulatory paralysis, that was to kill him, Manet became incapable of producing anything more ambitious than a series of small still lifes of similar quality. A master of PASTEL-painting, he also produced about a hundred PRINTS, most of them after paintings, which remained unpublished in his lifetime. They were not mere reproductions, nor were they 'original' prints, like those produced by artists such as Pissarro, and he had intended them to be published. Conveniently labelled an Impressionist, Manet transcends any such narrow categorization, and his works contribute perhaps more than those of any of his fellow painters to incorporating the movement in the mainstream of European art. *See also* BALLEROY, BATIGNOLLES, BRAQUEMOND, BÜRGER, CALLIAS, CHESNEAU, DANCING, DESNOYERS, DRAWING, ENGLAND, FAURE, GERVEX, GONZALÈS, ILLUSTRATION, ITALY, JAPANESE ART, LAURENT, MELLON, MEURENT, MOORE, PHOTOGRAPHY, POLITICS, PORTRAITURE, PRICES, SOCIAL BACKGROUND [*16, 20, 23, 28, 34, 40, 46, 58, 65, 86, 90, 102, 105, 107, 110, 113, 126, 138, 159, 168, 171, 173, 174, 178, 183, 215, 217, 221, 224*]
□ E. Moreau-Nélaton, *Manet raconté par lui-même*, 2 vols. (1926); A. Tabarant, *Manet et ses*

oeuvres (1947); *Manet*, Metropolitan Museum, New York; Grand Palais, Paris, exhibition catalogue (1983); K. Adler, *Manet* (1986)

Manet, Julie *see* MORISOT

Mantz, Paul (1821–95) Art critic, historian, man of letters and successful civil servant, he contributed articles about art to a wide variety of reviews, including L'ARTISTE and *Le Temps*. He also wrote extensively for Charles BLANC's *Histoire des peintres*. At one time he was Director-General of Fine Arts. In an article in the *Gazette des Beaux-Arts*, he praised one of MONET's sea-paintings enthusiastically, writing 'the taste for harmonious schemes of colour in the play of analogous tones, the feeling for values, the striking point of view of the whole, a bold manner of seeing things and of forcing the attention of the spectator. These are qualities that M. Monet possesses in the highest degree. From now onwards we shall certainly be keen on following the progress of this painter.'
□ Hamilton (1954)

Manzi, Michel (1849–1915) Of Italian origin, and a friend of DEGAS, he was an engraver and a printer, who eventually became a dealer in partnership with Maurice JOYANT. Between 1881 and 1893 he directed the shop that GOUPIL ran for the sale of reproductions at 9 rue Chaptal. In 1896 he published a remarkable volume of reproductions of drawings by Degas, in close collaboration with the artist, using a technique that he had developed himself. He had a small but important collection of paintings, which included works by MANET, PISSARRO, Degas and GAUGUIN, and was auctioned in 1911.
□ J. Rewald, *Studies in Post-Impressionism* (1986); *Degas*, Grand Palais, Paris, exhibition catalogue (1988)

Marion, Antoine Fortuné (1846–1900) An ardent amateur artist who was a childhood friend of CÉZANNE, he went on painting excursions with him in the 1860s. Basically, however, he was a scientist by inclination and became a professor of zoology at the University of Marseilles, and director of the Musée d'Histoire Naturelle in that city. Marion was also a keen geologist and made some interesting discoveries in the area around AIX. He became friendly with a German musician Heinrich Morstatt (1844–1925), who was working in Marseilles and who later became director of a music school in Stuttgart. The correspondence between the two is full of information about Cézanne.

□ A. Barr, 'Cézanne as seen in the correspondence from Marion to Morstatt', in *Gazette des Beaux-Arts* (Jan. 1937); Rewald (1984)

Marlotte *see* CABARET DE LA MÈRE ANTHONY

Martelli, Diego (1838–96) An Italian painter and art critic, he had been introduced to the Macchiaioli at the Caffè Michelangiolo in Florence in 1855, and became their strongest protagonist and supporter, affording them publicity in the magazines he edited, as well as hospitality on his estate at Castiglioncello. By the 1870s, his horizons were widening beyond ITALY and, though he had become an enthusiastic admirer of the BARBIZON School as a result of visits to Paris in 1863 and 1869, his contacts with ZANDOMENEGHI made him more conscious of the significance of the Impressionists, to whose work he had until then been rather hostile. He made a protracted stay in Paris for the Exposition Universelle of 1878, acting as correspondent for a number of Italian papers, and by 1879 he was beginning to explain the Impressionists to his fellow countrymen in terms of their resemblances to the Macchiaioli. He praised MONET as 'the model of the young modern artist' and became a close personal friend of DEGAS, whom he persuaded to send two works to an exhibition in Florence. (They were unsold, but Martelli bought them for his own collection.)

Although Martelli was not successful in persuading his fellow Italians of the significance of the works of the Impressionists, which they found 'formless', he himself developed an acute awareness of what they were doing. This was expressed especially in a lecture he gave at Livorno in 1879 (subsequently printed in pamphlet form), in the course of which he expressed the view that 'Impressionism is not only a revolution in the field of thought, it is also a revolution in the physiological understanding of the human eye. It is a new theory which depends on a different mode of perceiving the sensation of light and of expressing impressions. The Impressionists did not construct their theories first and then adapt their paintings to them after the fact, but on the contrary, as is always the case with real discoveries, the paintings were born of the unconscious processes of the artist's eye.'

Degas' portrait of **Martelli** exists in two versions. This one was painted in 1879.

□ *Scritti d'arte di Diego Martelli*, ed. A. Boschetti (1952); P. Dini and A. de Soldato, *Diego Martelli* (1978); N. Broude, *The Macchiaioli* (1987)

Martin, 'Père' (*c*.1810–*c*.1880) A small-time dealer, upon whom the Impressionists frequently relied during the early stages of their careers. He used to handle the works of COROT and almost exclusively those of JONGKIND. He also bought works from PISSARRO, RENOIR, MONET and CÉZANNE. During the late 1860s he was paying artists sums of between 20 and 40 francs for their works, and selling them at between 60 and 80 francs. When in 1868 Monet wanted 100 francs for a landscape, Martin offered him 50 plus a small painting by Cézanne, which he accepted. As late as 1874 he was only prepared to give Renoir 450 francs for his *La Loge* (Courtauld Institute, London). Moreover, he had the unpleasant habit of telling his painters what was wrong with their work, and how they could improve it. But until his death some of them, notably Pissarro, continued to sell paintings to him.

□ Rewald (1973)

Martinet, Louis (1810–94) A painter and etcher, who pursued a successful career as a picture-dealer, and who invited MANET in 1861 to exhibit at his gallery in the boulevard des

Italiens, where he also arranged concerts. From 1861 to 1863 he issued a lively art magazine, the *Courrier artistique*, which fought vigorously for the SALON DES REFUSÉS. Predominantly interested in Romantic painters, such as DELACROIX, he actively promoted the work of currently neglected 18th-c. painters, including Watteau and Chardin, and it was possibly through his gallery that Manet absorbed their influence, which is most apparent in his work between 1865 and 1872. Martinet's etching activities must have stimulated Manet at this time to join the Société des Aquafortistes, a collective undertaking to promote etching as an art form independent of its reproductive function, which was sponsored by BAUDELAIRE, LEGROS and BRACQUEMOND. *See also* PRINTS
□ A. Tabarant, *Manet et ses oeuvres* (1947); H.C. and C.A. White, *Canvases and Careers; Institutional Changes in the French Painting World* (1967)

Mauclair, Camille (1872–1945) Born Camille Faust, he was a novelist, poet and dramatist associated with the Symbolist movement and for many years art critic of that movement's magazine, the *Mercure de France*. In addition to monographs on Rodin, MONET and PUVIS DE CHAVANNES, he published in 1903 a book devoted to the Impressionists which, despite its many imperfections, contributed much to the appreciation of the movement, especially in ENGLAND and the USA. (The English translation of 1903 by P.G. Konody preceded the French version, *L'Impressionnisme, son histoire, son esthétique, ses maîtres*, Paris, 1904.) Also in 1903 he published a novel, *La Ville lumière*, which presents a thinly disguised portrait of DEGAS as the artist Hubert Feuillery. An ardent defender of Impressionism, he was, however, contemptuous of PISSARRO (he was a fervid anti-Semite) and condescending towards CÉZANNE.
□ T.R. Bowie, *The Painter in French Fiction* (1950); J. Seznec, *Literature and the Visual Arts in Nineteenth-Century France* (1963)

Maus, Octave (1856–1919) The most influential Belgian art critic of his time, who founded the weekly review *L'Art moderne* and was one of the organizers of two associations, the Cercle des Vingt (1884–93) and Les Vingt. These groups organized exhibitions in Brussels showing the work of avant-garde artists from all over Europe, including especially the Impressionists, notably MONET, PISSARRO, CÉZANNE,

GAUGUIN and MORISOT. He was largely responsible for mounting these exhibitions, and the introductions that he provided for the catalogues were remarkable for their lucid explanations of what the Impressionists were trying to achieve. He was especially interested in problems concerning the depiction of light and colour. He was also a protagonist of Wagner, and of progressive MUSIC in general. *See also* BELGIUM, JOYANT *[29]*
□ M.O. Maus, *Trente années de lutte pour l'art, 1884–1914* (1926); *Post-Impressionism*, Royal Academy, London, exhibition catalogue (1979)

May, Ernest (1845–1925) A successful businessman who features in DEGAS' *Portraits in the Bourse* (1878–79; Musée d'Orsay). He was interested in the arts and had a large collection that was originally comprised of old masters and 18th-c. French paintings. In the late 1870s, however, under the influence of Jean-Baptiste FAURE and CAILLEBOTTE, he started collecting Impressionist paintings, in addition to building up an important group of early COROTS. He was a committee member of the Amis du Louvre and on his death left all his paintings to the museum.
□ 'Nécrologie: Ernest May', in *Bulletin de l'art ancien et moderne* (Jan. 1926); 'Donation May au Musée du Louvre', *L'Amour de l'art* (March 1926)

Médan In 1878, as a result of his growing prosperity, ZOLA bought a rather ugly house at Médan, on the Seine north-west of Paris, which he began to use as a country retreat. It was close to the railway, which cut across part of the

The Seine at Poissy, near **Médan**, where Zola had his country retreat.

Manet's *The Plum* (*c.* 1878) came into the possession of the **Mellon** family in the early 1960s.

Meurent, Victorine (1844–*c.*1885) She was a professional model, who had first posed for COUTURE's students and had a reputation for being talkative and argumentative when she was posing. She was 18 when first asked by MANET to sit for him; he had seen her in a crowd outside the Palais de Justice and written her address in his notebook as 'rue Maître-Albert 17'. His first portrait of her (Museum of Fine Arts, Boston) was painted in 1862. She also posed for *Mlle V. in the Costume of an Espada* (1862; Metropolitan Museum, New York) and was the main female figure in the *Déjeuner sur l'herbe* (1863; Musée d'Orsay), *Olympia* (1863; Musée d'Orsay) and, some ten years later in 1873, the female figure in *The Railroad* (National Gallery of Art, Washington).

She had various other talents, being a gifted guitarist, and took up painting, having a self-portrait accepted at the SALON in 1876 – ironically the year in which Manet's entries were entirely rejected. She had a passionate affair with Alfred STEVENS. Eventually she became an alcoholic, and died in abject poverty. [*134, 183*]

property. There he was able to indulge his passion for photography, to write and entertain his friends, and make the place a kind of unofficial headquarters of the REALIST movement. Médan is some 15 kms (9½ miles) from PONTOISE and in the centre of a region much frequented by MONET, PISSARRO, RENOIR and others, who were frequent visitors. Zola's most regular house guest, however, was CÉZANNE, who until the break between them in 1886 spent several weeks a year there.
□ E. Zola, *Correspondance*, ed. M. Le Blond (1928); Rewald (1984)

Mellon, Paul (b. 1907) Son of the famous Andrew (1885–1937), a formidable collector whose fortune was based on coal, real estate and banking concerns, and who founded the National Gallery of Art in Washington, opened in 1941. Paul began his collecting career with the Impressionists, acquiring a superb selection of paintings by MANET, most of which he has given to his father's foundation.

Victorine **Meurent** posed for *Mlle V. in the Costume of an Espada*, 1862, in Manet's studio on the rue Guyot.

Millet's *Angélus*, painted between 1858 and 1859, reflects the painter's peasant roots and his memories of rural life in Normandy.

□ B. Farwell, *Manet and the Nude, A Study in Iconography in the Second Empire* (1981); K. Adler, *Manet* (1986)

Millet, Jean-François (1814–75) The son of a small peasant farmer of Gréville in Normandy, Millet showed a precocious interest in drawing, and arrived in Paris in 1838 to become a pupil of Paul Delaroche. He had to fight against great odds, living for long a life of extreme penury. He exhibited at the SALON for the first time in 1840, and married two years later. At this time, the main influences on him were Poussin and Eustache Le Sueur, and the type of work he produced consisted predominantly of mythological subjects or portraiture, at which he was especially adept (*Portrait of a Naval Officer*, 1845; Musée des Beaux-Arts, Rouen).

His memories of rural life, and his intermittent contacts with Normandy, however, impelled him to that concern with peasant life that was to be characteristic of the rest of his artistic career. In 1848 he exhibited *The Win-nower* (now lost) at the Salon, and this was praised by Théophile GAUTIER and bought by Alexandre Ledru-Rollin, the Minister of the Interior. In 1849, when a cholera epidemic broke out in Paris, Millet moved to BARBIZON on the advice of the engraver Charles-Emile Jacque (1813–94) and took a house near that of Théodore ROUSSEAU. Devoted to this area as a subject for his work, he was one of those who most clearly helped to create the Barbizon School. His paintings on rural themes attracted growing acclaim and between 1858 and 1859 he painted the famous *Angélus* (Musée d'Orsay), which 40 years later was to be sold for the sensational price of 553,000 francs.

Although he was officially distrusted because of his real or imaginary Socialist leanings, his own attitude towards his chosen theme of peasant life was curiously ambivalent. Being of peasant stock, he tended to look upon farmworkers as narrow-minded and oblivious of beauty, and did not accept the notion that 'honest toil' was the secret of happiness. In fact, his success partly stemmed from the fact that, though compared with most of his predecessors and, indeed, his contemporaries, he was a 'Realist', he presented this reality in an acceptable form, with a religious or idyllic gloss. Nevertheless, he became a symbol to younger artists, to whom he gave help and encouragement. It was he who, on a visit to Le Havre to paint portraits, encouraged BOUDIN to become an artist, and his work certainly influenced the young MONET, and even more decidedly so PISSARRO, who shared similar political inclinations.

Although towards the end of his life, when he started using a lighter palette and freer brushstrokes, his work showed some affinities with Impressionism, his technique was never really close to theirs. He never painted out-of-doors, and he had only a limited awareness of tonal values, but his draughtsmanship had a monumentality that appealed to artists such as SEURAT and VAN GOGH, who was also enthralled by his subject-matter, with its social implications. Millet's career was greatly helped by DURAND-RUEL. See also PASTELS, POLITICS, REALISM

□ E. Moreau-Nélaton, *Millet raconté par lui-même*, 3 vols. (1921); R.L. Herbert, 'Millet revisited', *Burlington Magazine* (July and Sept. 1962); Clark (1973a)

Mirbeau, Octave (1848–1917) A novelist from Calvados who lived and worked in Paris, Mirbeau was also an art critic. He became an impassioned defender of Impressionism, and was especially linked with MONET, RENOIR and PISSARRO, though he did not approve of the latter's excursion into SEURAT's style. In 1889 he wrote the introduction to Monet's first retrospective at the gallery of Georges PETIT, and also to the exhibitions later organized by DURAND-RUEL of works by the same painter on the themes of London and Venice. In *L'Art des deux-mondes*, a magazine financed by Durand-Ruel, he also wrote the first important assessment of Pissarro's paintings. He was especially perceptive about the work of Renoir, to which he devoted an important study, published in 1913. His collected art criticism was published posthumously in 1921 as *Des Artistes*.

Although he did not write much about DEGAS, he clearly used him as the model for the character Lirat in a novel, *Le Calvaire*, published in 1886, which depicts the artist as an embittered, satirical misanthrope, dominated by a relentless drive to artistic perfection. One of Lirat's statements in the book – 'One works for oneself and for some two or three friends who are alive, and a few more who are dead' – sounds like a statement by Degas himself. Most of Mirbeau's novels might be described as decadent, several of them revelling in the perversity and cruelty of modern life (*Le Jardin des supplices*, 1899). The first critic to recognize the genius of GAUGUIN, he was also most helpful in promoting his work. See also FÉLIX PISSARRO
□ F. Cachin, 'Un défenseur oublié de l'art moderne', *L'Oeil* (June 1962); M. Schwarz, *Octave Mirbeau, vie et oeuvre* (1966)

Monet, Claude (1840–1926) The most consistently explorative and prolific of the Impressionists, Monet represents the movement and all it stood for perhaps with greater clarity than anyone else. The eldest son of a Parisian shopkeeper, who moved to Le Havre when he was five, he went to Paris at the age of 19 to study at the ACADÉMIE SUISSE, where he met PISSARRO. After a period of military service in Algeria, he returned to Le Havre and commenced painting landscapes, coming into fruitful and encouraging contact with BOUDIN and JONGKIND. In 1863 he returned to Paris to study at the atelier of Charles GLEYRE, where he met BAZILLE, RENOIR and SISLEY. With these artists he went to paint in the forest of Fontainebleau, where they evolved many of the ideas that were to be fundamental to Impressionism.

Monet had some success at the SALON, and, with a mistress, Camille Doncieux, and an illegitimate child to support, the notion of achieving success through official channels to alleviate his penury was to be a complicating factor in his creative evolution until the 1880s, when he started to win acceptance for those works that really represented his creative intention. At one point, in 1868, he tried to commit suicide, but his confidence was restored by help from Bazille. When war broke out in 1870 he went to London, where he came into contact with DURAND-RUEL, who started to exhibit his works. It was here that he made his first contact with the works of Turner, the full impact of which was to be felt in the 1890s; by then he was experimenting more freely with the expression of light, which had already begun to be his main concern (*Impression; Sunrise*, 1872; Musée Marmottan, Paris).

Back in France, he went to live at ARGENTEUIL, where he painted regattas, life on the

Monet painting waterlilies in his garden at Giverny, *c.* 1920: the supreme *plein-air* painter at the height of his powers.

river, RAILWAYS and bridges, and was frequently joined by Renoir and MANET, all of them learning from each other and exploring the recently discovered potential of PLEIN-AIR painting (Renoir, *Monet Working in his Garden at Argenteuil,* 1873; The Wadsworth Athenaeum, Hartford, Conn.). Although throughout his career he was to visit many places, including HOLLAND, Norway and ITALY, and although he was to devote a good deal of time and attention to seeking suitable painting sites – in his house at GIVERNY there is still a large collection of guidebooks – his main output was concerned with those places in the Seine valley north of Paris where he spent most of his life.

His landscapes seldom have a prime focus, and sometimes he edits what he sees – leaving out, for instance, in some of his pictures of Argenteuil, the factory chimneys which were, in fact, so essential a part of the landscape. In 1876 he painted the three views of the Gare Saint-Lazare that encapsulate his achievement in the depiction of translucency, and in the animation of brushwork and colour to create an overpowering sense of visual vitality. He exhibited these at the 1877 IMPRESSIONIST EXHIBITION, but it is curious that, though he was the supreme exponent of the artistic ideals of the movement, his relations with the group as a whole were irregular, and tinged, on his part, with a certain diffidence. He did not participate in the exhibitions of 1880, 1881 or 1886 and, though he was on the closest possible terms of intimacy with Renoir and, intermittently, with Pissarro, many of his main contacts were with artists such as SARGENT and CAROLUS-DURAN, with whom he came into contact through Georges PETIT's Expositions Internationales.

In 1878 he moved to VÉTHEUIL, and two years later a one-man exhibition of his works organized by CHARPENTIER was a failure. In the mean time he had been painting a series of seascapes around the Channel coast; these expressed a side of his creative character that revelled in the violent and, drawing its inspiration largely from DELACROIX, verged on the confines of Expressionism (*Rough Sea, Etretat,* 1883; Musée des Beaux-Arts, Lyons). A great change took

Monet, *The break-up of the ice at Lavacourt*, 1880.

place in his life when Durand-Ruel again began to buy his paintings and so secured him a regular and adequate income. By 1881 he was receiving some 20,000 francs from the dealer, and in the following year 35,000 francs; this was in addition to those paintings he sold on his own. Partly as a result of this upturn in his fortunes, he moved in 1883 to GIVERNY, where he was to live for the rest of his life, and which was to be the centre and inspiration of his work for some 40 years. Meanwhile, he had met the HOSCHEDÉ family, first as patrons, then as friends — and in the case of Mme Hoschedé, who came to live at Giverny with her children, something more — a relationship that was legalized on the death of their respective spouses, when they married.

In Giverny Monet found the kind of focus of familiarity that had always been one of his preoccupations, though he was to continue painting subjects from other places (e.g. *Twilight, S. Giorgio Maggiore, Venice*, 1908; National Museum of Wales, Cardiff). In the 1880s he had for a while tried figure painting, under the influence of Sargent, and still-life painting, but as his financial position improved, he was able to dedicate all his creative activities to those explorations of light, atmosphere and time — he often indicated on the back of his canvases the hour of the day at which they were painted — that culminated in the great series of *Nymphéas*, or 'Waterlilies' (Musée d'Orsay; Musée Marmottan; Orangerie; Tate Gallery, London; Museum of Modern Art, New York). The preoccupation with single subjects surveyed under differing temporal and atmospheric conditions was also exemplified in the series of *Haystacks* (1890–91), *Poplars* (1891–92) and *Rouen Cathedral* (1892–93).

The *Nymphéas* series was based on the gardens of the house at Giverny, where Monet had reconstructed nature to suit his own pictorial needs, diverting a branch of the Seine to create a pond. The whole was in the JAPANESE style, and partly planned by a Japanese gardener who stayed with him in 1901. The walls of the house were covered with Japanese prints — Monet had been one of the first to collect them, having seen them in shops in Le Havre in his youth. The composition of his paintings was deeply influenced by these prints. This is seen at its most evident in *Terrace at Sainte-Adresse* (1867; Metropolitan Museum, New York), but is often perceptible in his habit of reversing the customary European system of convergent perspective to create a divergent space that spreads out on either side of the central feature, suggesting that the pictorial space is continued beyond the limits of the canvas. Japanese influence is also apparent in his concern with the complex relationship between space and surface. The main preoccupation of his whole career had been to give visual permanence to the evanescent, to halt time — not that involved in human action, but in those fluctuations of light and movement which make nature a living thing. No other painter has been so consistently effective in doing so. *See also* ANTECEDENTS, ASTRUC, BOUGIVAL, BRASSERIE DES MARTYRS, BRUYAS, CAFÉ GUERBOIS, COLOUR, DRAWING, ENGLAND, ETRETAT, GAUDIBERT, GEFFROY, LA GRENOUILLÈRE, LOUVECIENNES, LUXEMBOURG, MANTZ, MUSIC, PASTELS, PHOTOGRAPHY, PORTRAITURE, PRICES, PRINTS, SAINTE-ADRESSE, SOCIAL BACKGROUND, TECHNIQUE, VILLE D'AVRAY [*19, 28, 34, 50–1, 52, 54, 56, 81, 85, 86, 99, 108, 114, 168, 191, 195, 227*]

□ J.P. Hoschedé, *Monet; ce mal-connu*, 2 vols. (1960); D. Wildenstein, *Monet, biographie et catalogue raisonné*, 4 vols. (1974–85); J. House, *Monet: Nature into Art* (1986)

Montmartre Deriving its name from three Christians who were martyred there in the 3rd c. AD, Montmartre is one of the hills surrounding PARIS. A major point of military defence, it played such a role in the early 19th c., when the gypsum quarries, whose miles of underground galleries threatened to undermine the hill, were abandoned, as were the 30 mills driven by wind power which gave the place its distinctive appearance. At this time Montmartre was very much as ZOLA described it in *L'Assommoir* — 'looking as though it were part of the country-

The junction of the rues des Abbesses and Lepic, **Montmartre**, c.1890. The quarter attracted many of the Impressionists, and Renoir lived there in 1875.

side, with green trees shading the cheap taverns'. It was the writers who first started living there, including Nerval, Murger and Heine, but artists were already making their appearance by the time of the Commune, when the people of Montmartre, refusing to surrender to the government the 171 canons that had been used against the Prussians, precipitated the bloody uprising that has become part of the legendary history of the Left.

Access to the quarter had been made easier by the replanning of the city under Baron Haussmann, and its role as a place of entertainment was stimulated by its population, which consisted basically of shop assistants, workers in the minor trades and theatrical underlings. It was an ideal milieu for the Impressionists, with their passion for recording contemporary life. PISSARRO had been sketching there as early as 1860, and in 1869 SISLEY painted a memorable view of Montmartre (Musée de Grenoble). But of all the Impressionists it was RENOIR who was really devoted to the place. Coming as he did from a

family of petty craftsmen – his father was a tailor – he found the social milieu especially attractive and in 1875 he rented for 100 francs a month a small house in the rue Cortot, near the Place du Tertre. It had a charming, luxuriantly overgrown garden, which appears in *The Swing* (1876; Musée d'Orsay), and in *Garden of the rue Cortot* (1876; Carnegie Institute, Pittsburgh). The house was close to the Moulin de la Galette, one of the three surviving mills on the hill. Originally used for grinding iris roots for perfume, it had been converted by the Debray family into a café-restaurant at which balls – if the word is not too pretentious – were held on Sundays from three in the afternoon until midnight, with an entrance fee of 30 centimes. It was one of these Sunday dances that Renoir depicted with such loving attention in his *Dance at the Moulin de la Galette* (1876; Musée d'Orsay). It was obvious why, when he was in Naples in 1881, Renoir could write to his friend, the collector Charles DEUDON, 'I feel quite lost when I am away from Montmartre.

An illustration by Théodore Steinlen from Paul Delmet's *Chansons de **Montmartre*** (1898).

. . . I am longing for my familiar surroundings, and think that even the ugliest Parisienne is preferable to the most beautiful Italian girl.'

The main centre of artistic life in Montmartre at this time was the Nouvelle-Athènes, where DEGAS painted *L'Absinthe* (Musée d'Orsay), and which was situated in the Place Pigalle. MANET, Renoir, Pissarro, DESBOUTIN, FORAIN and ZANDOMENEGHI were also frequent visitors, and it was probably there that Manet painted *At the Café* (1878; Winterthur, Oskar Reinhart Collection) and *The Plum* (c.1878; National Gallery of Art, Washington, D.C.). An interesting indication of the growing importance of Montmartre in the art world was the fact that the small print-selling shop GOUPIL had established at 19 boulevard Montmartre was transformed in 1880 by BOUSSOD AND VALADON (who had taken over from Goupil) into a proper gallery, of which THÉO VAN GOGH was put in charge. The full flowering of Montmartre as an artists' quarter was to occur after the heyday of Impressionism, but by that time it had lost much of its spontaneous charm

and authenticity as an integral part of the life of Paris. *See also* CAFÉS, TANGUY *[17, 53, 101, 138, 187, 204]*

□ J. Hillairet, *Dictionnaire des rues de Paris*, 2 vols. (1964); R. Courtine, *La Vie parisienne; 1814–1914* (1984); Milner (1988)

Moore, George (1852–1933) A novelist who was largely responsible for introducing the concept of REALISM into English writing, notably in *Esther Waters* (1894). He was born and brought up in Ireland and then attended Oscott College in Birmingham. His early ambition was to be a painter and at the age of 21 he went to Paris, where he studied under Cabanel. During the ten years he lived there, he did not do a great deal to promote his career as an artist, but became infatuated with the poetry of BAUDELAIRE and the prose of Flaubert. A socially gregarious person, he was an habitué of the Nouvelle-Athènes, and was on intimate terms with most of the Impressionists. MANET painted three portraits of him in 1879; two of them, one an oil sketch on canvas, the other a pastel, are in the Metropolitan Museum, New York. He saw at least three of the IMPRESSIONIST EXHIBITIONS, and is the only Englishman to have written an account of the final one, at which SEURAT exhibited his *Grande Jatte*.

His quite copious reminiscences of the Impressionists and their context are to be found in *Confessions of a Young Man* (1888), *Modern Painting* (1908), *Reminiscences of the Impressionist Painters* (1906), *Memoirs of My Dead Life* (1906) and *Avowals* (1919). He was not greatly liked by the artists themselves, and in some ways had no very clear idea of what they were trying to do, though he tended to boast of the PATRONS he could obtain for them. On the other hand, despite some imaginative elements in his accounts of what went on, he has succeeded in conveying very clearly the ambience of the Impressionist movement.

From 1891 to 1895 he was art critic of the *Speaker* and a great supporter of the various forms of Impressionism that were being practised by English artists at the time (*see* ENGLAND); but some of his comments on the Parisian artists he knew verged on the asinine. He suspected RENOIR of 'a certain vulgarity'; of DEGAS he said (surveying the contents of his own sitting-room in Ebury Street) 'of what value are Degas' descriptions of washerwomen and dancers and racehorses compared with that fallen flower, that Aubusson carpet, and above all the footstool?'; and he dismissed MONET by saying that 'he sees clearly, and he sees truly, but does he see beautifully? Is his an enchanted vision?' After becoming involved for some time in the Irish literary renaissance centred around the Abbey Theatre, he settled down to become the 'Sage of Ebury Street', duplicating in London the role that MALLARMÉ had played in Paris. See also CAFÉS, LITERATURE

☐ W. Rothenstein, Men and Memories, 2 vols. (1932); D. Cooper, 'George Moore and Modern Painting', in Horizon (Feb. 1945); Cooper (1954); J.-P. Collet, George Moore et la France (1957)

Moreau, Gustave (1826–98) The son of an architect, an admirer and pupil of Chassériau, whose influence he never escaped, he spent three years in Italy, where he was greatly attracted by the works of Benozzo Gozzoli and Vittore Carpaccio. By the time he returned to Paris, he had evolved his own very personal style, exotic, allusive and bearing many characteristics of what was later to be known as the 'fin-de-siècle' style, as exemplified, for instance, in the works of Aubrey Beardsley.

In 1864 his Oedipus and the Sphinx (Metropolitan Museum, New York) had an enormous success at the SALON, and he became a popular figure in literary and artistic circles. Two years later The Apparition had an even greater success. An emotive painting in watercolour, it depicted the story of Herod and Salome, which was to grip so powerfully the imagination of the latter half of the century, and to find expression in the writings of Oscar Wilde and others. Moreau's works indeed had a great appeal to writers, including especially HUYSMANS, who featured descriptions of them in his influential novel A Rebours. He commenced various large canvases, few of which were completed. In 1892 he became a professor at the ECOLE DES BEAUX-ARTS, and numbered amongst his students Matisse, Rouault, Pierre-Albert Marquet and Manguin, all of whom owed much to his enlightened teaching.

Although the Impressionists tended to despise his works, this reaction was not universal. MANET was a friend and admirer, and was largely responsible, through his friend Antonin PROUST, for ensuring that Moreau received the Legion of Honour. To another friend, DEGAS, Moreau once confessed 'After all, I may be wrong, but I see things a certain way and must work that way, and I simply cannot see you any

more. You upset and discourage me.' Unlike that of the Impressionists, Moreau's sensuality was of the mind rather than of the eye. See also FANTIN-LATOUR

☐ Gustave Moreau, Louvre, Paris, exhibition catalogue (1961); J. Pierre, Gustave Moreau (1972); Catalogue, Musée Gustave Moreau, Paris (1974)

Morisot, Berthe (1841–95) Morisot's interest in art was initiated by her father, a top-ranking civil servant at the Cour des Comptes, who taught her to draw. She was then given painting lessons, together with her sister Edma, by Joseph Guichard, a friend of COROT, in whose studio she herself worked for some time. She was also in contact with FANTIN-LATOUR, whom she met in 1859.

All who came into touch with her at this time were impressed not only by her skill and facility, but by her sensitivity to changes that were taking place in the world of art. On the advice of Corot, she and Edma went to work at AUVERS and Fontainebleau, where she met DAUBIGNY, Antoine GUILLEMET and Daumier. In 1864 she made her first submissions to the SALON; two of her works were hung and admired by the critics. She exhibited regularly there until 1873, and her remarkable Paris Seen from the Trocadéro (1872; Kirkland Collection, Palm Beach, Fla.) attracted a great deal of praise and attention as a technical tour de force.

In 1868 she met MANET through Fantin-Latour, and he immediately became a warm admirer, getting her to pose for some memorable paintings, notably The Balcony (1869; Musée d'Orsay) and Repose (1870; Rhode Island School of Design). She greatly encouraged Manet's move towards PLEIN-AIR painting, while his influence on her is apparent in such paintings as The Artist's Sister Edma and Their Mother (1870; National Gallery of Art, Washington). In 1874 Berthe married Eugène, Manet's brother, and they had a daughter Julie, who later kept a fascinating diary, published in an English translation as Growing Up with the Impressionists (1987).

This was the year of the first IMPRESSIONIST EXHIBITION, at which Morisot exhibited several works, including the now famous The Cradle (1873; Musée d'Orsay). She was to participate in all the exhibitions during her lifetime, and was one of the mainstays of the group. Preferring on the whole interior and domestic subjects, she developed an execution free from

Berthe **Morisot** at work in her studio. In 1877 Paul Mantz wrote: 'There is only one impressionist in the whole revolutionary group – and that is Mlle Morisot.'

preoccupation with irrelevant details and marked by a spontaneous brushstroke that distributed dashes of colour almost at random. Her works are always bathed in a luminous light, similar in quality to that which had been exploited by Corot, but more complex in its colours, more various in its gradations. She exhibited in PETIT's Expositions Internationales, at DURAND-RUEL's New York exhibition and elsewhere, and obtained a wide degree of acceptance before most of her male contemporaries did.

Above all else, she provided a social and inspirational centre for the Impressionists. Initially at her house in the rue Villejust (now rue Paul-Valéry), every Thursday she entertained DEGAS, MONET, CAILLEBOTTE, PISSARRO and WHISTLER, as well as writers such as MALLARMÉ (one of her most devoted admirers), DURET and ZOLA. After the death of Eugène in 1892 she continued these social activities from a smaller flat in the rue Weber. In the mean time her work began to show the strong influence of RENOIR, who had become an intimate friend of

Morisot's *The Artist's Sister Edma and Their Mother*, 1870, was retouched by Manet.

her family (*In the Dining-Room*, 1884; National Gallery of Art, Washington). During the remaining three years of her life she travelled a great deal, and held a very successful exhibition at BOUSSOD AND VALADON. Her daughter Julie married Ernest Rouart, the grandson of Degas' friend, and her niece Nini Gobillard became Mallarmé's wife. *See also* BOUGIVAL, ENGLAND, GOBILLARD, GONZALÈS, GUICHARD, JOYANT, LEROLLE, PASTELS, PORTRAITURE, SOCIAL BACKGROUND *[105, 156]*
□ A. Fourreau, *Berthe Morisot* (1925); H. Perruchot, *La Vie de Manet* (1959); *Correspondance de Berthe Morisot*, ed. D. Rouart (1950; English trans. 1986); K. Adler and T. Garb, *Berthe Morisot* (1987); *Berthe Morisot: Impressionist*, National Gallery of Art, Washington, exhibition catalogue (1987)

Morozov, Mikhail (1870–1903) and **Ivan** (1871–1921) Members of a family of successful Russian textile manufacturers in Tver, they were both passionate collectors of French painting. From 1890 onwards Mikhail developed an interest in the Impressionists and bought important works by MANET, RENOIR, MONET, and Toulouse-Lautrec. These were hung in his house in Glazovsky Lane, Moscow, which became a meeting-place for those with advanced literary and artistic interests. He inspired his younger brother Ivan with the same passion which, in the latter's case, was all the more enthusiastic for his having been a student at the Ecole Polytechnique Supérieure in Paris. They became dedicated customers of DURAND-RUEL and employed an agent in Paris to buy from other sources. As they were advised by a number of critics, their purchases were always judicious, and included works by SISLEY (Ivan's favourite artist), Renoir, Monet, PISSARRO and CÉZANNE. They also went on to collect works by VAN GOGH, SIGNAC, Bonnard, Denis, Matisse and Picasso. Their collection, like that of SHCHUKIN, was later distributed between the Pushkin and Hermitage Museums.
□ M. Ginsburg, 'Art Collectors of Old Russia', *Apollo* (Dec. 1973); *Impressionist and Post-Impressionist Paintings in Soviet Museums*, ed. M. Bessonova (1985)

Murer, Eugène (1845–1906) A schoolfriend of GUILLAUMIN, through whom he got to know the rest of the Impressionists, he was a pâtissier by trade and was so successful that he opened a small but very successful restaurant at 95 boulevard Voltaire. There he held dinners for his painter friends every Wednesday night, assisted by his sister Marie. Loyal and supportive, he amassed a large collection of Impressionist paintings – bought, so his detractors said, at very low prices. They included 15 RENOIRS, 8 CÉZANNES, 25 PISSARROS, 10 MONETS, 28 SISLEYS, 22 Guillaumins, 2 GACHETS, as well as works by DELACROIX and Constantin GUYS – an allocation that seems to suggest that, in part at least, he was influenced by the poverty or pertinacity of the relevant artist – Sisley and Pissarro being respectively representative of these qualities. His portrait was painted by Renoir (1877; Collection of Mrs Enid A. Haupt, New York) and Pissarro (1878; Museum of Fine Arts, Springfield, Mass.).

Later, he bought a hotel at Rouen, where Pissarro stayed for a lengthy period and where Murer frequently entertained Monet, who was living nearby at GIVERNY. Murer was also a novelist of some originality, if not significance, and when he retired to AUVERS-SUR-OISE he took up painting seriously, holding exhibitions at the Théâtre de la Bodinière in 1895 and at VOLLARD's gallery in 1898. He was very intimate with the playwright and critic Paul ALEXIS, who helped his career as a painter. On his tombstone at Auvers are inscribed the words: 'Ouvrier – Littérateur-Peintre'. *See also* CABANER, CAFÉS
□ P. Gachet, *Deux amis des Impressionnistes; Le Docteur Gachet et Murer* (1956), M. Reilly Burt, 'Le pâtissier Murer', in *L'Oeil* (Dec. 1975)

Music The relationship between Impressionism and music can be considered on two levels; the simpler is the personal one, of the interest which the Impressionists as individuals took in music and musicians; the second, more complex, is that concerning the existence of Impressionism in music.

Most of the Impressionists had an interest in music, which was common amongst artists of their time. MANET's wife Suzanne (*see* LEENHOFF) was the daughter of a well-known organist and herself a gifted pianist. One of her closest musical friends was Emmanuel Chabrier (1841–94), who, though mainly known as the composer of comic operas such as *Le Roi malgré*, was also a distinguished conductor and is regarded by some, in his piano music, as a predecessor of Debussy and Ravel. He was a regular attender at the musical evenings that the Manets used to hold at their home, which was near his own, and he dedicated his *Impromptu in*

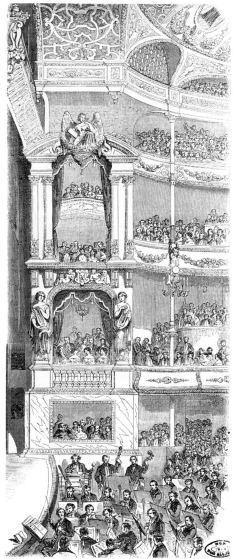

Musicians figure frequently in Manet's works; it is believed, for example, that the model for *The Spanish Singer* (1860; Metropolitan Museum, New York) was the famous Andalusian guitarist Huerta. In 1862, when the dance group from the Royal Theatre in Madrid came to Paris, Manet had them pose for him in the studio of Alfred STEVENS (drawing in the Szépművészeti Múzeum, Budapest), and later painted one of the main dancers, Lola Meleas, known as Lola de Valence (1862; Musée d'Orsay). Some 18 years later he continued the Spanish theme with a portrait of Emilie AMBRE in the title role of *Carmen*, an opera of which he was especially fond. He was friendly with Offenbach, whose portrait appears, appropriately enough, in *La Musique aux Tuileries* (1862; National Gallery, London); he is seated at the foot of a tree, together with his wife. When in Rome in 1885, Debussy admitted that he was homesick and yearned 'to see Manet and hear Offenbach'. Another close friend of Manet in the musical world was the singer Jean-Baptiste FAURE, who collected his works and whom he painted in the role of Hamlet in Ambroise Thomas' opera of that name (1865; National Gallery of Art, Washington).

BAZILLE was a musical enthusiast, who organized concerts in his studio in the rue de la Condamine, and in his well-known painting of it (1870; Musée d'Orsay) Edmond MAÎTRE, the music critic and composer, is seen at the piano. Maître was also a friend of RENOIR, and the three shared a passion for German music, being especially fond of the works of Wagner, which they used to discuss at great length. Renoir's enthusiasm led him in 1882 to visit the composer in Palermo, where they discussed musical subjects (somewhat inaccurately, as Renoir confused Auber with Meyerbeer), and where Renoir painted Wagner's portrait (Musée d'Orsay). MONET's early musical tastes are not documented, but by the time he was living in GIVERNY he had become fond of opera, frequently visiting Garnier's fairly new Opéra on his visits to Paris. When in the 1910s Diaghilev's Russian ballets came to Paris he was also entranced by them.

The Impressionist most closely associated with music in the popular mind is DEGAS, largely because of his ballet pictures, though it is interesting to note that as late as 1880, when he wrote to Albert HECHT asking him for a ticket admitting him to the examination of prospective ballet-dancers at the Opéra, he confessed

Music: Garnier's Opéra, *c.* 1870. The orchestra pit appears in Degas' painting, opposite.

C Major to Mme Manet. His portrait by Manet (1881) is in the Fogg Art Museum, and he was also a considerable collector of Impressionist paintings; the sale of his collection in 1896 included seven works by Manet, including the *Bar at the Folies-Bergère* (1882; Courtauld Institute, London).

Music: Renoir's portrait of Richard Wagner, painted in Palermo in 1882.

organist and teacher of music who achieved considerable popularity for his versions of Spanish songs. The painting remained in the Degas family until 1933, and Degas once showed it to one of his close friends, the lawyer Paul Poujad, who was an ardent defender of the school of younger musicians, including Debussy, d'Indy, Duparc and Chausson, and who introduced the artist to their works.

The concept of musical Impressionism is one that is widely accepted, but which serves to underline once again the amorphous meaning of the word. In this context it is usually applied to the music of Debussy, Ravel, Dukas, Roussel and Ibert, the general idea being that they wrote music that conveys an 'impression' of something, such as the sea or a hot afternoon, in a rather imprecise and unstructured way. A typical example of this interpretation of the word can be found, for instance, in Debussy's *L'Après-midi d'un faune*, in which a tonal impression is given of the poem by MALLARMÉ. There are, however, closer analogies between music and painting in this context. One of the most typical Impressionist techniques was the use of small, juxtaposed brushstrokes to build up a total effect, and in music those composers who are described as Impressionists used parallel thirds, fourths and fifths to create very much

that he had never been present at such an event. His range of acquaintances in the musical world was very large indeed, and some idea of it can be gauged from *L'Orchestre de l'Opéra* (1870; Musée d'Orsay); the work was bought and probably commissioned by Désiré Dihau, bassoonist at the Opéra from 1862 to 1889, who occupies the dominant position in the picture. Amongst the 'players' are Chabrier, the cellist Louis-Marie Pilet, the Spanish tenor Lorenzo Pagans, Louis Souquet (a doctor who was an amateur musician and composer), the flautist Henry Altès, and others who were actually members of the Opéra orchestra. *Musiciens à l'orchestre*, painted at about the same time, is a more documentary work (Städtische Galerie, Frankfurt-am-Main). A sense of the intensity of Degas' interest in music can be derived from the recently discovered fact (catalogue of the Degas exhibition at the Musée d'Orsay, 1988), culled from the Archives Nationales, that he attended Meyerbeer's opera *Robert le Diable* six times between 1885 and 1892, and the fact that he painted the *Ballet de 'Robert le Diable'* (Metropolitan Museum, New York) in 1871–72 seems to indicate that he must also have seen it several times before these dates. At about this time, too, Degas painted a portrait of Lorenzo Pagans, now in the Musée d'Orsay, with the artist's own father. Pagans was a singer, guitarist,

Music: *L'Orchestre de l'Opéra*, by Degas, 1870. Dihau, who bought the work, appears centre.

the same effect, tending to avoid broad, melodic lines in favour of a shimmering type of sound. This effect was one also sought by several later composers such as Delius, Vaughan Williams and Respighi, all of whom produced works that expressed in sound 'Impressionistic' visual experiences. *See also* CABANER, DANCING, FANTIN-LATOUR, HECHT, MAUS *[16, 20, 28, 90, 131, 144, 159]*

□ A. Stokes, *Monet* (1958); E. Lockspeiser, *Music and Painting* (1973); *New Grove Dictionary of Music and Musicians*, 20 vols., entry on 'Impressionism' (1980)

Muybridge, Eadweard *see* PHOTOGRAPHY

N

Nadar (Gaspard-Félix Tournachon) (1820–1910) One of the most remarkable figures of 19th-c. French cultural life, Nadar, as he called himself, was primarily an artist who became a photographer. As a caricaturist he worked for CHARIVARI and *Le Rire*, and in 1849 founded the short-lived *Revue comique*. He projected a four-volume series of caricatures of leading characters of his time, entitled *Le Panthéon Nadar*, but only one volume was published (1854). He was an impassioned collector, possessing an especially large number of works by Constantin GUYS. Deeply involved in the total cultural and social life of Paris, his main circle of contacts belonged to an older generation that included BAUDELAIRE, DELACROIX, Daumier and Doré, but he came to know the Impressionists mainly through the CAFÉ GUERBOIS. He does not seem to have bought any of their works, however.

The fact that the first IMPRESSIONIST EXHIBITION was held in his old studios at 35 boulevard des Capucines has tended to give a distorted impression of his connection with the movement. At the time when the exhibition was held, he was working from a new studio at 51 rue d'Anjou, and his old studio had been rented by Gustave Le Grey. The situation was first misinterpreted by MONET, who had met Nadar with BAZILLE, who knew him well, in 1864. Sixteen years later he said to a friend, 'The

Daumier's caricature of the Parisian photographer **Nadar** on one of his famous balloon flights.

Haussmann presenting his plans for the rebuilding of Paris to **Napoleon III**.

The Empress Eugénie, consort of **Napoleon III**, and her ladies, painted by the successful society portraitist F.X. Winterhalter *c.* 1853.

dealers didn't want us, yet we had to exhibit. But where? Nadar, the great Nadar, who is as good as fresh bread, lent us his place.' It is, of course, possible that Nadar persuaded his tenant to be accommodating, but he was not person- ally responsible for the exhibition.

There can be little doubt that Nadar's remarkable photographs of contemporary life, including his aerial views of Paris, had an influence on the Impressionists' visual imagina- tion. (The whole question is carefully and accurately discussed in A. Scharf, *Art and Photography* (1975); *see also* PHOTOGRAPHY.) It is an interesting coincidence that the year of the first Impressionist exhibition also saw the first industrialization of bromide plates for cameras, thus bringing photography within the range of a wider group of practitioners. *[133, 163]*
□ Nadar, *Quand j'étais photographe*, preface by L. Daudet (1900, repr. 1976); *Nadar*, Biblio- thèque Nationale, Paris, exhibition catalogue (1965); J. Prinet and A. Dilasser, *Nadar* (1966)

Napoleon III (1808–73) Charles Louis Napo- leon Bonaparte was the third son of Louis Bonaparte, King of Holland and brother of Napoleon I. In 1832 he became head of the Napoleonic family and in 1848, after an earlier attempt to seize power, became President of FRANCE. In 1851, as the result of a coup d'état, he

assumed personal control of the government, and in the following year was proclaimed Emperor.

The early years of his reign were marked by considerable political repression and censor- ship; in 1869 MANET's lithograph of the shooting of the Emperor Maximilian in Mexico – the result of one of Napoleon's ill-fated schemes – was censored; opponents of the regime, such as Victor Hugo, went into exile, and there was a general air of repression. On the other hand, the price of bread was regulated; immense public works, including the rebuilding of large areas of Paris, were undertaken; agriculture was subsi- dized; and the wars against Russia, Austria and China stimulated national self-confidence. France was also reassured by the spectacularly successful Exposition Universelle of 1862, which underlined the extent to which the nation was, somewhat tardily, benefiting from the Industrial Revolution, and which empha- sized the new position of PARIS as one of the most spectacular of European capitals.

Napoleon and his Empress Eugénie formed the centre of a court life as brilliant in appear- ance, if not in fact, as that which had flourished under the *ancien régime*, and he presided over a comparatively enlightened and certainly gener- ous system of art patronage, which he saw as one of the props of his power. Inevitably, the art forms he most favoured were of the ACADEMIC variety, and one of the results of the patronage that he dispersed was to widen still further the already apparent gulf between official and avant-garde art, and to link each with an attitude of political conformity or political dissent which, inevitably, neither possessed. His strong and forcibly expressed dislike of the works of COURBET – shared incidentally by NADAR, who drew some savage caricatures of the painter – almost certainly had political as well as aesthetic foundations – Courbet was a notorious opponent of his rule. On the other hand it was Napoleon III who was responsible for creating the SALON DES REFUSÉS of 1863, seen as an official snub to the hide-bound members of the SALON jury and a gesture towards artistic freedom. An efficient Ministry of Fine Arts, under the Comte de NIEUWERKERKE, not only dispensed patronage, supervised art education, created a nationwide system of museums and art galleries and promoted industrial art in all its forms, but undertook the preservation or restoration of France's heritage of national monuments. After all, Napoleon's was the last political regime in France to give its name to a style of fashion and design.

Tempted foolishly into war with Prussia when he was liberalizing his government, he was crushingly defeated, and died in exile in London. *See also* FRANCO-PRUSSIAN WAR, LA GRENOUILLÈRE, POLITICS *[215]*
□ P. La Gorce, *Histoire du Second Empire* (1899–1905, repr. 1970); D. Pinkney, *Napoleon III and the Rebuilding of Paris* (1958); A. Dansette, *Naissance de la France moderne, le Second Empire* (1976)

Nieuwerkerke, Emilien, Comte de (1811–92) Probably the most important, and certainly one of the most interesting, figures in the cultural life of the Second Empire. Born of an aristocratic Dutch family, he started his career as a sculptor, but with the advent to power of NAPOLEON III, his charms and abilities – no less than the fact that he was the lover of Princesse Mathilde Bonaparte, daughter of the great Napoleon's brother Jérôme – led him to a position of considerable power in the world of art. In 1849 he was appointed Director-General of National Museums, and in 1869 the Emperor created for him the post of Superintendent of Fine Art. His apartments in the Louvre were the location of a salon frequented by everybody who was anybody, and his activities, as well as

those of the Princess, were lovingly recorded by the GONCOURTS.

He had great influence on such things as the choice of pictures at the SALON: in 1868, for instance, after one of DAUBIGNY's pictures had been accepted and another was presented, Nieuwerkerke remarked 'Oh no, we've had enough of that kind of painting.' His views were, indeed, usually reactionary, and he tended to identify artistic with political radicalism, commenting on COURBET and the BARBIZON School, 'This is the painting of democrats, of people who don't change their linen, who want to deceive men of the world. It is an art which displeases and disgusts me.' Although he was reluctantly involved in the SALON DES REFUSÉS, he rejected two letters from CÉZANNE in the spring of 1866 suggesting a repeat of the experiment. It is worth noting, however, that Paul ALEXIS, in an article that appeared in 1873, commented, 'Many artists are now beginning to regret the passing of the Empire, and of M. Nieuwerkerke.' *See also* POLITICS
□ F. Henriet, *Le Comte de Paris* (1893); S.C. Burchill, *Imperial Masquerade; The Paris of Napoleon III* (1971); P. Mainardi, *Art and Politics of the Second Empire* (1987)

Nittis, Guiseppe de (1846–84) Born at Barletta in the south of ITALY, he studied painting at Naples and soon became involved in various anti-academic art movements, such as the Macchiaioli. In 1867 he visited Paris for the first time, and finally settled there in 1872. A friend of MANET and DEGAS, he participated in the first IMPRESSIONIST EXHIBITION, though most of the others had a very low opinion of his work; Paul ALEXIS described it as 'more like pastry than painting'. Though he remained on friendly terms with most of the Impressionists, De Nittis realized that his own gifts lay elsewhere, and started to produce those paintings, predominantly of high society, that were to make him famous and successful (*On the Banks of the Seine*, 1874; Galleria d'Arte Moderna, Milan). In 1878 he was awarded the Legion of Honour, much to Degas' disgust, and possibly envy.

De Nittis continued in his prosperity to support the Impressionists by buying their works extensively, and was especially appreciative of the paintings of MONET. In 1879 he held an exhibition of his own works at the offices of LA VIE MODERNE, which was run by the CHARPENTIER family and had become one of the main outlets for the Impressionists. It was the

De Nittis, *The Little English Girl*. His modified Impressionism proved highly successful.

most successful held there, attracting 2000–3000 people a day. In 1882 he entered into partnership with Georges PETIT, DURAND-RUEL's great rival, to found the Expositions Internationales, which had a warm reception from Parisian high society.

There can be no doubt that De Nittis was greatly influenced by Impressionism, even though he diluted it to suit his own style. As the Danish author Georg Brandes pointed out, in a letter written after he had seen an Impressionist exhibition in Berlin in 1882, 'Painters such as De Nittis, who, without siding completely with the Impressionists, have let themselves be influenced by, and have learned much from them, are likely to have a great success.' Towards the end of his life De Nittis made frequent visits to London, where he had a success comparable to that he enjoyed in Paris.
□ M. Pittaluga, *Guiseppe de Nittis* (1968); N. Broude, *The Macchiaioli* (1987)

Nouvelle-Athènes *see* CAFÉS

O

Oller y Cestero, Francisco (1833–1917) Born in Puerto Rico, he went to Paris and became a student at the ACADÉMIE SUISSE. Here he became friendly with PISSARRO and CÉZANNE, with whom he shared lodgings at 22 rue Beautreillis. He returned to South America for several years, but came back to France in 1895 and went to stay with Cézanne at AIX, until they had one of those rows that tended to mark the latter's relationships with others. Oller nevertheless maintained his friendship with Pissarro.
□ E. Bénézit, *Dictionnaire des peintres, sculpteurs, dessinateurs et graveurs* (1966); Rewald (1984)

P

Paris The Paris that the Impressionists knew in their childhood was basically the same as it had been in the reign of Louis XIV, an admixture of great houses and palaces surrounded by buildings of immense squalor, many of them still medieval in construction, with narrow streets, and roads without pavements – the Place de la

Baron Haussmann armed with the pick and trowel with which he was rebuilding **Paris**.

The Maison du Pauvre Diable was one of the many new department stores in **Paris**.

Concorde, for instance, was a sea of sand or mud, according to the season. There was little or no drainage or sanitation, little or no street lighting. The cholera epidemic of 1836, which killed 5500 of London's 1,778,000 inhabitants, killed 20,000 of Paris' 861,400. Yet the Paris of their maturity was one of the wonders of the modern world, with great boulevards, bright street lighting, and immense vitality. Despite the siege of 1870 and the subsequent ravages of the Commune, Paris had become the cultural capital of Europe, providing the subject-matter of many of their paintings and, by the unique qualities it had acquired, giving Impressionism characteristics it would not have possessed had it evolved elsewhere.

Very largely this was due to Baron Haussmann (1809–91) who, as Prefect of the Department of the Seine, ruthlessly, efficiently and magnificently rebuilt whole sections of the city, mainly but not exclusively in the western area of the Right Bank. He created a network of 50 kms (31 miles) of boulevards, which may have had some strategic purpose, in making the building of barricades more difficult and facili-

tating the rapid movement of troops in case of insurrection, but which provided a magnificent setting for that 'life of the streets' that has become so typical of Paris, and caught the imagination of the Impressionists in a way no other urban theme has ever enthralled a group of artists. In 1864 A. Césena (in *Le Nouveau Paris*) described the boulevard des Italiens as 'a long open-air room, where waves of humanity follow one another; a room that is enlivened in the evenings by innumerable gas-jets'.

CAFÉS proliferated; splendid restaurants catered for every taste and every purse; a multitude of theatres and music-halls provided entertainment for an ever-growing population, which more than doubled in the course of the century, very largely due to the influx of people from the provinces and the surrounding countryside. This had been facilitated by the expansion of the RAILWAYS. Paris was the centre of a railway system – by 1870 it was the terminus of ten lines – that helped to make it the world's greatest manufacturing city, with nearly half a million workers employed in its various industries. These, no less than the flurry of economic activity engendered by the rebuilding of the city, created a vast inflow of wealth, reflected in the growth of a banking system far in advance of that in any other European capital, with the possible exception of London. Mirrored in the pages of ZOLA's novels, the affluent bourgeois society which emerged during the second half of the century provided the majority of the patrons of the Impressionists.

It was a society, too, which was mirrored in the splendour of its public buildings. Appropriately enough, railway stations were built like cathedrals, and the type of interaction they provoked is exemplified in the Gare Saint-Lazare, the subject of paintings by MONET and CAILLEBOTTE, which stimulated the growth of the BATIGNOLLES area in which it was situated. This became an area greatly favoured by the Impressionists in the early stages of their development, and the station, by offering easy egress to the surrounding countryside, promoted the growth of weekend pleasure places and country retreats such as ARGENTEUIL, PONTOISE and BOUGIVAL, as well as giving easy access to the Channel ports and seaside resorts. Garnier's grandiose Opéra gave architectural expression to the importance which that institution always possessed, and the growth of large department stores such as the Bon Marché (1872) not only enhanced the urban landscape,

The Eiffel Tower on its way to dominating the **Paris** skyline in 1888. The pavilions for the centenary Exposition Universelle can be seen in the background.

but gave Parisians the opportunity of acquiring smart but cheap clothes of a kind that make, for instance, the shopgirls of DEGAS or the dancing midinettes of RENOIR so engagingly attractive (a phenomenon somewhat dramatically described by Zola in *Au Bonheur des dames*, 1882).

Paris had always been famous for its cultural amenities, especially as far as the fine arts were concerned. The Louvre had been a great gallery since the time of the first Napoleon, and its treasures had been significantly enhanced – with special relevance for the Impressionists – by the addition of Louis-Philippe's Spanish Gallery. The Palais du LUXEMBOURG, originally the residence of Marie de'Medici, had become since 1818 a gallery of 'living French art', drawing its new acquisitions mainly from the SALONS by a system that was constantly varying. Other public galleries and museums opened during the latter half of the century. In 1879 the Musée des Monuments Français offered to artists, especially sculptors, a repertoire of works of art, mainly medieval, that was to exert an important influence on people such as Rodin. In 1889 Emile Guimet, a collector and

scholar, founded the museum that bears his name, and in 1891 Henri Cernuschi, a friend of Gambetta, bequeathed his fabulous collection of Chinese art to the nation; the creation of a Museum of Decorative Arts, based on the collections of the Duchesse de Galliéra, opened up a new dimension of artistic experience.

Less permanent exhibitions were a constant feature of the Parisian calendar. Every year the Salon showed some 5000 paintings by close on 2000 painters, attracting in 1884, for example, 238,000 visitors. By 1861 there were 104 commercial art galleries in the capital mounting, on average, 8 exhibitions a year. But more specific to Paris was the series of international exhibitions, more frequent and more popular than similar events in London, Berlin or Vienna, which not only attracted large numbers of foreign tourists, but enhanced the reputation of French art and stimulated collectors from other countries to buy French paintings. Exhibitions of this kind were put on in 1855, 1867, 1878, 1889 and 1900. Each of them had a section devoted to art – that in the 1855 exhibition was visited by 982,000 people –

where visitors could see a conspectus of all that was happening in the world of art, not only in France but in the whole of Europe. Nor were these exhibitions as conservative in their content as one might have expected: the art section of the centennial exhibition of 1889 contained works by MONET, PISSARRO, CÉZANNE, FANTIN-LATOUR, TISSOT and RAFFAËLLI, and indirectly enhanced the reputation of the Impressionists.

These exhibitions also opened up new art forms. France's preoccupation with colonialism prompted the introduction of sections devoted to her various colonies. That of 1855, for instance, laid emphasis on ALGIERS and Morocco, and the influence of their cultures became immediately apparent not only in the Salon but in the works of RENOIR and others. The most exotic international exhibition, and the one that had the greatest display of non-European cultures, was that which celebrated the first centenary of the Revolution; Muslim minarets, Cambodian temples, Javanese and Tahitian dancers, Senegalese tomtoms and Polynesian flutes exposed artists – notably GAUGUIN – to areas of aesthetic experience which they might not otherwise have known, and created a realization amongst the general public that there were ways of seeing and expressing things, other than in the language of Western painting and sculpture. *See also* NAPOLEON III *[24, 25, 39, 50–1, 89, 90, 91, 92, 101, 106, 117, 126, 130, 143, 144, 160, 166, 202]*
□ M. Girouard, *Cities and People* (1985); J. Seigel, *Bohemian Paris; Culture, Politics and the Boundaries of Bourgeois Life, 1830–1930* (1986); Zeldin (1988)

Pastels The sketch-like quality that was of the essence of Impressionism, and the movement's accentuation of the process of creation rather than of the completion and finishing of a work of art, naturally attracted many of its practitioners to the medium of pastel. It provided a simple way of enclosing, within an outline, flat areas of colour created by rapid, spontaneous strokes, of emphasizing highlights, producing half-tones by 'scuffing' to reveal the ground, and allowing the artist to keep an immediate check on colour effects. Its impermanent nature, and its capacity of being manipulated by the fingers and altered quickly, gave it a quality that even watercolour did not possess.

There had been a growing interest in pastel, due in part at least to the rehabilitation of artists of the 18th c., especially great pastellists such as

Morisot, *Portrait of Madame Pontillon*, 1871: an accomplished and sensitive **pastel** of her sister.

Quentin de Latour, Nattier, Greuze and Chardin; and in part to the way in which English artists had exploited its landscape potential. Some indication of this revival is provided by the fact that in 1870 the Société des Pastellistes was founded in Paris, and ten years later the first exhibition of the Pastel Society, at which WHISTLER exhibited, was held in London.

MILLET had been one of the first of his generation to use pastel. MANET experimented with it a great deal, though somewhat exceptionally, of the 89 of his works in this medium that have survived, more than 70 are portraits of women, such as, for instance, *La Viennoise*, a portrait of Irma Brunner (*c.*1880; Cabinet des Dessins, Musée du Louvre). Although he occasionally used paper as a ground, most of the pastels are on canvas or board. In all cases they have a dazzling freshness, a sense of spontaneity, and a freedom from pretentious analysis that is entirely delightful. These qualities are also apparent in the pastels of MORISOT, who used very much the same technical devices but introduced a more perceptible element of analysis into her portraits.

RENOIR tended to use chalk in his explorative work, but pastel played an important role too, especially in the 1880s, when he produced such works as the *Young Woman with a Muff* (Metropolitan Museum, New York), and explored the elements of his great *Baigneuses* of 1884–87 in a huge pastel and wash sketch (The Art Institute of Chicago). This largeness of concept is very much an innovation of the Impressionists and is to be found again in Renoir's *Two Young Women* (1895; Private collection, Switzerland), which measures 79 × 65 cms (31 × 25½ ins.) and in which he uses complex criss-crossing lines to create a pattern of highlights, catching an extraordinary feeling of instantaneous observation.

MONET inherited an interest in pastel from his preceptor BOUDIN, who used it extensively to produce remarkable studies of vast expanses of cloud and sea; these sketches aroused the admiration of BAUDELAIRE, who commented on the fact that each recorded the date and time of execution. Monet's own pastels partook of the same explorative nature as Boudin's and were clearly preliminary explorations for paintings. In the sketch for Waterloo Bridge in the Cabinet des Dessins in the Louvre, he seized on various transitory combinations of colour and form with a vigour of apprehension that brings him close to an artist such as Munch.

PISSARRO began to use pastels in 1870, but saw them as independent works, rather than as preparatory sketches for another medium, and

Degas' **pastel** *After the Bath*, c. 1900, is one of several variations on the same theme.

also as sellable works of art for those who could not afford his oil paintings. But it was DEGAS who not only used pastel extensively but, from the 1880s onwards, raised it to the level of a major art form, using it to depict volume and to create pictorial freedom of the most innovative kind, in a manner that makes his works in this medium as important as the paintings of CÉZANNE in opening up to art the way to the future. His technical experiments were endless. He rejected the smooth, unbroken application of colour in favour of animated, broken up, tessera-like strokes, with the pastel applied unevenly to allow underlying colour or the ground to show through. As in all his works, form remained predominant, reinforced rather than dissolved by colour. Massive in size (the memorable *After the Bath* of 1895–98 in the Kunstmuseum Solothurn measures 94.5 × 80.5 cms; 37 × 32 ins.) and heroic in composition, not all of them are 'sketches', either in appearance or intent. Works such as *The Coiffure* (1884–86; Metropolitan Museum, New York) or *The Injured Jockey* (c.1897; Kunstmuseum, Basle) are of subjects that many other artists would have used for oil paintings.

CASSATT, who was so close to Degas, also produced a great number of pastels, mostly of intimate and domestic subjects, closer in feeling to Manet's works in the medium, but showing strong Japanese influence. *See also* ILLUSTRATION □M.L. Bataille and G. Wildenstein, *Catalogue raisonné of the Oil Paintings, Pastels and Water-colours of Berthe Morisot* (1961); J. Leymarie, *Impressionistische Zeichnungen von Manet bis Renoir* (1969), A. Callen, *Techniques of the Impressionists* (1982); Adriani (1985)

Patrons and collectors 'Every rich family', commented Georges de Sonneville in 1893, writing about the art collections of Bordeaux, 'is necessarily obliged to collect a gallery of pictures, and this for two compelling reasons; first, from a natural taste for modern luxury, and second, because the possession of wealth has its obligations.' There can be no doubt that the acquisition of wealth, and the upward social mobility it implied, meant that in the 19th c. FRANCE had more patrons and collectors of art than at any previous time in its history. Though only a very small proportion of them were sufficiently adventurous to buy works by the Impressionists and other artists of that type, this proportion did reflect the overall pattern. It was composed very largely of those who were

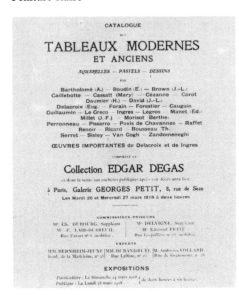

CATALOGUE

TABLEAUX MODERNES
ET ANCIENS

AQUARELLES — PASTELS — DESSINS

PAR

Bartholomé (A.) — Boudin (E.) — Brown (J.-L.)
Caillebotte — Cassatt (Mary) — Cézanne — Corot
Daumier (H.) — David (J.-L.)
Delacroix (Eug. — Forain — Forestier — Gauguin
Guillaumin — Le Greco — Ingres — Legros — Manet (Ed.)
Millet (J.-F.) — Morisot Berthe
Perronneau — Pissarro — Puvis de Chavannes — Raffet
Renoir — Ricard — Rousseau Th.
Serret — Sisley — Van Gogh — Zandomeneghi

ŒUVRES IMPORTANTES de Delacroix et de Ingres

COMPOSANT LA

Collection EDGAR DEGAS

et dont la vente aux enchères publiques après son décès aura lieu

à Paris, Galerie GEORGES PETIT, 8, rue de Sèze

Les Mardi 26 et Mercredi 27 mars 1918 à deux heures

COMMISSAIRES-PRISEURS

Mᵉ Ch. DUBOURG, Suppléant | Mᵉ DELVIGNE, Suppléant
Mᵉ F. LAIR-DUBREUIL, | Mᵉ Edmond PETIT
Rue Favart nᵒ 6 mobilier | Rue Grammont nᵒ 25 mobilier

EXPERTS

MM. BERNHEIM-JEUNE |MM. DU RANDBEUL M. Ambroise VOLLARD
Bould. de la Madeleine, nᵒ 25 | Rue Laffitte, nᵒ 20 | Rue de Grammont, nᵒ 28

EXPOSITIONS

Particulière : Le Dimanche 24 mars 1918 } de deux heures à six heures
Publique : La Lundi 25 mars 1918

Patrons and collectors: catalogue of the Degas sale at the Galerie Georges Petit, 1918.

either moving into the middle classes or who, having already got there, were progressing upwards in that social category. There were very few collectors of the upper classes; the Prince de WAGRAM and the Bibescos were very much the exception. A large number were professional people: doctors, such as GACHET and DE BELLIO; teachers, such as the Abbé GAUGAIN; musicians, such as FAURE and Chabrier; lawyers, such as Emile Blémont; publishers, such as CHARPENTIER; and civil servants, such as CHOCQUET. Then there were the upwardly mobile *nouveaux riches*: the department store magnate Ernest HOSCHEDÉ; the successful pâtissier and restaurant-owner Eugène MURER; François DÉPEAUX, the successful Rouen merchant who left a large part of his collection of Impressionists to his native city; and the Swiss Oscar Schmitz (1861–1931), who built up a large and successful cotton industry in Le Havre and was of vital help to MONET during a difficult period. All these patrons and collectors were very typical of the dominant social class in late 19th-c. France, and almost any of them could have figured in the pages of ZOLA's novels.

An important category of collector, however, and one that is often disregarded, is that of artists, who often, as soon as they began to be successful, bought paintings on quite a lavish scale, sometimes out of considerations of friendship, but more frequently because they had a real interest in, and admiration for, the works of their contemporaries. Of these the most outstanding is CAILLEBOTTE, who was of course a rich man – but there are others. ROUART built up a collection which consisted of works by COROT, COURBET, Daumier, MILLET, ROUSSEAU, JONGKIND, CÉZANNE, DEGAS, MANET, Monet, MORISOT, PISSARRO and SISLEY. In addition to his important collection of JAPANESE prints, Monet had some 30 works by his contemporaries and friends, especially Renoir and Cézanne. Degas was a collector of drawings by old masters, but also of works by some of his fellow Impressionists, and was an early patron of GAUGUIN. Official patronage was largely absent until the 20th c. *See also* AROSA, BARNES, BÉRARD, CHAMPFLEURY, DAVIES COLLECTION, DORIA, DURAND–RUEL, EPHRUSSI, FLORNOY, GANGNAT, GAUDIBERT, HAVEMEYER, HECHT, HÔTEL DROUOT, KHALIL BEY, LANE, LATOUCHE, PÈRE MARTIN, MARTINET, MAUS, MAY, MELLON, MOROSOV, NADAR, PELLERIN, PETIT, PHILLIPS COLLECTION, PORTRAITURE, PRICES, PROUST, SHCHUKIN, VOLLARD *[47, 57, 124, 138, 208]*
□ H.C. and C.A. White, *Canvases and Careers* (1965); A. Boime, 'Entrepreneurial Patronage in Nineteenth-Century France', in *Enterprise and Entrepreneurs in Nineteenth- and Twentieth-Century France*, ed. E.C. Carter (1976); Zeldin (1988)

Peinture claire A method of painting evolved and much used by MANET, which creates a high-key colour configuration by first applying loose-flowing and *grasse*, or fat, pigment onto the canvas and then, whilst the paint is still wet, adding the half-tones and darker passages. This was the reverse of the accepted ACADEMIC process, which worked from the dark passages towards the light. The resulting effect is one of sparkle and vitality, seen for instance in *A Bar at the Folies-Bergère* (1882; Courtauld Institute, London), one of his last works, in which the TECHNIQUE is at its most highly developed. The technique was adopted by other Impressionists, especially Manet's own personal followers, MORISOT and GONZALÈS. *See also* COLOUR
□ A. Callen, *Techniques of the Impressionists* (1982)

Pellerin, Auguste (1852–1929) A successful margarine manufacturer who built up a significant collection of Impressionist paintings. It was

especially rich in works by CÉZANNE, amongst which are to be included the *Still Life with Onions* (1895), *Woman with a Coffee-Pot* (1890–95), and *Achille Emperaire* (1868–70), which he and his children bequeathed to the Louvre and which are now in the Musée d'Orsay. In 1910 he sold part of his collection to a group of dealers, including DURAND-RUEL, Bernheim-Jeune and Paul Cassirer, for the record sum of one million francs. [*218–19*]
□ S. Monneret, *L'Impressionnisme et son époque*, vol. 4 (1981)

Perrot, Jules (1810–92) Starting his DANCING career at the age of 20, he became one of the most important dancers and choreographers of the 19th c. Until 1834 he danced with Marie Taglioni at the Paris Opéra, and then undertook an extensive European tour with Carlotta Grisi. From 1842 to 1848 he was choreographer and *maître de ballet* at Covent Garden, and then took the same job at the St Petersburg opera.

A lithograph showing Carlotta Grisi and the youthful **Perrot** in *The Polka* (1844).

Manet's sparkling portrayal of the *Bar at the Folies-Bergère*, 1882, shows extensive use of *peinture claire*, a technique Manet himself evolved.

The eye is drawn inwards through Caillebotte's dramatic use of **perspective** in *Le Pont de l'Europe* of 1876.

In 1873 he met DEGAS, who made him the central figure in *The Dance Class* (*c.* 1875; Musée d'Orsay, and *c.* 1876; Metropolitan Museum, New York). Degas also drew various sketches of him in different media (Fitzwilliam Museum, Cambridge, in pencil; Art Institute of Chicago, watercolour, ink and oil wash). *[67]* □ I. Guest, *The Ballet of the Second Empire, 1858–70* (1974), *Jules Perrot; Master of the Romantic Ballet* (1984)

Perspective Although it would not be true to say that the Impressionists introduced a new type of perspective, their attitude towards its conventional forms was explorative and innovative. CÉZANNE was not the only one to notice that objects in close proximity to the eye do not follow the laws of classical perspective, a fact that has been exploited by many more recent artists. The experiments in perspective carried out by CAILLEBOTTE are the subject of detailed analysis in K. Varnedoe's monograph of the artist, in which it is pointed out that in works such as *Le Pont de l'Europe* (1876; Musée du Petit Palais, Geneva) the following stages were involved:

1. A small drawing of an empty architectural setting, made without a straight edge.

2. A careful perspectival drawing of the above, made with a straight edge.

3. Drawings of figures and architectural details.

4. Oil sketches for the component parts of the picture which pay only cursory attention to the perspective construction, intended to work out the colour arrangements.

5. A modification, achieved in the finished picture, of the figures and the perspectival construction, arrived at in such a way that an artificially achieved structure is presented as an objective depiction.

There is evidence that the fidelity with which Caillebotte depicted his sites may have owed a good deal to PHOTOGRAPHY, or the use of an optical drawing aid such as the *camera lucida*. The camera did indeed have a great influence on the perspective of the Impressionists – as well as on that of their more traditional contemporaries. Wide-angle lenses, with their potential for expanding space, were available from the 1860s onwards, and the camera generally presented artists such as MANET, who had already acquired many of the perspectival techniques perfected by Velazquez and other Spanish 'realists', with a model of REALISM that, by its spontaneous observation of people and objects in space, provided them with an essential element of their pictorial language. DEGAS had an intimate knowledge of the theory and practice of photography, and clearly made use of it in many of his works, but his perspective was basically of a traditional kind based on his predilection for drawing and his close study of the old masters. His fondness for viewing people and objects from a low vantage-point (e.g. the *Portrait of Diego Martelli*, 1879; Museo Nacional de Bellas Artes, Buenos Aires) provided obvious opportunities for his virtuosity, and his most remarkable display of this technique of *sotto in sù*, which reached a Tiepolo-like dexterity, is the *Miss La La au cirque Fernando* (1879; National Gallery, London). It is worth noting, however, that in a copy of Sensier's *La Vie et l'oeuvre de J.-F. Millet* (1881) in the library of University College, London, there is a note in the hand of SICKERT, to whom the book once belonged, saying that Degas told him that he had used the services of a *perspecteur* – an architectural draughtsman specializing in perspective – in planning the work.

Another powerful influence on the way in which the Impressionists approached the problems of perspective was provided by the discovery of JAPANESE prints. The use of close-up viewpoints, the creation of a dynamic tension between figures and space, and the exploration of Japanese compositional conventions, such as bridges to introduce the spectator into the pictorial space, became common devices amongst all the Impressionists. *See also* TECHNIQUE *[128, 136, 222, 223]*
□ Rewald (1973); A. Callen, *Techniques of the Impressionists* (1982); K. Varnedoe, *Gustave Caillebotte* (1987)

Petit, Georges (c.1835–1900) Usually thought of as DURAND-RUEL's chief rival, Petit was in fact a dealer who had a much wider range of interests, and a good deal less commitment to the Impressionists as a group. Though, on the whole, he was interested in 'modern' movements in painting, his stance would be described in political terms as 'slightly left of centre'. He owned a very luxurious gallery at 8 rue de Sèze, which was much frequented by polite society, and his speciality was the works of the more advanced traditionalist painters such

The use of **perspective** in Japanese art: Hiroshige's *Shower at the Ohashi Bridge* (1857).

as RAFFAËLLI, Albert Besnard and DE NITTIS.

In collaboration with the latter he commenced in 1882 a series of annual Expositions Internationales de Peinture, and by 1885 MONET and RENOIR had started exhibiting at them, though not without some misgivings. By so doing they were brought into contact with a wider range of patrons and fellow artists; it was through Petit, for instance, that Monet met SARGENT. Petit was responsible for persuading Monet to submit to the Salon again, and advised him to keep his prices low. At the 1886 exhibition all of his paintings sold and the following year he was on the selection committee. Petit's involvement with the Impressionists increased with their success, and SISLEY signed a contract with him. One of his most imaginative gestures was when he organized a joint Rodin–Monet exhibition in 1889, which enhanced both their reputations and suggested the existence of 'Impressionist SCULPTURE'. *See also* HÔTEL DROUOT, MIRBEAU, MORISOT
□ Rewald (1973); J. House, *Monet; Nature into*

Renoir's *Déjeuner des canotiers*, pride of the **Phillips Collection**, was bought from the artist in 1881, and remained in Durand-Ruel's private collection until 1923, when his sons sold it to Duncan Phillips.

Art (1986); J. Rewald, *Studies in Post-Impressionism* (1986)

Phillips Collection The combination of a fortune made out of manufacturing window glass and the influence of the writings of Walter Pater on a sensitive Yale undergraduate, who had come to see art as 'an escape from the boundaries of the self', was responsible for the creation of an art collection housed in a pleasant, but not remarkable, family mansion in Washington. Rich in many phases of art history, it is especially so in its holdings of works by the Impressionists and their immediate successors.

Duncan Phillips and his brother Jim, who died at an unexpectedly early age, persuaded their parents in 1916 to devote the not inconsiderable sum of $10,000 a year to the purchase of works of art. By the time the collection was opened to the public in 1921, it contained some 250 pictures, many of them works by American painters such as Ryder, Eakins and Winslow

Homer, as well as works by Chardin, Ingres, DELACROIX and COURBET. Duncan, now actively supported and encouraged by his artist wife Marjorie, was however becoming increasingly concerned with more recent art. This concern was fostered by DURAND-RUEL's sons, who in 1923 invited them both to lunch; facing them at the table was RENOIR's *Le Déjeuner des canotiers* of 1881, which they bought for the then fantastic sum of $125,000. It became the centrepiece of an impressive collection of Impressionist works, including CÉZANNE's *Self-portrait* of 1878, DEGAS' *Women Combing their Hair* of 1875, and a larger number of POST-IMPRESSIONIST works, with a strong emphasis on VAN GOGH and Bonnard. Duncan Phillips wrote a number of illuminating books about art and collecting, before his death in 1966.

□ D. Phillips, *A Collection in the Making* (1943), *The Phillips Collection* (1952)

Photography 'From today painting is dead': although Paul Delaroche's comment on photography was, as befitted a Romantic painter, slightly melodramatic, there can be no doubt that it had an immensely important influence on the development of art. Joseph Nicéphore had first fixed images on metal plates in the 1820s, and his discoveries were exploited and publicized by his partner Louis Daguerre, who published details of his photographic process in January 1839. Within ten years half a million photographic plates were being sold in Paris; the 'daguerrotype' had altered peoples' apprehension of visual reality, and artists were beginning to take serious note of the possibilities and the dangers inherent in this 'pencil of nature', which was seen as a direct threat to the art of the painter; indeed, the category of jobbing portrait-painter virtually vanished.

DELACROIX thought that 'the photograph is a demonstration of the true idea of nature, something of which otherwise we would have only the flimsiest notion'. Ingres was one of the first to utilize the camera for portrait-painting, and by 1867 ZOLA was attacking artists purely because their works were too much like photographs. But resemblances were not always direct. By the late 1840s many of COROT's paintings were marked by a massing of light and shadow areas into flat, unarticulated planes, and the edges of his foliage started to show a fuzziness at precisely the time (c.1848) when the coated glass plates which began to supplant the daguerrotype showed just that particular characteristic. On his death more than 300 photographic plates, mostly of landscape subjects, were found in his studio.

Most of the BARBIZON painters depended quite heavily on this new adjunct to their technique, and so it was inevitable that when the Impressionists began, in their different ways, to adopt attitudes to natural reality, they should explore the potential of the camera. There is more than an accidental significance in the fact that their first exhibition should have been held in a building which had once been a photographer's studio. Its landlord NADAR, who had commenced his own career as an artist, was not only one of the most innovative and enterprising photographers of his time, but was an active and loquacious member of the circle which gathered at the CAFÉ GUERBOIS. One of MANET's etched portraits of BAUDELAIRE was made from a photograph taken by Nadar, and his portrait of Edgar Allen Poe, and another of that writer, intended for the French poet's translation of Poe's stories, was based on an

13508
La photographie sollicitant une toute petite place à l'Exposition des beaux-arts.

Nadar's caricature (1855) emphasizes the claims of **photography** to be considered a form of fine art.

American daguerrotype. The execution of the Emperor Maximilian unleashed a whole series of photographs of the event – many of them montages – and in his painting of the scene (Mannheim Museum) Manet relied on several of these. BAZILLE used a combination of sketches and photographs for certain of his outdoor groups, a fact which is very evident in the varying poses of Summer Scene, Bathers (1869; Fogg Art Museum, Cambridge, Mass.), and MONET's Women in the Garden (1867; Musée d'Orsay), painted for Bazille, into whose collection it passed, was based on two photographs taken at Bazille's home at Méric, near Montpellier.

It is known that by the 1880s Monet possessed no fewer than four cameras, and he was on very friendly terms with Theodore ROBINSON, who had a clearly avowed policy of using the photographic image and who must almost certainly have had some influence on him. But Monet belonged to a generation that saw something slightly reprehensible in a

A photograph of Cézanne and the self-portrait he based on it in 1866. Unlike many artists of his day, Cézanne felt no qualms about relying on **photography**.

painter's using a camera; he was especially sensitive about the merits of PLEIN-AIR painting, a technique he did not invariably use, despite his protests to the contrary. He certainly possessed photographs of Rouen cathedral, and more than probably used them when reworking pictures from the series at GIVERNY. In 1905 he wrote angrily to DURAND-RUEL on the subject, which had apparently been brought up by William Rothenstein: 'I know a Mr. Harrison, whom SARGENT asked to make me a little photograph of the Houses of Parliament, which I have never used. But that is of no significance, and whether my cathedrals, my Londons and other canvases are painted from nature or not is nobody's business and is of no importance.'

CÉZANNE, on the other hand had no qualms about relying on the camera, and his friend and supporter Émile BERNARD was astonished that he executed portraits from photographs, just as he painted flower pictures from illustrations in magazines. His self-portrait of 1866 (Private collection) is painted from a photograph, and c.1868 Marion wrote to their mutual friend Heinrich Morstatt, 'Cézanne is planning a painting for which he will use some snaps . . . . I have your photograph and you will be in it.' His *Melting Snow at Fontainebleau* of about 1880, and the *Male Bather* of 1885–90 (both Museum of Modern Art, New York), were based on photographic images.

The influence of the camera went beyond its use on specific occasions, however. The quest for REALISM, which was one of the motivating drives of Impressionism, involved more than subject-matter chosen from ordinary life; it called for a realism of gesture and action – as opposed to the stylized syntax of movement which the Academy had inherited from the Carracci and the Mannerists – and a recording of spontaneous rather than contrived movements. Until the 1840s artists intent on catching such moments in time had been dependent on a rapid sketching ability, which not all possessed. The camera provided an 'image of magical instantaneity', as DEGAS described it. It was not merely that this image could on occasion be transferred to canvas or paper, but that the visual paradigms created by the photographic image, with its abrupt and often compositionally gauche bisections of vision and oddities of gesture, became an accepted part of the Impressionists' technique. Especially influential was the 'snapshot' type of photograph available to the general public in the mid-1880s (the Kodak camera was first marketed in 1888). Additional support was supplied from more historic sources by the similar compositional brutalities which occurred in the currently popular JAPANESE prints. The extensive series of drawings which CAILLEBOTTE made for his exercise in the immediacy of observation, *Peintres en bâtiment* (1877; Private collection, Paris), show just how far he was prepared to go in his quest for the instantaneous eye, while his *Rue de Paris; temps de pluie* (1877; Art Institute of Chicago) shows a scene in which the perspective might have been based on the wide-angle lens, which had been invented in the previous decade. The camera had indeed made available to artists a whole new range of visual experience which hitherto had not been patient of analysis by the unaided eye, including views from a considerable height or distance, such as those provided by the pictures Nadar took from his balloon, and detailed views of such normally inaccessible subjects as the gargoyles of Notre-Dame.

The *locus classicus* of the impact of the camera on art in general, and on Impressionism in particular, is the effect that the photographic vision had on Degas. In 1878 the magazine *La Nature* published a series of illustrations documenting the work which Eadweard Muybridge had been carrying out by photographic sequences of horses in motion, and this was followed by an article about his discoveries in *L'Illustration*. His work in this field had, to a certain extent, been paralleled in France by that of the French physiologist Etienne-Jules Marey, who had endeavoured to analyse the sound of hoof beats. The whole subject fascinated both artists and horsemen, and it seems probable that Degas attended the illustrated lecture given by Muybridge in the studio of the famous battle-painter Ernest Meissonier, certain aspects of whose work he greatly admired, on 26 November 1881. But it was not until the publication of Muybridge's great work, *Animal Locomotion*, in 1887 (of which he bought a copy) that Degas began to apply these discoveries to his own work. He made at least two drawings of the Muybridge plate illustrating 'Annie G. at the trot', and from that point onwards his depiction of horses in motion, in both two and three dimensions (e.g. the sculpture *Horse Rearing* of c.1890, Musée d'Orsay), reflected the photographic discoveries of Muybridge. In about 1896 Degas bought an easily portable Kodak camera, and he was one of the first to use a spool of film. From then onwards he became an enthusiastic photographer,

though he continued to utilize the old glass plates with a tripod-based camera. In this field, especially in his photographs of the HALÉVY family and of friends such as MALLARMÉ, he showed a real skill and creative brilliance, even though over-enthusiastic experimentation sometimes led to technical imperfections. *See also* BAYARD, TECHNIQUE *[24, 27, 52, 150, 198, 221, 222, 231]*

☐ D. Halévy, *Degas parle* (1960); V.A. Coke, *The Painter and the Photograph* (1972); A. Scharf, *Art and Photography* (1974)

Piette, Ludovic (1826–77) A landscape-painter, who was a pupil of COUTURE before attending the ACADÉMIE SUISSE, where he became friendly with PISSARRO and started to follow the tendencies of Impressionism. He participated in the third and fourth IMPRESSIONIST EXHIBITIONS during a period when his works were almost indistinguishable from those of Pissarro, who often stayed with him in his house at Montfoucault in Brittany, and where Pissarro painted a number of landscapes. Around 1870 Piette painted a picture in gouache of Pissarro at work, which later belonged to Camille, the painter's son; now lost, it is known only through a photograph.

☐ L.R. Pissarro and L. Venturi, *Camille Pissarro, son art, son oeuvre*, 2 vols. (1939)

Pissarro, Camille (1830–1903) The most vocal, the most literate, the most active of all the Impressionists, Pissarro has an importance for the movement that transcends his undeniable artistic achievements. He was at once an irritant and an inspiration to his fellows, constantly pushing his own painting style in all possible directions, in response to changes in the wind of taste. At times almost unduly modest and unsure of himself, he was at others assertive and challenging in his attitudes. Given to analysing and questioning his own creative processes, he was remarkably undogmatic in the plentiful advice he gave to others. His own career encapsulated all the different elements that gave Impressionism its individual qualities. A radical in politics, with a strong leaning towards those anarchistic beliefs that at the time were causing such alarm in European society, he had a concern with the welfare of humanity shared by few, if any, members of the artistic community in which he lived.

Born in Saint-Thomas in the West Indies of a fairly affluent family, he was sent to Paris when

Boulevard des Italiens; Morning, Sunlight (1897): in the last decade of his life **Pissarro** painted some of his greatest works, including this vivid picture of a crowded boulevard.

young to complete his education, and there showed his first skills in drawing. After his return to the West Indies, his determination to be an artist led his father eventually to desist from forcing him into the family business. In 1855 he returned to Paris and studied painting at the ACADÉMIE SUISSE, where he met MONET. An assiduous searcher-out of suitable contacts, he frequently visited the CAFÉ GUERBOIS and got to know MANET, CÉZANNE, RENOIR and the rest. Enraptured at first by the work of DELACROIX, he soon discovered COROT, who gave him advice and encouragement, and under whose auspices he had works regularly accepted at the SALON between 1864 and 1869. His paintings showed the deep influence of Corot in his concern for light and atmosphere, the wide-angle view of landscape and an overall dark, but silvery tonality (*The Marne at Chennevières*, 1864; National Gallery of Scotland). In 1863 the paintings he had sent to the SALON DES REFUSÉS were praised by CASTAGNARY and three years

later, ZOLA, in his review of the Salon of that year, picked out his works for a laudatory mention.

On the outbreak of war Pissarro came to London, where a branch of his family had already established itself. Whilst there he produced some fine landscapes, predominantly of Norwood and the area in South London around the Crystal Palace (*Penge Station, Upper Norwood*, 1870; Courtauld Institute, London). He also met Monet again, and both were in contact with DURAND-RUEL, who exhibited Pissarro's works at his London gallery and with whom he was to maintain a lasting connection.

When he returned to LOUVECIENNES, where he had been living just before the war, Pissarro found that only about 40 paintings out of a total of 1500 – an extraordinary comment on the facility with which he must have worked – had been left undamaged by the Prussians who had occupied his house. The following year he moved to PONTOISE, where he was visited by

Cézanne. To the latter he expounded the merits of painting in the open air, a technique in which he had always been interested. Pissarro was deeply involved in the discussions and planning which went into preparing for the first IMPRESSIONIST EXHIBITION in 1874, and he participated not only in that, but in all the subsequent exhibitions. Later in life, however, he was to confess about this period 'I remember that, though I was full of ardour, I did not have the slightest idea, even at the age of 40, of the profound aspect of the movement which we pursued instinctively. It was in the air.' His vague discontent with the Impressionist exhibitions found some expression in 1875 when he became associated with Alfred Meyer in setting up an alternative group, L'UNION, but by the time its first exhibition had been arranged in 1877 at the Grand Hôtel on the boulevard des Capucines, he, as well as Cézanne and GUILLAUMIN, had resigned.

Pissarro had for some time been discontented with what he called his 'rough' technique, and c.1885, having come under the influence of SEURAT, he began, to everybody's surprise, to adopt a modified and softened form of Pointillism (*Springtime in Eragny*, 1886, Brooks Memorial Art Gallery, Memphis). By 1892, however, when he had an important and successful one-man exhibition at Durand-Ruel's, he had judiciously reverted to his earlier Impressionistic style. Henceforward his financial position was secure: he bought a house at ERAGNY and spent the rest of his life in patriarchal serenity. Amongst other activities, Pissarro was an active engraver, watercolourist and painter of porcelain designs. *See also* AROSA, BRAQUEMOND, COURBET, DRAWING, ENGLAND, GACHET, GAUGUIN, GUILLEMET, ILLUSTRATION, ITALY, PASTELS, PIETTE, PLEIN-AIRISME, PORTRAITURE, PRICES, PRINTS, ROUSSEAU, SOCIAL BACKGROUND, VIGNON *[15, 37, 55, 75, 84, 179]*
□ L.R. Pissarro and L. Venturi, *Camille Pissarro, son art, son oeuvre*, 2 vols. (1939); *Camille Pissarro; letters to his son Lucien*, ed. J. Rewald (1943); *Correspondance de Camille Pissarro*, ed. J. Bailly-Herzberg, vol. 1, 1865–85 (1980); *Pissarro: 1830–1903*, Arts Council, London, exhibition catalogue (1980)

Pissarro, Félix (1874–97) Born in the year of the first Impressionist exhibition, Camille's son Félix became a painter, engraver and caricaturist, using the pseudonym Jean Roch to avoid confusion with other members of the family.

His work was enthusiastically praised by Octave MIRBEAU, and his father commented warmly on the force and originality of his paintings. He died of tuberculosis in London. There is a portrait of him by Camille in the Tate Gallery, London (1881).

Pissarro, Julie (1838–1922) Camille Pissarro met Julie Vellay, the daughter of a Burgundian farmer and vine-grower, in 1860 when she was working as his mother's maid, and started to have an affair with her. This estranged the painter from his family, who cut off his allowance. The couple married in London in 1870, when Pissarro was a refugee there, by which time they had already acquired two children; four more were to follow. Julie loyally supported her husband during years of privation. In 1879 he painted a moving portrait of her sewing close to a window (Ashmolean Museum, Oxford).

Pissarro, Lucien (1863–1944) The eldest son of Camille, he was brought up, as it were, in the bosom of Impressionism and was taught painting by his father, with the assistance of others, especially MANET and CÉZANNE. As a young man, he came to England and worked under LEGROS, of whose teaching, however, his father

Lucien and Félix **Pissarro** with their father, c. 1900.

was very wary. He exhibited at the Impressionist exhibition of 1886, but by this time he had adopted a Pointillist style, having fallen under the influence of SEURAT, as indeed his father had.

His move to ENGLAND, where he had become permanently settled by the early 1890s, however, removed him from French influences, and in 1896 he founded the ERAGNY Press at Hammersmith. This published illustrated books, predominantly of French origin. Many of the works produced were illustrated by himself in woodblocks, mainly of a decorative nature; but in some works, such as the coloured frontispiece to Coleridge's *Christabel* (1904) and the 12 illustrations to an adaptation of a French fairy tale, *The Queen of the Fishes*, he transcended the less admirable mannerisms of the current *fin-de-siècle* style. Hand-printed, small in format, these books were issued in very limited editions. The press ceased publishing in 1914. Thereafter his main activity was painting intimate views of the English landscape. He had a very real influence on securing the complete acceptance of Impressionism in England, and the correspondence between his father and himself is of primary importance to the history of Impressionism. *See also* ILLUSTRATION
□ W.S. Meadmore, *Lucien Pissarro* (1962)

Plein-airisme (Open-air painting) The notion of the importance of painting landscape *in situ* was in a sense a legacy bequeathed by Romanticism to REALISM. Part of its motivation was that belief in the inspiring and almost sacramental quality of nature which had been an integral part of the anti-classical bias of art and literature since the last quarter of the 18th c.: here in the open air was a truth far removed from the stuffy restraints of the studio, the conventions of the academic; here too was reality perceived through the eyes, not conceived in the remoteness of the mind. The notion was not entirely new, especially amongst English painters, and the story of Turner being strapped to the mast of a ship so that he could paint a storm at sea recurs frequently in the writings and letters of many later artists – it had an especial appeal to MONET. The attraction of this approach was also stimulated by a technical innovation of the 1840s: the invention of collapsible tin tubes in which paint could easily be carried about and manipulated in the open air.

It would be a gross oversimplification to think of *plein-airisme* as an innovation of the

Manet, *Monet Working in his Studio-Boat*, 1874, shows the painter's passion for **plein-airisme**.

Impressionists. Delaroche emphasized the need to paint in the country and encouraged his students to make trips into the environs of Paris. COUTURE did the same, and even took his students on paintings trips to Normandy and the Channel coast to paint seascapes. GLEYRE also advised his students, including BAZILLE, RENOIR and Monet to work *en plein air*. By the early 1860s it had become the accepted thing (as recorded in the GONCOURTS' novel about artistic life at the period *Manette Salomon*) for students of each atelier to club together to provide funds for country painting expeditions, usually to the area around BARBIZON. All the painters connected with that place practised some kind of open-air painting – with the curious exception of MILLET, who said that he could remember everything he had seen when he got back to his studio – but it was mostly in the form of sketches or rough outlines which served as a basis for more considered working up. This was even true of JONGKIND, whose paintings so often give the feeling of having been painted on the spot. Only BOUDIN and DAUBIGNY consistently painted complete works in the open air. Their influence on the younger generation was significant.

In 1866 Monet decided at VILLE D'AVRAY near Saint-Cloud to paint a picture entirely in the open air; he dug a trench to accommodate the lower portions of the very large canvas he was using, so that he could easily reach the upper part. Renoir at this time was painting landscapes in the open, predominantly with a palette-knife technique, and when he exhibited his portrait of *Lise* (Folkwang Museum, Essen), in 1867, a critic commented on the fact that his accurate rendition of the colouring of the shadows showed that it had been painted out of doors. The group of paintings which Monet, Renoir and SISLEY produced at ARGENTEUIL in the late 1860s was the most spectacular vindication of *plein-air* painting, of which PISSARRO had by this time become an enthusiastic advocate.

The approach seemed to have emotional as well as artistic undercurrents. There was the largely literary feeling of direct communion with nature in the Romantic tradition; there were suggestions of that passion for the open air which had started to affect society in the first half of the century, and which ensured the popularity of country excursions and seaside resorts; there were even moralistic dimensions, especially apparent in the case of Monet, who became vehement in his insistence that he did paint his pictures out-of-doors, even when it was evident that he had not. He became indignant when he heard from DURAND-RUEL that it was being suggested he had used photographs for his paintings of the Houses of Parliament, adding rather lamely that in any case it was nobody's concern but his own. It was only in his smaller paintings that he used the *plein-air* approach, however, and it was not until the waterlily pictures of 1914 that he undertook large works in the open; his paintings of Venice were all completed at Giverny from sketches done in Italy. On the other hand, his insistence on accuracy of observation of light effects was remarkable. Often he noted the times of day on the back of canvases, and he said that seven minutes was the length of time he could work on any one of the *Poplar* series 'until the sunlight left a certain leaf'. He often had a number of canvases in progress at the same time, so that he could work on each according to the appropriate time of day. In 1889 he wrote to a friend, 'I've got everything under control and things are progressing nicely with different motifs chosen for the morning and the afternoon, sunlight and grey weather.' On occasions he would get up before dawn to catch a particular effect, and could spend as many as 60 sessions on the same painting.

It is improbable that any of his contemporaries, with the possible exception of Sisley, whose life is not well documented, were quite as besotted with the creative ideology of the open air as Monet was. CÉZANNE, for instance, though he spent endless days painting under the hot sun of Provence, was quite prepared to rely on magazine illustrations for some of his flower paintings. But all in all it can be said that *plein-airisme* contributed an essential element to Impressionism. It can indeed be seen as playing the same role that drawing and painting from the life had played for earlier generations of artists as a pictorial discipline, as a field of experimentation and discovery, and as a stimulus to creativity. *See also* COLOUR, MANET, PHOTOGRAPHY, TECHNIQUE *[49, 52, 195, 213]*
□ *Painting from Nature; The Tradition of Open-Air Oil-Sketching from the Seventeenth to the Nineteenth Century*, Arts Council, London, exhibition catalogue (1980); A. Callen, *Techniques of the Impressionists* (1982); J. House, *Monet; Nature into Art* (1986)

Pointillism *see* SEURAT, SIGNAC

Politics For a variety of reasons, left-wing politics and art in 19th-c. PARIS had become inextricably linked. This was partly due to geographical factors. The centre of the art world was on the Left Bank, around the ECOLE DES BEAUX-ARTS, an area identified by authority as troublesome, and unsanitized by the urban renewal which NAPOLEON III had inflicted on Paris to make the building of barricades impossible, and to facilitate the movement of the forces of law and order. In addition, artists tended to frequent the same cafés and social centres used by writers and what were generically known as 'agitators'. Moreover, the Romantic image of the artist as rebel, intent on pursuing his own aims contrary to the wishes of his family and society, had become firmly established by the 1830s and was enshrined in books such as Henri Murger's *Scènes de la vie de Bohème* (1847–49) and ZOLA's *L'Oeuvre* (1886). Official art, on the other hand, heavily subsidized and highly organized, with its elaborate hierarchy of institutions from the Ecole des Beaux-Arts downwards, was seen and used as one of the main props of society. By its imagery it sanctified the power of the state and the rightness of the social order, providing pictures of the Emperor or the President to confirm their significance, commemorating battles, perpetuating the Napoleonic myth, bodying forth the eternal verities of religion, and codifying, in meticulously painted detail, those sartorial and other niceties which established the different ranks of society. Any variation from these officially sanctioned icons, any infraction of the stylistic syntax that governed their expression, was seen as a threat to society.

Politics: a cartoon of 1870 shows the current French view of the European political scene. France is resisting the invasions of Prussia, who has one hand on Holland and the other on Austria.

There was, too, during the latter half of the 19th c., especially in France, a heightened sensitivity to such putative dangers as a consequence of a series of outrages, usually committed by, or attributed to, anarchists. In 1858 an attempt was made to assassinate Napoleon III, and at regular intervals during the next five decades bombs were thrown into cafés, politicians were assassinated, banks were blown up. The worst fears of the middle classes were realized in the establishment of the Commune in Paris in 1871, even though it was rapidly and bloodily suppressed. Even before this, the paranoia of the establishment had been succinctly expressed by the sensitive and otherwise highly cultivated Count NIEUWERKERKE, Napoleon III's Minister of the Arts, when he referred to the works of MILLET and the BARBIZON School generally: 'This is the art of democrats, of those who don't change their linen, and who want to put themselves over on men of the world. This art disgusts and displeases me.' In fact, Millet was a political sceptic, a religious agnostic, whose peasants were closer in feeling to the bucolic fantasies of the 18th c. than to any wild revolutionary principles. The identification of political and artistic unreliability with dirty clothes is especially revealing, and it is interesting that when Zola and others defended MANET's works they laid special emphasis on the artist's smart clothes and gentlemanly demeanour.

COURBET's political stance, however, helped to identify artistic with political revolution in the public mind, and confirmed the Emperor's expressed dislike of his work. When the Commune was established he was elected a representative of the people and became president of the Assembly of Artists, which abolished the Ecole des Beaux-Arts, the awarding of medals and the fine arts section of the INSTITUT. In this capacity he ordered the destruction of Napoleon's column in the Place Vendôme, and when government forces occupied Paris on 28 May 1871 he was imprisoned, then moved to a hospital. He was condemned to rebuild the column at his own expense, and understandably fled to Switzerland, where he died in 1877.

None of the Impressionists, however, showed the least degree of involvement in the politically significant events that were taking place at this time. MONET and PISSARRO were safely ensconced in London; RENOIR and SISLEY had gone back to the forest of Fontainebleau;

Politics: sentence being pronounced by a military court on those involved in the Commune; Courbet is in the back row on the left. From *Le Monde illustré*, 4 September 1871.

DEGAS stayed with his friends the Valpinçons in their country house; Manet and CÉZANNE were in Provence; Zola was in Bordeaux. The only visual record of the Commune made by any of the group are two lithographs by Manet, who, in spite of his earlier brush with the Imperial censors over a lithograph of the execution of the Emperor Maximilian – an event which irritated Zola a good deal more than it did him – tended to take a detached, cynical, dandyish attitude to politics.

Generally, the political opinions of the Impressionists, insofar as they had any, reflected the attitudes of that bourgeois society to the destruction of which they were popularly thought to be dedicated. Renoir and Degas could generally be thought of as fairly right of centre. Both were anti-Semitic; Renoir always referred to Pissarro as 'that Israelite', and discussed at length with Wagner the evil influence of Jewish composers. Some of the sentiments he expressed, which were lovingly recorded by Julie Manet in her *Journal*, are almost ludicrously reactionary: 'Socialism has taken everything away from the workers. Religion, which for them was such a consolation, has been replaced by an extra 25 centimes a

Politics: Manet's *The Barricade* illustrates the violent suppression of the Commune, 1871.

day'; 'Education is the downfall of the people'; 'We are living in an age of decadence, where people think of nothing but travelling at dozens of kilometres an hour'; 'Jews come to France to earn money, but if there is any fighting to be done they hide behind a tree' – and then, a few lines later, 'There are a lot of Jews in the army because they like to walk about wearing uniforms.' During the early part of his life, Degas seems to have had no very strong political views, beyond a certain scepticism. But the Dreyfus affair of 1893–94, which did so much to polarize French public opinion, revealed him as a confirmed conservative who rejected all his Jewish friends, even those of long standing such as the HALÉVYS. Cézanne, who had also gone back to his earlier religious beliefs in the cosy provincial security of AIX-EN-PROVENCE, was an anti-Dreyfusard. Monet, on the other hand, signed the so-called 'Petition of the Intellectuals' calling for a new trial, though this was due rather to his friendship with CLEMENCEAU than to any very deeply held left-wing opinions. Pissarro, the exception, was a convinced radical with anarchistical leanings; always concerned about injustice, he produced a number of impassioned cartoons for left-wing journals.

Facts have little to do with opinions, and in the public mind the Impressionists were seen as political revolutionaries; their art was condemned invariably as being an onslaught on the established order. Nor was this attitude confined to France. Reviewing the 1883 Durand-Ruel exhibition in London, *The Times* critic commented on the artists as being 'the chosen representatives of the Extreme Left', and ten years later the *National Observer* characterized Monet's art as 'the very anarchy of painting'. In 1904 E. Wake Cook published a book, *Anarchy in Art and Chaos in Criticism*, in which he underlined quite clearly, with special reference to the Impressionists, the notion that change in art involved social revolution.

Although the Impressionists – with the exception of Pissarro – had no settled revolutionary stand in organized politics, it must be acknowledged that their artistic practice implied a generally democratic stance. They painted contemporary life, and made no attempt to validate the present by reference to the patriotic achievements of the past; they never painted religious pictures; their portraits depicted people as they were, in casual poses, without trying to emphasize or enhance their

official standing or social status; they frequently chose subjects depicting aspects of working-class life – though the main source of imagery was the life of the middle classes – and it is ironic that it was Degas, probably the most reactionary member of the group, who went furthest in breaking down accepted conventions by his preoccupation with working girls, prostitutes and other representatives of those 'lower orders' who were thought to constitute a potential threat to society. *See also* CASTAGNARY, DURET, FÉNÉON *[89, 92, 150, 215]*

□ Clark (1984); J. Seigel, *Bohemian Paris: Culture, Politics and the Boundaries of Bourgeois Life 1830–1930* (1986); P. Mainardi, *Art and Politics of the Second Empire. The Universal Expositions of 1855 and 1867* (1987); Zeldin (1988)

Pontoise A small village on the river Oise near AUVERS that first became popular with painters of the BARBIZON School. PISSARRO first settled there in 1866 (*The Hermitage at Pontoise*, 1867; Solomon R. Guggenheim Museum, New York), and returned again after the FRANCO-PRUSSIAN WAR. There he met DAUBIGNY, and on at least one occasion they painted very similar versions of the same area (Pissarro: *The Côte du Jallais, near Pontoise*, 1867; Metropolitan Museum, New York, and Daubigny, *The*

Pontoise, *c.* 1875, before increasing industrialization in the 1880s diminished its rural charms.

Hermitage near Pontoise, 1866; Kunsthalle, Bremen). In 1872 CÉZANNE came to visit Pissarro there, and during his stay developed the Impressionistic elements in his work; it was there, too, in 1877 that GAUGUIN began to paint seriously. In 1873, when the idea of the first group exhibition was being mooted, Pissarro pressed enthusiastically for the creation of an association of those who were going to participate, basing an elaborate constitution for such a body on the regulations and rules which the bakers of Pontoise had drawn up for their own co-operative association. By 1883, however, Pontoise was becoming urbanized, and Pissarro left, first for Osny and then ERAGNY, where he settled permanently. *See also* GUILLAUMIN, MÉDAN, SOCIÉTÉ ANONYME DES ARTISTES
□ *See bibliographies for* ARGENTEUIL *and* AUVERS

Portraiture Despite the fact that their main interest was in either natural or man-made landscape, portraiture played an important part in the work of many of the Impressionists, and they have created some of the most outstanding exercises in the genre. Unlike their more academic contemporaries, however, they did not rely on commissioned portraits as a source of income, and often works of this kind were undertaken either as a gesture of patronage on the part of the sitter, or as a demonstration of friendship on the part of the artist. RENOIR's portrait of Madame CHARPENTIER and her children (1878; Metropolitan Museum, New York), for example, owes it existence to the fact that she and her husband were warm supporters of the painter. Despite its Impressionistic handling and the fact that the faces of the children especially were already conforming to the stereotype that Renoir was to make so specifically his own, the picture had a considerable success when it was exhibited at the SALON of 1879.

Analogous in many ways was MANET's 1877 portrait of FAURE as Hamlet in Ambroise Thomas' opera, the work with which, as a singer, he was most closely identified, and to which he owed some of his phenomenal success. Faure was one of the most active collectors of works by the Impressionists, an activity not untinged with speculative considerations – and so, in a sense, it was an act of patronage. But it was also something of a publicity exercise, since it was clearly good for an actor or musician to have his or her portrait in the Salon. In the event, the work was not a success; it was slated by the critics, and Faure

Detail from Degas' **portrait** of Manet listening to his wife playing the piano, *c.* 1865.

refused to accept it, though this did not prevent him from commissioning another portrait four years later, when he and Manet received the Legion of Honour.

Commissioned portraits were comparatively rare for the Impressionists, and their greatest achievements in the field were portraits of members of their family or friends, or sometimes, as with Manet's portrait of the hostile art critic Albert WOLFF, intended to flatter those who might be useful. Members of the artist's family – constantly observed, suffused with affection or respect – appear as icons of domestic felicity: MONET's pictures of his wife; CÉZANNE's of his father; Renoir's of his children; and DEGAS' remarkable series of the Italian members of his family, grave, with echoes of the Renaissance in their stately posed profiles and their clear limpid gaze – all these are milestones in the history of portraiture. Then they painted portraits of each other: BAZILLE painted Monet after his accident at the Inn in Chailly (1866; Musée d'Orsay); Renoir painted SISLEY in the CABARET DE LA MÈRE ANTHONY (1866; Nationalmuseum, Stockholm) and with his wife (1868; Wallraf-Richartz-Museum, Cologne), as well as Bazille at his easel (1867; Musée d'Orsay); GUILLAUMIN showed PISSARRO apparently painting some blinds (1868; Musée

Municipal, Limoges); Manet found in Berthe MORISOT a constant source of inspiration (e.g. *Repose*, 1870; Rhode Island School of Design); and Degas painted Manet, sprawled in a chair, listening to his wife playing the piano (*c.* 1865; Kitakyushu City Museum, Japan). The next most popular category included those who were intimate with them and gave them support, either in the form of patronage or favourable reviews. Degas' numerous portraits of the HALÉVY family, Manet's of ASTRUC, MALLARMÉ, George MOORE and ZOLA; Renoir's of CHOCQUET, DURAND-RUEL, Eugène MURER and VOLLARD; Cézanne's of Chocquet and Vollard, and Bazille's of Edmond MAÎTRE and Astruc, are all part of the accepted iconography of Impressionism.

All these portraits conformed with what Degas proclaimed to be the true purpose of portraiture, 'To depict people in familiar and typical attitudes, above all to give their faces the same choice of expression as one gives to their bodies.' This, of course, may be partly attributable to the influence of PHOTOGRAPHY, though it should be noted that until the invention of a cheap, portable camera in the late 1880s, most portrait photographs were of a stiff and posed kind. There was also the spontaneity of pose in so many Japanese portraits – or their equivalents – of the kind that were so popular in Impressionist circles. Both these influences must also have contributed to another very characteristic feature of many Impressionist portraits – the unusual viewpoint which the artist adopts to his sitter, usually from a much lower, or a diagonal position. Degas was especially adventurous in this respect: his portrait of Diego Martelli (1879; National Gallery of Scotland) seems to have been painted from an almost crouching position; in that of Ludovic Halévy and Albert Boulanger-Cavé, the latter's body is sliced in two by the right and the two are seen in an almost voyeuristic way (1879; Musée du Louvre); and in *L'Absinthe* (1875–76; Musée d'Orsay) – virtually a portrait of Marcellin DESBOUTIN and the actress Ellen ANDRÉE – the two figures are confined within less than half of the total picture space. In Monet's *Corner of an Apartment* (1875; Musée d'Orsay) his wife and son sink like half-seen shadows into the deep recesses of the picture space, whereas CAILLEBOTTE's top-hatted oarsman so dominates the forefront of the picture *Partie de bateau* (1877; Private collection, Paris) that he seems to be rowing into the spectator's space.

Manet's **portrait** of the engraver Bellot in a Dutch-inspired genre scene, *Le Bon Bock* (1873).

On the whole the Impressionists did not paint portraits of 'ordinary' people, using them rather for genre-like themes, as with Manet's *Le Bon Bock* (1873; Philadelphia Museum of Art), or the curious *Interior* (1868–69; Philadelphia Museum of Art) by Degas, sometimes called *The Rape*. One remarkable contribution, however, that the Impressionists made to the art of portraiture was the revitalization of the concept of the conversation-piece, a group painting in which identifiable individuals are portrayed engaged in some specific social activity or situation. During the first 20 years of the movement there was a whole sequence of such paintings, most of them implicitly recording stages in the progress towards coherence amongst the artists involved, hinting at student loyalties and a sense of camaraderie. Manet's *La Musique aux Tuileries* of 1862 (National Gallery, London) is perhaps too large to fall neatly into this category, even though all the figures in the foreground are identifiable portraits, but Renoir's *Inn of Mother Anthony* of four years later, in its informality, its emphasis on a social activity and its sense of a moment seized in time, most certainly does do so. This was painted in 1866, and in the following year Monet's *Terrace at Sainte-Adresse* (Metropolitan Museum, New York) adapted something of the same approach to what is essentially a group portrait. Bazille's group essay in the same genre, showing ten members of his family on the terrace of their house near Montpellier (1868–69; Musée d'Orsay), comes closer in feeling to the carefully staged set pieces of a Winterhalter, and is in sharp contrast to his view of his own studio in the rue de la Condamine (Musée d'Orsay) painted the following year, with its sense of spontaneous observation. How explicit this 'conversation piece' element often was in the Impressionists' approach can be realized from the fact that when Degas painted the interior of the Cotton Exchange in New Orleans, he deliberately entitled it *Portraits in an Office* (1873; Musée des Beaux-Arts, Pau). Even to the most apparently straightforward portraits, such as that of himself and Evariste de VALERNES (1865; Musée d'Orsay), he gave an added suggestion of recently spoken words and unfinished dialogue. Renoir's great group portraits – for this is what they really are – *The Boating Party at Chatou* (1879; National Gallery of Art, Washington), *Dancing at the Moulin de la Galette* (1876; John Hay Whitney Collection, New York) and the *Déjeuner des canotiers* (1881;

Phillips Collection, Washington) involve the same degree of interpersonal relationships.

In their portraits the Impressionists looked for a degree of psychological REALISM, and were just as concerned with the depiction of personality as their more traditionalist contemporaries. But they used a weaponry more extensive than the usual 'expressive' eyes and stylized features to achieve this. The whole body of the sitter, his or her pose, the clothes, the accoutrements with which the sitter is surrounded: all these were utilized to depict people not *sub specie aeternitatis*, but as sentient human beings alive at one particular moment in time. *See also* TECHNIQUE [*17, 28, 30, 37, 47, 57, 65, 90, 131, 162, 164, 205, 208, 222*]

□ T. Reff, 'Pissarro's portrait of Cézanne', in *Burlington Magazine*, CIX (1967); D. Gordon, *Edgar Degas; Hélène Rouart in Her Father's Studio* (1984); M. McQuillan, *Impressionist Portraits* (1986)

Post-Impressionism Although obviously meaning anything that happened after

Post-Impressionism: Cézanne's *Bathers* of 1876 shows that quest for structural solidity which was, in a sense, alien to much Impressionist thinking.

Impressionism, the word is of imprecise and sometimes contradictory meaning. It was popularized in the English-speaking world after it was first used to describe an exhibition held at the Grafton Galleries in London in 1910, entitled, 'Manet and the Post-Impressionists'. This contained 21 works by CÉZANNE, 41 by GAUGUIN, and two each by SEURAT and SIGNAC, whom the French more accurately describe as 'néo-impressionnistes', in that they pushed to their logical extremes many of the basic technical devices and attitudes of the Impressionists, and so eventually negated them.

In the preface to the catalogue of the second Post-Impressionist exhibition of 1912, Roger Fry commented on the 'classic spirit' of the work on show, and anchored it to Cézanne. He put forward the plausible theory that Post-

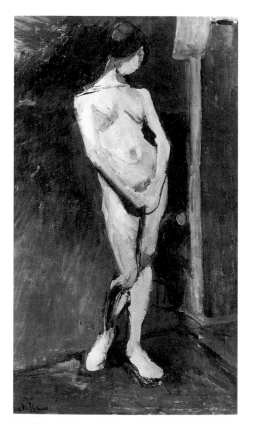

Detail of *Nude Study in Blue*, 1900; an early work by the **Post-Impressionist** Matisse.

Impressionism was a reaction against the apparently formless nature of Impressionist painting, and an attempt to create plastic form rather than to describe it – a view popularized by Clive Bell in his *Art* of 1914. The relationship to Cézanne was well taken, and much play was made about his well-known reference to Poussin. Artists such as Picasso and Matisse were included in the category of Post-Impressionists, and there was a clear link with Cubism. More recently, however, the word has been used as an umbrella description for many different tendencies between about 1890 and 1914 which express a stylistic reaction against one or other of the characteristic features of Impressionism. *See also* BERNARD, ENGLAND, FÉNÉON, INDÉPEN-DANTS, VOLLARD *[31, 101, 197, 210]*

□ S. Lovegren, *The Genesis of Modernism* (1959); *Post-Impressionism*, Royal Academy, London, exhibition catalogue (1959); R. Shattuck, *The Banquet Years* (1959); J. Rewald, *Post-Impressionism* (1956)

Prices The initial problem in examining the prices which the Impressionists got for their works is to translate them into the monetary values of the late 20th c. One has to take into account, for instance, not only the cost of living, but standards of living. A very rough and ready formula is to multiply sums by four, but this is at best an approximation. A more indistinct, but at the same time more accurate, picture can be obtained by comparison with other prices: a return ticket from PARIS to ARGENTEUIL cost 3 francs in 1890; a miner at the same period paid 2 francs a month to his union; a solicitor's clerk got 1200 francs a year; admission to the SALON was 50 centimes; postage for a letter, 10 centimes; and a comfortable middle-class income was about 80,000 francs a year. Paintings by artists such as Meissonier, COUTURE and Rosa Bonheur fetched prices around 40,000 francs. Another complication is the fact that in the late 20th c. the price of Impressionist paintings has soared into the realms of fantasy. A MONET can reach £3 million, a RENOIR £5 million and a CÉZANNE £4.5 million. Faced with such figures, it is difficult to assess the prices the artists received in their own lifetime, without making comparisons which introduce an unsettling dimension of melodrama.

Most of the Impressionists, with the possible exception of SISLEY, eventually received reasonable, if not excellent prices for their works, despite initial hardship. There is no certain relative pattern. In 1895, for instance, Renoir's *Déjeuner des canotiers* sold for 7500 francs at a time when Monet was getting as much as 13,000 per picture, whereas some ten years previously the position had been reversed. Monet's financial career is very revealing. In 1865 he sold the first two paintings that had been accepted into the Salon for 300 francs each, but three years later he got 800 francs for a larger one that had also been exhibited there. In the next decade his income from picture sales varied between 10,000 and 20,000 francs a year, and in the 1880s between 25,000 and 30,000 francs. But then, as a consequence partly of the success of his exhibition with Rodin in 1889, partly of his growing popularity with American collectors, his annual income in 1891 topped 100,000 francs. By the beginning of the 20th c. he had saved enough to be almost independent of sales, and so was able to indulge in those pictorial experiments which produced the *Nymphéas* series. In the salerooms the rise in values was even more spectacular. In 1913, for instance, DURAND-RUEL bought *The Terrace at Sainte-Adresse* (1867; Metropolitan Museum, New York) for 42,400 francs, and at the end of the First World War American dealers were asking as much as $50,000 for Monet's larger works. After his death, however, there was a sharp fall in the prices his pictures fetched — in 1926 the Tate Gallery, London, bought *Dame assise dans un parc* for a mere £525 — and it was not until the 1950s that the rise to today's astronomic figures really got under way.

One thing is obvious, that as far as the artists themselves were concerned, longevity was the key to financial success. MANET, who died early, never received high prices during his lifetime. In 1872 Durand-Ruel bought a number of works from him, including the following:

L'Espagnol: 1500 francs; sold to HOSCHEDÉ for the same amount; then to FAURE for 650 francs, and finally to HAVEMEYER for 100,000 francs.

Le Liseur: 1000 francs; sold to Faure for 1500 francs; bought back in 1907 for 100,000 francs, and sold to the Museum of Cincinnati for 150,000 francs.

Bullfight: 500 francs; not sold at 5000 francs in a New York exhibition of 1886, but sold ten years later to the art gallery of Chicago for 70,000 francs.

In 1924 the Tate Gallery paid £10,000 for *La Serveuse de bocks*, which had cost £100 in 1884, and £3292 in 1919.

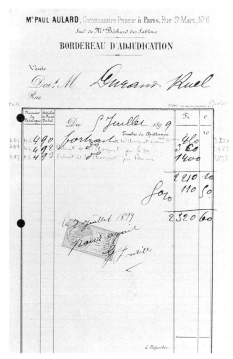

Prices: an invoice from the Durand-Ruel archives for works acquired at the Chocquet sale in 1899.

DEGAS' prices followed a more complex pattern, dictated by a variety of factors, some peculiar to himself, some due to the fact that his art was more accessible. In 1872 Faure commissioned a ballet painting from him at the comparatively high price of 5000 francs. Some years later Durand-Ruel bought it from Faure for 100,000 francs, and almost immediately sold it to Colonel Payne of Boston for 125,000 francs. In 1892 Alexander Reid, the Scottish dealer, bought *L'Absinthe* for a mere £180 and sold it at a considerable, though undisclosed, profit to Count Isaac de Cammondo, who bequeathed it to the Louvre. At the end of the century SICKERT made a humble 500 francs profit when he sold to Durand-Ruel a Degas he had bought in 1889 for 1500 francs. Ten years later Durand-Ruel sold it to Senator Clark of Washington for 80,000 francs. The sale that took place in 1918 after the painter's death produced mixed results. The LUXEMBOURG museum, for instance, paid the considerable sum of 300,000 francs for Degas' *Portrait of the*

Bellelli Family of 1858, but only 60,000 for the *Battle Scene* of 1865. Almost from the beginning, Degas' pastel works fetched comparatively high prices. Three years before the artist's death, Sir William Eden, WHISTLER's patron, bought one for £4620, and at the studio sale in 1918, the pastels, though much fewer in number than the oil paintings, made comparatively more. This tendency has persisted into quite recent times. In 1928 William Cargill paid £12,800 for a ballet painting in oils and £4200 for one in pastel. In 1963 the pastel sold for £105,000, a 25-fold rise, whilst the oil made only £55,000, a 4-fold rise.

The pattern of Renoir's financial success was similar to that of Monet, though his early triumphs at the Salon meant that he got off to an earlier start. In 1912 the *Ride in the Bois de Boulogne* of 1873 was sold for 52,500 francs, and after his death the contents of his studio, consisting of 103 paintings and drawings, were acquired by the Galerie Barbezanges for 1½ million francs. PISSARRO, on the other hand, never really commanded high prices. In the Durand-Ruel archives there is a copy of the catalogue of the second IMPRESSIONIST EXHIBITION of 1876, in which are pencilled the prices of his works; they range from 1000 francs for *Printemps; soleil couchant* to 400 francs for *Neige, côteaux de l'Hermitage*. Even in 1912, five of his landscapes only made a total of 23,000 francs at the ROUART sale, though *The Thames at Charing Cross*, which in 1937 was bought by Cargill for £2600, reached £47,000 sixteen years later. *See also* DEUDON, DURET, ENGLAND, GAUGUIN, THÉO VAN GOGH, HÔTEL DROUOT, KHALIL BEY, PÈRE MARTIN *[17, 30, 40, 162]*
□ Venturi (1939); H.C. and C.A. White, *Canvases and Careers* (1965); G. Reitlinger, *The Economics of Taste*, 3 vols. (1970)

Prints The invention of lithography, the growth of a popular illustrated press – over 1300 illustrated periodicals were launched in France between 1830 and 1900; improvements in the tools, machinery and paper used for traditional print-making activities such as etching: all these combined to create a great upsurge of interest in reproductive art forms from the 1840s onwards, and artists such as Honoré Daumier and Charles Meryon were known to the generality mainly for their graphic work. Another important factor was operating, too. As the art market became larger and more intricate in its operations, the need for large-

scale personal publicity became apparent; until the invention of photogravure by Karl Klič in Vienna in 1879 there were no satisfactory ways of mass-producing images beyond those controlled by manual dexterity, and GAUGUIN was expressing a common thought in 1899 when he wrote to tell VAN GOGH that he 'had commenced a series of lithographs for publication in order to make myself known.'

MANET was one of the first to exploit the idea, and was a founding member of the Société des Aquafortistes, established in 1862 to promote interest in etching. He produced two portfolios of etchings at the time, most of them based on his paintings, and in 1867 did a version of *Olympia* in the same medium to accompany a projected booklet by ZOLA, defending the independent exhibition that Manet had organized in that year. He also produced a number of lithographs, sometimes using the same work for differing techniques: the painting *Berthe Morisot with a Bunch of Violets* (1872; Private collection), for instance, was translated into an etching, in which Manet followed the original quite closely, and into two lithographs, in which the painting was used mainly as a pretext for experimenting with the juxtaposition of masses of black and white. It seems that when making prints from his paintings Manet used photographs of them, several of which survive

Prints: The frontispiece to Manet's portfolio of etchings published in 1874.

Woman with a Wheelbarrow (1880): etching by Pissarro, an enthusiastic producer of **prints**.

in the DURAND-RUEL archives, sometimes touched up with watercolour.

It was DEGAS who produced the greatest number of prints, in the widest possible range of techniques. He had his own printing press, and between 1876 and 1893 he produced some 500 monotypes – single prints obtained by putting a drawing executed in an oily ink through the press. Some of these he translated into lithographs, others he used as the foundation of multi-media works involving, for instance, PASTEL and charcoal. With most of his lithographs Degas started with a completely inked stone, from which light forms were then extracted, sometimes with an elaborate system of smudging to create a *sfumato* effect. His concern with the minutiae of the processes involved is reflected in his letters to CASSATT, who herself produced a large number of prints, very much under his influence, and to PISSARRO, who became an enthusiastic producer of prints in almost every medium.

It was Degas who by constant encouragement after 1878 impelled Pissarro to greater adventurousness and to experiment with such unconventional tools as wire brushes and sandpaper. When Degas proposed (the project never came to anything) to found a magazine, *Le Jour et la nuit*, to consist entirely of artists' prints, Pissarro set himself the task of producing a print of his *Wooded Landscape at l'Hermitage, Pontoise* (1879; Nelson Atkins Museum of Art, Kansas City), an undertaking of great technical complexity. The resulting work, which combines soft-ground etching, aquatint and drypoint, succeeds in transposing into various shades of black and white the rich chromatic effect of the painting, and even the shimmering brushwork. He was clearly very pleased with the result, and showed four stages in the development of the print framed together at the IMPRESSIONIST EXHIBITION of 1880.

Pissarro was also in touch with DR GACHET, who was deeply interested in etching and created a studio, complete with presses and the like, in his house overlooking the Oise, which he made available to the painters he had met at the CAFÉ GUERBOIS. He persuaded CÉZANNE, who stayed with him at certain times, to make some excursions into the medium, and the artist produced a few prints, notably a portrait of GUILLAUMIN sitting cross-legged on the ground. He was not sympathetic to the medium, however, and most of his efforts are fairly inept.

There were also those, such as MONET and SISLEY, whose concern with light and atmosphere was so intense that the linear austerity of graphic art did not appeal to them. *See also* BRAQUEMOND, GOUPIL, ILLUSTRATION *[20, 43, 46, 106, 110, 113, 134]*

☐ R. Passeron, *Impressionist Prints* (1974); F. Carey and A. Griffiths, *From Manet to Toulouse-Lautrec: French Lithographs 1860–1900* (1978); C.S. Ives, 'French Prints in the Era of Impressionism and Symbolism', in *Metropolitan Museum of Art Bulletin* (Summer 1988)

Prix de Rome *see* ECOLE DES BEAUX-ARTS

Proust, Antonin (1832–1905) He was a fellow pupil of MANET's at the Collège Rollin in 1842, and they remained close friends throughout their lives; Proust's eventual success as a politician and as an influential figure in Parisian society was to prove of great value to Manet specifically, and to the Impressionists generally.

He started his career as the founder of a magazine, *La Semaine universelle*, and became secretary to Gambetta as the latter was rising to power. As a consequence, during the FRANCO-PRUSSIAN WAR of 1870–71 he became minister in charge of the refugees who were flocking into

PARIS, and subsequently rose through the political hierarchy of the Third Republic, becoming Minister of Fine Arts 1881–82, and Commissioner for Fine Arts at the Paris Exposition Universelle of 1889. In 1892 he was implicated in a financial–political scandal, but acquitted.

In 1880 he obtained the Legion of Honour for Manet, and he pronounced an oration at a banquet organized by Manet's family and friends to celebrate the commemorative exhibition of his works held at the ECOLE DES BEAUX-ARTS in 1884. In 1897 he wrote a lengthy article in the *Revue blanche*, entitled, 'Souvenirs de Manet', which in an expanded form was published posthumously as a book in 1913. Manet painted a portrait of Proust in 1880 (Toledo Museum of Art, Ohio), which was damned with faint praise by ZOLA and HUYSMANS. In the following year Proust commissioned Manet to paint four portraits of women to represent the four seasons. Only two were finished: *Jeanne; Spring* (Fogg Art Museum, Cambridge, Mass.) and *Autumn* (Musée des Beaux-Arts, Nancy); the former was a portrait of the young actress Jeanne Demarsy, the latter of the popular and successful demi-mondaine Méry LAURENT, who enjoyed the unique distinction of having been the mistress of Marshal Canrobert, of Crimean War fame, and of the Empress Eugénie's dentist. *[110]*

Puvis de Chavannes, Pierre (1824–98) Trained as an engineer, he took up painting as a result of the impressions made on him by a journey to Italy. He was basically a Romantic, preoccupied with rather naïve idealistic concepts, but driven to express them in an ACADEMIC idiom, which owed a great deal to Ingres. Theoretically, he was hostile to the notion of the academic tradition, though he was very largely fettered by it; theoretically, too, he was opposed to the spontaneous naturalism of the Impressionists, though he was very friendly to them, and indeed was regarded by the general public as part of that avant-garde of which the Impressionists were the most outstanding exemplars.

He was one of the first to appreciate the works of DEGAS, with whom throughout his life he was to remain on very friendly terms. He was also very close to MORISOT, who was always ready to take his advice on technical matters; he met RENOIR, MANET and others at the house of Alfred STEVENS, and in 1888 made a generous contribution to the fund which MONET was raising to buy Manet's *Olympia* for the nation. Preoccupied with mural and large-scale public art, which he painted in flat areas of colour, often with symbolic undercurrents to the subject-matter, he came to exert a considerable influence on the generation of SEURAT and GAUGUIN, as well as on painters such as Odilon Redon and the Nabis. One of his favourite models was Suzanne VALADON *[134]*.

□ L. Worth, *Puvis de Chavannes* (1926); R.J. Wattenmaker, *Puvis de Chavannes and the Modern Tradition* (1975); *Puvis de Chavannes*, Grand Palais, Paris, exhibition catalogue (1983)

R

Puvis de Chavannes' *Hope* (1872) was copied by Gauguin in 1895.

Raffaëlli, Jean-François (1850–1924) Even though he participated in the IMPRESSIONIST EXHIBITIONS of 1880 and 1881, and although his work showed considerable affinities with that of MANET's early period, and in certain ways with that of CAILLEBOTTE, he was really closer to an older tradition of REALISM. Except towards the end of his life, his colours were sombre and lacked that sparkle which was so characteristic of quintessential Impressionism. He was an habitué of the CAFÉ GUERBOIS, and, because his works dealt predominantly with urban genre

Raffaëlli, *Guests Waiting for the Wedding.*

popular success, he disassociated himself from the Impressionists, and even DEGAS, who had been his most enthusiastic, and indeed sometimes only, supporter in the group, dropped him. In a book, *Etude des mouvements de l'art moderne*, published in that year, he denounced Impressionism as being 'too scientific'. A painter, lithographer and writer, he was also a sculptor, but his most lasting achievement is as an illustrator of Parisian life in publications such as *Les Types de Paris* (1889). *See also* ILLUSTRATION, ITALY, PETIT

□ L. Bénédite, *Great Painters of the Nineteenth Century* (1910); G. Lecomte, *Raffaëlli* (1927)

and landscape scenes, they were greatly applauded by writers such as HUYSMANS; some of his most impressive works as an illustrator were those he produced for the works of MALLARMÉ.

In 1886, partly because of his growing

Railways Of all the applications of steam power that affected life in the 19th c., one of the most significant was the railway, celebrated in the architectural flamboyance of its stations, as well as in books such as ZOLA's immensely popular *La Bête humaine* (1879). It made possible that type of total warfare first demonstrated in 1870; it gave people a mobility they had never

The **railway** bridge at Asnières in the late 19th c., by which time vast expansion of the rail network had brought many towns along the Seine within easy reach of Paris.

before possessed, making possible, for instance, the development of those more remote Parisian suburbs that provided the Impressionists with one of their favourite themes. It opened up to painters a range of landscape possibilities that in the past would have been closed to them, and in bringing the resorts of Provence and the Mediterranean coast within reach of all, it provided painters such as RENOIR with subject-matter that radically changed the nature of their art. MONET travelled as far afield as England, HOLLAND, Norway, SPAIN, Switzerland, ITALY and Africa. When CÉZANNE first went from AIX to PARIS, the journey took the best part of three days. By the 1890s it took a day.

The railway appealed to the Impressionists as a symbol of progress and of modern life. Monet was especially intrigued by trains, even when living in the country, and produced in 1870 *Le Train dans la campagne* (Musée d'Orsay), in 1872 *Le Convoi du chemin de fer* (Private collection), and in 1875 *Le Train dans la neige à Argenteuil* (Private collection). Then he turned his attention to the Gare Saint-Lazare, exhibiting eight paintings of it at the 1877 Impressionist exhibition (one of the most powerfully evocative is in the Fogg Art Museum, Cambridge, Mass.). In 1871 PISSARRO painted two pictures of engines of the London Dover and Chatham Railway leaving Penge station in South London, and two years later MANET evoked the Gare Saint-Lazare in a painting of a woman and child seated outside the station; through the railings behind them can be seen the steam of passing engines (National Gallery of Art, Washington). A work that perhaps better than any other epitomizes the Impressionists' reaction to railways is CAILLEBOTTE's remarkable *Pont de l'Europe* (Musée du Petit Palais, Geneva) of 1876, which presents an ingenious perspectival view of the bridge that spans the lines emerging from the Gare Saint-Lazare, considered one of the most outstanding engineering achievements of the age. Another version, showing the silhouette of the station's roof, is in the Kimbell Art Museum, Fort Worth, Texas. *See also* FRANCE, POLITICS *[31, 49, 50–1, 160]*

□ P. Dauzet, *Le Siècle des chemins de fer en France* (1948); F. Braudel and E. LaBrosse, *L'Avènement de l'ère industrielle; 1789–1880*, 2 vols. (1977); J.M. Merriman, *French Cities in the Nineteenth Century* (1982); Zeldin (1988)

Rashdall, Edward (1860–1888) After leaving Oxford, he went to Paris, and studied painting under Francis Bate. A friend of MONET, he was acquainted with the other Impressionists, and was especially interested in the analysis of their TECHNIQUE, about which he wrote extensively in the columns of the *Artist*. In the year of his early death he contributed to that magazine a most percipient study of Monet's work.

Realism is a word with several meanings in the context of art, most of them overlapping or close enough to create an element of ambiguity. There is the initial sense of the faithful depiction of perceived reality, seen as the antithesis of abstract or non-figurative art. Secondly, realism can be taken to mean those styles of art that eschew distortion, and present acceptable 'photographic' images. Finally, it can be used to describe the work of those artists who choose 'real' subjects drawn from ordinary, usually lower-class or prosaic surroundings. Within this range of definitions can be included a very wide variety of artists – Bruegel, Caravaggio, Chardin, Hogarth, Murillo, Zurbarán, Holman Hunt, Wilkie, Copley and Hockney; all represent different dimensions of 'realism'.

Zola, the Emperor of **Realism**, rides on top of the Vendôme Column, 1880.

In the context of Impressionism, however, the word has a more specific meaning. It describes a movement, or perhaps one might better describe it as an attitude, which played an important role in art, and indeed in literature, during a large part of the 19th c. Time and time again critics, painters and writers emphasized both its historical precedents and its current relevance. Claude Lantier, ZOLA's artist-hero of *L'Oeuvre* (1886), expressed the underlying notion with the author's usual vigour when he said that he preferred painting a pile of cabbage to all the historical bric-à-brac of the Romantics, and that a bunch of carrots honestly and directly painted on the spot was preferable to all the high-faluting subject-matter of ACADEMIC painters: 'The day is coming when a single original carrot will be pregnant with revolution.' Théophile THORÉ wrote in 1863, 'If a painter is possessed of an original feeling for nature and a personal method of execution, even if he applies them to the most inferior subjects, he is master of his art and in his art. Murillo in his *Young Beggar* is as much a master as in his *Assumption of the Virgin*. Brouwer and Chardin painting pots are as much masters as Raphael painting Madonnas. . . . The portrait of the worker in his smock is certainly worth as much as that of a prince in his golden robes.'

There were many impulses that made artists and writers of the 19th c. look more closely at contemporary reality. The population explosion of the first half of the century and the rapid growth of conurbations brought much larger numbers of people into intimate contact with each other. In addition, there was an inevitable stylistic revulsion against the escapist fantasies which had characterized so much Romantic art. And there were important political dimensions: Realism was equated with radicalism, with the left wing; it was the art of an embattled democracy, and this was highlighted by the career of the most vociferous of the early apostles of Realism. COURBET went out of his way not only to paint scenes of ordinary life, but to do so with a technique that by its frequent 'brutality', as his critics called it, emphasized the lack of those seductive graces that characterized Salon paintings. But though there was a political dimension to Realism, it

Manet, *Déjeuner sur l'herbe*, 1863: the painting was criticized for its excessive **realism**, and for replacing graceful historical dress with 'the horrible modern French costume'.

did not necessarily imply, as it would do in the next century, political conviction. MANET, many of whose earlier works (e.g. *Boy with Cherries*, 1859; Calouste Gulbenkian Foundation, Lisbon) were idealized, went on to make what was possibly the most publicized statement of Realism in the *Déjeuner sur l'herbe* (1863; Musée d'Orsay); the painting aroused such horror, not because of the naked woman, but because, in the words of Philip HAMERTON, a contemporary English critic, 'Some wretched Frenchman has translated the *fête champêtre* into modern French realism, and with the horrible modern French costume instead of the graceful Venetian one.' Manet continued to concern himself with modern life, but though he was sceptical about the political establishment, he could by no means be thought of as a propagandist of democracy, still less as an admirer of the proletariat.

This was even more true of DEGAS, whose quest for the realism of brothels and the intimacies of the boudoir and bathroom was equalled only by that of another aristocratic observer, Toulouse-Lautrec. The sense of something approaching disdain, with which this pre-eminently conservative and even reactionary man viewed the subjects that he was so concerned to describe, had very close analogies with the GONCOURTS' approach to similar themes in literature.

Without pursuing so vigorously the less entrancing aspects of Realism, all the Impressionists chose subjects from ordinary life, if not of the proletariat, at least of the *petite bourgeoisie*: boating parties, seaside excursions, public dances. They painted Parisian streets, railway stations, the boulevards; never before had a whole group of painters been so devoted to the urban scene. There were, of course, occasional lapses. Though MONET could bisect his landscapes with railway viaducts, and PISSARRO could depict railway engines in South London, both were quite capable of tidying up the scenes they were painting by removing unsightly factory chimneys.

But Realism was not necessarily confined to the choice of subject-matter. It betrayed itself in attitudes to PORTRAITURE, in the quest for the unposed, revelatory stance, in the careless array of accessories – scraps of notepaper, opened books, pipes and the impedimenta of daily life. Such aspects of Realism were clearly related to the spread of PHOTOGRAPHY and the example of the unselective eye of the camera. So, too, was

what might be described as 'temporal realism', the abandonment of the older convention of pictorial sequence of action, for the disjointed observation of a moment in time. In CAILLEBOTTE's *Rue de Paris; temps de pluie* (1877; Art Institute of Chicago) the viewpoint has been chosen purely arbitrarily; it imposes no perspectival unity on the composition; the various figures walking in different directions, regardless of each other – as in 'real' life – have not been cajoled into any pictorial pattern, and no attempt has been made even to hint at visual logic – in fact one pedestrian is indicated only by his left side, part of his arm, the side of his face, and his umbrella. By contrast, the vortex-like pull of the architectural setting imposes a sense of the dominance of an urban scene which was part of the psychological reality of contemporary life.

In a wider sense, of course, the century was hypnotized by that concept of a tangible and measurable reality which could be expressed in scientific terms. The aim of the Impressionists, both in technique and choice of subject-matter, could be described as the quest for objective truth – what Zola, in his review of the 1866 SALON described as 'the exact study of facts and things'. The exact study of light and shade, the exact analysis of how colour actually appears to the eye, the exact impact the landscape makes on the eye when painted out of doors, and the overall substitution in art of the perceptual for the conceptual, seemed to those who were involved the very essence of that pursuit of reality which characterized the activities of the scientist. Realism in all its aspects was to the Impressionists not so much a programme, more a way of life. *See also* BURTY, CASTAGNARY, CHAMPFLEURY, DAUDET, LITERATURE, MÉDAN, MOORE *[24, 183]*

□ L. Rosenthal, *Du Romantisme au réalisme* (1914); L. Nochlin, *Realism* (1971); Clark (1973b)

Renoir, Edmond (1849–c. 1943) Eight years younger than his more famous brother, Edmond spent much of his earlier life with Auguste, joining him, for instance, on trips to the CABARET DE LA MÈRE ANTHONY at Marlotte. In 1867 Edmond started a career as a journalist, but the FRANCO-PRUSSIAN WAR intervened and both brothers, after serving in the army, met again in PARIS shortly afterwards. It was during this period that Edmond participated most closely in his brother's work, sometimes asking

Crayon and ink drawing of **Edmond Renoir** at a Mediterranean resort, by his brother, 1881.

passers-by to stop so that he could incorporate them into his paintings. He posed frequently for Auguste, and appeared most notably in *La Loge* (1874; Courtauld Institute, London). In the mean time his own career had prospered; he had become editor of the daily *La Presse*, and when the CHARPENTIERs founded the magazine LA VIE MODERNE, he was put in charge of the art gallery that was situated on the magazine's premises, in a disused wine warehouse on the boulevard des Italiens. Edmond travelled a good deal on his journalistic assignments, especially in the south of France (he was a correspondent of *La France méridionale*, which was published in Nice); he was frequently accompanied by his brother, who did a drawing of him at Menton as an illustration for a story by Edmond that appeared in *La Vie moderne* on 15 December 1883. However, they gradually began to drift apart, partly because Edmond aroused a degree of hostility amongst the Impressionists themselves, because of his over-enthusiastic trumpeting of his brother's works. The crisis came in 1884, when PISSARRO wrote bitterly to MONET, 'Renoir's younger brother is really unbearable. . . . He has treated me in a fine way, making out that I am an untalented schemer, a greedy Jew, surreptitiously plotting to replace both you and

Renoir.' Monet replied soothingly, 'It is very unpleasant, but don't get upset since I have the feeling that not many people like him.' From this time onwards Edmond ceased to be closely involved in the movement, and once *La Vie moderne* ceased publication in 1893, they no longer had any common point of contact. *See also* BATIGNOLLES

□ M. Robida, *Le Salon Charpentier* (1958); J. Rewald, 'Auguste Renoir and his brother', in *Studies in Impressionism* (1985)

Renoir, Pierre-Auguste (1841–1919) Son of a tailor and a dressmaker, he was born in Limoges; three years later the family moved to PARIS. In 1854 he was apprenticed to a porcelain-painter, and took drawing lessons at an *école gratuite de dessin* (free drawing school). At the end of his apprenticeship, he started working for a blind-maker, but in 1861 he began to attend GLEYRE's studio, and in the following year, the ECOLE DES BEAUX-ARTS, coming 68th out of 80 candidates in the entrance examination. In the mean time, he had formed a close friendship with SISLEY, MONET and BAZILLE, and became an habitué of the CAFÉ GUERBOIS. He started to have a reasonable success at the SALON, especially in 1868, when his *Lise* (Folkwang Museum, Essen) attracted almost uniform praise from the critics. He was mobilized in 1870 and spent a year in the cavalry. In 1872 DURAND-RUEL started buying his paintings, and in 1873, he was also taken up by DURET, who bought a painting from him for 1200 francs. At this time he was very close to Monet and stayed with him at ARGENTEUIL, each stimulating the other to new departures in their work.

Renoir took part in the 1874 IMPRESSIONIST EXHIBITION and in three subsequent ones, but he was neither a compliant nor an enthusiastic member of the group, largely because, unlike most of the others, he had built up an affluent and supportive body of patrons, including Victor CHOCQUET, the CHARPENTIERs and the BÉRARDS. The Charpentiers were especially effective, as the journal LA VIE MODERNE, which they founded, gave Renoir a great deal of publicity, and in 1879 he had a one-man exhibition at the art gallery associated with the magazine. In the same year his portrait of *Madame Charpentier and her Children* (Metropolitan Museum, New York) was given a prominent position in the Salon and attracted very favourable comments. A visit to ALGIERS in 1881 was followed by one to ITALY, where he visited

Photograph of **Renoir**, *c.* 1885, at the time when he was painting *Les Grandes Baigneuses*.

Venice, Florence, Rome, Naples and elsewhere, as well as painting a portrait of Wagner (Musée d'Orsay). In 1882 he refused to take part in the *Exposition des artistes indépendants* at 251 rue Saint-Honoré, on the grounds that it was inconsistent with his exhibiting at the Salon, and to recuperate from an attack of pneumonia he spent another six weeks in Algiers. In 1883 Durand-Ruel gave him a one-man show of 70 works and sent three to Boston for the American 'Exhibition of Foreign Products, Arts and Manufactures', as well as 10 to the Dowdeswell Gallery in London. In the autumn Renoir also had works on show at the Gurlitt Gallery in Berlin.

In the meantime, his style had been undergoing certain changes: the bright, vivid colours, the 'rainbow palette', and the rapidly applied free brushwork were replaced in the 1880s by a more dry and acrid colouring (as in *Les Parapluies*, 1884; National Gallery, London) and by a linear refinement and Raphaelesque classicism revealed at its most impressive in the *Grandes Baigneuses* (1884–87; Philadelphia Museum of Art). Durand-Ruel did not approve of this 'new style', and though it was reinforced by Renoir's close contact with CÉZANNE during this period – he visited him in 1885, 1888 and 1889 – he began to feel the strength of the reaction against his attempts to escape from his earlier, more Romantic idiom. In 1887 PISSARRO related to his son Lucien, 'I had a long talk with Renoir. He told me that everyone, from Durand-Ruel to his old collectors, is criticizing him, and attacking his attempts to escape from his old manner.'

In 1892 Renoir visited SPAIN, where he was greatly impressed by the works of Velazquez and, after spending a good deal of time in Brittany and on the Channel coast, he decided to live predominantly in the south of France. He bought a house at Essoyes, later moving first to Grasse then to Le Cannet in 1902, and finally to Cagnes-sur-Mer in 1905. Very largely this predilection was influenced by a variety of physical ailments which were besetting him, notably partial atrophy of a nerve in the right eye and the onset of rheumatoid arthritis, both of which afflictions had a perceptible influence on his painting, making it increasingly loose and 'expressionist' in appearance. As he himself said, he could only paint 'broadly' but, at the same time, he managed to combine this with great delicacy of effect, as can be seen in *The Concert* (1919; Art Gallery of Ontario), in which the figures of two girls seem almost to be distilled from the luminous haze of the background. At the same time, however, in portraits such as that of Maurice GANGNAT (1919; Private collection), he was able to maintain a firm and accurate line. In 1913 VOLLARD persuaded him to take up SCULPTURE – six years previously Renoir had done a relief medallion of his son Claude's head. He worked through the hands of an assistant, and two works, *Venus Victorious* (1914; Tate Gallery) and *Standing Venus* (1913; The Baltimore Museum of Art), were exhibited at the Paris Triennale in 1916. He also did designs for a tapestry for the city of Lyons and reverted to his first profession, ceramics.

No other Impressionist incorporated so much of the traditional spirit of the European tradition into his work. He was clearly the heir of Raphael, of Rubens and of DELACROIX. He translated into the visual idiom of his time the ideals of the humanist tradition. Few painters have expressed so felicitously images of an anxiety-free sensuality. Yet in many ways this was a contrast to his personality. Georges RIVIÈRE said of him, for instance, 'Though he

Renoir, *The Moulin de la Galette*, 1876. Though this sparkling painting evokes a random moment in time, the strength of the composition reveals Renoir as heir to the mainstream European tradition.

gave women a seductive appearance in his paintings, and conferred charms on those who had none, he generally took no pleasure in converse with them. With a few exceptions he only liked women as models'; and he himself once said 'I paint women as I would paint carrots.' He was often moody and introverted; his political ideas were both naïve and reactionary, and he vaguely subscribed to a series of rather muddled religious beliefs. His schemes for a 'Société des Irrégularistes', drawn up in 1884, give some indication of his ingenuousness. At the same time, however, he was quite widely read, an able and often witty letter-writer, interested in contemporary MUSIC as well as LITERATURE. He wrote a long and interesting introduction to a French translation of Cennino Cennini's *Il Libro dell'Arte* in which he expounded a rather Romantic credo based on the notion that art was decaying through its 'lack of an ideal'. More specifically, however, in an interview with the American Walter Pach, published in *Scribner's Magazine* in May 1912, he was explicit about the element of traditionalism that underlay his work: 'There is nothing outside the classics. To please a student, even the most princely, a musician could not add another note to the seven on the scale. He must always come back to the first one again. Well, in art it is the same thing. But one must see that the classic may appear in any period. Poussin was a classic; Père COROT was a classic.' Renoir died on 3 December 1919 and was buried next to his wife Aline in the cemetery at Essoyes. *See also* BARNES, BAUDOT, BÜRGER, CABARET DE LA MÈRE ANTHONY, COURBET, DIAZ, DORIA, ENGLAND, L'ESTAQUE, FAIVRE, GOBILLARD, LA GRENOUILLÈRE, ILLUSTRATION, L'IMPRESSIONNISTE, ITALY, LECOEUR, MONTMARTRE, MUSIC, PASTELS, PHILLIPS COLLECTION, PORTRAITURE, RESTAURANT FOURNAISE, SOCIAL BACKGROUND, VILLE D'AVRAY [*28, 31, 37, 47, 48, 49, 53, 86, 117, 149, 162, 185, 188, 199, 208, 213, 220, 225*]

□ G. Rivière, *Renoir et ses amis* (1921); B.E. White, *Renoir* (1984); *Renoir*, Hayward Gallery, London, exhibition catalogue (1985)

Renoir family In 1879 Renoir met Aline Charigot, a 20-year-old girl from Essoyes in Burgundy, who was living with her mother, a

The **Restaurant Fournaise** at Chatou, from a 19th-c. photograph.

Renoir family: *Maternity* (*c.* 1905): Renoir's wife Aline with their son Pierre, born in 1885.

dressmaker. Aline was contributing to the family income – the father had left them – by doing laundry work for both Renoir and MONET, who were living nearby. She rapidly became Renoir's favourite model, and then his mistress. In 1885 they had a son, who was named Pierre, but Renoir hid their existence from those of his friends, such as Berthe MORISOT and the MANETS who, he thought, might be repelled by Aline's obvious peasant origins. This attitude persisted even after their eventual marriage in July 1890.

Three years after their marriage they had another son, named Jean, and then in 1901, when the painter was 60, a third, Claude, nicknamed 'Coco'. Renoir found in Aline and the children a constant source of inspiration, and produced numerous paintings and drawings of them. An almost compulsive eater, she died of a heart-attack in 1915. Pierre, who died in 1952, was buried in the same grave as his father and mother. Jean, the famous film-producer, wrote a number of interesting books about his father.

Restaurant Fournaise Situated on an island in the Seine at CHATOU, it was a celebrated and fashionable restaurant for the oarsmen who used that stretch of the river, and was much frequented by artists and journalists. It was especially favoured by RENOIR, who painted the *Déjeuner des canotiers* (Phillips Collection, Washington) on its upstairs terrace. He also painted portraits of the owner, Alphonse Fournaise, and of his wife. *[162]*

□ M. Catinat, *Les Bords de la Seine avec Renoir et Maupassant* (1952); Herbert (1988)

Rivière, Georges (1855–1943) Writer and art critic, he was a close friend of RENOIR, who painted him as one of the figures in *Dancing at the Moulin de la Galette* (1876; Mr and Mrs John Hay Whitney, New York) and more prominently as one of five figures in *The Artist's Studio, rue Saint-Georges* (1876; Collection Santa Marina, Buenos Aires). It was Renoir who in 1877 persuaded Rivière to bring out a periodical to defend the Impressionists, a notion that had been canvassed some four years earlier in the original charter of the group. The resulting *L'Impressionniste, journal d'art* ran to five issues between 6 and 28 April. It was almost entirely written by Rivière, who was not the most inspired of critics, and it attracted little attention. Some 40 years later, however, he produced a number of books of considerable value, including *Renoir et ses amis* (1921); *Le Maître Paul Cézanne* (1923) and *M. Degas, bourgeois de Paris* (1935). *See also* L'ARTISTE, HOUSSAYE, L'IMPRESSIONNISTE *[116]*

□ G. Rivière, *Renoir et ses amis* (1921); Venturi (1939)

Robinson, Theodore (1852–96) An American painter, whose early works are in an ACADEMIC REALIST style, he first studied at the school of the National Academy of Design in New York, and came to work in France in 1887, staying there until 1892. He became a close friend of MONET, whose style he partly imitated and with whom he worked a great deal in GIVERNY, keeping an invaluable diary, now in the Frick Art Reference Library. In the Detroit Institute of Art there is a painting of a haystack by him (1890), which can be compared with a similar one by Monet painted the previous year, now in the Hill-Stead Museum, Farmington, Conn.

Robinson was especially interested in the relationship between PHOTOGRAPHY and painting, and several of his works are virtually translations of photographs into paintings (e.g. *Two in a Boat*, Phillips Collection, Washington, D.C.; the relevant photograph is in the Brooklyn Museum, New York). It is more than possible that this interest was transferred to Monet, who at about this time had two darkrooms constructed in his house at Giverny. On his return to America Robinson became an impassioned protagonist of the Impressionists, especially, of course, of Monet. *See also* USA

□ J. Baur, *Theodore Robinson* (1946); P. Toulgouat, 'Peintres américains à Giverny', in *Rapports France–Etats-Unis* (May 1952); *Americans in Brittany and Normandy 1860–1910*, Phoenix Art Museum, AZ, exhibition catalogue (1982)

Rouart, Henri (1833–1912) It is one of the injustices of history that Rouart, who participated in most of the IMPRESSIONIST EXHIBITIONS, took part in all their discussions, and helped the group enormously with money and advice, is hardly known to the generality in this context. A successful industrialist who had always practised painting, he was at school with DEGAS, and their friendship was cemented when they both served in the same unit in one of the Paris forts during the FRANCO-PRUSSIAN WAR. They were in constant contact, and the letters that Degas wrote to Henri and his brother Alexis are of primary importance to the history of the movement. Rouart built up a collection that was rich not only in the works of Impressionists and their immediate predecessors, but also in works by El Greco, Goya, Poussin and Bruegel. *See also* PATRONS AND COLLECTORS, PRICES

□ P.A. Lemoisne, *Degas et son oeuvre*, 4 vols.

Robinson's, *Sunlight and Shadows* (1896) shows considerable Impressionist influence.

(1946–49; repr. 1984); J.S. Boggs, *Portraits by Degas* (1962); *Degas*, Grand Palais, Paris, exhibition catalogue (1988)

Rousseau, *A Marshy Landscape*, 1842: an atmospheric work typical of the Barbizon school.

Rousseau, Théodore (1812–67) Impassioned since his childhood by the attractive landscape in Compiègne, he took up an anti-ACADEMIC stance from the very beginning of his career, and was constantly preoccupied with many notions that were later to exercise the Impressionists, such as the effects and pictorial nature of light and shade. In the 1830s he made a tour of France in search of appropriate landscapes, showing in his work at this time the combined influences of Constable and of Dutch painters such as Ruysdael and Van Goyen. Having discovered the visual delights of the forest of Fontainebleau and become disillusioned by the Parisian art scene, he went to live at BARBIZON and, slightly to oversimplify matters, it might be said that he became the leader of the school that took its name from that village.

Rousseau's vision of nature, the spontaneity of his composition, and his technique of using very small brushstrokes can be seen, for instance, in his *Outskirts of the Forest of Fontainebleau* (1850; Louvre). In the 1860s, when most of the Impressionists were working intermittently in and around Barbizon, they all reflected his influence in various ways, but it was most clear in the works of PISSARRO. By this time Rousseau's work was becoming widely accepted, and he made no further technical advances in his painting. *See also* ARROWSMITH
□ A. Sensier, *Souvenirs sur Théodore Rousseau* (1872); A. Terrasse, *L'Univers de Théodore Rousseau* (1976)

Rouvière, Philibert (1809–65) Trained originally as a painter, and working in the atelier of Baron Gros, he exhibited at the SALON between 1831 and 1837. Then he turned to acting and established his reputation playing the title role in *Hamlet* in 1846–47. His acting was marked by a very personal style of costume and make-up, based very largely, in the case of Hamlet, on DELACROIX's painting; he was also extravagant in his gestures. However, after a string of successes, followed by a contract with the Comédie Française, and despite the award of a pension by the government, he had great difficulty in finding work. In 1865 MANET produced a memorable portrait of him (National Gallery of Art, Washington) in the role of Hamlet, entitling it *The Tragic Actor*. Rouvière died before it was completed, and the artist modelled the hands on those of Antonin PROUST, the legs on those of Paul Roudier.
□ A. Tabarant, *Manet; Histoire catalographique* (1931); D. Solkin, 'Philibert Rouvière; Edouard Manet's "L'Acteur Tragique"', *Burlington Magazine* (Nov. 1975)

Rutter, Frank (1876–1937) Art critic of the *Financial Times* and the *Sunday Times*, he was a fervent protagonist of the Impressionists and in 1905 campaigned vigorously for the purchase of some of their works for the national collections of Britain. In 1909 he launched *Art News*, a progressive art journal that was the mouthpiece of the Allied Artists' Association, which was committed to modern art. *See also* CRITICS, ENGLAND
□ Cooper (1954); Flint (1984)

S

Sainte-Adresse A beach, with a few scattered houses, 4 kms (2½ miles) from Le Havre, which had been discovered by the English in the 1820s. Visited by COROT, Isabey, JONGKIND and others, it was publicized by the journalist and writer Alphonse Karr, who also established various new plants and flowers along the bay. Its other amenities included a casino and two lighthouses. Basically it was a fishing village, and MONET, having first visited it in his childhood, returned there in 1867 and produced a whole series of paintings, including *The Beach at Sainte-Adresse* (Art Institute of Chicago) and *Terrace at Sainte-Adresse* (Metropolitan Museum, New York).

Monet, *The Beach at **Sainte-Adresse***, 1867: the resort was also popular with Jongkind.

☐ E. Chapus, *De Paris au Havre* (1855); Herbert (1988)

Salon Originally this was the exhibition of works by members of the French Académie Royale de Peinture et de Sculpture, founded by Colbert in the 17th c. In 1791, with the advent of the Revolution, it was thrown open to all artists, and a system of awards of medals and the like was initiated. But the creation of a jury originally intended to organize the exhibition – soon led to a process of selection. With the Restoration of the monarchy this jury came to be nominated from members of the newly reconstituted Academy by the Director of Museums, and thus became a mere outlet for a restricted circle of officially approved artists, bitterly resented by the rest.

It was inevitable, therefore, that with the 1848 revolution the jury should have been abolished and replaced by a hanging committee, chosen by 801 artists. The result was confusion: some 5000 works of art were selected. A return to the old system occurred, and remained in force until 1870, although during this period several changes took place. NAPOLEON III tried to court popularity with the artists by allocating them seats on the selection jury. In 1852 they were given half, and in 1864 nine out of fourteen. A certain conservatism, however, still remained, because only those artists who had previously won medals at the Salon were allowed to sit on the jury. In 1861, 7000 works were submitted and only 4097 accepted, while in 1863 the figures were 5000 and 2217. In the latter year it had been announced that those who had won first- or second-class medals need no longer submit to the jury, but the number of works that could be sent in was limited to three. This meant, for instance, that MILLET, not a favourite figure in official circles, was able to exhibit his *Man with a Hoe*, since he had won a second-class medal in 1855. The general outcry about the choice of works this year led to the one-off experiment of the SALON DES REFUSÉS. With the advent of the Third Republic things went on very much as before, though the state gradually started to reduce its own role in the selection of juries, a process which was completed in 1880, when the organization of the Salon was handed over to a Society of Artists, consisting of 90 members elected by all those who had previously exhibited. By this time, however, the Salon was losing some of its prestige and had split into two bodies, one run by the Société Nationale des Beaux-Arts, the other by the Société des Artistes Français. During the formative period of Impressionism, however, there was no doubt about the prestige and importance of the Salon, and this is emphasized by the fact that MANET, RENOIR and MONET especially were very much concerned with having their works accepted there. It was the single most effective way of obtaining recognition, the most important single source of commissions and livelihood. An artist's fortune could be made by a single success, and the fact that Manet's *Le Bon Bock* and Renoir's *Madame Charpentier and her Children* were favourably received at the Salon had a significant effect on their careers. Every Salon received an enormous amount of publicity, attracting long notices in all the national papers. The Salon of 1863, for instance, was covered by 12 extensive articles from Ernest CHESNEAU in *Le Constitutionnel*, 13 articles in *Le Moniteur universel* by Théophile GAUTIER, and Louis LEROY, who was responsible for popularizing the title of 'Impressionists', wrote or drew something about it in 18 different issues of CHARIVARI. Books and explanatory pamphlets were also published.

Although originally the opening date of the Salon had varied, by 1830 it had become established that it should open between 1 March and 15 June. In the 18th c. the Salon had been held in the Salon Carré of the Louvre – hence its name – but it soon outgrew that restricted space, and various other locations were tried. A more or less permanent home was not found until after the Exposition Universelle of 1855, when the Palais de l'Industrie, built for the exhibition, was converted into a public gallery

Gervex, whose speciality was recording scenes from current life, painted this view of the jury of the **Salon** des Artistes Français at work in 1885.

housing the annual showing of the Salon. The actual opening day was one of the major events in the Parisian calendar, and was enthusiastically described in the *Fine Arts Quarterly Review* for May 1863 by Philip HAMERTON: 'Entering there, the visitors find themselves at the foot of a magnificent staircase of white stone, on ascending which they arrive at the exhibition of pictures, which is on the upper floor and extends the whole length of the room, with tent-like ceilings of white canvas to subdue the glare from the glass roof. There are three large halls, one in the middle and one at each end of the building, with a double line of lower rooms between. The halls at the two ends open upon two other magnificent staircases, where the wearied traveller may refresh himself with brioches and babas and Malaga or Xerxes to his liking. A plan much to be recommended is to eat a baba and drink a glass of Malaga at one end, then to march steadily to the other, and repeat the dose. You then descend at the other end of the building into the garden, which occupies the whole of the immense nave and

there, under the broad glass roof, you see a great number of statues . . . after looking at these the majority of the spectators stop at the restaurant there established.' There were variable charges for entry, according either to the time of day or the day of the week (Sundays, and sometimes Thursdays, were free). In 1876, for instance, there were 518,892 visitors, of whom 185,000 paid admission fees.

It was clearly an agreeable context in which artists, journalists, dealers and PATRONS met to their mutual advantage. But it was immensely popular, too; a unique opportunity, in a world where reproduction processes offered the general public only a rough approximation of what contemporary art looked like, to see actual paintings. *See also* BOUSSOD AND VALADON, COROT, CRITICS, DURET, INDÉPENDANTS, NIEUWERKERKE, WALEWSKI, ZOLA *[47, 174]*
□ Lethève (1972); Boime (1986); Milner (1988)

Salon des Refusés On 15 January 1863 the Comte de NIEUWERKERKE announced new regulations for entry to the SALON. The good news –

for some at least – was that artists who had already won first- or second-class medals in previous Salons no longer had to submit their entries to a jury. The bad news was that entries for all were limited to three. On the whole, therefore, this was a move that favoured established artists at the expense of newcomers. This became apparent in April when the jury's decisions were announced. Some 5000 works had been submitted, 2217 accepted; the number of exhibitors had fallen from 1289 in 1862 to 988. Because of the death of Horace Vernet, a famous ACADEMIC artist, there had been 13 rather than the usual 14 members of the jury, but at least two of them, Ingres and DELACROIX, had taken no part in the deliberations, and the most influential voice had been that of the embattled traditionalist Emile Signol, who was renowned for his history paintings. Amongst the artists who had been rejected were MANET, who had submitted three works including his *Déjeuner sur l'herbe* (1862; Musée d'Orsay), LEGROS, WHISTLER, Harpignies, PISSARRO, JONGKIND and FANTIN-LATOUR, who, although he had one work accepted, had two others thrown out.

The outcry was immediate and vociferous, because numerous other regular exhibitors had also been rejected. Notable amongst these was Paul César Gariot, who had submitted four decorative panels, commissioned for the Empress Eugénie's salon in the Elysée Palace. Perhaps it was this as much as the more general outcry that prompted the Emperor to visit the Salon at the Palais de l'Industrie, in the company of Philippe de CHENNEVIÈRES, who had been responsible for hanging the exhibition. He expressed great surprise at the severity of the jury. On his return to the Elysée he sent for Nieuwerkerke, who could not be found. Instead, he had to deal with a subordinate, whom he told that the jury must be recalled and asked to reverse some of their decisions. It was pointed out to him, however, that if such a course were adopted the jury might resign *en bloc*, which would create an awkward situation, with possible political undercurrents. The Emperor decided, therefore, on an entirely novel solution. On 24 April the *Moniteur universel* contained the following notice: 'Numerous complaints have reached the Emperor on the subject of works of art which have been refused by the jury of the Exhibition. His Majesty, wishing to let the public judge the legitimacy of these complaints, has decided that the rejected works shall be exhibited in another part of the Palais de l'Industrie. This Exhibition will be voluntary, and artists who do not wish to participate need only inform the administration of the exhibition, which will hasten to return their works to them.'

The reaction amongst artists was curiously ambivalent. In the words of CASTAGNARY: 'When the news broke, the studios were thrown into a state of frenzy; people laughed, cried and embraced each other. But the first rush of feeling gave way to doubt. What should an artist do? To exhibit might mean exposing oneself to the derision of the public. Not to exhibit meant confessing to one's lack of ability and, from another point of view, it could mean admitting that the jury was right.'

In the event, quite a considerable number of artists did withdraw their works, but those who decided to participate in what was coming to be known unofficially as the Salon des Refusés, formed a committee to look after their interests. The rooms used in the annexe, designed for the exhibition, were decorated in the same style as the official Salon, but there was no ordered hanging of the pictures, a fact which tended to accentuate the sense of stylistic confusion. The exhibition opened on 17 May and over 10,000

Salon des Refusés: Daumier cartoon, 1848. An artist's work is rejected by the Salon.

people turned up on the first day, a figure that was more than maintained subsequently. In fact, it was noted that more people were visiting this exhibition than the official Salon; Cham had a cartoon showing two artists in conversation, one saying 'My painting has been accepted, but nobody is looking at it', whereat the other replies, 'Mine is with those that have been refused, and there is a crush to see it.' The popularity of the exhibition did not reflect a heightened aesthetic sensibility amongst the Parisian public. ZOLA's subsequent account in L'Oeuvre, the preliminary draft of which was drawn up in 1869, emphasized the general atmosphere of ostentatious hilarity, especially in front of Manet's Déjeuner sur l'herbe, which came to be seen as the star turn of the exhibition: 'Shafts of wit fell thicker here than anywhere else. It was the subject that was the main target for jokes. Nobody understood it. Everybody thought that it was "mad" and "killingly funny".' Nor were most of the CRITICS any more reasonable, most of them believing that Manet had deliberately set out to annoy and provoke. Whistler's White Girl, however, which the year before had been rejected by the Academy in London, was well received, and so too were the works of Jongkind, Harpignies and even Pissarro.

One cannot judge the Salon des Refusés merely in terms of the good paintings in it; there were – there must have been – many that were execrable, no matter what style they displayed, and it is easy to understand what Castagnary meant when he wrote, 'Before the Salon des Refusés we could not imagine what a bad painting was. Today we know. We have witnessed and seen it.' The official view was later expressed in 1866 when, in replying to CÉZANNE's request for another Salon des Refusés, Nieuwerkerke wrote, 'What he asks is impossible. We have already seen how unsuitable the exhibition of the rejected was for the dignity of art. It will not be re-established.' What the Salon des Refusés did do, however, was to publicize the existence of a gulf between official, or academic, and 'modern' art, which has persisted into the 20th c., to place Manet and his followers firmly in the latter group, and to endow the Impressionists, once they became a more or less coherent group, with a reputation for stylistic anarchy that they had done little to deserve. See also ASTRUC, DESNOYERS, MARTINET [183, 229]

□ A. Tabarant, La Vie artistique au temps de Baudelaire (1944); I. Dunlop, The Shock of the New (1972); Rewald (1973)

Sargent, John Singer (1856–1925) An expatriate American, he showed remarkable technical precocity as a painter. After studying with CAROLUS-DURAN, he achieved a great reputation for his portraits, employing a style that could be seen as derived from Velazquez by way of MANET. Moving in the circle of the Impressionists, he came to know most of them, and they reacted to his work in varying ways. DEGAS, as might have been expected, was brutally dismissive; PISSARRO, in sending his son to see him in London, where Sargent spent the major part of his working life, described him as 'an adroit performer'; but with MONET he had a close and mutually profitable relationship. In the 1880s he began to paint landscapes that were overtly Impressionist in technique and approach, despite a certain superficiality. At this time he visited Monet at GIVERNY on several occasions, painting two memorable portraits of him: Claude Monet Painting at the Edge of a Wood (c.1885; Tate Gallery, London) and Claude Monet in his Bateau-Atelier (1887; National Gallery of Art, Washington). Although Monet was later to deny that Sargent was an Impressionist, this was unjust, especially in relation to some of his works in the 1880s and 1890s. Indeed, Sargent's technique for painting large canvases out of doors, as evinced in Carnation, Lily, Lily, Rose (1885–86; Tate Gallery, London), was to be of use to Monet in his larger compositions. Sargent persuaded Monet to exhibit at the New English Art Club (see ENGLAND), and at the Leicester Galleries in London. See also ITALY, JAMES, USA [124]
□ E. Charteris, John Sargent (1927); S. Olson, John Singer Sargent (1986)

Scandinavia There were, in the first instance, personal ties between Scandinavia and the Impressionists. MONET's stepson Jacques lived in Norway, and he himself arrived there in 1895, deep in the heart of winter, to paint its landscape, though he had also made earlier visits in the 1880s when the elements were not so hostile. During the later excursion he gave a lengthy interview at Sandviken to the young Norwegian poet Henri Bang, which was published in its entirety in the Bergens Tiede for 5 April 1895. He also established contact with the person who was to be mainly responsible for consolidating the reputation of the Impressio-

Sargent's view of Monet painting at the edge of a wood (1888), a companion piece to Manet's view of him at work in his studio-boat, emphasizes Monet's taste for open-air painting.

nists in Scandinavia, Prince Eugen (1865–1947), a son of King Oscar II, and one of the most important Swedish painters of his generation. Eugen's own painting owed a great deal to the Impressionists, though he adumbrated it with a mysterious quality, which seems at times to suggest the influence of Odilon Redon. He bought from Monet works for his own private collection, as well as for the Swedish National Gallery, and in 1913 CASSATT told DURAND-RUEL that he had paid 25,000 francs for a DEGAS for the gallery at Stockholm.

The Scandinavians as a whole had a natural affinity for landscape painting, even though they were apt to overlay the purely descriptive element with implications of deeper significance. The reaction against the tradition of academic painting which took place in most of the Nordic countries in the late 1870s was initiated by artists such as the Swedes Karl Frederick Hill (1849–1911) and Nils Kreuger

(1858–1930), who had studied in Paris but who showed more of the influence of Bastien-Lepage and COROT than of the Impressionists themselves. The same rather half-hearted concern with the true nature of the Impressionist discovery was also shown in the work of the artistic colonies – the Swedes and Finns at Onningeby on Lemland, the largest of the Åland Islands, and the Norwegians on the farm of Erik Wrenskiold – which in the latter quarter of the 19th c. became centres of contemporary Scandinavian art.

Edvard Munch (1863–1944) had made his first trip from Norway to Paris in 1885 and was impressed by the work of CAILLEBOTTE, a friend of his mentor Christian Keogh. On his return he was hailed by a fellow artist as 'the first and only Impressionist of Norway', but it would seem that the word 'Impressionist' was being used loosely, as indeed it often was, merely to indicate general avant-garde tendencies. In any

Kreuger, *Old Country House*, 1887: the brushwork reveals the extent to which the techniques of Impressionism influenced painters from **Scandinavia**.

case, by the time he returned to Paris, for a more protracted stay in 1889, he had come under the influence of the heirs of Impressionism.

One of these, Paul GAUGUIN, had Danish connections through his wife Mette, and spent some time in that country. His reactions were negative. In 1882 he wrote to Emile SCHUFFE-NECKER, who, having worked in the same bank as he, was now earning a precarious living as art master in a school, 'Here it is like anywhere else. I meet painters who say they do not see nature like us, but that doesn't keep them from consulting us. The other day I caught one doing a painting for an exhibition with a picture of mine, which he borrowed from me, and which he says he can't understand. The result of his efforts you can imagine! Impressionist colours with *Ecole des Beaux-Arts* drawing.' In 1882, the Danish critic Georg Brandes (1842–1927), who married Mette Gauguin's sister Ingeborg, saw his first Impressionist paintings in Berlin and was of the opinion that 'Impressionism as such could never become a predominant style. For

Scandinavia: Munch, *The Sick Child*, 1886: though hailed as 'the first and only Impressionist of Norway', Munch was to have great influence on the German Expressionists.

Scandinavia: Gallen-Kallela, *Démasquée*, 1888: the boldness of the gaze is reminiscent of *Olympia*.

this it is too close to dilettantism. Its main principle throws open the gateway to preciousness and slovenliness; one must fear that the works of its masters will drown in the flood of its amateurs.' One of the curious things is that the Finnish artist Akseli Gallen-Kallela (1865–1931), who most clearly showed the direct influence of Impressionism (e.g. 1888; *Démasqué*, Ateneumin Taidemuseo, Helsinki) was always most vociferous in rebutting the notion. The point was that the historic Scandinavian cultural tradition inclined to an art of feeling rather than of visual analysis and, just as the Italians tended to find Impressionism too 'loose', so the people of the northern countries found it too 'tight'; too rational; too controlled.
□ M. Jacobs, *The Good and Simple Life; Artist Colonies in Europe and America* (1985); N. Kent, *The Triumph of Light and Nature; Nordic Art, 1740–1940* (1987)

Scholderer, Otto (1834–1902) Born in Frankfurt, where he attended the local art school, he arrived in Paris in 1857 and became friendly with COURBET and FANTIN-LATOUR, who included him in MANET, MONET and RENOIR in his *Studio in the Batignolles Quarter* (1870; Musée d'Orsay). From 1871 until 1899 he lived in London and became very friendly with SIC-

KERT, on whose work he had a considerable influence. His own paintings were close in feeling to those of Fantin-Latour and could most easily be categorized as essays in a form of Romantic REALISM [86].
□ W. Rothenstein, *Men and Memories* (1932); W. Baron, *Sickert* (1973)

Schuffenecker, Emile (1854–1912) Working in the same bank as GAUGUIN in the late 1870s, he too decided to become an artist, as well as the older man's devoted disciple. Securing a job as an art teacher in a school, he offered Gauguin constant help and accommodation, and was in part rewarded by being asked to participate in the 1884 exhibition of the Société des Artistes INDÉPENDANTS. In 1889 he was largely responsible for organizing the exhibition held in the Café Volpini next door to the fine arts section of the Exposition Universelle. On the whole, Gauguin was contemptuous of Schuffenecker's painting – which might loosely be described as sub-standard SISLEY – though his correspondence with him was affectionate and frequent. He painted a revealing portrait of the Schuffenecker family and produced a remarkable vase-portrait of Madame Schuffenecker, with whom he was probably having an affair at the time.
□ *Lettres de Gauguin à sa femme et ses amis*, ed. M. Malingue, 2 vols. (1949); J. Rewald, *Post-Impressionism* (1956); W. Anderson, *Gauguin's Paradise Lost* (1972)

Sculpture Although sculptors often express themselves in graphic form – the very nature of

Gauguin, *The Schuffenecker Family*, 1889: Emile became both a patron and disciple of the painter.

Degas' bronze **sculpture** *Horse Rearing, c.* 1890, is based on a photograph by Muybridge.

their art postulates at least some preliminary exploration of their subject on a two-dimensional scale – painters do not frequently venture into sculpture. And this, it would be thought, applies especially to the Impressionists, whose innovations were based largely on COLOUR, and on purely painterly concepts, such as working in the open air. Two of them, however, DEGAS and RENOIR, did make significant forays into sculpture. There was a difference between them: Renoir, with considerable technical assistance, translated figures from his paintings into three-dimensional objects, whereas Degas created new notions in sculpture, explored its possibilities, and used it to enrich his paintings and pastels.

It is not known precisely when Degas started producing sculpture. Albert BARTHOLOMÉ, himself a sculptor who helped the painter greatly in this medium, remembered him having produced a bas-relief of girls picking apples before 1870, and in a letter to a friend written on his first Italian trip, Degas wrote 'I often wonder whether I shall become a painter or a sculptor. I must confess the problem bothers me.'

By about 1869 he had started to produce models of horses in wax, which were cast in bronze after his death by A.A. Hébrard (Metropolitan Museum, New York, and Musée d'Or-

say). In 1878, however, at a period when he was heavily involved in some of his most celebrated ballet pictures, he undertook a figure of the 14-year-old Marie van Goethem dressed as a ballet-dancer, which he had finished by the following year in time for inclusion in the fifth IMPRESSIONIST EXHIBITION. It was an extraordinary achievement, remarkable for its REALISM, the vitality of the pose and, perhaps above all else, for the variety of media used. Standing 95.2 cm (37½ ins.), the original figure was made in wax with satin ribbon, net and cotton; the textile materials were also waxed to produce the right kind of tension. He took enormous pains over the work; there are many drawings for it (e.g. in the Musée d'Orsay, The Art Institute of Chicago, and the Metropolitan Museum, New York) as well as a nude statuette (National Gallery of Art, Washington).

In 1882 Degas did a bas-relief in wax on wood (National Gallery of Art, Washington) of the apple harvest, presumably a renewed version of the very early work referred to by Bartholomé. Two years later, in the course of an outburst of pastels depicting bathing women and ballet-dancers, he produced a sculptural sketch in bronze-coloured wax of a dancer in the role of Harlequin, related to a pastel of the same subject now in the Art Institute of Chicago. By its very nature as a 'study' this work shows something of the vitality of Degas' plastic vision, and hints at affinities with the work of Rodin. He also produced, originally in some form of plaster, a head of Bartholomé's dead wife, loosely based on the statue that the sculptor had produced for her tomb at Crépy-en-Valois (Musée d'Orsay). At the end of the 1880s came a statuette of a horse, made originally in wax, with a wire reinforcement, based on an illustration from Muybridge's *Animal Locomotion* (1887), and another of a horse rearing from the same work (both Musée d'Orsay). He then turned his attention to a more complex and ingenious subject, *The Tub*, which showed a young woman examining her foot, in a shallow bath tub of the kind that appears in several pastels of the period. A final figure of the period, impossible to pinpoint to a specific year, was again in the same roughly 'expressionist' style of the Harlequin, showing a ballet-dancer with her right leg extended in front of her, and her arms *en attitude*.

Other studies of ballet-dancers, bathers and horses accumulated in Degas' studio, but he was very reluctant to have them cast, finding in the

Together they produced a portrait and a medallion of Renoir, a standing 58-cm (23-in.) statue of Venus holding an apple, and a variant some 183 cms (72 ins.) high; a 71-cm (28-in.) high mounting for an overmantel-clock, representing a hymn to life, or triumph of love; and a bas-relief based, with some modifications, on his *Judgment of Paris* (Hiroshima Museum, Japan) – indeed, of the 14 statues and bas-reliefs that were produced as a consequence of the Renoir–Guino partnership, half were related to this painting. The other important works were a bust of Madame Renoir and a seated *Mother and Child* (Musée d'Orsay), both dated 1915, and a series of medallions of famous artists,

Sculpture: clock case designed by Renoir and entitled *Hymne à la vie*, produced *c*. 1914.

mutability of wax a constant invitation to explore form. In 1919, however, A.A. Hébrard, a dealer who had been involved with the artist, started to cast 73 of the wax models. The actual work was done by a brilliant Italian founder, Albino Palazzolo (who eventually received the Legion of Honour for his work with the sculpture of Degas and Rodin), under the supervision of Bartholomé. From these casts some 22 more were made in bronze, those intended for sale being marked A–T, those reserved for the artist's family HERD, and those for Hébrard himself HER.

Renoir's early interest in sculpture had been rekindled in 1906, when Aristide Maillol came to Essoyes to execute a bust commissioned by VOLLARD. Renoir was deeply absorbed in the process and the techniques involved, and gave up painting entirely until the bust was finished. Seven years later, Vollard turned up at Renoir's home with the suggestion that Richard Guino, a 23-year-old Spaniard who had been Maillol's assistant, should collaborate with the painter on the production of a number of pieces of sculpture, which would be signed by the artist when they were to his satisfaction. At first Renoir rejected the idea, but then succumbed.

Rodin's innovative **sculpture** *Monument to Balzac* of 1898.

including DELACROIX, Rodin, CÉZANNE and Ingres, which were executed 1916–17.

In several of these sculptures there is more than a hint of the influence of Maillol, due, in part at least, to the role played by Guino. Inevitably, therefore, the question arises as to whether there was a sculptural equivalent to Impressionism. If one accepts the narrow meaning of the word (*see also* MUSIC) it seems impossible, but then in common usage the word is seldom used in so restricted a sense. In its wider connotation, as implying (at the time) something 'modern' that gave an impression of a visual experience rather than a literal description, it has come to be applied to the work of sculptors such as Jules Dalou (1838–1902), whose *Fraternity*, a bas-relief on the *mairie* of the 10th arrondissement, presents such a contrast to so much contemporary urban neo-classicism, and of course to the work of Rodin, who shared an exhibition at Georges PETIT's with MONET. To many of his contemporaries Rodin's statue of Balzac must have seemed as disturbing as MANET's *Déjeuner sur l'herbe* had been some 30 years earlier.

Medardo Rosso (1858–1928) was in a position analogous to that of Rodin as a sculptural 'Impressionist'. Their styles were in fact very similar, and Rosso always claimed that the compositional idea of the latter's *Balzac* was derived from his own works, such as *The Bookmaker* (1894; Museum of Modern Art, New York). Although Italian by birth, Rosso spent much of his time in Paris, and was friendly with Degas, ZOLA and the collector ROUART. His creative career virtually ended when he was 41. *See also* ASTRUC *[70, 98, 188]*

□ V. Belrose-Huyghues, 'Impressionnisme en Sculpture', in *Connaissance des arts* (Jan. 1974); H.W. Janson, *Nineteenth-Century Sculpture* (1985); *Degas*, Grand Palais, Paris, exhibition catalogue (1988)

Seurat, Georges (1859–91) A Parisian of solid middle-class background, Seurat entered the ECOLE DES BEAUX-ARTS when quite young, but was not happy there, although he absorbed its discipline of drawing. He spent much time studying in the Louvre and, from the very beginning, showed a thoughtfulness and a

Seurat's Pointillist masterpiece, *Sunday Afternoon on the Island of La Grande Jatte*, 1884–86, created a sensation when it was shown at the last Impressionist exhibition of 1886.

Cartesian passion for analysis, which led him to create from within Impressionist visual empiricism a new system that would supplant it, and act as a catalyst for a whole spectrum of 20th-c. art. He claimed that ever since the age of 16 he had been searching for a method of rationalizing colours to create form, and he became deeply immersed in the theories of CHEVREUL and other scientists on the simultaneous contrasts of COLOUR, the effects of juxtaposed colours, and the fact that each colour can impose its own complementary on its neighbour.

These ideas first found expression in *Bathing at Asnières* (1883–84; National Gallery, London), which he exhibited at the Salon des INDÉPENDANTS, of which he was one of the first members, and through which he came to know SIGNAC, who did so much to promulgate his theories. His next major work, *Sunday Afternoon on the Island of La Grande Jatte* (1886; Art Institute of Chicago), which measures 206 × 259 cms (81 × 102 ins.), created a sensation when it was shown at the last Impressionist exhibition of 1886, along with six seascapes. PISSARRO was immediately impressed, writing to his son Lucien, 'Seurat has something new to contribute, which these gentlemen (his fellow exhibitors), despite their talent, are not able to appreciate. I am totally convinced of the progressive nature of his art, and certain that in time it will yield extraordinary results. . . . I do not accept the snobbish judgments of "romantic" Impressionists in whose interest it is to fight against new tendencies. I accept the challenge, that's all.' He did, in fact, 'accept the challenge' and for a period painted in what was coming to be known as the Pointillist style.

The other Impressionists had been extremely reluctant to accept Seurat's work, and eventually his paintings, together with works of Signac, Pissarro himself and his son Lucien, were shown together in a separate room. Both factions were right in their own ways. Seurat represented an entirely different attitude, closer, in terms of the old dichotomy, to Ingres than to DELACROIX, and he was, by implication, assailing the 'softness' of Impressionism in very much the same way that CÉZANNE was.

Seurat died of an infection at the age of 32 and so was not able fully to realize the implications of his revolution and the effects it would have. Nevertheless, he became the precursor of all 'hard-edge' painting that occurred throughout most of the following century, giving special encouragement through his works and ideas to Cubism and to painters such as Léger, whereas the traditions of Impressionism were transmitted to Expressionism and its derivatives. *See also* BLANC, EMPERAIRE, GAUGUIN, LUCIEN PISSARRO, LA VIE MODERNE

☐ J. Rewald, *Seurat* (1948); J. Rewald, *Post-Impressionism* (1956)

Shchukin, Sergei (1851–1936) came from a dynasty of Moscow traders; all four of his brothers were assiduous art collectors, but none more adventurous or more enthusiastic than he. He did not, however, start collecting on a large scale until after the death of his father in 1890, when he became head of the Shchukin Trading House and bought a princely residence, which he proceeded to stack with French paintings. In 1897 Fiodor Botkin, one of his mother's relatives, drew his attention to MONET, and he bought from DURAND-RUEL *Lilac in the Sun*, the first Impressionist painting to reach Moscow. He continued to buy Monets extensively up to about 1906. He relied heavily on Durand-Ruel and had a special gallery built for his collection of RENOIRS. He also collected PISSARRO and CÉZANNE, and had a superb collection of pastels by DEGAS. Later he went on to acquire works by GAUGUIN, Picasso and especially Matisse. Most of his collection is now in the Hermitage, Leningrad, or the Pushkin Museum, Moscow. *See also* MOROSOV

☐ M. Ginsburg, 'Art Collectors of Old Russia', *Apollo* (Dec. 1973); M. Bessonova (ed.), *Impressionist and Post-Impressionist Paintings in Soviet Museums* (1985)

Sickert, Walter Richard (1860–1942) Born in Munich of mixed English and Danish descent, Sickert was the outstanding example of an artist on the fringes of Impressionism, friendly with many of its leading practitioners while yet remaining an individualist, taking from the movement those technical devices and attitudes that were best attuned to his own creative personality. Commencing his career as an actor, he soon found that painting was his real métier. He became a student at the Slade School of Art, under Alphonse LEGROS, who was close to the Impressionists, and then worked in WHISTLER's studio.

In 1883 Sickert went to Paris, where he became intimate with DEGAS, deriving from his work an interest in the depiction of contemporary urban life that was to remain one of the

Sickert's *St Jacques, Dieppe*: Sickert lived in the town 1899–1905.

characteristics of his work, as well as a predilection for using drawings to create the basic structure of his paintings – in opposition, for instance, to Whistler's technique of direct painting. In 1885 he was involved in an exhibition at the GOUPIL Gallery of the so-called 'London Impressionists', and in his introduction to the catalogue he defined Impressionism in a manner which emphasized those qualities that were best exemplified in the works of Degas – and Whistler. He was averse to the works of MONET, though he himself at this time was painting with broken brushstrokes. Between 1899 and 1905 he lived in Dieppe, where he came into contact with GAUGUIN, who also had some influence on his work, and it was during this period that he bought a significant number of works by Degas.

Involved in the New English Art Club (*see* ENGLAND), he did much to popularize Impressionism, mostly through his provocative, but stimulating, writings. In his own work, however, he tended to move away from the ideals it stood for, and there was something dourly nationalistic in his approach to the movement. *See also* HALÉVY

□ W. Sickert, *A Free House; or the Artist as Craftsman: Being the Writings of Walter Sickert* (1947); W. Baron, *Sickert* (1973)

Signac, Paul (1863–1935) His well-to-do parents had originally intended him to be an architect, but eventually agreed to his desire to be a painter. Whilst still in his teens he wrote an enthusiastic letter to MONET asking for advice: 'I have always worked regularly and conscientiously, but without help or guidance, for I know no Impressionist painter who could guide me, living as I do in a mainly unfriendly environment'. Monet was indeed most helpful, and Signac was always to remain grateful, writing to the older artist in 1912, 'Always a Monet has moved me profoundly. Always I have found something to learn from in one of your works, and in my days of doubt and discouragement, Monet has always been for me a friend and a guide.'

Painting originally in the mainstream Impressionist style with a heavy dependence on Monet, his membership of the Société des Artistes INDÉPENDANTS, to all of whose nine exhibitions he contributed, brought him into close and friendly contact with SEURAT, whose newly formed doctrines and techniques he absorbed with such fervour that for some time their works were almost identical in appearance.

An outgoing character, unlike his friend Seurat, he defended Pointillism, or neo-Impressionism, as it was coming to be called, with a fervour based on profound intellectual conviction. His book *D'Eugène Delacroix au néo-impressionnisme* (1899) was a convincing and impressive attempt to see the evolution of 19th-c. painting as a steady progression from the chromatic Romanticism of Delacroix, through Impressionism, to the apparently

Signac, *The Seine, Grenelle*, 1899: an industrial landscape in Pointillist technique.

ordered visual rationalism of Pointillism. It was a theory that has informed much artistic thinking ever since. In 1927 he published an important book on JONGKIND (a painter whom Monet had greatly admired and learnt from), and his article on 'Les Besoins individuels et la peinture' for the 1935 *Encyclopédie française* was a remarkable piece of imaginative interpretation.

Inferior to Seurat in magnificence of conception and in the ability to handle complicated compositions, he produced a great number of eminently pleasing and even impressive paintings, though his style and technique showed little or no development. *See also* CHEVREUL, GAUGUIN

□ P. Signac, *D'Eugène Delacroix au néo-impressionnisme* (1899); 'Extraits du journal inédit de Paul Signac', intro. and notes by J. Rewald, *Gazette des Beaux-Arts* (July–Sept. 1949; April 1952; July–Aug. 1953); J.U. Halpérin, *Félix Fénéon* (1988)

Silvestre, Armand (1837–1901) Critic, novelist, playwright, poet and journalist, Silvestre figures largely in the history of Impressionism because of his vivid reminiscences of the participants, especially in the pages of his autobiographical excursus *Au Pays des souvenirs* (Paris, 1892), which contains a particularly fascinating account of life in the CAFÉ GUERBOIS: MANET in his conversation, 'naturally ironical and frequently cruel'; DEGAS, 'an innovator of sorts, whose ironic modesty of bearing saved him from the hatred that his more outspoken colleagues provoked'; the critic DURANTY, 'a man of incredible dignity, who spoke very slowly and softly, with an almost imperceptible English accent. Nothing about him suggested wealth, yet he had an air of real breeding and dignity.'

When DURAND-RUEL published his three-volume *Receuil d'estampes* in 1873, which was to contain 300 reproductions of works from his own stock, including examples of works by Manet, MONET, PISSARRO, SISLEY and Degas, he commissioned Silvestre to write the introduction, a tribute to the percipience that the latter had shown in his general criticism of the Impressionists. His judgments may be faulted, but they did present the general public with an appropriate framework into which individual artists could be fitted: 'Monet, the most adept and daring'; Sisley, 'the most harmonious and hesitant'; Pissarro, 'the most genuine and

naïve'; whilst Manet 'still belongs to the field of discussion, but not of bewilderment'. His general judgment of the group as a whole is 'that the success of these newcomers is that their pictures are painted according to a singularly cheerful tonality. A blond light illumines them, and everything in them is gaiety, clarity and joyfulness.' On the other hand, in a review published in the same year, Silvestre complained that the Impressionists' insistence on painting any kind of landscape, rather than selecting an obviously beautiful one was 'an awkward affectation, based on the concept that everything in nature is of equal beauty, an artistically erroneous idea'. *See also* CRITICS

□ A. Silvestre, *Au Pays des souvenirs* (1892); Rewald (1973)

Silvestre, Théophile (1823–76) Originally a Republican, who became a supporter of NAPOLEON III, he played an important part in the art world of the Second Empire. He wrote for *Figaro* about art, and edited a satirical journal, *Le Nain jaune*. His most famous work was his *Histoire des artistes vivants* (1856–58). He was a great supporter of COROT.

Sisley, Alfred (1839–99) Sisley was born in Paris of English parents. After his schooldays, his father, a merchant trading with the southern states of America, sent him to London for a business career, but finding this unpalatable, Sisley returned to Paris in 1862 with the aim of becoming an artist. His family gave him every support, sending him to GLEYRE's studio, where he met RENOIR, MONET and BAZILLE. He spent some time painting in Fontainebleau, at Chailly with Monet, Bazille and Renoir, and later at Marlotte with Renoir. His style at this time was deeply influenced by COURBET and DAUBIGNY, and when he first exhibited at the SALON in 1867 it was as the pupil of COROT.

By this time, however, he had started to frequent the CAFÉ GUERBOIS, and was becoming more deeply influenced by the notions which were creating Impressionism. During the FRANCO-PRUSSIAN WAR and the period of the Commune, he spent some time in London and was introduced to DURAND-RUEL by PISSARRO, becoming part of that dealer's stable. In the mean time, his father had lost all his money as a result of the war, and Sisley, with a family to support, was reduced to a state of penury, in which he was to stay until virtually the end of his life.

Sisley, *Vue de Montmartre prise de la Cité des Fleurs*, 1869. An early landscape showing the influence of Courbet and Corot.

He now saw himself as a full-time professional painter and part of the Impressionist group, exhibiting with them in 1874, 1876, 1877 and 1882. His work had by this time achieved complete independence from the early influences that had affected him. In the 1870s he produced a remarkable series of landscapes of ARGENTEUIL, where he was living, one of which, *The Bridge at Argenteuil* (1872; Brooks Memorial Gallery, Memphis, USA) was bought by MANET. Towards the end of the decade Monet was beginning to have a considerable influence on him, and a series of landscape paintings of the area around Paris, including Marly, BOUGIVAL and LOUVECIENNES (1876; *Floods at Port-Marly*, Musée d'Orsay), shows the way in which his dominant and evident lyricism still respects the demands of the subject-matter. From his early admiration for Corot he retained a passionate interest in the sky, which nearly always dominates his paintings, and also in the effects of snow, the two interests often combining to create a strangely dramatic effect (*Snow at Véneux*, 1880; Musée d'Orsay). Naturally diffident, he did not promote himself in the way that some of his fellow Impressionists did, and it was only towards the end of his life, when he was dying of cancer of the throat, that he received something

approaching the recognition he deserved. *See also* DRAWING, ENGLAND, FAURE, MOROSOV, PLEIN-AIRISME, PRICES, PRINTS, SOCIAL BACKGROUND *[37, 56, 82]*
□ Venturi (1939); F. Daulte, *Alfred Sisley* (1959); J. Leymarie and M. Melot, *Les Gravures des impressionnistes* (1971)

Social background It is generally accepted that the French Revolution transferred real political power to the bourgeoisie, and that this transfer was confirmed by the suppression of the Commune after the fall of the Empire (*see* FRANCE, POLITICS). But this is clearly an oversimplification. The growth of industrialization and all that went with it was enlarging the bourgeoisie both in size and in wealth, a phenomenon which was so convincingly documented in the novels of ZOLA. The advent of the Third Republic after 1870, however, was characterized by the emergence of a powerful 'middle' as opposed to a 'grand' bourgeoisie, and its members became the most characteristic representatives of the period. It was from their ranks that most of the Impressionists were drawn, and Impressionism was very largely concerned with their life and its background.

MANET came from a family of magistrates; MORISOT was the daughter of a monarchist

Bazille's painting of his family on the terrace of their home near Montpellier in 1867 reflects the leisured life of the bourgeoisie, which formed the **social background** of most of the Impressionists.

high-ranking civil servant; DEGAS came from a banking family of aristocratic origins; SISLEY's father was a rich English businessman; CASSATT's was a wealthy railway magnate, BAZILLE's a prosperous vineyard owner. CÉZANNE's father had started off as a hatter but, by lending money to the farmers from whom he bought the skins then used in his trade, made himself into the most important banker in AIX-EN-PROVENCE. PISSARRO came from a wealthy West Indies family, which eventually settled in Paris. CAILLEBOTTE's family was typical of the very affluent bourgeois of the Second Empire; extremely wealthy textile manufacturers who had moved to Paris from Normandy, they took a stake in the development of the French capital that happened under NAPOLEON III, and further increased their riches.

RENOIR and MONET were the only exceptions: Renoir's father was a tailor who, like many of the inhabitants of Paris at the time, had migrated to the capital from the provinces, while Monet's father adopted the reverse procedure and left Paris in 1845 to work in his brother's wholesale grocery business in Le Havre. In their subsequent careers neither artist showed the least sign of their 'humble' beginnings. *See also* PARIS, PATRONS

□ Rewald (1973); Zeldin (1988)

Société Anonyme des Artistes It is important in the first instance to realize that the phrase 'société anonyme' cannot be translated literally; it is the French equivalent of 'limited company'. In 1873, largely as a consequence of the economic depression that hit France around this time, and which forced DURAND-RUEL to stop buying any more paintings, MONET, PISSARRO and others decided that it would be worth while trying to sell their paintings at a group exhibition, consisting of those who formed the so-called BATIGNOLLES group and others connected with them. Much of the drive towards the exhibition came from Pissarro, who was almost obsessively concerned with administration and organizational details. He himself, in 1860, had joined the Association des artistes peintres d'histoire et de genre, sculpteurs, graveurs, architectes et dessinateurs, which had been founded 16 years earlier as a kind of provident society, offering help and pensions to its members. This formed one of the prototypes for the association of artists he had in mind to arrange exhibitions and indulge in other mutually beneficial activities. Another even more bizarre precedent he advanced was that of the bakers' union, which he had studied in PONTOISE, and which harmonized with his own POLITICAL views. However, RENOIR and others

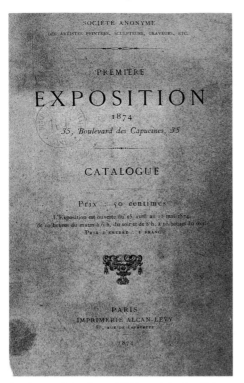

Catalogue of the first exhibition of the **Société Anonyme** des Artistes, 1874.

objected forcibly to so elaborate a structure, and it was decided to create a joint stock company, the capital of which would be replenished by each member paying one-tenth of the income from sales organized by the company, with the running costs being covered by subscriptions.

The agreement to found this 'société anonyme' was signed on 27 December 1873. Amongst the original members were Monet, Renoir, SISLEY, DEGAS, MORISOT, PISSARRO, BÉLIARD, GUILLAUMIN, and Degas' friends LEPIC, Levert and ROUART. Having secured the studios recently vacated by NADAR and started to arrange their first exhibition, they had to find a name for themselves, and it is significant, in view of the later history of what came to be known as 'Impressionism', that there was considerable opposition to any title with stylistic connotations. This was led by Degas, who suggested that they should call themselves 'la Capucine' – which means nasturtium – and adopt the flower as their emblem. Eventually

the decision was reached to call themselves simply 'Une Société anonyme des artistes'.

Philippe BURTY recorded the basic facts in an article on the exhibition in the columns of *La République française* on 16 April: 'Thirty artists have founded a co-operative society, whose rules exclude choice by a jury as being inimical to the true spirit of artistic personality. As a consequence of this attitude, too, the idea of prizes and awards has been rejected. Hanging is decided by drawing lots, and paintings are grouped together according to size.' Later exhibitions were described merely as 'An Exhibition of Paintings by MM. . . .' On 17 December 1874, a general meeting was held in Renoir's apartment, with him in the chair, and it was decided to wind up the Society because of its financial liabilities. *See also* IMPRESSIONIST EXHIBITIONS

☐ Venturi (1939); Rewald (1973)

Société des Artistes Indépendants *see* INDÉPENDANTS

Society of French Artists Between 1870, when he first came to ENGLAND, and 1875 DURAND-RUEL mounted at his gallery at 168 New Bond Street, ten annual exhibitions of the so-called Society of French Artists. The Society was, in fact, very largely a public relations concoction of his own, invented to give authenticity to what he described as 'a considerable body of masterpieces by our most distinguished French artists'. There was, in fact, a 'Committee of Honour', which included the names of many well-known French artists, including LEGROS, but its function was at best of a lightly advisory kind. Quite apart from anything else, Durand-Ruel included in the exhibitions works by English artists, such as Mark Fisher, Burne-Jones, Alma Tadema (and his wife) and Wilkie.

The majority of the artists represented were of the kind in which his Parisian gallery specialized, reaching as far back as Ingres and DELACROIX, but including predominantly COURBET, Isabey, COROT, BOUDIN, JONGKIND, Harpignies and FANTIN-LATOUR, whose works were bought in England by such collectors as Louis Huth, Constantine Ionides and John W. Wilson. But he also included in every exhibition except the second (1871), works by the Impressionists. MONET and PISSARRO were the first, then in 1872 came MANET, DEGAS, SISLEY and RENOIR. In 1874 MORISOT and GONZALÈS

appeared. Manet's representation in these exhibitions was the most formidable, and his works
were priced the highest, 400 guineas being
asked for works such as *The Spanish Singer*
(1860; Metropolitan Museum, New York) and
Dead Christ with Angels (1864; Metropolitan
Museum, New York). Pissarro's *Upper Norwood* (1871; Courtauld Institute, London),
however, was priced at only 25 guineas, and the
same kind of amounts were charged for
Monet's works, as well as those of Sisley. Degas
occupied a median position, his *Robert le Diable*
(1872; Metropolitan Museum, New York)
being priced at 100 guineas, and eventually
being bought in Paris by FAURE for 1500 francs.

Although the exhibitions exposed the
Impressionists to the English public for the first
time, they do not seem to have secured any
immediate sales, and having closed his London
gallery in 1875, when Durand-Ruel returned
again to the English scene in 1883 he no longer
employed the 'Society of French Artists' as a
front for his commercial activities.
□ Venturi (1939); Cooper (1954)

**Sommier, François-Clément (Henri
Somm)** (1844–1907) Born in Rouen, he
quickly built up in Paris a reputation as an
illustrator, caricaturist and designer, his work
appearing in fashionable journals such as *Le
Monde parisien* and *Tout-Paris*. In 1879 he
submitted two prints and a group of book
illustrations to the 1879 IMPRESSIONIST EXHIBI-
TION. He was deeply influenced by JAPANESE art,
and was a close friend of Félix BRACQUEMOND.
□ E. Bénézit, *Dictionnaire des peintres, sculpteurs,
dessinateurs et graveurs* (1966)

Spain Nineteenth-century France was hypnotized by Spain, a fact documented in the

Spain: Goya's *Executions of 3 May 1808*, painted six years after the event, shares many similarities with
Manet's *Execution of the Emperor Maximilian*, 1867, an equally political work.

Spain: In 1917 Renoir painted Vollard in the unlikely garb of a toreador.

following year the first biography of Goya appeared in French. In the same year the Louvre acquired at auction works by Velazquez, Zurbarán and Ribéra. Nobody could have been more receptive to this vindication of the Spanish spirit than Manet, and, when he held his first retrospective at MARTINET's in 1867, 28 of the 53 works had Spanish themes or models. There were, of course, two distinct elements: the subject-matter and the style. His first success at the SALON, *The Spanish Singer* of 1860 (Metropolitan Museum, New York), shows a model dressed in some of the Spanish clothes that, as ZOLA pointed out at the time, Manet kept in great quantities in his studio. All these early 'Spanish' works were indeed costume pieces, and it was not until 1862, when Mariano Camprubi's troupe of Spanish dancers made an appearance in Paris, that Manet was able to paint authentic Spaniards. He invited the company to pose for him, using the studio of Alfred STEVENS, as his own was too small. The outstanding production of this episode was the portrait of Lola de Valence (Musée d'Orsay, Paris), 'a beauty at once darkling and lively in character', as Baudelaire described her. It was not until 1865 that Manet first visited Spain, though, quite apart from any Spanish paintings he had seen in Paris, he had been aware of the many prints and engravings of such works as Velazquez' *The Drinkers*, an etching of which – attributed to Goya – can be seen in the background of his portrait of Zola (1867; Musée d'Orsay). Manet was himself producing numerous etchings at this period very much in the style of Goya, some of which were reproductions of works such as Velazquez's *Philip IV* and of the painting in the Louvre, then falsely attributed to him, *A Gathering of People of Rank*. On his first trip to Spain Manet intended following an itinerary mapped out for him by Zacharie ASTRUC, a Hispanic enthusiast, but in the event, he only stayed ten days. Most of his time was spent in Madrid, where he met Théodore DURET, with whom he was to maintain a close friendship, though he also visited Burgos, Valladolid and Toledo, where he praised El Greco's portraits.

The influence of Spanish painters, especially Velazquez, on Manet is obvious – in the choice of subject-matter; in that sense of REALISM he had begun to transfer from studio-pictures such as *The Spanish Singer* to the life of his own time, as in the *Déjeuner sur l'herbe* (1863; Musée d'Orsay) and *The Old Musicians* (1862; Natio-

writings of Théophile GAUTIER, BAUDELAIRE, Prosper Mérimée and others; by the music of Bizet, and by the paintings of MANET and, to a lesser extent, of other Impressionists, as well as such peripheral figures as Constantin GUYS, WHISTLER and SARGENT. On a more prosaic plane, three times as many Frenchmen holidayed in Spain in the 1860s as they did in ITALY; Spanish musicians and entertainers were extremely popular, and the peninsula represented an image of Romantic beauty and abandoned passion that conformed perfectly to the fantasies of an industrial society. Napoleon's Hispanic policies, and the collecting activities of his uncle Cardinal Fesch, had introduced a number of Spanish paintings into the Louvre, and Louis-Philippe, largely because of his designs to set his family on the Spanish throne, fostered an interest in Spanish art and created an entire gallery in the Louvre dedicated to it. This collection was eventually broken up on his downfall and sold at Christie's in 1850, many of the works going into public collections.

Manet was only 16 when the Galerie Espagnole was dismantled, but its contents had exerted a powerful influence on COURBET, and Spanish art became accepted as the very epitome of the Romantic spirit. In 1857 Baudelaire published his essay on Goya's prints, and in the nal Gallery of Art, Washington, D.C.), in which there are also echoes of Murillo; in a kind of visual seriousness, and in the dramatic manipulation of black. More problematic are technical influences, such as brushwork, where some apparent similarities might be more convincingly attributed to the influence of Frans Hals, with whose works Manet had a closer first-hand experience through his visits to HOLLAND. But as late as 1881, when he painted *The Bar at the Folies-Bergère* (Courtauld Institute, London), he was still remembering Velazquez's interplay of the viewpoints of spectator and implied spectator, to be found in *Las Meninas* (1660; Prado, Madrid). The influence of Goya was also apparent in *The Execution of the Emperor Maximilian* (Museum of Fine Arts, Boston, and National Gallery, London) and in *The Balcony* (1869; Musée d'Orsay, based on the *Majas on the Balcony*, a version of which he saw in 1867.

In 1862 Manet found DEGAS in the Louvre, making an etching directly onto copper of the portrait of the Infanta Marguerita by Velazquez. He was greatly impressed by the skill and ingenuity that Degas was displaying in the task. On the whole, however, it was to Goya rather than to the earlier artist that Degas looked. Several of his group portraits show the frontal simplicity of composition that marked Goya's *The Family of Charles IV*, and the year after the encounter with Manet, Degas bought the newly published edition of *The Disasters of War*. Time and time again, contemporary critics likened his pictures of prostitutes and working women to the works of the Spaniard, and portraits such as *Woman with the Umbrella* (National Gallery of Canada, Ottawa) show more formal influences.

CÉZANNE, on the other hand, was more impressed by the dramatic effects of Zurbarán and Ribéra, the influence of the latter being especially apparent in the sombre *Preparation for the Funeral* (1868; Private collection); it is clearly based on Ribéra's *Entombment*, which had recently been acquired for the Louvre. RENOIR visited Spain in 1892, but there was little evidence of any Spanish influence on his works, though he kitted out the plump Ambroise VOLLARD in the unlikely dress of a matador when he painted his portrait in 1917.

DURAND-RUEL carried on a brisk trade in Spanish paintings from the 1860s onwards, though the works of Goya and Velazquez which he sold seem to have been of question-

able authenticity. There does not seem to have been any considerable market for the works of the Impressionists in Spain, and the influence of the movement on Spanish painting was so late and so diffused as barely to merit attention. *See also* ANTECEDENTS *[20, 105, 159, 215]*

□ F. Jímenez-Placer, *La Pintura española en la época del realismo y del impresionismo* (1944); J. Isaacson, *Manet and Spain*, Art Museum, University of Michigan, exhibition catalogue (1969); *Le Musée espagnol de Louis-Philippe*, Louvre, exhibition catalogue (1981)

Stevens, Alfred (1823–1906) A Belgian artist, who lived and worked in Paris for most of his life, he became immensely popular as a society portraitist, and was one of the first living artists to be accorded an exhibition at the ECOLE DES BEAUX-ARTS. He was a great friend of MANET, and it was in Stevens' studio that he first met BAZILLE. Especially towards the latter part of his career he was much influenced by the Impressionists, adopting a loose style of brushwork analogous to that of SARGENT. With his friend BRACQUEMOND, he was one of the first devotees

Stevens, *Ophelia*: a successful portraitist, he was a great friend of Manet.

of JAPANESE art, elements of which he introduced as bric-à-brac into his society paintings (*The Visit*, 1876; Sterling and Francine Clark Art Institute, Williamstown, Mass.). His book, *Impressions sur la peinture* (1886), was a considerable success. His brother Joseph was a critic and animal painter who did quite a lot to help the Impressionists. *See also* CAFÉS, CRITICS, MEURENT
□ G. van Zype, *Les Frères Stevens* (1936)

Stevenson, R.A.M. (1847–1900) Painter and art critic who, along with D.S. MACCOLL, helped explain Impressionism to the English public. A cousin of Robert Louis Stevenson, after graduating at Cambridge he studied art in Edinburgh, Paris and Antwerp, became Professor of Fine Art at University College, Liverpool, from 1880 to 1893 and was, for the last ten years of his life, art critic of the *Pall Mall Gazette*. His major work was *The Art of Velazquez*, published in 1895, the first intelligent appreciation of that artist to appear in ENGLAND; and it was his concern with this artist, who had so much influenced MANET and others, that led him to a sympathetic understanding of what Impressionism was all about. He also greatly encouraged the work of those English and Scottish artists who adopted Impressionist techniques and approaches. *See also* CRITICS
□ *Dictionary of National Biography*, supplement iii (1914); Cooper (1954); Flint (1984)

Stora, Clémentine (1845–1917) A well-known hostess, and the wife of a dealer in antiques and Middle Eastern wares, whose shop in the boulevard des Italiens was very popular amongst those who favoured the current taste for exotic bric-à-brac. RENOIR painted a portrait of her dressed in Algerian costume (Fine Arts Museum, San Francisco), which was exhibited at the 1870 SALON and which formed part of a sequence of similar works he was painting at this period, all showing the very clear influence of DELACROIX. The painting was acquired by MONET in 1906.
□ *Renoir*, Hayward Gallery, London, exhibition catalogue (1985)

T

Tanguy, Julien (Père Tanguy) (1825–94) A colour merchant, originally of the peripatetic variety, Tanguy first came into contact with the vital elements in 19th-c. painting in 1870, in the forest of Fontainebleau, where he met RENOIR, PISSARRO and MONET. A republican radical in POLITICS, he fought on the side of the Communards, was captured by the troops of Thiers and deported to Brest, but was released through the intervention of ROUART. He then opened a shop in the rue Clauzel in MONTMARTRE. Friendly and intelligent, he was ready to exchange artists' materials for paintings and drawings by his friends, and they saw in his efforts to promote their works an artistic expression of his natural revolutionary instincts. Introduced to CÉZANNE by Pissarro, his shop became a virtual gallery for the painter from AIX, and it was there that Renoir took CHOCQUET to persuade him of Cézanne's neglected talents. It is interesting to note that as late as 1885 Cézanne owed Tanguy 4015 francs 40 centimes, and Tanguy had to beg the painter to repay him as he was facing eviction.

Van Gogh's portrait of Père **Tanguy**, the colour merchant, surrounded by Japanese prints, 1887–88.

Eventually, as Emile BERNARD expressed it, 'People would go there as they might go to a museum, which had unexpectedly become a Parisian legend, the talk of every studio.' Tanguy was to be especially helpful to VAN GOGH, with whom his name is most commonly associated, and who painted two portraits of him. His collection was sold at the HÔTEL DROUOT in 1894.

□ J. Rewald, *Post-Impressionism* (1956); Rewald (1985); J. Rewald, *Studies in Post-Impressionism* (1986)

Technique The techniques of Impressionism inevitably varied a great deal from artist to artist, and from period to period. It clearly requires a great deal of economizing with the truth to find much common technical ground between, say, DEGAS' *Bouderie* of 1869 (Metropolitan Museum, New York) and RENOIR's *The Promenade* (National Gallery of Scotland) of the same year, or between MANET's *Olympia* of 1863 (Musée d'Orsay) and his portrait of MONET working in his studio boat, painted 11 years later (Bayerische Staatsgemäldesammlungen, Munich).

There were, however, certain changes that the Impressionists jointly brought about in the nature of painting and its objectives, which depended on technical devices, including their use of COLOUR and PERSPECTIVE, as well as their actual manipulation of the paint surface. It was this latter quality which most antagonized their critics, who saw in their works a lack of 'finish', a 'roughness', and a general lack of skill, which they attributed to technical incompetence rather than deliberate intention.

Two of the most cherished ideals of the Impressionists determined the nature of their brushwork. The first was the idea of PLEIN-AIRISME, of working out-of-doors in direct contact with nature. This had not been unknown amongst the artists of the ACADEMIC tradition, but they had used it merely to produce *pochades*, or sketches, which were later worked up into finished paintings. The Impressionists, however, placing emphasis on the notion of spontaneity, saw in this approach an honesty and directness of expression that were central to their beliefs. Closely connected with this was a concern with catching the fleeting moment, the precise time at which changing light and atmosphere influenced the actual appearance of a place, a person, or an object. To achieve such instantaneous imagery, the slow,

deliberate application of paint with fine brushes in the unhurried quiet of the studio was impossible. Rapidly applied strokes were necessary, set down with a certain vehemence, sometimes with the palette-knife, sometimes with the brush. The necessity for such a technique was emphasized, too, by the colour preoccupations of the Impressionists: the notion of using colours in such a way that they blended in the eye of the spectator through appropriate juxtaposition on the canvas, and the realization that pigment applied in varying degrees of thickness could catch and reflect light, giving the finished work an impression of brightness and vivacity.

Such an approach to the manipulation of paint was not entirely new. Renoir, especially in his early days, had been greatly impressed by the fluent brushstrokes and dynamism of some of COURBET's works, but by the 1870s he and Monet had become converted to a much smaller brushstroke, creating in their painting a pattern of dots and dashes, which could be manipulated in colour and opacity to create an overall image of persuasive coherence. In the period between 1876 and 1878 Monet was selling to his colleagues, as well as to dealers, works that were in actual fact mere *pochades* – to the detriment of his reputation at the time; in the 1880s, however, he started to apply a greater degree of finish to his paintings, working up the out-of-door sketches in the studio with more elaborate forms of brushwork and a greater integration of colour.

There was, in fact, throughout the comparatively short history of the movement a growing reaction against the ideal of technical spontaneity. It was to find ultimate expression in the Pointillism of SEURAT, and in PISSARRO's temporary conversion to it, no less than in the works Renoir was producing in the 1880s, marked as they were by smoother brushwork and harder outlines, which seemed at times almost to look back to Ingres. The reaction against the loose techniques of the earlier period could be seen as a consequence of ageing. But it was due, at least in part, to pressures from both dealers and even friendly critics. DURAND-RUEL had for long been complaining about the Impressionists' lack of finish, and in 1880 Zola had commented tartly 'M. Monet has given in too much to his facility of production. When one is too easily satisfied, when one delivers sketches that are scarcely dry, one loses the taste for works that have been worked on for a long

time. It is study which produces solid paintings, and henceforward he must devote himself to *solid* works meditated upon over a lengthy period.' (*Salon de 1880*) The wheel had come full circle, and techniques which had once seemed wild exercises in expression had been converted into what was rapidly becoming an accepted pictorial language. *See also* COLOUR, FLOCHETAGE, JAPANESE ART, PEINTURE CLAIRE, PERSPECTIVE, PHOTOGRAPHY *[134, 168, 217–24]*
□ J.C. Webster, 'The Technique of Impressionism', *College of Art Journal* (Nov. 1944); O. Reuterswärd, 'The accentuated brushwork of the Impressionists', *Journal of Aesthetics and Art Criticism* (March 1952); T. Reff, 'Cézanne's Constructive Stroke', *Art Quarterly* (Autumn 1962); Rewald (1973); A. Callen, *Techniques of the Impressionists* (1982)

Thoré, Théophile *see* BÜRGER, WILHELM

Tillot, Charles (b. 1825) He took part in the exhibitions of 1876, 1877, 1879, 1881 and 1886, mainly through the good offices of DEGAS, whose friend he was. In a letter to MONET, PISSARRO commented that, of the whole group of followers whom Degas insisted on dragging into the IMPRESSIONIST EXHIBITIONS, only Tillot and ROUART were worth anything. Few other people seem to have thought so, and his work was never mentioned by the critics.

Tissot, Jacques Joseph (James) (1836–1902) After first achieving success as a painter of historical pictures dealing with the Middle Ages, he turned his attention to modern life, choosing subjects from polite society rather than from the ordinary walks of life, and built up a successful practice as a portrait-painter. He struck up an early friendship with WHISTLER and was superficially influenced by his style, as well as by JAPANESE art; in 1867 he was appointed drawing master to the 14-year-old brother of the last Shōgun when he was on a visit to Paris.

Tissot was a close friend of DEGAS until 1895, when they broke contact with each other because Tissot had sold a painting of Degas', which the latter had given him. At one point they seemed to have a reciprocal influence on each other's style, and Degas was reputedly jealous of Tissot's success. In the Metropolitan Museum, New York, there is a portrait of Tissot by Degas (1868). He was also friendly with MANET, and remained so until the latter's death.

Tissot, painted by Degas in 1868. Note the Japanese picture above.

After the fall of the Commune, in which he had been involved in some inexplicable way, he spent eleven years in ENGLAND, specializing in pictures of London life, especially on or near the Thames, and being dubbed by the *Daily Telegraph* art critic as 'the Watteau of Wapping'. On the death of his English mistress Kathleen Newton, of whom he did endless portraits, he returned to France and spent the latter part of his life as the painter of religious works characterized by a portentous bathos. *See also* ITALY
□ M. Wentworth, *James Tissot* (1984); C. Wood, *Tissot* (1986)

Tréhot, Lise (1848–1924) RENOIR's mistress between 1865 and 1872, she was the model for many of his paintings during that period. The sister of Jules LE COEUR's companion, Clémence Tréhot, she was born in Paris of a humble family that had moved there from the country. She soon established herself on terms of intimacy with both Renoir and SISLEY, who gave her one of his paintings. She first appeared prominently in Renoir's *Diana* (1867; National Gallery of Art, Washington), and in 1868 was the sitter for a work sometimes known as *The*

Renoir, *Lise **Tréhot** with a Parasol*, 1867: an early *plein-air* portrait.

Gypsy Girl, but more frequently as *Lise* (Natio-nalgalerie, Berlin-Dahlem); this was the first of Renoir's works to attract the attention of DURET, who bought it. For lengthy periods she stayed with Renoir at his parents' house at VILLE D'AVRAY, and amongst the other important works for which she modelled were *Lise with a Parasol* (1867; Folkwang Museum, Essen), *The Bather* (1870; Museu de Arte Moderna, São Paulo, Brazil), and *The Algerian Woman* (1870; National Gallery of Art, Washington). In 1872 she married a young architect, who died in 1902. Outliving Renoir, she destroyed all their correspondence and photographs, though she kept the paintings that he and other artists had given to her.
□ D. Cooper, 'Renoir, Lise and the Le Coeur Family; i. Lise', *Burlington Magazine* (May 1959)

Trouville Described by a contemporary writer as 'Paris, with all its foibles, its vices transplanted for two or three months to the edge of the ocean', it was one of those Channel resorts opened up by the development of the RAILWAYS. It naturally attracted the attention of artists, partly because of its natural beauties, partly because it presented a fascinating perspective on society. It was also useful in that it allowed artists access to influential patrons, such as Prince Demidov, the Comte de Pour-talès and the Duchesse de Morny, all of whom had holiday homes there.

Guide books and other promotional litera-ture about the place emphasized the fact that it was popular with artists, who were given the credit for having discovered it. Alfred STEVENS recorded its social atmosphere in works such as his view of the promenade (*c.*1880; Private collection), and in 1865 WHISTLER painted a remarkable picture of COURBET (Isabella Stew-art Gardner Museum, Boston) standing on the sands there, a solitary figure on the edge of the sea. The place became a favourite haunt of BOUDIN, who wrote about its visitors, 'between ourselves, those bourgeois who promenade along the pier towards sunset, don't they have the right to be fixed on canvas, to be led towards the light?'; and he vindicated that right in innumerable works. It was at Trouville that MONET met DAUBIGNY, and during his several visits there he painted many aspects of its life. The most productive of these visits was in 1870, when he was accompanied by his wife and their three-year-old son Jean (e.g. *The Beach at Trouville*, National Gallery, London; *The Hôtel des Rochers Noirs*, Musée d'Orsay). *[33]*
□ D. Rouillard, *Le Site balnéaire* (1984); Herbert (1988)

Families on the beach at **Trouville**, *c.* 1890: Paris 'transplanted' to the Channel coast.

U

L'Union In August 1875 PISSARRO, with his passion for organization, conceived the idea, together with his friend Alfred Meyer, of founding a group called L'Union to succeed the SOCIÉTÉ ANONYME DES ARTISTES etc., which the Impressionists had formed as a 'joint stock company' in 1873, and which had been dissolved in the following year. Meyer became the secretary and was soon being accused of plotting against the original Impressionists – especially MONET. CÉZANNE refused to exhibit with the new group. The company, for that was the financial form it assumed, was incorporated on 18 August 1875, with Pissarro as one of the board of directors.

In 1877, to forestall the Impressionists' own exhibition, due to open in April, Meyer staged one by the members of the Union at the Grand Hôtel on the boulevard des Capucines, and on 24 February GUILLAUMIN wrote to DR GACHET, 'You know that the exhibition of the Union has opened at the Grand Hôtel. We were supposed to be in it, Pissarro, Cézanne and me, but at the last minute we resigned.' Cézanne had indeed written to Pissarro the previous summer expressing distrust of Meyer and adding, 'First, too many exhibitions one after another seem to me a bad thing, and second, people who think that they are going to see Impressionists see nothing but co-operatives.' The CRITICS in fact paid no attention to the Union and it faded into oblivion. *See also* LATOUCHE
□ P. Gachet, *Lettres impressionnistes au Dr Gachet et à Murer* (1957); Rewald (1973); Rewald (1985)

USA The first contact between the Impressionists and the United States was on the occasion of DEGAS' visit to New Orleans in 1872, amply documented in his correspondence, and finding its most impressive monument in *Cotton Office, New Orleans* (Musée Municipal, Pau). Close contacts with America grew up in Paris, due very largely to people such as Mary CASSATT of Pittsburgh, who arrived there in 1868, settling permanently in 1874, and the American painter Theodore ROBINSON, who was most active in promoting the works of the Impressionists both amongst American expatriates and in the USA itself.

The first Impressionist painting to be exhibited in America was MANET's *Execution of the Emperor Maximilian* (1868; Kunsthalle, Mannheim), which, for political reasons, Manet had not been allowed to show in Paris. This was brought to New York and Boston by Emilie AMBRE, a singer, and exhibited in the one city at the Clarendon Hotel on the corner of 8th Street and Broadway, in the other at the Studio Building Gallery. Despite the fact that the subject was of historical interest, and that the exhibition was advertised by a poster which proclaimed 'Come in! Come in and see the famous picture of the famous painter Ed Manet', there was little enthusiasm, even though the press was not overtly hostile.

In 1883, however, a so-called 'International Exhibition for Art and Industry' was held in the Mechanics' Building in Boston, which was declared a bonded warehouse, thus exempting exhibits from customs duty. A number of Impressionist paintings were exhibited: 2 by Manet, 3 by MONET, 6 by PISSARRO, 3 by RENOIR and 3 by SISLEY, as well as works by BOUDIN, COURBET and COROT. It is assumed that these were sent by DURAND-RUEL, though this is not certain. A drawing after Manet's *Dead Christ with Angels* (1864; Metropolitan Museum, New York) appeared as a frontispiece to the catalogue, and was the first work of the school to be reproduced in America. Also in 1883, an exhibition was arranged at the National Academy of Design, to help secure funds for the pedestal for the Statue of Liberty, largely under the direction of William Merrit Chase. Many Impressionist paintings were included, and Manet was given the position of honour. Then in 1885 the American Art Association approached Durand-Ruel, asking him to arrange an exhibition of the Impressionists in New York. This opened on 10 April 1886, and included 23 works by Degas, 17 by Manet, 48 by Monet, 42 by Pissarro, 38 by Renoir, 3 by SEURAT, 5 by Cassatt, 6 by CAILLEBOTTE and 15 by Sisley. Press reaction was varied, but much less hostile than it had been in Paris or London. About 20 per cent of the works exhibited were sold.

Some of the paintings in the exhibition were lent from American sources, and a considerable body of collectors had by now started to show interest in the work of the Impressionists. These included – in addition to the HAVEMEYERS – Albert Spencer, who sold his collection of older paintings in 1888 to concentrate on the Impres-

Manet's *Execution of the Emperor Maximilian* (1867), the first Impressionist painting to be exhibited in the **USA**, was brought from Paris by Emilie Ambre.

sionists; Desmond Fitzgerald (1846–1928), who wrote the introduction to an exhibition of works by Monet, Pissarro and Sisley held in New York in 1891, and was instrumental in arranging the loan exhibition of Monet held by the Copley Society of Boston in 1905; James S. Inglis, who headed the New York art dealers Cottier and Co. and was the owner of Manet's *Bullfight* (1867; Art Institute, Chicago) and *Dead Toreador* (1863; National Gallery, Washington); and William H. Fuller, who arranged a one-man exhibition for Monet – by far the most popular of the Impressionists in America – and sold many of his works directly to American collectors. Durand-Ruel, in collaboration with James F. Sutton of the American Art Association, held another exhibition in May 1887, but because of complications concerning customs duties, no pictures were sold. At the Columbian Exposition of 1893, the Impressio-

nists were not included in the official French section, but a privately arranged Loan Collection of Foreign Masters owned in the United States presented 18 pictures by Degas, Manet, Monet, Pissarro and Sisley. The exhibition had been largely arranged by Mrs Berthe Honoré Palmer, who had been an early collector of Impressionist paintings, most of which are now in the Art Institute of Chicago. By the 1890s Impressionism had become firmly established as an influence amongst painters and this led to a greater interest amongst collectors generally.

A good deal of their success was due to various publications, such as *Scribner's, Modern Art*, the *Art Amateur* and others, which gave the Impressionists a good deal of publicity, most of it objective, if not positively favourable. Personal contacts also played an important role. Cassatt was very active in promoting the works by her friends and colleagues amongst a circle

Chase, *A Friendly Call*, 1895. Chase encouraged the spread of Impressionism to the **USA**.

to give it a sense of colonialism in regard to Europe, and a lack of self-reliance epitomized by Charles Eliot Norton's remark to his class at Harvard, 'There are handsome landscapes in our country, but in America even the shadows are vulgar.' *See also* BARNES, JAMES *[222]*

☐ Venturi (1939); H. Huth, 'Impressionism comes to America', *Gazette des Beaux-Arts* (April 1946); *Americans in Brittany and Normandy, 1860–1910*, Phoenix Art Museum, AZ, exhibition catalogue (1978)

which included the Havemeyers, and it was largely due to SARGENT that a whole series, *La Creuse*, by Monet was sold in the United States. By the first decades of the 20th c., American collectors of the Impressionists such as the PHILLIPSes had become so numerous and so active as to require more extensive coverage than a work of this kind can hope to give.

The custom of American artists going to Paris to study had become established by the middle of the 19th c., and it was inevitable that the exciting new ideas of the Impressionists should have had an influence on some of them, especially as they were conscious of the close relationship between the Impressionists and American-born artists such as WHISTLER and Sargent. Two of the first important figures to show this influence, though in a diluted form, were W.M. Chase (1849–1916), and Theodore Robinson, who lived and worked for some time with Monet and was responsible indirectly for the whole host of American students who used to descend on GIVERNY in the 1890s, often to the discontent not only of Monet, but of the citizens of the place.

In 1895 a group of New York and Boston painters led by John W. Twatchman (1852–1902) formed a group under the name 'The Ten American Painters' and projected an image of themselves as the transatlantic guardians of the Impressionist tradition. On Twatchman's death Chase took over leadership of the group. In fact, however, the influence of Impressionism was very diluted. Subdued colours, mainly decorative in intention, an all-pervading luminosity rather than an intense study of light, and a tendency to use the dashing brushwork beloved by Sargent: these were the main characteristics of the 'Ten'. A side-effect of the Impressionist impact on American painting was

Technique
(See entry on p. 211)

The aspect of the Impressionists' work most often criticized by contemporary critics was their technique. Under the influence of Monet they adopted the style of the academic *ébauche*, employing free and unblended brushstrokes to create an illusion of spontaneity. The bold modelling of Manet, the feathery surfaces of Renoir and the flat, blocked brushwork of Cézanne stressed the potential of the painterly trace as a pictorial element in its own right. Equally unsettling for those attuned to the conventions of Salon art was the Impressionists' experimental use of composition. Inspired by photographic effects and the devices of Japanese art, they favoured unexpected, startling perspectives and apparently unposed, arbitrary views that were wholly alien to the logical ordering principles of the classical tradition. Through their technique they aimed to invent a new language by which to express what was strongly felt to be an entirely new era: the age of modernity.

See also COLOUR, JAPANESE ART, PEINTURE CLAIRE, PERSPECTIVE, PHOTOGRAPHY, PORTRAITURE

It was above all Manet who, through his radical transformation of traditional practices and the freedom of his brushwork, paved the way for the technical innovations of the Impressionists. This late still life of Pinks and Clematis in a Crystal Vase *(c. 1882) reveals him at the very height of his powers. He appears to have followed his usual practice of applying colour directly onto pale-primed canvas, adding the background at a later stage to sharpen the outlines of the central subject. The abrupt disjunctions in tone that often resulted from this technique are softened here by the subtle range of colours – blond, pastel shades of pink and grey are accented by the single clematis bloom – but the great delicacy of effect belies the virtuosity of Manet's technique. Each expressive brushstroke, applied with the spontaneity of a sketch, creates at once colour, form and texture, with a supreme economy and sureness of touch.*

Concerned by the lack of
structure apparent in the
Impressionists' technique,
Cézanne sought to recapture a
more classical sense of balance –
in his own words, 'to re-do
Poussin from nature'. In his
Still Life with Onions and
Bottle (1895–1900) he creates
a composition of great
permanence and solidity by
building up a complex web of
visual relationships. The broad,
bare wall provides a foil to the
closely packed forms and faceted
colour blocking of the
foreground, where a series of
rhythmic curves and tilting axes
are echoed in the scalloped
curves of the table, the bottle,
the glass, and the twisting
onion leaves. As part of the
continuing search for a means
of producing an accurate record
of reality, Cézanne aimed to
express the contradictions of
binocular vision, rather than
adhering to the convention of
single-point perspective. This
causes the forms in his paintings
to appear broken and unfinished
– as in the lip of the wine-glass
– or to shift disconcertingly in
their relationships. Thus, the
knife handle leads the eye into
the image, yet the viewer is
brought up against the rigid,
decorative flatness and secure
horizontality of the table. The
table-top tilts up towards the
picture plane, and the bottle,
plate and glass are not clearly
anchored to the table surface.
Cézanne thereby establishes a
powerful tension between the
apparent solidity of the three-
dimensional forms and the
emphatic flatness of the linear
design.

'I want a red to be sonorous, to sound like a bell': in his late works Renoir reduced his palette as far as possible in order to obtain greater control over his materials, and to exploit the richest possible effects from the simplest possible means. Gabrielle with Roses (1911) is constructed from a series of clear colour contrasts united by a pattern of equally weighted accents: the warm red of the roses, lips and table against the cooler tones of the flesh; the crisp white highlights of the blouse and cheeks against the pure black of the hair and eyes. The vigorous handling of the blouse and flowers contrasts with the fine web of separate, blended strokes, which introduce subtle variations of red and white, and animate the soft flesh – always a source of fascination for Renoir, who employed Gabrielle largely because 'her skin took the light well'.

It was Manet's technique as much as the subject-matter of Déjeuner sur l'herbe *that so outraged visitors to the* Salon des Refusés *in 1863. His use of frontal lighting, which eliminates shadows, allowed him to dispense with the painstaking academic procedure of building up a* series of half-tones from dark to light. His massing of light and dark areas, reminiscent of studio photography, and the freedom of his handling must have seemed crude by comparison with the subtle chiaroscuro and tightly worked surfaces of contemporary Salon paintings.

Degas' relationship with Impressionism, like that of Manet, is highly problematic. His traditional training had imbued him with an Ingresque sense of line and with an enduring faith in the value of preparatory studies: 'There is nothing less spontaneous than my art'. Unlike his fellow contributors to the Impressionist exhibitions, his paint was often thinly and smoothly applied , his forms were more clearly modelled, his contours more sharply defined, and his compositions more tightly structured; colour was by no means his main concern, and he continued to use earth colours and black. What does connect him with the avant-garde of the age is his love of contemporary subjects and his experimental, anti-academic approach to composition.

Cotton Office, New Orleans *(1873)* is both a modern genre scene and an informal group portrait of members of the American branch of the De Gas family. By presenting his 'sitters' in their familiar everyday surroundings, in their characteristic clothes and poses, Degas, like many of the Impressionists, sought to revitalize the stiff and rather staid conventions of Salon portraiture, conveying more fully the entire personality of the subject.

The influence of another Impressionist enthusiasm – photography – is also clearly reflected in the unfocused grouping of the figures and in the way the man on the right is cut through by the picture frame; it is as if a single, passing moment has been captured in a snap-shot. Yet the apparently arbitrary arrangement conceals a precisely constructed composition. The repeated verticals of the window frames and shelving balance the almost frieze-like disposition of heads across an above-centre horizontal. This rigid grid is then crossed by the powerful diagonal of the steeply rising floor, repeated in the cotton table, the arms of the foreground chair and the stretched-out legs of the man reading the newspaper. A secondary, opposing diagonal is set up by the tilted hat of the foreground figure and echoed in the man lounging against a wall on the left.

The complex geometrical framework, the linearity of the image, and the subdued, limited colour range mark the gulf between Degas and, say, Monet or Renoir; but like his fellow Impressionists Degas was seeking, in the manner best suited to his own taste and temperament, to provide a convincing response to Baudelaire's call for a 'painter of modern life'.

In Racehorses in Front of the Stands (c. 1869–72)
Degas shows Parisians taking the air at the newly
opened racecourse at Longchamp in the Bois de
Boulogne. The complex forms of the horse provided a
supreme challenge to Degas' skills of draughtsmanship,
and proved an enduring source of inspiration – from his
early studies of Uccello, Gozzoli and Géricault, to his
fascination with the photographic experiments of
Eadweard Muybridge, first published in 1878, and
his own sculptures of leaping horses.

Japanese art, with its emphasis on line and two-
dimensional design, particularly appealed to Degas'
artistic sensibilities, and – combined with the possible
influence of English sporting prints, which were popular
in France at the time – it seems to have set the stylistic
tone for this painting. The clearly outlined areas of
bright colour, unmodulated by light or atmosphere; the
decorative patterns of the horses' legs; the broadly
painted flatness of the ground and sky, contrasted with
the detailed depiction of the crowd; the cropping of the
slanting shadows and of the horse on the right: all these
are typical Japanese devices.

The power of the image lies in the visual tension
between this Japanese-inspired flatness of design and the
traditional Western perspective construction, which
simultaneously creates a convincing illusion of depth.
The sharply drawn diagonals seem to lead the eye to
some significant pictorial climax, but the bolting horse,
the distracted gazes of the jockeys and the random
directions of the horses provide centripetal forces which
counteract the implied focus of the image. This would
have been considered heresy by upholders of the
rational, classical approach to composition still
favoured in academic circles.

In many ways the thoroughbred racehorses of
Longchamp express Degas' attitude to his art:
concealing in their elegant motion the strain and effort
of months of training, they mirror the painter's reliance
on careful preparation and past experience as he clears
with apparent ease the series of pictorial hurdles he has
devised for himself.

References to Japanese art occur in many of Manet's paintings – in the background to his portrait of Zola, for example, and here, in the portrait of Nina de Callias, known as Woman with Fans (1873–74). It is not the actual style of Japanese art that is borrowed here, so much as the atmosphere of domestic intimacy found in many Japanese prints, and the use of Japonaiserie to evoke an aura of exoticism. The fans form a decorative and richly coloured backdrop to the figure, their varied axes balancing the tilt of the woman's head and echoing the sweeping curves of her dress and shawl. The feathers in her hair link her with the plumage of the crane in the wallpaper, implying a pun on the French word grue, which also means courtesan.

The portrait seems to invite direct comparison with Olympia (1863) – in the similarity of the pose, and in the placing of the dog at Callias' feet – but the similarities only serve to point up the change in Manet's technique. The painting reveals him at his most 'Impressionistic': the harsh frontal lighting and 'playing card' forms of the earlier work are softened by a golden light, accented by scattered splashes of pure red, white and turquoise. The lightening of Manet's palette and the increasing freedom of his brushwork clearly reveal the influence of Impressionism, but he nevertheless maintains his faith in expressive contour and makes striking use of intense black. The vibrant, broken brushmarks create an effect of lively movement around the steady gaze of the sitter, which directly engages the attention of the spectator. This was one of Manet's favourite devices, but here the gaze invites a sense of intimacy and sympathetic psychological penetration, rather than challenging, and so distancing the viewer, as in Déjeuner sur l'herbe (1863).

V

Valabrègue, Antonin (1845–1900) A boyhood friend of CÉZANNE in AIX-EN-PROVENCE, he moved to Paris in 1867 to become a writer, publishing some 13 years later a fairly successful book of poetry, *Petits Poèmes parisiens*. Much of his output was devoted to art criticism, though his most important work, a study of the Le Nain brothers, was not published until four years after his death. He was marginally involved in the politics of his native town, and on the downfall of NAPOLEON III was elected municipal councillor. A close friend of ZOLA, he maintained a regular correspondence with him and with Cézanne throughout his life. Cézanne painted two portraits of Valabrègue, one of which (1869) is in the J. Paul Getty Museum, Malibu; the other (1866) shows him in the open air with the zoologist and amateur painter Antoine Fortuné Marion. *See also* CRITICS

□ *Encyclopédie des Bouches-du-Rhône*, vol. xi *Les Biographies* (1913); Rewald (1984)

Valadon, Marie Clémentine (Suzanne) (1867–1938) A favourite model of RENOIR, DEGAS, PUVIS DE CHAVANNES and Toulouse-Lautrec, her most memorable appearance as a model is in Renoir's *Bathers* of 1887 in the Philadelphia Museum of Art. She commenced her career in a circus, but soon established herself as a personality in artistic circles. Toulouse-Lautrec brought her drawings to the attention of Degas, who encouraged her to continue her own artistic activity, and she was one of the few people with whom he kept in close contact during the latter years of his life. In 1908 she began painting landscapes and still lifes, in a style marked by brisk REALISM, strong contours and clear, vivid colouring. She was the mother of Maurice Utrillo. *See also* ILLUSTRATION

□ R. Rey, *Suzanne Valadon* (1922); M. Mermillon, *Suzanne Valadon 1867–1938* (1950); J. Warnod, *Suzanne Valadon* (1981)

Renoir, *The Bathers*, 1887: Suzanne **Valadon**, who is the figure on the left, was encouraged by Degas to pursue her own artistic career.

Suzanne **Valadon**, artist and model, from a photograph, *c.* 1890.

Valernes, Evariste de Bernardi de (1816–96) The impecunious son of a nobleman, Valernes had studied painting under DELACROIX, and his work first appeared in the SALON in 1857. He became friendly with DEGAS in 1855, and shared with him not only a genuine love of art, but an appreciation of things Italian. It was probably this aspect of Valernes to which Degas was referring in 1865 when he painted a portrait of them both against a window showing a view of Rome (Musée d'Orsay). Valernes was very conscious of the significance of Impressionism, and had been an enthusiastic reader of DUR-ANTY's *Nouvelle Peinture* when it appeared in 1876. He eventually retired to Carpentras in the south of France, and in 1890 Degas wrote him a moving letter in which he said, 'You have always been the same person, nothing in you has changed, my old friend. There has always survived in you that delightful spirit of Romanticism, which clothes and colours art'; he went on 'I would like to ask your forgiveness that I was *harsh* to you, or seemed to be so

during our long friendship. I was mainly being hard with myself. . . . I was harsh against the world because brutality became an attitude which can only be explained by my state of mind and bad temper. I felt so badly equipped, so unprepared, so weak.' *See also* ITALY

□ *De Valernes et Degas*, Musée de Carpentras, exhibition catalogue (1963); E. Lipton, 'Deciphering a friendship; Edgar Degas and Evariste de Valernes', *Arts Magazine* (June 1981); T. Reff, 'Degas and Valernes in 1872', *Arts Magazine* (Sept. 1981)

Venturi, Lionello (1885–1961) Son of the well-known art historian Adolfo, he became in 1915 Professor of Art History at the University of Turin, but resigned his chair in 1931, having refused to take an oath of loyalty to the Fascist state. He went to Paris, where he made his great contribution to the history of Impressionism, the two-volume *Archives de l'impressionnisme* (Paris and New York, 1939), based on the archives of the firm of DURAND-RUEL. The work contains a wealth of relevant material, including a history of the firm by Venturi, as well as reminiscences by Durand-Ruel himself, information about collectors and exhibitions, extracts from contemporary criticism of a serious nature, and details of sales and PRICES. There is also a large collection of letters to Durand-Ruel from the Impressionists: 213 from RENOIR, 411 from MONET, 86 from PISSARRO, 16 from SISLEY, 31 from CASSATT, and 27 from DEGAS. The majority of them tend to be tedious demands for money and other trivia, which, though they throw light on the day-to-day concerns of the writers, contribute little to a general understanding of their aesthetic preoccupations.

On the outbreak of the war, Venturi went to the USA, where he held posts at various universities. In 1945 he returned to ITALY and held a professorship at Rome University until his death.

□ Venturi (1939); L. Venturi, *Histoire de la critique d'art*, with biographical note (1969)

Vétheuil A village on a loop of the Seine between MÉDAN and GIVERNY, where MONET rented a house in 1878 and where he lived until 1883. For the most part it was a difficult time for him. He was in bad financial straits – he had to borrow money from DR GACHET to pay the removal men who were waiting outside his door. His wife was ill – she died in 1879 – but he

Monet, *Vétheuil*, 1880: Monet lived for several years in the village of **Vétheuil** on the Seine between Médan and Giverny.

and the children were looked after by Madame HOSCHEDÉ. He found the neighbourhood a source of inspiration, epitomized by two paintings he did from the riverbank there, one in winter (1878; Albright Knox Art Gallery, Buffalo) and one in summer (1880; Metropolitan Museum, New York).
□ J. House, *Monet, Nature into Art* (1986); Herbert (1988)

La Vie moderne A periodical dealing with art, literature and social life, founded in the spring of 1879 by the publisher Georges CHARPENTIER on the prompting of his wife Marguerite, who was encouraged in this direction by her favourite protégé, RENOIR. Although the magazine played some part in promoting the reputation of the Impressionists, its major significance lay in the art gallery opened in its offices on the boulevard des Italiens, which set out as its aim 'to transfer the artist's studio to the boulevard'. EDMOND RENOIR was in charge of the gallery, and the first exhibition, devoted to DE NITTIS, was highly successful, with some 2000 visitors a day. This was followed by an exhibition of pastels by Renoir, the catalogue for which had an introduction by his brother. Subsequent exhibitions were devoted to MANET, MONET (not

The house where Monet lived at **Vétheuil**.

one of his pictures was sold, though Mme Charpentier acquired one at a reduced price), SISLEY and Odilon Redon. The gallery made a great impression on the young SEURAT. *See also* CRITICS
□ M. Robida, *Le Salon Charpentier* (1958); Rewald (1985)

Vignon, Victor (1851–1917) Although he exhibited – sometimes as many as 15 or 20 paintings – at the IMPRESSIONIST EXHIBITIONS of 1880, 1881 and 1886, Vignon was regarded by most of his fellow Impressionists as a boring artist, who kept reverting to his early dependence on COROT. A landscape of his in the Ny Carlsberg Glyptotek in Copenhagen does not, however, bear this out entirely; dated 1883, it reveals considerable vigour and freshness. He was a friend of PISSARRO and was generally accepted as belonging to his 'faction' rather than to that of DEGAS.

□ E. Bénézit, *Dictionnaire des peintres, sculpteurs, dessinateurs et graveurs* (1966)

Ville d'Avray A village near Saint-Cloud where COROT spent much of his time. MONET also lived there in the late 1860s, and it provided the background for his *Women in the Garden* (1866; Musée d'Orsay), which was bought by BAZILLE after being rejected by the SALON of 1867. COURBET, who worked in the nearby forest, was a frequent visitor, and RENOIR stayed there in the summer of 1868 with Lise TRÉHOT. *See also* PLEIN-AIRISME [52]

Les Vingt *see* BELGIUM

Vollard, Ambroise (1868–1939) One of the great art dealers of the golden age of French painting, he was born in the Ile de la Réunion, the son of a notary, and read law at the University of Montpellier, preparing his thesis in Paris. A gregarious and sociable character, he started his career in the art world by buying prints from the quayside stalls by the Seine and, seduced by the idea of being an art dealer, became an apprentice at the gallery of the Union Artistique.

He opened his first gallery in the rue Laffitte, with an exhibition of sketches by MANET. In the following year he moved to more extensive premises, and started to interest himself in CÉZANNE, whose work had been introduced to him by Maurice Denis. This was at a time when Cézanne was the only Impressionist who had not really attracted the attention of the dealers, and Vollard's first exhibition of his works in 1895 turned out a marked success, establishing him as the leading dealer in the avant-garde; he also exhibited PISSARRO, RENOIR, DEGAS and Rodin. He then went on progressively to keep abreast of what was happening in French art, exhibiting works by painters such as Bonnard

and Vuillard, as well as by VAN GOGH, Picasso and Matisse. Although his fame rests largely on his promotion of the styles that followed Impressionism, his activities generally raised the prestige of that movement, and continued to increase the value of its works. *See also* THÉO VAN GOGH, ILLUSTRATION, SPAIN [208]

□ A. Vollard, *Recollections of a Picture Dealer* (1936), *En écoutant Cézanne, Degas et Renoir* (1938)

Wagram, Louis-Marie Philippe Alexandre Berthier, Prince de (1883–1917) An omnivorous collector of Impressionist paintings, described by Proust in *Du Côté des Guermantes* as 'a young prince who liked impressionist paintings and motoring'. Between 1905 and 1908 he bought several hundred paintings on the advice of Adrien Hébrard, a bronze-caster who worked for Rodin and Degas, and who acted as an intermediary with dealers. Wagram's collection, which included 50 works by RENOIR, 11 by DEGAS, 12 by MANET, 40 by MONET, 47 by VAN GOGH and 28 by CÉZANNE, was too large to be hung either in his house in the avenue des Champs-Elysées or his apartment on the quai d'Orsay, and much of it was left in store. After his death several of his paintings were bought by Alfred BARNES. *See also* PATRONS AND COLLECTORS

□ M.G. de la Coste-Messelière, 'Un jeune prince amateur de l'impressionnisme', *L'Oeil* (Nov. 1969); *Renoir*, Hayward Gallery, London, exhibition catalogue (1985)

Walewski, Comte Alexandre (1810–61) The natural son of Napoleon by his Polish mistress, he became for a while Minister of State with responsibility for the arts under NAPOLEON III, and it was to him that a petition about the nature of the SALON was presented by MANET and Gustave Doré in 1863.

□ Comte Fleury and L. Sonolet, *La Société du Second Empire*, 4 vols. (1928); A. de Monzie and L. Febvre, *Encyclopédie française* (1937)

Wedmore, Sir Frederick (1844–1921) A writer, perhaps over-influenced in his style by the purple prose of Pater, Wedmore was for 30 years the art critic of the *Evening Standard* and contributor to a large number of both English and French periodicals. In January 1883 he contributed a mainly favourable article about the Impressionists to the *Fortnightly Review*, the first piece of any substance in English to be devoted to the movement. It is marred, however, by the fact that he confused MANET with MONET. *See also* CRITICS, ENGLAND

□ Cooper (1954); Flint (1984)

Whistler, James Abbott McNeill (1834–1903) The American-born painter, who was one of the most publicized and colourful figures in the English art world of the 19th c., hovered on the brink of Impressionism for a considerable period in the early 1860s, and was on close personal terms with MANET, DEGAS, MONET, and the CRITICS and writers associated with them.

Discharged from the West Point Military Academy for 'deficiency in chemistry', he became for a while a cartographer in the US Navy Department, where he acquired those skills in etching that he was later to put to such admirable use. In 1855 he left America and went to study art in Paris at the studio of GLEYRE, acquiring at the same time an admiration for Velazquez and other Spanish painters, which was to remain one of the dominant influences in his work, and to bring him very close to Manet. One of his early friends was FANTIN-LATOUR, and one of his early heroes was COURBET, to whose brand of REALISM he was for some time attached. He was one of the first to acquire a passion for JAPANESE art, which provided a consistent element in his painting and occasional decorative excursions.

In 1863 he exhibited at the SALON DES REFUSÉS his *White Girl* (1862; National Gallery of Art, Washington), which had been rejected at the Royal Academy the previous year, and for which HOUSSAYE made an offer that Whistler did not consider adequate. There are signs of the painting's influence on Manet's portrait of Berthe MORISOT (1870; Rhode Island School of Design), and Whistler's influence is also to be seen in some of RENOIR's views of Venice (e.g. *View of St Mark's*, 1881; Sterling and Francine Clark Art Institute, Williamstown). He did not meet Monet until 1885, but their friendship became so close that Monet travelled to visit him in London two years later. Even before this there are signs of the influence of Whistler's *Nocturnes* on some of Monet's works.

Whistler, *The White Girl*, or *Symphony in White*, 1862, exhibited at the Salon des Refusés.

DEGAS had been copying works by Whistler (as well as by Meissonier and Menzel) as early as 1854, and was always to be influenced by his etchings, whilst works such as his *Seascape* (Musée d'Orsay) of 1869, though a pastel, show clear signs of Whistler's compositional techniques; in 1872 he confessed to his friend Paul Poujad, 'in the beginning Whistler, Fantin and I were all following the same path'. There were indeed obvious affinities between Degas and Whistler; both were dandies, both possessed a caustic wit. Whistler, however, was contaminated by an exuberant egomania, which led to such crises as the lawsuit with Ruskin, the controversy with Sir William Eden, and other

Bastien-Lepage's portrait (now lost) of the critic Albert **Wolff**, c. 1880.

imbroglios that obscured rather than enhanced his remarkable gifts. By the 1880s he had moved to a kind of Symbolism, identified in ENGLAND with the Aesthetic movement, and which he defended with wit and eloquence in *The Gentle Art of Making Enemies* (1890). *See also* JAPANESE ART, USA *[23, 78]*
□ J. and E. Pennell, *The Life of James McNeill Whistler* (1908), *The Whistler Journal* (1921); D. Sutton, *Nocturne; the art of James McNeill Whistler* (1963); S. Weintraub, *Whistler; a biography* (1974)

Zandomeneghi, *Place d'Auvers*, 1880: the Italian artist exhibited frequently with the Impressionists.

Wolff, Albert (1835–91) Of German origin, he was a writer and journalist who became the secretary of Alexandre Dumas *père*. A prolific writer of plays, novels and essays, he became art critic of *Figaro* and in this capacity a venomous opponent of Impressionism, especially of MANET, whom he reviled even in his obituary of the artist. Georges RIVIÈRE once said, 'When I see Albert Wolff I can forgive him the harsh words he has written about my friends. Nature has treated him far worse.' *See also* CRITICS, PORTRAITURE
□ A. Wolff, *Mémoires du boulevard* (1866); Hamilton (1954)

Z

Zandomeneghi, Federico (1841–1917) A painter who came from a family of sculptors, he was involved in his early life with the struggle for Italian independence, and became associated with the Macchiaioli group in Florence (*see* ITALY). In 1874 he came to PARIS, where he met RENOIR, PISSARRO and DEGAS, the last-named exerting a great influence on his style, reflected in works such as *Sleeping Girl* (1878; Galleria d'Arte Moderna, Florence). Thanks to the help of Degas, he participated in the IMPRESSIONIST EXHIBITIONS of 1879, 1880, 1881 and 1886, and DURAND-RUEL took him up and promoted his works. His pastels were highly praised. *See also* CAFÉS, PASTELS
□ M. Cinotti, *Zandomeneghi* (1960); N. Broude, *The Macchiaioli* (1987)

Zola, Emile (1840–1902) Born in PARIS, but brought up in AIX-EN-PROVENCE, where his father was building an aqueduct, he went to school with CÉZANNE, who was for long to remain one of his closest friends. Returning to Paris in his twenties, he became a clerk in the publishing house of Hachette and then, after unsuccessfully attempting to become a play-wright, turned his attention to fiction and journalism, becoming in 1866 the literary editor of the radical daily *L'Evénement*.

His early novels show the extent to which he adhered to the 'Naturalist' school of Flaubert,

A keen photographer, **Zola** took this picture of himself holding a box camera, *c.* 1889.

A contemporary poster advertising the serial publication of **Zola**'s *Germinal*.

DAUDET, Turgenev and the GONCOURTS. It was not, however, until after the fall of the Empire that he began the great cycle of novels on which his fame is largely based: the *Rougon-Macquart* series, which in some 20 books set out to give a complete picture of virtually every section of French society in the latter half of the 19th c. His reputation was further enhanced in 1897–98 when he became embroiled in the Dreyfus affair, was sentenced to a year's imprisonment for insulting the army – a fate he escaped by taking refuge in England for a short time – and, virtually single-handed, succeeded in obtaining the Captain's eventual vindication as a result of one of the most famous polemics of all time, the pamphlet *J'accuse*.

A man of enormous mental energy and unflagging application, Zola was tireless in his criticism of the establishment, and assiduous in his opposition to injustice. It was these concerns that were partly responsible for his impassioned defence of the Impressionists. He had become friendly with the group thanks to his contacts with Cézanne, and to the fact that he was a frequent visitor to the CAFÉ GUERBOIS and similar haunts. He came to see them as 'fighters', and for long the vocabulary of his

criticism was tinctured with metaphors chosen from the battlefield rather than the art gallery. Published for the most part in the columns of *L'Evénement*, a selection of his art reviews appeared in book form in 1880, under the significant title of *Mes Haines* (My Hates).

He also saw the Impressionists as exemplars of the new spirit of REALISM in the arts, which he and his colleagues were expressing in literature. Devoid, on the whole, of any marked visual sensibility, he interpreted this 'realism' as the actual essence of the movement, whereas to the painters themselves it was peripheral, their major innovation being a new way of seeing things. When it came to describing or evaluating individual paintings, his vocabulary became imprecise and laudatory in the most generalized way. Essentially a literary man, he tended on the whole to see painters as doing what writers did, but in a less satisfactory way. On the other hand, he was a superb publicist and an eminently readable writer, and it is almost impossible to overestimate the value of his support for the Impressionists up to 1868, when he was relieved of his post on *L'Evénement*.

From then until 1880, when he reviewed the SALON of that year, his writings on art were

confined to a Russian journal in St Petersburg, but it was obvious that he was becoming less enthusiastic about the Impressionists, as, indeed, they were about him. DEGAS had always found his novels vulgar, too packed with meaningless statistics, and infinitely preferred the writings of the Goncourts; PISSARRO found his work too 'photographic', and accused him of running with the hare and hunting with the hounds. Then in 1886 there appeared L'Oeuvre, which is basically a portrait of a painter – identified by most contemporaries as Cézanne – who kills himself because of his inability to realize his artistic ideals. Quite apart from the fact that it ruined Zola's life-long friendship with Cézanne, it did little to improve his standing with the group as a whole, especially as it encapsulated a judgment he had expressed in his review of the 1880 Salon: 'The tragedy is that there is not one artist of the group who has forcibly and definitively expressed the formula which all of them share, and which is scattered throughout their individual works.' Ironically, whereas Zola upbraided the Impressionists for not being consistently naturalist, the greatness of his own work lies in the fact that it transcends naturalism. *See also* CRITICS, DURANTY, LITERATURE, MÉDAN, MONTMARTRE, PHOTOGRAPHY, PRINTS, RAILWAYS *[15, 28, 65, 86, 182]*
□ J. Rewald, *Cézanne, sa vie, son oeuvre, son amitié pour Zola* (1939); Hamilton (1954); L.R. Furst, 'Zola's art criticism', in U. Finke (ed.) *French Nineteenth-Century Painting and Literature* (1972)

General bibliography

The following works will provide the reader with relevant background information. For titles covering more specialized aspects of the movement, consult the bibliographies which follow individual entries. Bibliographical references given in abbreviated form after the entries are indicated by a ★.

Adams, S. (1989): *The World of the Impressionists*, London and New York.
★Adriani, G. (1985): *Degas; Pastels, Oil Sketches, Drawings*, London and New York.
Blanche, J.-E. (1937): *Portraits of a Lifetime*, London.
Blunden, M. and G. (1981): *Impressionists and Impressionism*, Geneva and London.
★Boime, A. (1971): *The Academy and French Painting in the Nineteenth Century*, New Haven and London.
Braudel, F., and E. La Brousse (1977–82): *Histoire économique et sociale de la France. L' Avènement de l'ère industrielle 1789–1880*, 2 vols., Paris.
Callen, A. (1982): *Techniques of the Impressionists*, London.
Catalogue sommaire illustré des peintures du Musée du Louvre et du Musée d'Orsay, Réunion des Musées Nationaux, vols. 3–5 (1979–86).
Centenaire de l'impressionnisme, R. Huyghe et al., Grand Palais, Paris (1974).
★Champa, K.S. (1973): *Studies in Early Impressionism*, New Haven and London.
★Clark, T.J. (1973a): *The Absolute Bourgeois*, London and Princeton, New Jersey.
★Clark, T.J. (1973b): *Image of the People*, London and Princeton, New Jersey.
★Clark, T.J. (1985): *The Painting of Modern Life; Paris in the Art of Manet and his Followers*, London and New York.
★Cooper, D. (1954): *The Courtauld Collection*, London.
Crespelle, J.-P. (1981): *La Vie quotidienne des impressionnistes*, Paris.
The Crisis of Impressionism, 1878–82, J. Isaacson et al., University of Michigan, Ann Arbor (1980).
Dauberville, J. (1967): *La Bataille de l'impressionnisme*, Paris.
A Day in the Country; Impressionism and the French Landscape, R. Brettell et al., Los Angeles County Museum of Art (1984).
Degas, J. Sutherland Boggs et al., Grand Palais, Paris (1988).
★Denvir, B. (1987): *The Impressionists at First Hand*, London and New York.
Dufwa, J. (1981): *Winds from the East: A Study in the Art of Manet, Degas, Monet and Whistler, 1856–86*, Stockholm.
Dunlop, I. (1972): *The Shock of the New*, London.
Finke, U. (ed.) (1972): *French Nineteenth-Century Painting and Literature*, Manchester.
★Flint, K. (1984): *Impressionists in England; The Critical Reception*, London.
French Paintings II and III, C. Sterling and M. Salinger, Metropolitan Museum of Art, New York (1966, 1967).
French Prints in the Era of Impressionism and Symbolism, C. Ives, Metropolitan Museum of Art, New York (1988).
From Manet to Toulouse-Lautrec; French Lithographs 1860–1900, F. Carey and A. Griffiths, British Museum, London (1978).
Garb, T. (1986): *Women Impressionists*, Oxford.
Gaunt, W. (1970): *The Impressionists*, London.
Gerdts, W.H. (1980): *American Impressionism*, University of Washington, Seattle.
Gimpel, R. (1963): *Journal d'un collectionneur, marchand des tableaux*, Paris.

*Hamilton, G.H. (1954): *Manet and his Critics*, New Haven and London.

Hamilton, G.H. (1967): *Painting and Sculpture in Europe, 1880–1940*, London.

*Harrison, C.A, and H.C. White (1965): *Canvas and Careers; Institutional Change in the French Painting World*, New York.

*Herbert, R.L. (1988): *Impressionism; Art, Leisure, and Parisian Society*, New Haven and London.

Hillairet, J. (1964): *Dictionnaire historique des rues de Paris*, 2 vols., Paris, 2nd edn.

Impressionism, J. House, Royal Academy of Arts, London (1974).

Impressionism in 1877, Dixon Gallery, Memphis (1977).

*Lethève, J. (1972): *Daily Life of French Artists in the Nineteenth Century*, London.

Levine, S.Z. (1976): *Monet and his Critics*, New York and London.

*Lloyd, C., and R. Thomson (1986): *Impressionist Drawings*, Oxford.

McQuillan, M. (1986): *Impressionist Portraits*, London and Boston.

Manet, 1832–83, F. Cachin et al., Metropolitan Museum, New York and Paris (1983), and London (1984).

*Milner, J. (1988): *The Studios of Paris; the Capital of Art in the Late Nineteenth Century*, New Haven and London.

Monneret, S. (1978–81): *L' Impressionnisme et son époque*, 4 vols., Paris.

The New Painting; Impressionism 1874–86, C.S Moffett et al., The Fine Arts Museums, San Francisco (1986).

Nochlin, L. (ed.) (1966): *Impressionism and Post-Impressionism, 1874–1904; Sources and Documents*, Englewood Cliffs, New Jersey.

Nochlin, L. (1971): *Realism*, London.

Pool, P. (1967): *Impressionism*, London and New York.

Reff, T. (ed.) (1981): *Modern Art in Paris 1855–1900*, New York and London.

Renoir, J. House, Arts Council of Great Britain, London (1974).

*Rewald, J. (1942): *Pissarro's Letters to his Son Lucien*, London; revised edn, New York (1972).

*Rewald, J. (1973): *The History of Impressionism*, 4th revised edn, London and New York.

*Rewald, J. (1984): *The Letters of Cézanne*, revised edn, New York, first pub. Paris, 1937; Engl. trans. London, 1941.

*Rewald, J. (1985): *Studies in Impressionism*, London and New York.

*Rewald, J. (1986): *Cézanne; a biography*, London and New York.

Rewald, J. (1986): *Studies in Post-Impressionism*, London and New York.

*Roberts, R. de B., and J. Roberts (1987): *Growing up with the Impressionists*, London.

Roskill, M. (1970): *Van Gogh, Gauguin and the Impressionist Circle*, London.

Rothenstein, W. (1932): *Men and Memories*, London.

The Second Empire; Art in France under Napoleon III, J. Rishel, Philadelphia Museum of Art (1983).

Seigel, J. (1986): *Bohemian Paris; Culture, Politics and the Boundaries of Bourgeois Life, 1830–1930*, New York.

Shiff, R. (1984): *Cézanne and the End of Impressionism*, Chicago and London.

*Sloane, J.C. (1951): *French Painting between the Past and the Present*, Princeton.

*Venturi, L. (1939): *Les Archives de l'impressionnisme*, 2 vols., Paris.

Vollard, A. (1936): *Recollections of a Picture Dealer*, London and Boston; Paris (1937).

White, B.E. (ed.) (1978): *Impressionism in Perspective*, Englewood Cliffs, New Jersey

*Zeldin, T. (1973 and 1977): *France, 1845–1945*, 2 vols., Oxford.

Comparative chronology

THE IMPRESSIONISTS

1855 Degas enters the Ecole des Beaux-Arts. Whistler arrives in Paris, as does Pissarro. Courbet finishes *The Artist's Studio*.

1856 Degas leaves for Italy and stays there for the best part of three years, making extensive trips to Rome, Florence and Naples, with occasional visits to Paris.

1857 Manet travels to Germany, Holland and Italy. Renoir starts attending evening classes in drawing. Sisley is in England to learn the language and prepare for a commercial career. Monet, in Le Havre, begins to attract attention with his caricatures.

OTHER EVENTS

1855 Paris World's Fair. Fall of Sebastopol. Baudelaire, reviewing the Exposition Universelle, lauds the work of Delacroix. Death of Kierkegaard.

1856 Duranty founds the magazine *Réalisme*. End of the Crimean War. Liszt publishes his *Préludes*, Victor Hugo *Les Contemplations*. Peace congress in Paris. Death of Schumann.

1857 Millet exhibits *The Gleaners*. Baudelaire publishes *Les Fleurs du mal*, and Flaubert *Madame Bovary*; both are prosecuted for offending public morality. Alfred de Musset and Glinka die. Bunsen and Kirchhoff make the first spectral analysis of light.

Comparative chronology

1858 Pissarro attends the Académie Suisse and meets Monet; Monet meets Boudin, who encourages him in his painting. Renoir gives up painting on porcelain. Morisot copies old masters at the Louvre, where Manet is also working.

1859 Manet rejected at the Salon. Degas returns from Italy. Monet goes to Paris and meets Pissarro at the Académie Suisse. Renoir starts working as an artist. Morisot becomes a disciple of Corot.

1860 Degas paints *Young Spartans Exercising*. Manet establishes himself in the Batignolles area. Pissarro is working in the countryside around Paris. Morisot begins out-door painting.

1861 Manet successful at the Salon; he meets Baudelaire and Duranty. Degas continues painting historical subjects. Pissarro meets Cézanne and Guillaumin at the Académie Suisse. Monet does his military service in Algeria.

1862 Manet comes into his inheritance; he paints *La Musique aux Tuileries* and meets Degas, who is beginning to paint race scenes at Longchamp. Cézanne in Paris fails the Ecole des Beaux-Arts entrance exam. Monet is working in Le Havre. Renoir enters Gleyre's studio, as do Sisley and Bazille.

1863 Manet marries and has an exhibition at Martinet's gallery. Degas is in Italy. Pissarro has a son. Cézanne studies at the Académie Suisse; Monet works in forest of Fontainebleau, and Morisot at Pontoise. The Salon des Refusés contains works by Manet, Cézanne, Pissarro, Guillaumin and Whistler.

1864 Manet is rejected at Salon; his portrait is painted by Degas. Pissarro exhibits at the Salon. Monet meets Courbet, works in Honfleur with Bazille, Boudin and Jongkind; Renoir meets Diaz when painting in the forest of Fontainebleau. Bazille decides to take up painting full-time. Morisot has two works accepted at the Salon.

1865 Manet's second exhibition at Martinet's is well-received, but *Olympia* at the Salon arouses a storm; he spends ten days in Spain. Pissarro is again successful at the Salon. Cézanne returns to Aix. Monet paints *Déjeuner sur l'herbe*. Renoir works in Fontainebleau and exhibits at the Salon. Bazille shares his studio with Monet. Morisot paints in Normandy and exhibits at the Salon.

1866 Manet meets Zola and Cézanne. Pissarro is praised by Zola, but breaks with Corot. Cézanne protests about his rejection by the Salon. Monet meets Manet and has success at the Salon; he works at Sainte-Adresse. Renoir shares Bazille's studio and paints views of Paris; Sisley spends some time with Renoir at the home of the Le Coeur family at Berck. Morisot is again successful at the Salon; she works in Brittany.

1867 Courbet and Manet arrange special exhibitions at the Paris World's Fair; Zola publishes articles about the latter. Degas has two portraits in the Salon. Pissarro signs a petition for another Salon des Refusés. Monet exhibits views of Paris; he also works on the Channel coast at Honfleur. Renoir, rejected at Salon, paints in the open air at Fontainebleau.

1858 Slavery is abolished in Russia. Plücker discovers cathode rays. The Virgin appears at Lourdes, Hiroshige dies. Puccini and Leoncavallo are born.

1859 The French acquire Indo-China. Darwin publishes his *Origin of Species*. The Suez Canal is started. First oil well drilled in the USA. Tennyson publishes *Idylls of the King*. Battles of Magenta and Solferino. Wagner starts to compose *Tristan und Isolde*.

1860 The rotary press is invented in England. The kingdom of Italy is formed; France acquires Nice and Savoy. Lister introduces modern antiseptic treatment. Free trade treaty between France and Britain. Lincoln becomes President of the USA. Death of Schopenhauer.

1861 Civil war in the USA. Siemens invents the electric furnace. Dostoevsky publishes *House of the Dead*. Prince Albert dies. French expedition to Mexico.

1862 Victor Hugo's *Les Misérables* and Turgenev's *Fathers and Sons* are published. Bismarck becomes prime minister of Prussia. Foundation stone of the new Paris Opéra by Garnier laid; Debussy born. The French annexe Cochin-China. Slavery abolished in Russia.

1863 Delacroix dies. Tellier invents refrigerators, Beau de Rochas the internal combustion engine. Nadar starts making balloon ascents. The Ecole des Beaux-Arts is reorganized. Haussmann commences his rebuilding of Paris. Jules Verne publishes *Five Weeks in a Balloon*. Poland revolts against Russia.

1864 The Goncourts publish their realist novel *Germinie Lacerteux*, Chevreul his *Notes sur les couleurs*. Socialist congress in London. The first petrol-driven car appears in France. The Geneva Convention lays down rules for war and the Red Cross is born. The right to strike becomes legalized in France. Maximilian is proclaimed emperor in Mexico.

1865 Wagner finishes *Tristan und Isolde*. Lewis Caroll publishes *Alice in Wonderland*, and Mendel his researches on heredity. Abraham Lincoln is assassinated and Palmerston dies. Rockefeller opens his first petrol refinery in Ohio. Educational reforms in France.

1866 Zola publishes his book of Salon reviews, Daudet his *Lettres de mon moulin*, Verlaine his first book of poems, and Swinburne his *Poems and Ballads*. Strauss publishes his Blue Danube waltz; Offenbach's *La Vie parisienne* receives its first performance. The Prussians defeat the Austrians at Sadowa. The Swede Alfred Nobel invents dynamite, and the Americans Sholes and Schoule, the typewriter. The French abandon Mexico.

1867 Karl Marx publishes *Das Kapital*, and Ibsen's *Peer Gynt* has its first performance. Baudelaire dies, as do Ingres and Théodore Rousseau. Bonnard, Galsworthy, Pirandello, Toscanini and Nolde are born. There are constitutional reforms in Hungary, Austria and Germany, and there is trouble in Ireland. Monier invents reinforced concrete. Gounod's *Romeo and Juliet* has its first performance at the Paris Opéra. Execution of the Emperor Maximilian in Mexico. Financial crisis in France.

1868 Manet paints his portrait of Zola; he takes a trip to England where he meets Morisot. Daubigny helps Pissarro get two works accepted at the Salon. Monet also accepted at the Salon thanks to Daubigny, yet apparently attempts suicide. Renoir is accepted at the Salon and praised by the critics. Morisot becomes friendly with Degas and Puvis de Chavannes.

1869 Café Guerbois becomes the favourite centre of the Impressionists. Eva Gonzalès becomes a pupil and model of Manet. Pissarro settles in Louveciennes, and Cézanne falls in love with Hortense Fiquet. Monet has his paintings in Le Havre seized by his creditors, and becomes an habitué of the Café Guerbois; he works at Bougival with Renoir, who has one work accepted by the Salon.

1870 Manet is turned down as a Salon juror, and figures in Fantin-Latour's *Studio in the Batignolles Quarter*; he joins the National Guard when war breaks out and serves under Meissonier. Degas, on the other hand, joins the infantry, and Cézanne dodges conscription. Monet and Pissarro solve the problem by leaving for England; Renoir becomes a cuirassier and is posted first to Bordeaux and then to Tarbes. Bazille is not so lucky and is killed on active service on 28 August.

1871 Courbet is involved in destruction of the Napoleonic column in the Place Vendôme. Manet moves to Bordeaux; Degas travels to Normandy and, briefly, London, where Pissarro and Monet have works rejected by the Royal Academy, but are taken up by Durand-Ruel. At the end of the year Monet goes to Holland; Pissarro returns to Paris. Renoir is in Paris for most of the time, but works at Bougival with Sisley. Morisot moves to Saint-Germain during the troubles.

1872 Manet sells 29 paintings to Durand-Ruel for 51,000 francs; he travels in Holland and exhibits at the Salon. Degas is introduced to Durand-Ruel and leaves France with his brother for the USA. Pissarro settles in Pontoise and is intermittently joined by Cézanne, who has just had a son. Monet, living at Argenteuil where he settled after a visit to Holland, is joined by Renoir. Morisot visits Spain.

1873 Manet's *Bon Bock* is well received at the Salon, and he meets Mallarmé for the first time. Degas, after a visit to New Orleans, returns to France and has one of his pastels bought by the American Mrs Havemeyer. Pissarro has a good year, his pictures fetching fairly high prices at auction. Monet, now working in Argenteuil, takes up the plan first suggested in 1867 for a group exhibition. Renoir enters the Durand-Ruel stable, meets Guillaumin, and has a considerable success at the Exposition des Refusés.

1874 First Impressionist exhibition held at 35 boulevard des Capucines. Durand-Ruel stages an Impressionist exhibition in his London gallery. Manet starts to reap the benefits of his friendship with Mallarmé, who protests about the rejection of his paintings by the Salon. Refusing to participate in the Impressionist exhibition, Manet works at Argenteuil with Monet. Pissarro insists on Cézanne being allowed to participate and, though he sells one of the works he shows, he arouses derision with his *Modern Olympia*. Renoir joins the others at Argenteuil, and Sisley visits England. Morisot, who exhibits nine works, spends part of the year with the Manet family at Fécamp and marries Eugène, Edouard Manet's brother.

1868 Wagner's *Meistersinger*; death of Rossini. Dynamo and synthetic perfumes invented. Gladstone becomes Prime Minister. Dostoevsky publishes *The Idiot*, and Maxim Gorki is born. Japan opened to the rest of the world. First cycling race at Saint-Cloud. Charles Cros invents colour photography. Grieg composes his piano concerto.

1869 Berlioz, Lamartine, Saint-Beuve and Overbeck die. Flaubert publishes *L'Education sentimentale*. An international art exhibition is held in Munich. The Vatican Council, which declares the infallibility of the pope, opens in Rome, and hydroelectric power is used for the first time. Matisse and Frank Lloyd Wright are born. Suez Canal opened.

1870 Outbreak of the Franco-Prussian War. French defeated at Sedan; Third Republic proclaimed in Paris. Dickens, Dumas and Jules de Goncourt die. Millais' *Boyhood of Sir Walter Raleigh* and Frith's *The First Cigarette* are the most popular exhibits at the Royal Academy Summer Show in London. The first synthetic material is manufactured in the USA, where the first turbine motor also makes its appearance. Rome becomes the official capital of Italy. Paris besieged.

1871 France surrenders to the Prussians. The Commune in Paris is bloodily repressed in May by governmental forces. Thiers becomes President. The first of Zola's great series of novels on the Rougon-Macquart family is published, and Nietzsche publishes his first book. Ruskin becomes the first Slade Professor at Oxford, and Verdi's *Aida* is given its first performance at the opera house in Cairo. Darwin's *Descent of Man* is published.

1872 Business boom in France, despite defeat and the payment of heavy reparations to the Germans. Durand-Ruel arranges an exhibition in London. An international congress is held at The Hague to seek a universal peace. Daudet publishes *Tartarin de Tarascon*, and Samuel Butler *Erewhon*. Whistler paints a portrait of Carlyle. Grant is re-elected president of the USA. César Franck becomes professor at the Conservatory.

1873 The beginning of a period of economic recession, which hits picture sales and eventually gets Durand-Ruel into difficulties. Courbet takes refuge in Switzerland, and Marshal Mac-Mahon becomes President. Rimbaud publishes his *Saison en enfer*, and Hans Andersen his *Fairytales*. Napoleon III dies in England, and a short-lived republic is set up in Spain. Thomas Eakins finishes *The Biglen Brothers Turning the Stake*, and Tolstoy publishes *Anna Karenina*. End of German occupation of France.

1874 Foundation stone of the church of Sacré-Coeur on Montmartre laid. Winston Churchill is born, and Disraeli becomes Prime Minister. Stanley commences his major African exploration, and Verdi conducts the first performance of his *Requiem*. Alfonso XII becomes king of Spain. Lady Butler paints *The Roll Call*. Gleyre dies.

Comparative chronology

1875 A largely unsuccessful sale of works by Impressionists at the Hôtel Drouot. Durand-Ruel closes his London gallery. Degas has financial problems, and Pissarro gets involved in a new association of artists, which he persuades Cézanne to join. Monet goes through a worse than usual financial period, but Renoir's lot is improving slightly, thanks to the support of Chocquet and Caillebotte. Morisot visits England and spends some time on the Isle of Wight.

1876 The second exhibition is held at 11 rue Le Peletier, with 20 participants. Degas exhibits 24 works, and, by bailing his brother out of financial difficulties, loses most of his personal fortune. Monet finds no way out of his financial problems, while Renoir's fortunes continue to mend as a result of meeting Charpentier. Seurat decides, with family support, to become a painter. Mallarmé publishes a flattering article about Manet.

1877 Third exhibition, at 6 rue Le Peletier; 18 participants. Degas invites Cassatt to join the group, and Pissarro and Cézanne leave L'Union. Monet, still in dire straits, exhibits 30 paintings, Renoir 17, and Morisot 19. Rivière edits L'Impressionniste during the run of the exhibition. The Nouvelle-Athènes becomes the favourite meeting place of the Impressionist group. On 28 May another auction sale is held, at which the average price obtained is 169 francs.

1878 Manet moves studio to the rue d'Amsterdam and helps Monet, who has a second child and is now living at Vétheuil, where he is joined by Mme Hoschedé and her children. Renoir continues to enjoy Charpentier's patronage, and paints a portrait of Mme Charpentier. Pissarro rents a room in Montmartre to show his pictures to possible clients, and also sends two pictures to Florence for an exhibition organized by Diego Martelli. Cézanne has a bitter row with his father, and is helped by Zola.

1879 Fourth exhibition at 28 avenue de l'Opéra; 15 participants. Manet exhibits 2 works at the Salon, though the exhibition is savaged by Huysmans; all Cézanne's entries are rejected. Renoir's Mme Charpentier and her Children is not only accepted but highly praised, and later in the year he has a one-man exhibition at the offices of La Vie moderne. Pissarro invites Gauguin to submit to the group exhibition, and he shows 1 sculpture and 7 paintings. Morisot, who is pregnant, does not participate.

1880 Fifth exhibition at 10 rue des Pyramides; 18 participants. Manet's Execution of the Emperor Maximilian is exhibited successfully in the USA and he has a one-man exhibition of pastels at La Vie moderne; his health continues to deteriorate. Degas works with Cassatt and Pissarro on etchings, and Cézanne, living mainly in Paris, makes several visits to Zola at Médan. Monet also has an exhibition at La Vie moderne.

1881 Sixth exhibition at 35 boulevard des Capucines; 13 participants. Manet, now seriously ill, is awarded the Legion of Honour. Pissarro is working in Pontoise with Gauguin and Cézanne, who at the end of the year returns to Aix. Renoir travels a great deal, first to Algiers, and then to Italy, where, after visiting Venice and Florence, he goes to Pompeii. Morisot, now living at Bougival, spends the winter in Nice.

1882 Seventh exhibition at 251 rue Saint-Honoré; 9 participants. Manet shows the Bar at the Folies-Bergère at the Salon. Degas makes a trip to Spain. Pissarro moves from Pontoise to Osny, where Cézanne, in Paris most of the year, moves to the Jas de Bouffan in September. Renoir stays in L'Estaque, and then goes to Algiers to recuperate from an illness. Seurat is painting Barbizonesque landscapes around Paris.

1875 Corot, Millet, Bizet and Hans Andersen die, and Ravel is born. The Third Republic is formally constituted by a series of constitutional laws. Chromosomes are discovered by a German and a Scot. Grieg produces Peer Gynt. Pierre Savorgnan de Brazza explores those parts of Africa north of the Congo, and so makes possible an extension of the French empire.

1876 The telephone is invented in the USA by Bell. Mallarmé publishes L'Après-midi d'un faune, illustrated by Manet. Strindberg visits Paris and is impressed by the work of the Impressionists. Wagner finishes The Ring, and Brahms his first symphony. Mark Twain publishes the Adventures of Tom Sawyer. First Socialist International dissolved. Bakunin and Georges Sand die.

1877 Turkey and Russia at war; Queen Victoria becomes Empress of India. Edison invents the phonograph, and Thomson electric welding. Thiers and Courbet die, and Saint-Saëns composes Samson et Dalila. Durand-Ruel is again in severe financial difficulties, owing to the bankruptcy of a financier who was supporting him. Grosvenor Gallery opens in London. Pateri's The Renaissance popularizes Leonardo's Mona Lisa. France colonizes the Congo.

1878 Paris World's Fair. Duret publishes Les Peintres impressionnistes, and Romania becomes an independent kingdom. The population of the USA tops that of any European country except Russia. The Congress of Berlin attempts to settle the affairs of Eastern Europe and, as a result, Britain acquires Cyprus. Leo XII becomes pope. And When Did You Last See Your Father? makes a big hit at the Royal Academy, London. Whistler v. Ruskin case. Telephones are installed in Paris.

1879 Daumier and Couture die. Paul Klee is born. Zola publishes Mes Haines, containing much of his earlier art criticism. Charpentier starts La Vie moderne, the offices of which also house art exhibitions. Bouguereau exhibits his sensational Birth of Venus, and Meredith publishes The Egoist. In America Edison invents the electric light bulb, and Hughes the microphone, whilst in Germany Siemens produces the first electric locomotive. Reform of the French educational system is inaugurated. The French socialist party is formed.

1880 Flaubert, Duranty, Offenbach and George Eliot die. Panama Canal Company founded. Napoleon III's only son, the Prince Imperial, is killed in Britain's war against Zulus. Maupassant publishes Boule de suif, and Dostoevsky The Brothers Karamazov; Ibsen's The Doll's House is first performed. Gladstone introduces a bill for Home Rule for Ireland. Lawson and Starley invent the modern bicycle.

1881 The Boer War breaks out. Tsar Alexander II is assassinated. Dostoevsky, Carlyle and Mussorgsky die; Picasso is born. Offenbach's Tales of Hoffmann has its first posthumous production. The technique of process-engraving is invented in Germany by Meisenbach, and the first electric tramway is inaugurated in Berlin. The French occupy Tunisia. Antonin Proust becomes Minister of Fine Arts.

1882 Garibaldi, Rossetti, Darwin, Longfellow and Emerson die. The folding camera is invented in the USA. A Triple Alliance is formed between Germany, Austria and Italy. The Catholic Union Internationale bank, which supported Durand-Ruel, crashes in Paris. Oscar Wilde publishes his Poems; Wagner finishes Parsifal; Gaudí begins La Sagrada Familia in Barcelona.

1883 Manet dies on 30 April. Durand-Ruel arranges a series of one-man exhibitions in his new gallery: Monet in March, Renoir in April, Pissarro in May, Sisley in June. He also organizes exhibitions in London, Rotterdam, Berlin, Boston and New York. Pissarro works closely with Gauguin. Renoir visits Guernsey and the south of France, where he and Monet meet Cézanne. Caillebotte draws up his will, leaving his collection to the Louvre. Monet moves to Giverny.

1884 Manet's affairs are tidied up and the contents of his studio are sold at auction for 115,000 francs; a memorial exhibition is held at the Ecole des Beaux-Arts. Durand-Ruel is still having financial difficulties. Monet, whose own affairs are on the mend, exhibits at Petit's Exposition Internationale. Pissarro moves to Eragny. Renoir seeks for a new style. Morisot paints in the Bois de Boulogne, and Signac, Redon and Seurat get involved in the new Société des Indépendants.

1885 Degas meets Gauguin and Sickert at Dieppe. Pissarro falls under the influence of Seurat and Signac. Cézanne, who is mainly working in and around Aix, visits Zola and goes to La Roche-Guyon to see Renoir, who has by now evolved what he feels is a satisfactory new style. Monet exhibits at Petit's fourth Exposition Internationale. Sisley has great financial problems, despite his contact with Théo van Gogh; Durand-Ruel is also in difficulties. Gauguin returns from Denmark, and Seurat produces La Grande Jatte. Durand-Ruel organizes an Impressionist exhibition in Brussels.

1886 Last exhibition at 1 rue Laffitte; 17 participants. Durand-Ruel has a successful American exhibition. Degas visits Naples. Pissarro exhibits his first Pointillist-style works and insists that Seurat and Signac exhibit with the Impressionists. Because of the presence of Seurat's works, Monet refuses to participate and, along with Renoir, exhibits at Petit's fifth Exposition Internationale. Cézanne breaks with Zola after the publication of L'Oeuvre and marries Hortense Fiquet. Vincent van Gogh arrives in Paris.

1887 Gauguin leaves France for Martinique. Pissarro and Seurat exhibit with Les Vingt in Brussels. Renoir shows examples of his new style, as exemplified in the Bathers, at Petit's and, though praised by Van Gogh, it is not well received either by Huysmans or Astruc. Dealers begin to find that it is easier to sell work by the Impressionists.

1888 Durand-Ruel organizes an important exhibition and opens a gallery in New York. Still anxious about his new style, Renoir has begun to suffer from arthritis. Under the influence of Muybridge Degas is creating sculptures of horses. Gauguin meets Bernard at Pont-Aven, and they hammer out the principles of Synthetism. Monet visits the south of France, and refuses the Legion of Honour.

1889 The International Exhibition attracts many visitors to Paris. Durand-Ruel organizes an exhibition of painter-engravers, including the Impressionists. The collection of Impressionist paintings amassed by Henry Hill of Brighton is sold at Christie's, averaging 60–70 guineas each. Monet has an exhibition at Boussod and Valadon's, followed by a joint exhibition with Rodin at Petit's.

1890 Pissarro abandons Divisionism and has a one-man exhibition at Boussod and Valadon's. Monet, with growing economic success, buys the house at Giverny. Dinner meetings at the Café Riche become a regular feature of the Impressionists' lives. Renoir begins to achieve real success, selling works to Durand-Ruel for 7500 francs each. Van Gogh dies, and his brother Théo leaves Boussod and Valadon.

1883 France's financial position improves. Wagner, Karl Marx and Gustave Doré die; Mussolini, Kafka and Utrillo are born. Whistler exhibits Portrait of the Artist's Mother at the Salon. Brazzaville, capital of the French Congo, is founded. Huysmans publishes L'Art moderne, Robert Louis Stevenson Kidnapped, and Maupassant Une Vie. The first petrol-driven car is produced in France, and the Maxim machine-gun appears in the USA. Marxist party founded in Russia.

1884 Smetana dies and Debussy wins the Prix de Rome. Bruckner's seventh symphony is given its first performance. The fountain-pen is invented by Waterman, the electric transformer by Gaulard, and Charles Algernon Parsons perfects the steam turbine; Chardonnet invents artificial silk. The Société des Vingt holds its first exhibition. Huysmans publishes A Rebours. Burne-Jones paints King Cophetua and the Beggar Maid. Trades unions are legalized in France.

1885 Victor Hugo dies and Ezra Pound is born. Whistler gives his Ten o'clock Lecture; first production of Ibsen's The Wild Duck. Creation of the Belgian Congo. Pasteur invents a vaccine against rabies. Mallarmé is appointed a teacher at the Collège Rollin. Zola publishes Germinal, Nietzsche Thus Spake Zarathustra, and Maupassant Bel Ami. Brahms completes his fourth symphony. Munch visits Paris. Millais becomes a baronet.

1886 Whistler retrospective exhibition held at Petit's. Liszt and Monticelli die. The New English Art Club is founded in London. Fénéon publishes Les Impressionnistes en 1886; Verlaine publishes Rimbaud's Les Illuminations, and Zola L'Oeuvre. First performance of D'Indy's Symphony on a Mountain Air. Henry James finishes The Bostonians.

1887 Verdi's Otello receives its first performance. Alfred Gilbert's Eros is unveiled in London; the foundations of the Eiffel Tower are laid. Fauré's Requiem is given its first performance. Lanston invents the monotype printing process; Hertz discovers the nature of electromagnetic waves. France signs a treaty with China.

1888 Wilhelm II becomes Emperor of Germany. George Moore publishes Confessions of a Young Man, containing recollections of his meetings with the Impressionists. Rimsky-Korsakov's Scheherezade and Richard Strauss' Don Juan are given first performances. Paper photographic films invented by Eastman, and hormones are isolated. Ruskin's Praeterita is published.

1889 Eiffel Tower opened. The Nabis emerge as a group. Robert Browning dies. The Symbolist magazine La Revue blanche starts publication. The chemist Chevreul, to whose discoveries the Impressionists owed so much, dies; haematology is discovered. As many as 32,250,297 people visit the International Exhibition in Paris to see the displays of 60,000 exhibitors. Boulanger flees the country.

1890 César Franck, Vincent van Gogh and Cardinal Newman die. Dunlop invents the rubber tyre. Bismarck is sacked. First performance of Ibsen's Hedda Gabler.

Gazetteer of the major Impressionist collections

BRAZIL

São Paolo, Museu de Arte The museum has a significant coll. of works from Courbet to Cézanne, and is esp. rich in works by Renoir (*Jules Le Coeur in the Forest of Fontainebleau*, *Baigneuse au griffon*, *Enfant portant des fleurs*). Also in the coll. are Manet's *The Artist*; Cézanne's *Paul Alexis Reading to Emile Zola* and *Rochers à L'Estaque*; Monet's *Japanese Bridge at Giverny*, as well as works by Degas, Gauguin and Van Gogh.

DENMARK

Copenhagen, Ny Carlsberg Glyptotek The coll. contains 5 Monets, 4 Renoirs, 3 Pissarros, 3 Sisleys, several oils and pastels by Degas, as well as a complete set of his 73 bronzes, works by Cézanne, Morisot and Guillaumin, and 3 important Manets; *The Absinthe Drinker*, *Execution of the Emperor Maximilian*, *Mlle Lemonnier*. Gauguin's Danish connections have resulted in a particularly large selection of 25 paintings and 2 wood reliefs.

FRANCE

Paris, Musée d'Orsay The Jeu de Paume coll., once part of the Louvre, now forms the core of this vast and magnificent coll. of 19th-c. French art and sculpture, housed in the converted Gare d'Orsay. A large number of important Impressionist works are to be found here, together with many pastels (by Cassatt, Degas, Manet and Morisot) and bronzes (Degas, Renoir). Highlights include Bazille's *Family Reunion*; Cézanne's *Still-Life with Onions*; Degas' *The Bellelli Family*, *L'Absinthe* and *L'Orchestre de l'Opéra*; Manet's *Olympia*, *Déjeuner sur l'herbe*, *Lola de Valence*, *The Balcony* and *Portrait of Zola*; Monet's *Women in the Garden*, fragments of *Déjeuner sur l'herbe*, several canvases in the Rouen cathedral series, a *Gare St-Lazare*, *Haystacks* and *Waterlilies*; Pissarro's *Woman in a Field*; Renoir's *The Swing*, *Nude in Sunlight*, *Dancing at the Moulin de la Galette*, *Gabrielle with a Rose*; Sisley's *Floods at Port-Marly*; Whistler's *Portrait of the Artist's Mother*;

Fantin-Latour's *Studio in the Batignolles Quarter*, and Denis' *Hommage à Cézanne* are also here.

Paris, Musée Marmottan In 1971 the museum received an exceptional legacy of works from Michel Monet, including 65 canvases by Claude Monet, painted mainly in Giverny, oils by Morisot, Pissarro, Renoir, Sisley, watercolours by Boudin and Signac, and an ink sketch of Monet by Manet. The Donop de Monchy bequest of 1950 provided the museum with its most famous painting, Monet's *Impression; Sunrise* (present whereabouts unknown).
The Cabinet des Dessins of the Louvre Museum and the Cabinet des Estampes of the Bibliothèque Nationale in Paris have important collections of Impressionist drawings, pastels and prints.

GERMANY, EAST

Berlin, Gemäldegalerie (Staatliche Museen, Preussischer Kulturbesitz) Before the Second World War Berlin possessed one of the world's finest colls. of 19th- and 20th-c. art. Although many French works have been lost, those few that remain in the Neue Sammlung are of very high quality. They include Degas' *Conversation*, Renoir's *Afternoon of the Children at Wargemont* and *Lise as a Gypsy Girl*, and 3 Cézannes. Corinth and Slevogt are esp. well represented.

GERMANY, WEST

Cologne, Wallraf-Richartz Museum Alongside an excellent coll. of the German Impressionists Leibl, Liebermann, Slevogt and Corinth, Cologne possesses Renoir's *Albert Sisley and his Wife*, Monet's *Rocks at Etretat*, Sisley's *Bridge at Hampton Court* and Pissarro's *L'Hermitage, Pontoise*.

Essen, Folkwang Museum Contains 4 Renoirs (incl. *Lise with a Parasol*), 2 Manets (incl. *Portrait of Faure as Hamlet*), 2 Cézannes and 1 work each by Monet (*Waterlilies*), Pissarro (*Snow at Louveciennes*) and Sisley. In addition there are 4 Gauguins, 4 Van Goghs, 5 works by Corinth, 3 by Liebermann and 1 by Slevogt.

Munich, Neue Pinakothek (Bayerische Staatsgemäldesammlungen) An exceptional coll. of works by Manet includes his *Luncheon in the Studio*, *Monet Painting in His Studio-Boat at Argenteuil*, *In the Conservatory* and the *House at Rueil*. There are also works by Monet, Degas (*Women Ironing*), Cézanne, Gauguin and Van Gogh.

GREAT BRITAIN

ENGLAND: London, Courtauld Institute Galleries An important coll. of works from the coll. of Samuel Courtauld: 10 Cézannes (incl. *Mont Sainte-Victoire* and *Card Players*), 3 Degas, 2 Manets (*Bar at the Folies-Bergère*, sketch for *Déjeuner sur l'herbe*), 3 Monets (*Seine at Argenteuil, Autumn*), 3 Pissarros, 4 Renoirs (*La Loge*, *Portrait of Vollard*) and 2 Sisleys.

London, National Gallery An impressive coll., some of which come from the SIR HUGH LANE bequest. There are 7 Cézannes (incl. *Large Bathers*), 9 Degas (*Young Spartans Exercising*, *Miss La La au cirque Fernando*, *Hélène Rouart in her Father's Study*), 4 Manets (*Music in the Tuileries*, *Eva Gonzalès*, *La Serveuse de Bocks*, fragments of the *Execution of the Emperor Maximilian*), 10 Monets (*La Grenouillère*, the *Gare St-Lazare*, *Waterlilies*), 6 Pissarros (*The Blvd Montmartre at Night*), 9 Renoirs (*Seine at Asnières*, *La Première Sortie*, *Les Parapluies*), and works by Sisley and Morisot (*Summer's Day*).

London, Tate Gallery The Modern Coll. includes 13 works by Degas (oils, pastels, and bronzes incl. the *Little Dancer Aged 14 Years*), a Manet, 3 Monets, 7 Pissarros, 1 Renoir painting and 3 bronzes (*Mother and Child*, *Washerwoman*, *Venus Victorious*) and 3 Sisleys. There are also many works by English artists influenced by the Impressionists: 39 Sargents (incl. *Monet Painting at the Edge of a Wood*), 42 Sickerts and 37 Wilson Steers.

SCOTLAND: Edinburgh, National Gallery of Scotland The Impressionist paintings here come mainly from the coll. of Sir Alexander Maitland (1958, 1960) and include 5 Renoirs, 4 Degas (incl. the *Portrait of Diego Martelli*), 2

Monets (*Poplars, Haystacks*), works by Morisot, Pissarro, Sisley, Whistler, Gauguin (*Vision After the Sermon*) and Van Gogh.

Glasgow, Burrell Collection The coll. of Sir William and Lady Burrell (1944) contains works by Degas (*Portrait of Duranty, The Rehearsal*), Manet, Monet and Renoir; it also includes others by Cézanne (*Château de Médan*), Pissarro, Sisley and Gauguin, as well as several drawings, prints and sculptures.

WALES: Cardiff, National Museum of Wales Almost all of the works held here are from the Gwendoline and Margaret DAVIES COLL. (1951, 1963): there are 12 Monets, 4 Cézannes, 3 Manets, 2 Pissarros, and works by Morisot, Renoir, Sisley, Sickert, Wilson Steer and Whistler, also sculptures by Degas and Renoir.

THE NETHERLANDS

Amsterdam, Rijksmuseum An outstanding coll. of Dutch art, incl. artists influenced by the Impressionists – Van Gogh, Isaac Israel, George Breitner, P.J.C. Gabriel, and Jacob Maris. There are 2 oils by Monet, and a superb coll. of prints and drawings by Degas, Manet and Renoir.

NORWAY

Oslo, Nasjonalgalleriet Works include 4 Manets (*Mme Manet in the Conservatory, L'Exposition Universelle of 1867, Portrait of de Nittis*), 3 Degas, 2 Monets (*Rainy Weather, Etretat*), 2 Renoirs, 2 Guillaumins, a Morisot and 6 Gauguins. Over half of the exhibition rooms are devoted to Norwegian artists, esp. Munch.

SWITZERLAND

Winterthur, Oskar Reinhart Foundation Reinhart's favourite artist was Renoir, and this is reflected in the high number of his paintings to be found here: 12 oils include the *Portrait of Chocquet* and numerous *plein-air* landscapes. The 11 works by Cézanne are a further indication of his taste. There are also 4 Manets (incl. *At the Café*), 2 Pissarros, a Sisley, a Monet (*Ice Floes on the Seine*) and works by Degas (incl. a drawing of Giulietta Bellelli). Van Gogh is represented by 4 paintings and 2 drawings.

UNITED STATES

Boston, Museum of Fine Arts One of the largest colls. in the US, comprising 40 Monets (incl. *Waterlilies, Haystacks, Rouen Cathedral, La Japonaise*), 20 Renoirs (*Rocky Crags at L'Estaque, Dance at Bougival*), 15 Degas (*Carriage at the Races, Edmondo and Thérèse Morbilli, The Artist's Father Listening to Pagans*), 7 Manets (*Portrait of Victorine Meurent, Street Singer, Execution of the Emperor*

Maximilian), 5 Sisleys (*Early Snow at Louveciennes*), 5 Cézannes, 4 Sickerts, 6 Gauguins (*D'où venons-nous? Que sommes-nous? Où allons-nous?*), 5 Van Goghs, a Caillebotte, a Guillaumin, a Morisot and some Cassatts (*Five o'clock Tea, Woman in Black at the Opéra*).

Chicago, Art Institute of Chicago A substantial holding of Impressionist works, incl. several donated in 1922 by Mrs Potter Palmer, a friend of Cassatt. Highlights include: a self-portrait by Bazille, Caillebotte's *Rue de Paris, temps de pluie*, Cézanne's *Bay of Marseilles, seen from L'Estaque*, several ballet scenes by Degas and his *Millinery Shop*, Manet's *Christ Mocked by Soldiers* and the *Races at Longchamp*, Monet's *Beach at Ste-Adresse*, Renoir's *Oarsmen at Chatou* and *Two Little Circus Girls*. It also houses Seurat's *Sunday Afternoon on the Island of La Grande Jatte*.

Cleveland Museum of Art Possesses 5 Monets (*Antibes, Waterlilies*), 5 Degas, 4 Renoirs (*Three Bathers*) and important works by Cassatt, Morisot, Pissarro and Sisley. There are 3 late landscapes by Cézanne, 3 Gauguins and 3 Van Goghs. The museum also has a good coll. of sculpture by Degas, Renoir, Rodin and Rosso.

Kansas City, Nelson-Atkins Museum The museum's coll. is esp. strong in works by the Impressionists, with works by Cézanne (*Mont Ste-Victoire*), Gauguin, Van Gogh, Manet, Monet (*Blvd des Capucines*, late *Waterlilies* canvas), Pissarro (*Jardin des Mathurins, Pontoise*), Renoir and Seurat. There are pastels by Cassatt and Morisot, and a gouache and pastel by Degas which was purchased by Cassatt's friend Louisine Elder (later Havemeyer); it was one of the first Impressionist works exhibited in the USA.

New York, Brooklyn Museum Together with works by the American Impressionist school (Merritt Chase, Robinson, Sargent, Twachtman), the museum owns Degas' *Mlle Fiocre in the Ballet 'La Source'*, Pissarro's *The Climbing Path, Pontoise* and Cassatt's *Mother and Child*, as well as 4 landscapes by Monet, a Renoir, a Cézanne and a Van Gogh self-portrait. There are also several graphic works by Cassatt and Degas.

New York, Metropolitan Museum of Art One of the world's greatest colls. of Impressionist works. A large group by Degas includes 19 paintings (*Portrait of Tissot, Bouderie, The Orchestra of 'Robert le Diable', Woman with Chrysanthemums*), pastels, drawings and sculptures filling 3 galleries. There are 35 paintings by Monet (incl. *La Grenouillère, Terrace at Sainte-Adresse, Poplars, Haystacks*, views of London, Venice and Giverny), 26 by Renoir (incl. *Mme Charpentier and her Chil-

dren*), 18 by Manet (*Dead Christ and Angels*, portraits of George Moore and Faure, *Boating, The Spanish Singer, Mlle Victorine as an Espada*), 18 by Cézanne (*Portrait of Hortense Fiquet*), 16 by Pissarro (*Côte du Jallais, Pontoise*), 5 by Sisley, 2 each by Lebourg and Guillaumin, 1 each by Morisot and Sickert; there are 9 Van Goghs and 4 Gauguins. The American Impressionists are also well represented: there are many prints and paintings by Cassatt – largely from the HAVEMEYER collection – incl. *Lady at the Teatable, The Cup of Tea* and *Young Mother Sewing*; Whistler portraits, and works by Robinson, Sargent and Twachtman.

New York, Museum of Modern Art The Lillie P. Bliss collection forms the nucleus of the museum's painting coll., which includes 11 Cézanne oils (*Melting Snow, Fontainebleau*) as well as prints and 11 watercolours, 5 Monets (a whole room is devoted to his *Waterlilies*), 3 Gauguins, 3 Van Goghs, 2 Sickerts, a Renoir and a Degas pastel (*At the Milliner's*). The museum also holds many prints and drawings by these artists.

Philadelphia Museum of Art Holds examples of all the major Impressionists, incl. Manet's *Le Bon Bock*, Monet's *Poplars*, Renoir's *Bathers* and a portrait of Aline Charigot, Degas' *Ballet Class*, Cassatt's *Woman and Child Driving, Family Group Reading*, and a portrait of her husband and son, and Cézanne's *Mont Ste-Victoire*; many are drawn from the Tyson bequest of 23 Impressionist and Post-Impressionist works. There are also 6 paintings by Sargent.

Washington, D.C., National Gallery of Art French 19th-c. painting is one of the National Gallery's outstanding areas, thanks largely to the Chester Dale and MELLON colls. The body of works by Manet is the most important: *Dead Toreador, The Old Musician, The Tragic Actor, Masked Ball at the Opéra, The Railroad, The Plum*. There are several Renoirs (*Diana, The Pont Neuf, Paris, Odalisque*) and an impressive group of Monets, incl. views of Argenteuil, Vétheuil, London and Rouen, also important works by Degas (*Edmondo and Thérèse Morbilli*), Pissarro (*Blvd des Italiens*), Bazille, Guillaumin, Sisley and Cézanne (*Portrait of the Artist's Father*). Cassatt (*The Boating Party, Girl Arranging her Hair, Mother Wearing a Sunflower*) and Morisot (*In the Dining Room, The Artist's Sister Edma and their Mother*) are also well represented.

Washington, D.C., Phillips Collection This small but excellent coll. includes perhaps the most famous painting by Renoir, his *Luncheon of the Boating Party*, several works by Degas and Cézanne, Monet's *Road to Vétheuil* and *On the Cliffs, Dieppe*, Morisot's

Two Girls, as well as works by Sisley, Seurat and Van Gogh. Americans outnumber Europeans by 4 to 1 in the coll. as a whole, and there are many works by Merritt Chase, Robinson, Twachtman and Whistler.

The University Art Museums of Harvard (Fogg Art Museum, Cambridge), Yale (New Haven) and Princeton also hold important Impressionist works.

USSR
Leningrad, The Hermitage The Hermitage was much enriched after the Revolution by works from the private colls. of MOROSOV and SHCHUKIN, and the Impressionist galleries are now one of its major strengths. (Manet is the only artist who is poorly represented.) There are many Monets, Renoirs, Degas pastels, and a small group of landscapes and city scenes by Pissarro and Sisley. The coll. is very rich in Cézannes – 11 in all – and Gauguins – 15.

Moscow, State Pushkin Museum Cézanne is strongly represented here, by 14 works (*The Jas de Bouffan, Still-life with Peaches and Pears, Pierrot and Harlequin*), as is Monet, by 11 (incl. *Déjeuner sur l'herbe, Blvd des Capucines*, views of Rouen cathedral and Vétheuil). There are 5 Renoirs, mainly late (*Portrait of Jeanne Samary, La Grenouillère*), 4 Degas (pastels of dancers, *Exercising Race-horses*), 1 Sisley (*Frosty Morning at Louveciennes*) and Pissarro's *Avenue de l'Opéra* and *Ploughland*. Only 2 unfinished works by Manet are on display.

Illustration credits

Numbers refer to the page on which the illustration is to be found. The following abbreviations have been used: *a* above; *b* below; *l* left; *r* right

Photo A.C.L. – 29*r*; Photo Bulloz – 61, 62, 64, 85, 106*a*, 139, 150*b*, 164*r*; Collection Durand-Ruel – 19*b*, 85; Photo Durand-Ruel – 77, 177; Photo Giraudon – 15*ar*, 23, 28, 79, 100, 104, 114, 130*b*, 151, 156, 180, 202*r*, 205; Photo Martin Hürlimann – 109; John G. Johnson Collection, Philadelphia – 18; Mansell Collection – 38; Photo Mas – 207; Stavros S. Niarchos Collection – 210; The Norton Simon Foundation – 117; Presumed destroyed – 126*b*; Private collection – 22*r*, 80, 88*a*, 131, 164*r*, 172, 185, 188*r*, 189, 190, 202*r*, 208; Photo Rheinisches Bildarchiv – 82; Photo Réunion des Musées Nationaux – 17*a*, 30, 32, 52, 53, 55, 56*a*, 56*b*, 65, 76, 134, 149*b*, 181*a*, 192, 197*b*, 217, 218–19, 220, 221, 223, 224; Collection Sirot-Angel – 137, 146*a*, 213*r*; Photo Roger-Viollet – 60*l*, 89*b*, 91, 143, 155, 181*b*; Collection Viollet – 148; Collection François Emile-Zola – 231*l*; Wildenstein Collection – 75; Amsterdam: Rijksmuseum – 108*b*; Vincent van Gogh Foundation/National Museum Vincent van Gogh – 100*r*, 120*b*, 161; Berlin: Nationalgalerie, Staatliche Museen, Preussischer Kulturbesitz – 31*a*; Birmingham: City Museum and Art Gallery – 74*a*; Brussels: Musées Royaux des Beaux-Arts – 29*l*, 29*r*, 209; Buenos Aires: Museo Nacional de Bellas Artes – 107; Cambridge, Mass.: Houghton Library, Harvard University – 120*a*; Cardiff: National Museum of Wales – 54, 84*b*; Chicago: The Art Institute – 24*br* (Charles H. and Mary F.S. Worcester Fund Income), 94 (Joseph Winterbotham Collection), 101, 200 (Helen Birch Bartlett Memorial Foundation), 132 (Albert H. Wolf Memorial Collection); Cologne: Wallraf-Richartz Museum – 82, 96; Columbus: Gallery of Fine Arts – 57; Compiègne: Musée National du Château de Compiègne – 151; Dublin: The Hugh Lane Municipal Gallery of Modern Art – 124; National Gallery of Ireland – 199*l*; Edinburgh: Lady Stair's House Museum – 24*al*; National Galleries of Scotland – 136; Essen: Folkwang Museum – 213*l*; Fort Worth: Kimbell Art Museum – 58*b*; Geneva: Musée du Petit Palais – 160; Glasgow: Burrell Collection – 33; Grenoble: Musée des Beaux-Arts – 204; Haarlem: Frans Halsmuseum – 17*b*; Hamburg: Kunsthalle – 97; Helsinki: Ateneumin Taidemuseo – 197*a*; Kitakyushu: Municipal Museum of Art – 173; Liverpool: Merseyside County Art Galleries – 44*b*; London: British Museum – 10–11, 12*a*, 179; Courtauld Institute Galleries (Courtauld Collection) – 45, 159*b*; National Gallery – 40*a*, 50–1, 90, 102, 128*l*, 157, 175; Tate Gallery – 70*b*, 176, 195; Madrid: Museo del Prado – 207; Manchester (New Hampshire): The Currier Gallery of Art – 34*a*; Mannheim: Kunsthalle – 215; Melbourne: National Gallery of Victoria – 199*r*; Milan: Pinacoteca di Brera – 118; Montpellier: Musée Fabre – 36; Munich: Neue Pinakothek, Bayerische Staatsgemälde-sammlungen – 126*al*, 168; Newcastle: Laing Art Gallery – 84*al*; New York: Metropolitan Museum of Art – 43 (Gift of Paul S. Sachs, 1917), 47 (Wolfe Fund, 1907), 68 (Bequest of Robert Graham Dun, 1911), 78, 88*b* (Bequest of Stephen C. Clark), 138*b* (Bequest of Mrs H.O. Havemeyer, 1929. The H.O. Havemeyer Collection) 191, 227*a* (Bequest of William Church Osborn, 1951), 212; Collection, The Museum of Modern Art – 31*b* (Grace Rainey Rogers Fund), 39*b* (Acquired by Exchange); The New York Public Library, Prints Division, Astor, Lenox and Tilden Foundations (S.P. Avery Collection) – 171*b*; Oslo: Nasjonalgalleriet – 196*b*; Oxford: Ashmolean Museum – 15*al*, 167; Paris: Bibliothèque Historique de la Ville de Paris – 150*b*; Bibliothèque Nationale – 15*b*, 20, 25, 39*l*, 46*b*, 58*a*, 67*b*, 110*a*, 111, 116, 127, 130*a*, 178, 206; Louvre – 100, 76 (Cabinet des Dessins); Formerly Musée Marmottan – 114; Musée d'Orsay – 17*a*, 23, 28, 30, 32, 40*b*, 52, 53, 55, 56*a*, 56*b*, 61, 62, 64, 65, 67*a*, 86, 98, 104, 105, 125, 134, 139, 149*a*, 149*b*, 156, 180, 181*a*, 183, 187, 192, 197*b*, 205, 217, 218–19, 220, 221, 223, 234; Musée du Petit Palais – 106*a*; Pau: Musée des Beaux-Arts – 222; Philadelphia: Museum of Art – 16 (Given by Edgar Scott), 34*b*, 174, 225 (Mr and Mrs Carroll S. Tyson Collection), 108*a*; Piacenza: Galleria d'Arte Moderna – 230*b*; Rhode Island: Museum of Art, Rhode Island School of Design, Providence – 81; Rome: Galleria Nazionale d'Arte Moderna – 153*a*; Rotterdam: Museum Boymans-van-Beuningen – 122; São Paolo: Museo de São Paolo – 15*ar*; Stockholm: Nationalmuseum – 37, 196*a*; Stuttgart: Staatsgalerie (Graphische Sammlung) – 106*b*; Toronto: Art Gallery of Ontario – 202*l* (Gift of The Contemporary Art Society, London, 1946); Toulouse: Musée des Augustins – 72; Tours: Musée des Beaux-Arts – 119; Washington, D.C.: National Gallery of Art – 48 (Gift of Sam A. Lewisohn 1951), 74*b*, 146*b*, 166, 216 (Chester Dale Collection 1962), 138*a* (Collection of Mr and Mrs Paul Mellon, 1971), 142, 229 (Harris Whittemore Collection, 1943); Phillips Collection – 162, 188*l*; Smithsonian Institution (National Portrait Gallery) – 42*r*; Williamstown, Mass.: Sterling and Francine Clark Art Institute 13.

The following illustrations are from books and journals:
L'Artiste 111 (1867) *La Caricature* 182 (1880); *Le Charivari*: 127 (1874), 46*a* (1877), 115 (1879); P. Delmet, *Chansons de Montmartre* (1898) – 144; E. de Goncourt, *Manette Salomon* (1896) – 128*r*; *Harper's Monthly Magazine* 38 (1889); *L'Impressioniste* 116 (1888); *Le Journal amusant* 103*a* (1873); *Le Monde illustré* 171*b* (1871); W.C. Morrow and E. Cucuel, *Bohemian Paris of Today* (1899) – 221*l*; E.A. Poe, *The Raven* (1875) – 113; *Paris illustré* 120*b* (1866); *Petit Journal pour rire* 163 (1855); *Psst . . . !* 89*a* (1898).